Book Reviews on *The Triunity of God Is Jewish*

I was delighted and fascinated with what I found in [John Metzger's book]. He has produced a very careful, exegetical study of not only the names of God and the plural descriptions of God, but he has given a strong case for the tri-unity of God in the Old Testament. Pastors and laypersons will find enormous help in discussions such as the *Angel of the LORD*, the meaning of the great *Shema* given in Deuteronomy 6:4, and a great discussion of the precise meaning of the phrase "Hear O Israel, the Lord our God is one." This is a much-needed tool to correct and inform the dialogue between Christians and Jewish people as well as for Christians to understand better their own doctrine of the Trinity. This work should bring great blessing to the body of Christ everywhere.
    Walter Kaiser, Former President
    Gordon-Conwell Theological Seminary

John Metzger makes his case and proves his point in a thoroughly convincing and scriptural manner. The treatment of the indivisibility and the plurality of God and the Hebrew names of God in this study are all convincing. We agree with the author that God has given ample evidences of His unity as well as His plurality. God is one God, and yet there is a tri-unity. The distinctions John Metzger makes between biblical and rabbinical Judaism are most helpful. The importance of this critical study cannot be separated from the eternal destiny of Jewish souls. John Metzger enlarges on this thought by saying, "One cannot separate the salvation that was provided in Messiah from his or her belief in the oneness, unity of God and the plurality of God." It isn't difficult to commend John Metzger for a thorough treatise and an excellent textbook.
    Peter W. Teague
    President of Lancaster Bible College and Graduate School

It is impossible to do Jewish ministries using only the New Testament. One must have an excellent knowledge of the tri-unity of God in the Old Testament, messianic prophecies of the First Coming of the Messiah and be able to answer Jewish objections on issues such as the virgin birth and the God/man concept, among other issues, while using only the Old Testament. After all, when the apostles proclaimed the Messiahship of Jesus from "the Scriptures," it meant from the Old Testament, since the New Testament had not yet been written. This work by John Metzger is an excellent presentation on the tri-unity of God, including many of the First Coming prophecies, which will give the reader not only expertise in messianic prophecies, but also on how they correlate with the other areas of biblical doctrine in the New Testament as well. This work is highly recommended.
    Dr. Arnold Fruchtenbaum
    Founder and Director of Ariel Ministries

This is an excellent work on the tri-unity of God which will help every Christian understand the theological perspective of the Jewish people and become more effective in his or her witness. This book uncovers the large body of evidence that God has given to us in the Hebrew Scriptures regarding the nature of His Person. An exceptionally well-informed and useful study!
    Les Lofquist
    Former Executive Director of IFCA Int'l; currently Assistant Professor of Practical Theology, Shepherds Theological Seminary, Cary, NC

Other Books by the Author

*Discovering the Mystery
of the Unity of God*

*God in Eclipse:
God Has Not Always Been Silent*

*God in Eclipse
Russian Translation*

*Israel's Only Hope:
The New Covenant*

*Poking God's Eye:
A Theological & Historical View of Anti-Semitism
Based on the Blessings and Curses
of Genesis 12:3*

*The Law, Then and Now:
What About Grace?*

THE TRI-UNITY OF GOD IS JEWISH

A Theological Study
on the Plurality and Tri-Unity of God
in the Hebrew Scriptures
(Second Edition)

This book is an abridged and updated version of the complete work *Discovering the Mystery of the Unity of God* by the same author.

THE TRI-UNITY OF GOD IS JEWISH

A Theological Study

on the Plurality and Tri-Unity of God

in the Hebrew Scriptures

(Second Edition)

This book is an abridged and updated version of the complete work *Discovering the Mystery of the Unity of God* by the same author.

by John B. Metzger, M.A.

The Tri-Unity of God Is Jewish (2nd edition)
First Edition © 2005 by John B. Metzger
Second Edition © 2019 by John B. Metzger

www.PromisesToIsrael.org

ISBN: 978-0-9912151-8-8

REL 067040 RELIGION - Christian Theology - Christology
REL 006210 RELIGION - Biblical Studies - Old Testament
REL 067030 RELIGION - Christian Theology – Apologetics

This book is an abridged and updated version of the complete work *Discovering the Mystery of the Unity of God* by the same author.

Unless otherwise noted, Bible quotations from the New Testament are taken from the King James Version (KJV), Published by Oxford University Press, The Scofield Reference Bible Edition (1996).

Unless otherwise indicated, Bible quotations from the Old Testament are taken from *Jewish Study Bible* (JSB), published by Oxford University Press (2004), for the Jewish Publication Society, *Tanakh* Translation.

As noted, Scripture quotations taken from the New American Standard Bible® (NASB), Copyright © 1960, 1962, 1963, 1968, 1971, 1972, 1973, 1975, 1977, 1995 by The Lockman Foundation. Used by permission. www.Lockman.org

All Rights Reserved. No part of this book may be reproduced, stored in a retrieval system or transmitted in any form or by any means – for example, electronic, photocopy, recording – without the prior written permission of the publisher. The only exception is for brief quotations in printed reviews.

Artwork by Amy Sheetreet
Cover design by Josh & Jesse Gonzales
Edited by Joni Prinjinski
Published by JHousePublishing, Keller, TX, under the Purple Raiment Label
www.JHousePublishing.com

Purple Raiment
Love Letters

DEDICATION

✼

To my Wife
Sharon of over 50 years of marriage
and her patience as I studied and for
her help in the original editing.

ACKNOWLEDGMENTS

**I would like to acknowledge four people
who have had a great impact on my life:**

Mabel Metzger
Who went home to be with the LORD in 2011 at the age of 103.
I am indebted to her for all her encouragement over the years.

Rev. J. Albert Ford
the first pastor of
McLean Bible Church, , VA
who preached the whole Scripture:
Doctrine, Book Studies, Prophecy.
Because of his ministry, a love of the Word of God
and a love for Jewish people and Israel took root in my heart
and gave me direction as a teenager and for the rest of my life.

Dr. Willis Bishop
Professor Emeritus of Old Testament Studies
at
Washington Bible College, Lanham, MD
For his faithfulness in teaching over the years
and for giving me the foundation
for my Old Testament understanding.
At age 99, he went home to be eternally with the LORD
that he so faithfully taught to others.

Dr. Arnold G. Fruchtenbaum
Founder and Director of Ariel Ministries, Tustin, CA,
Camp Shoshanah - Keeseville, NY,
and the Ariel School of Messianic Jewish Studies
For teaching me the *Tanakh* (Hebrew Bible) from a Jewish perspective.
God has used him to change my life ministry.

CONTENTS

DEDICATION vii

ACKNOWLEDGMENTS ix

PREFACE xvii

CHAPTER I: INTRODUCTION 1
    Statement of Purpose 1
    Need for the Study 7
    Scriptural and Theological Basis 14
    Limitations of the Research Project 17
    Organization of Study 18
        Image and Likeness of God – Chapter 2 18
        Names of God – Chapter 3 18
        Theophanies – Chapter 4 18
        Shema – Chapter 5 19
        Plural Terms – Chapter 6 19
        Holy Spirit – Chapter 7 20
        Messiah Is Divine – Chapter 8 20
        Summary and Conclusion 21

CHAPTER 2: IN THE IMAGE AND LIKENESS OF GOD 23
    צֶלֶם – *Tzelem* - IMAGE 23
    דְּמוּת - *Demut* - LIKENESS 25
        Distinction Between Man and Animals 26
        Comparisons of God in Man 27

How Mankind Is Like Elohim in His Person 30
Background for the Plurality of God that Mankind Reflects 32
Man and Woman, a Plurality and Tri-Unity in One 35
Anthropomorphism 40

CHAPTER 3: NAMES FOR GOD 49

אֵל *El* 50
אֵלִים *Elim* 53
אֱלָהּ *Elah* 54
אֱלוֹהַּ *Eloah* 55
אֱלֹהִים *Elohim* 56
    Arguments Against a Literal Understanding of Elohim 59
    Arguments for a Literal Understanding of Elohim 63
Dual Plurality 75
אֲדוֹן *Adonai* 81
יהוה *Yahweh* 82
    Two Yahwehs in the *Tanakh* 84
        Genesis 19:24 84
        Zechariah 2:8-9 86
        Hosea 1:1-7 86
        Isaiah 44:6 87

CHAPTER 4: THEOPHANIES 89

Theophany – The Angel of the LORD 90
    The Angel of *Yahweh* 92
        Genesis 22 94
        Judges 2:1 95
        Zechariah 3:1-10 97
    Yahweh Is Distinct from The Messenger (Angel) of The LORD 99

CONTENTS

Shechinah 101

CHAPTER 5: *SHEMA* 111

   Judaism 111

   Christianity 115

      Usages of *Echad* 119

         Two Becoming One 119

         Plurality without Unity 120

      Comments by Christian Authors on *Echad* 121

      Echad Not Seen as Compound Unity 122

      Echad Seen as Compound Unity 126

   Yachid - יָחִיד 130

   Author's Position on *Echad* 133

CHAPTER 6: PLURAL DESCRIPTIONS 135

   Pronouns 135

      Genesis 1:26 136

      Genesis 3:22 140

      Genesis 11:7 142

      Isaiah 6:8 145

   Opposition to Plural Pronouns 145

      The Heavenly Court Argument 147

      The Plural of Majesty Argument 151

      The Plural of Deliberation Argument 152

   Plural Verbs Used With *Elohim* 156

      Genesis 20:13 157

      Genesis 35:7 158

      2 Samuel 7:23 159

      Psalm 58:11(12) 159

- Other Plural Descriptions 160
  - Deuteronomy 5:23 160
  - Deuteronomy 10:17 161
  - Joshua 24:19 161
  - Ecclesiastes 12:1 162
  - Psalm 149:2 164
  - Isaiah 54:5 (comparing KJV with NASB) 164
  - Isaiah 50:1-6 165
  - Zechariah 11:4-14 167
- Tri-Unity in Isaiah 168
  - Isaiah 48:12-16 169
  - Isaiah 61:1-2a 172
  - Isaiah 63:7-14 173

CHAPTER 7: THE HOLY SPIRIT IN THE *TANAKH* 175

- Difficulties with the Term *"Spirit"* רוּחַ 175
  - The Use of the Term *"Spirit"* 178
- Personality and Work of the Holy Spirit in the *Tanakh* 180
  - The Holy Spirit Is a Person 180
- The Holy Spirit in Creation 184
- Holy Spirit Is Distinct from the Father and Son 188
- Holy Spirit's Coming Upon and Indwelling 190
  - Holy Spirit's Ministry to Individuals in the *Tanakh* 192
    - Bezaleel 192
    - Unnamed Tailors 192
    - Seventy Elders 193
    - Balaam 194
    - Joshua 194
    - Othniel 195

CONTENTS

    Gideon 196

    Jephthah 197

    Samson 198

    Saul 199

    David and Saul 201

    David 202

    Micah 203

    Isaiah 203

    Ezekiel 204

Inspiration of the Scriptures 207

Methods of Revelation 213

OT and NT comparisons of the Holy Spirit 214

    Psalm 110:1 with Matthew 22:42-44 214

    Psalm 41:9[10] with Acts 1:16 215

    Isaiah 6:9-10 with Acts 28:25-27 215

    Psalm 95:9-11 with Hebrews 3:7-11 216

    Jeremiah 31:33 with Hebrews 10:15-16 216

New Covenant 217

CHAPTER 8: MESSIAH DIVINE? 219

Olam עוֹלָם 220

'Ad - עַד 226

First Coming Messianic References 227

Messiah Divine! 229

    2 Samuel 7 and 1 Chronicles 17 230

    Isaiah 9:6-7 232

    Micah 5:2 239

    Jeremiah 23:5-6 244

    Psalm 110:1-7 249

  Daniel 9:24-27 254

  Isaiah Chapters 7 through 12 265

  Isaiah 50:1a, 4-6 266

  Isaiah 52:13 – 53:12 267

  Zechariah 11:12-14; 12:10; 13:7 269

  Zechariah 12:10 272

  Zechariah 13:7 276

CHAPTER 9: SUMMARY 281

APPENDIX 1: HOW TO BECOME ONE WITH G-D 291

APPENDIX 2: MOSES' USE OF ECHAD IN THE TORAH 307

APPENDIX 3: THE WORD: VERBAL PLENARY INSPIRATION 333

APPENDIX 4: THE SERVANT OF THE LORD 353

APPENDIX 5: THE DRIFT AWAY FROM THE BIBLE, A SUMMARY .. 357

BIBLIOGRAPHY 367

AUTHOR INDEX 389

SCRIPTURE INDEX 395

PREFACE
Words from the Author

I love the Jewish people and am deeply grieved by the atrocities that the "Christian" Church has committed against the Jewish people over the centuries. I intentionally set out to investigate what the Hebrew Scriptures say about the primary issue that separates Judaism from Christianity: Judaism espouses an absolute monotheistic perspective of God that attempts to discredit the Christian perspective of God as indivisibly One and yet a plurality at the same time. The Christian term for this concept is the word *trinity*, but in this work I will use what I consider to be a more accurate term: *tri-unity*.

I am well aware that on one hand, the Jewish people have little historical and theological incentive to personally investigate the Christian "Jesus"; and on the other hand, Christians lack clear perception that God's program for reaching the world is through the Jewish people. Judaism completely rejects with every ounce of strength the whole idea that God is a plurality and that the Messiah could be God. I also know that few Christians appreciate the evangelistic possibilities that would quite naturally open up if God's Oneness and plurality (tri-unity) could be proven from the Hebrew Scriptures alone, without the aid of the New Testament. Therefore, I engaged in a two-year study of the primary question, "Does the Old Testament clearly teach both monotheism and plurality, or is that combination found only in the New Testament? This volume is an extension of my findings regarding that intensely-researched question.

Since the publication of the first edition of *The Tri-Unity of God Is Jewish* in 2005, I have spent an additional 5 years, meaning a total of 10 years, in studying the plurality of God in the Hebrew Scriptures, because I realized that there was much more to study and investigate. In 2010, I wrote a comprehensive 914-page study on the plurality of God, entitled *Discovering the Mystery of the Unity of God*. Recently, I decided to republish my original book, *The Tri-Unity of God Is Jewish*, with a few more points and to correct some grammatical errors in the original volume. I will be using this 2019 update of it as the abridged study of the longer study from 2010.

Through this study I have become completely convinced that the Old Testament clearly presents God as both a monotheistic God and a plurality of three persons. Although the smallness of any human mind is incapable of logically explaining this tri-unity, I have discovered that in the Hebrew Scriptures, God presents Himself as "One" God who is plural.

I passionately desire to reach out to the Jewish people, asking them to consider what their Scriptures present as *HaShem's* message to them, His beloved, gifted, and talented people. I consider the Jewish people to be the most blessed nation on earth, the nation with some of the world's greatest intellects, the nation whose people consistently rise to the top in almost every field of endeavor. I desire to tap into that collective and individual giftedness by asking them to carefully considering the Hebrew Scriptures as God wrote them – simply as a direct message to them from *HaShem,* who longs to reveal Himself to them.

I was dismayed by a related but unexpected additional insight – that even many evangelical conservative Christians do not want to see the tri-unity of God in the Hebrew Scriptures – that they instead perform biblical and secular "gymnastics" which are based on humanistic, higher criticism applied to the Scriptures, to discount the verbal plenary aspects of Inspiration. In other words, the Bible is being increasingly sidelined as being less than the authoritative, inspired Word of God, so less emphasis is put on studying what God is saying to us literally from the Bible. I also discovered that many popular Christian commentaries ineffectively handle Scriptures related to the nature of God, especially the Trinity in the Hebrew Scriptures. The treatment is scanty, although much is revealed in the Old and New Testaments regarding God's nature.

I acknowledge my limitations as a Hebrew scholar; however, with contemporary Hebrew helps and computer technologies available in addition to my education and years of study, I am not a novice with the Scriptures. I am deeply passionate that this book encourage fundamental Bible believers to maintain their faith before it slips away in response to the pressures of Christian marketing that waters down the authority of the Bible and moves Christian error into the hearts and minds of believers. Steadfast believers need to turn the trend by countering it with solid Bible teaching and doctrine that encourages believers to hold firmly to the Scriptures.

I continue to be in awe of the Messiah (Christ) in the Hebrew Scriptures as Moses, David, and the Prophets wrote of Him, and then in the Gospels as He is revealed as the fulfillment of what the Hebrew Scriptures wrote of Him. I do continue to encourage all my readers to stand in awe of the Jewish Messiah, Jesus Christ, and the salvation that He has prepared for Israel as a nation, the Jewish people, and for Gentiles alike.

Still, beyond my concern for Christian believers to hold fast to their faith in Scripture is my most intense prayer – that this study may challenge Jewish people to study the claims of *HaShem* Himself. He is, after all, God.

John B. Metzger, M.A. - 2019

CHAPTER I: INTRODUCTION

Statement of Purpose

Within Judaism and biblical Christianity today, the foundational belief that both hold in common is that God is one and that there are no gods besides Him (Deuteronomy 6:4; Isaiah 44:6; 1 Corinthians 8:6). However, Judaism and biblical Christianity part company after that point. Judaism has an unmovable belief in monotheism, that God is one alone. Rabbi Stanley Greenberg of Temple Sinai of Philadelphia clearly contrasts the following statement of the Jewish belief in the oneness of God with the Christian belief of the tri-unity of God:

> Christians are, of course, entitled to believe in a Trinitarian conception of God, but their effort to base this conception on the Hebrew Bible must fly in the face of the overwhelming testimony of that Bible. Hebrew Scriptures are clear and unequivocal on the oneness of God….The Hebrew Bible affirms the one God with unmistakable clarity. Monotheism, an uncompromising belief in one God, is the hallmark of the Hebrew Bible, the unwavering affirmation of Judaism and the unshakable Faith of the Jew.
>
> Under no circumstances can a concept of a plurality of the Godhead or a trinity of the Godhead ever be based upon the Hebrew Bible.[1]

However, true New Testament faith views God as a Trinity. The term "trinity" is an inadequate term to describe God because it only emphasizes the three persons and not the unity within the Trinity. Hence the term *tri-unity* will be used because it is the best term to unite the oneness or unity of God with the plurality of God.[2] But even tri-unity is not palatable in the mind of Jewish people.

Jacob Jocz, a Jewish believer in Messiah, states that the differences between Judaism and New Testament faith center around a person and who He is:

---

[1] Arnold G. Fruchtenbaum, "Jewishness and the Trinity," n.p. [last accessed 11/4/2019]. Available online: www.Messiahnj.org/af-tri-unity.htm.
[2] Paul Enns, *The Moody Handbook of Theology,* 3rd edition (Chicago: Moody, 1989), 199.

> At the center of the controversy between Church and Synagogue stands the Christological question. This is not a question whether Jesus is the Messiah, but whether the Christian understanding of the Messiah is admissible in view of the Jewish concept of God. Here lies the dividing line between Judaism and the Church. On this point neither can afford to compromise.[3]

This controversy lies at the heart of this book: Who is Jesus (*Yeshua*)? How does Scripture present God and His Messiah? How does Judaism interpret those Scriptures, which have so much to say on the topic of God, His nature, and His Messiah? How do Bible believing Christians understand these Scriptures? Beyond that, what is the literal message that these same Scriptures deliver?

Ancient belief in the oneness of God is a major reason that Jewish people have resisted the advance of the Gospel of Christ (Messiah) for over twenty centuries. They rejected *Yeshua* the Messiah,[4] the promised Messiah of Israel, as God incarnate. In Old Testament times, unbelief was demonstrated by turning to other gods. Both Israel, in 722 B.C.E.,[5] and later Judah, in 586 B.C.E., suffered great defeats, resulting in the people being carried away into Assyria (Amos 7:10-17; Hosea 4:1-6; 9:1-9)[6] and Babylon (2 Chronicles 34:14-28; Jeremiah 2:5–3:10),[7] respectively. The Diaspora,[8] or scattering around the world that Moses spoke of in Deuteronomy (28:15-68 with Jeremiah 11:8; 30:1-10) had begun. These great defeats were a direct result of the unbelief of the Jewish people and their apostasy in relation to the Mosaic Law. They forsook God and His Law and worshipped false gods.

A second set of Jewish defeats (70 and 135 C.E.) further contributed to the Diaspora, in these instances not because they denied the oneness of God through idolatry as they had done previously, but because they had rejected their own Messiah who was prophesied by Moses and the prophets. This denial and rejection

---

[3] Jacob Jocz, "The Invisibility of God and the Incarnation," *Canadian Journal of Theology* (July 1958): 179-186.
[4] **Messiah:** Messiah comes from the Hebrew word Mashiach, meaning "anointed." When translated into New Testament Greek, Messiah is Christos, which becomes "Christ" in English.
[5] **Common Era**: These are alternate terms used as synonyms for the Latin adopted by the Church regarding the birth of Christ. B.C. and A.D. are the exact equivalent of B.C.E and C.E.
[6] Andrew E. Hill and John H. Walton. *A Survey of the Old Testament* (Grand Rapids: Zondervan, 1991), 359.
[7] Hill and Walton, *A Survey of the Old Testament*, 329.
[8] **Diaspora**: The dispersion of Jews throughout the world beginning with Israel (722 B.C.E.) and Judah (586 B.C.E.) through the fall of the Second Temple (70 C.E.) and their defeat in the revolt in 135 C.E. This term refers to all Jews living outside the Land of Israel; also known as the "Exile."

CHAPTER 1: INTRODUCTION

was partially a result of their absolute belief in the oneness of God compounded by the rabbinic teaching also known as the Oral Law (Daniel 9:26; Zechariah 11:1-17; 12:10; Matthew 24:1-2; Mark 13:1-2; Luke 21:5-6; 20-24).[9] The Oral Law made an even greater division between the Hebrew text and what first-century Pharisees taught in relationship to the Jewish concept of Messiah in the first century. That subject will not be dealt with here. For an informative study on the development of the Oral Law, review chapter seven in Arthur Kac's book, *The Spiritual Dilemma of the Jewish People*[10] (see appendix five for an overview). He presents insight regarding Jewish reasoning for transitioning to obeying the Oral Law instead of the Written Law.

Because of their rejection of *Yeshua* (Jesus), the Church has unjustly persecuted the Jewish people for over eighteen centuries in "Christian Europe."[11] More recently, Islam has persecuted Israel since the seventh century C.E. Yet today there is no indication that the Jewish people in general have changed their view relative to Jesus being the Messiah of Israel, the promised God/man who is one with God. Nevertheless, some Jewish people are coming to faith in Messiah *Yeshua* today, but the percentages are quite small, even in Israel. Even among some fringe messianic groups who profess faith in *Yeshua*, there is no belief that *Yeshua* is God as is reflected in this quote from Uri Marcus:

> Myself as well as our entire congregation of Believers in *Ma'aleh Adumim*, completely reject the Trinitarian notions of plural unity, and will not acquiesce to any theology which challenges the ONEness of *HaShem*[12] in any fashion.... *Yeshua* is the Son of the living G-d, never G-d the son, in our view.[13]

---

[9] **Oral Law**: Oral instruction beyond the written Torah, which was written down in the *Mishnah* (core of the Talmud) around 220 C.E. and is considered by Jewish people as authoritative, equal to the Scriptures. Rabbinic authorities use this argument to substantiate the Oral Law being as weighty as Scripture. They teach that Moses received more from God than the written Torah on Mount Sinai, that he received the Oral Law which was memorized and taught to Joshua, who taught it to the Judges, who then taught it to the Prophets and, finally, to the men of the Great Synagogue or the *Sophrim*. This Oral Law is the central reason *Yeshua* and the Pharisees were at odds.

[10] Arthur W. Kac, *The Spiritual Dilemma of the Jewish People* (2nd ed., Grand Rapids: Baker, 1983), 62-82.

[11] To understand the significance of the Christian persecution of the Jewish people over the centuries, I recommend reading from *Jews, God and History* by Max I. Dimont.

[12] *HaShem:* literally means "the name." Jewish people will refer to God as *HaShem* rather than mentioning the name of God.

[13] Richard Harvey, "Jesus the Messiah in Messianic Jewish Thought: Emerging Christologies," *Mishkan* (issue 39, 2003): 7.

That same belief is also seen in America by this statement of Joe Good:

> *Yeshua* was an attribute of the Father that was made flesh. But in being flesh, he was a man, totally man...*Yeshua* we do not see as being God when he walked here on earth. We see him as a man, a man anointed by God, sent by God to perform a function. Now in his resurrection, we do not see him as God. We see him as a man appointed by God and that has been restored back to what man was intended to be....I once believed in the Trinity; now I obviously don't.[14]

In Judaism, without question, the issue of the plurality of God is not embraced, and this disbelief also has spilled over to some Jewish "believers." Christianity treats this topic by either affirming the tri-unity of God in the Hebrew Scriptures or by affirming that this doctrine is foreshadowed in the Old Testament (*Tanakh*).

The core belief today in Judaism, or more precisely Rabbinic Judaism,[15] is one primary underlying point: that God is *one* (Deuteronomy 6:4). Their rejection of Messiah resulted in the unjust suffering of the Jewish people through the centuries at the hands of so-called Christians. A related point to this is the fact that the Pharisees[16] believed the Messiah would be a Pharisee and that he would help them build up the Oral Law[17] that served as a fence about the Written Law.[18] This fence was made up of man-made rules and regulations to protect the Written Law from being broken and the Jewish people from going into captivity. Between the years of the first generation of scribes that followed Ezra the Scribe up until Judah Ha-Nasi in 220 C.E., the memorized laws were written down into what is called the *Mishnah*.[19] The *Mishnah*,

---

[14] John Fischer, "*Yeshua:* The Deity Debate," Mishkan issue 39 (2003), 23.

[15] **Rabbinic Judaism**: There are two Judaisms: first, biblical Judaism, which is given in the Hebrew Scriptures without the Talmud, Oral Law, and rabbinic commentaries, and, secondly, Rabbinic Judaism with the Oral Law, which is the heart of the *Mishnah,* which is the core of the *Talmud.* Rabbinic Judaism follows the interpretations of the rabbis to the neglect of the Scriptures.

[16] **Pharisees**: Pharisees were the most well-known of several sects in Judaism in the first century. They are the ones primarily responsible for the Oral Law, consisting of man-made rules and regulations on how to keep the Law of Moses.

[17] Marc H. Tanenbaum and Marvin R. Wilson, eds., *Evangelicals and Jews in Conversation on Scripture, Theology, and History* (Grand Rapids: Baker, 1978), 60-61.

[18] J. Julius Scott, *Jewish Backgrounds of the New Testament* (Grand Rapids: Baker, 1995), 172-173.

[19] George Robinson, *Essential Judaism, a Complete Guide to Beliefs, Customs, and Rituals* (New York: Pocket Books, 2000), 341.

CHAPTER 1: INTRODUCTION

known as the fence that the rabbis built around the Written Law,[20] became known as the Oral Law, which became equal to Scripture.[21] The rabbis' teaching in regard to the Messiah was that he would be a great man, a gifted leader[22] and warrior, but he would not be God,[23] which contradicts the very *Tanakh*[24] they said they believed. So when Jesus came on the scene and tore down the fence, the rabbis were incensed.[25] They could have considered Jesus as the Messiah, but not as God. Their theological position was based on the Oral Law, and their reaction is clearly seen in John 10:32-33. The Messiah could not be God from their Pharisaic perspective.

The suffering of the Jewish people is not the result of believing in the unity and oneness of God. It is the failure to believe in the unity and oneness of God who presents Himself as a plurality of one God, who could and did appear as a man in the Hebrew Scriptures (Genesis 18). However, because of that belief, they would not believe that *Yeshua* was one with the Father, and, consequently, they also could not believe that *Yeshua* was the long-awaited, promised Messiah of Israel.

The foundation for the plurality of the Godhead was laid out in the Hebrew Scriptures.[26] The leadership of Israel did not recognize that; and, consequently, they rejected *Yeshua*, who clearly presented Himself as one with the Father. David Dockery's quote probably expresses the best way to view the tri-unity in the Hebrew Scriptures:

---

[20] A growing belief within Messianic Judaism is that in order to be a good Christian, many Messianic Jews (and Gentile believers) believe that the observance of the Written Law, or the Mosaic Law consisting of 613 laws, is necessary. This is a dangerous position of mixing Law and Grace together. These positions are expressed in *Torah Rediscovered* (a book) and *First Fruits of Zion* (a magazine published by Ariel and D'vorah Berkowitz). This is a very dangerous book and magazine and is not for a theological novice or person ungrounded in the faith.

[21] Jacob Neusner, *An Introduction to Judaism* (Louisville, Kent: Westminster/John Knox, 1991), 168.

[22] Louis Goldberg, *Our Jewish Friends* (Neptune, NJ: Loizeaux, 1983), 92-93.

[23] Emil Schurer, *A History of the Jewish People in the Time of Jesus Christ*, 2:160-162.

[24] **Tanakh**: the Hebrew Scriptures. The Hebrew term is an acronym derived from the three divisions of the Jewish Scriptures. The Hebrew words *Torah, Nevi'im* and *Ketuvim* or the Law, the Prophets and the Writings comprise the *"Tanakh."*

[25] This whole subject is beyond the scope of this paper but it does have a direct connection on why the Jewish leadership in Jesus' day rejected Him as the long awaited promised Messiah of Israel. There is a direct relationship between the Oral Law (fence) and its teaching and their rejection of Jesus.

[26] **Hebrew Scriptures**: The first 39 books of the Bible, called by many Christians the "Old Testament." The term "Hebrew Scriptures" is used to avoid alienating Jewish people by saying "*Old* Testament," which equates to them as being *old, out of date* or *no longer in force*.

> God did not reveal Himself in clearly defined trinitarian terms in the Old Testament. However, the Old Testament prepared the faithful for the doctrine of the Trinity.[27]

The New Covenant truths are not intended to be understood in a vacuum. Rather, they are clearly rooted in the teachings of the Hebrew Scriptures. The *Tanakh* will not necessarily prove in dogmatic terms the tri-unity of the Godhead until Isaiah, but it will lay a strong foundation for the unity of God and the plurality of God. Benjamin Warfield presents the concept of the tri-unity in the Hebrew Scriptures in the following statement:

> The Mystery of the Trinity is not revealed in the Old Testament; but the mystery of the Trinity underlies the Old Testament revelation, and here and there almost comes into view. Thus the Old Testament revelation of God is not corrected by the fuller revelation which follows it, but only perfected, extended and enlarged.[28]

Dockery and Warfield express the fact that the tri-unity is in the Hebrew Scriptures. It is the intent of this book to go one step further, demonstrating that the plurality (and tri-unity) was revealed but not as fully developed as it is in the New Covenant. Would Abraham, Moses, and David, to name a few, see the tri-unity and understand it? Probably they did not. But the Pharisees and Sadducees should have understood the fact of the plurality and unity of God in Jesus' day.

It has been the observation of this writer, over the last 60 years, that the Pauline Epistles seem to be the fuel for most of the messages in the Church today. Yet even Paul makes mention of only one mystery which the *Tanakh* did not teach, and that mystery was the mystery of the Church (Romans 16:25-26; 1 Corinthians 2:7, 10; Ephesians 3:4-10; Colossians 1:26-27).[29] Because of the Jewish insistence on the oneness of God, to the exclusion of the unity or plurality of God, they missed their Messiah and fell prey to 46 false messiahs over the centuries.[30] A current example of a false messiah is seen within the ultra-orthodox,

---

[27] David S. Dockery, *Biblical Illustrator, Monotheism in the Scriptures* (Nashville: Sunday School Board of the Southern Baptist Convention, Vol. 17, No. 4, Summer 1991), 27-30.
[28] Benjamin Breckinridge Warfield, *Biblical and Theological Studies* (Philadelphia: The Presbyterian and Reformed, 1968), 30-31.
[29] Robert L. Saucy, *The Church in God's Program* (Chicago: Moody, 1972), 59-60.
[30] James Smith, *The Promised Messiah*, (Nashville: Thomas Nelson, 1993), 470-474.

CHAPTER 1: INTRODUCTION

Lubavitch, Hasidic community, which believes that the late Rebbe Menachem Mendel Schneerson[31] is the Messiah.[32]

Need for the Study

This most critical study cannot be separated from the eternal destiny of Jewish souls. One cannot separate the salvation that was provided in the Messiah from his or her belief in the oneness (unity) of God and the plurality of God. Only their belief in the oneness of God is seen. Therefore, their belief in absolute monotheism rules out the whole redemptive plan of God, which was provided through the Messiah and includes the acceptance of the plurality of God. Since the Jewish people rejected *Yeshua ha Mashiach* as their Messiah, there is no possible way to deal with the question of sin and separation from God. They stumbled over the substitutionary sacrifice of the Servant of the LORD,[33] the Messiah of Israel, on the tree.

Contrary to what Jewish rabbis and liberal Christian theologians would have Christians believe, the Mosaic Covenant[34] is not a saving covenant for the Jewish

---

[31] **Messianic Scriptures**: (a) messianic passages tell us that the Messiah will be of Abraham (Genesis 12:1-3), (b) that the scepter will not depart from Judah until He is revealed (Genesis 49:10), (c) that He would be a prophet like Moses (Deuteronomy 18:15-19 with Numbers 12:5-8), (d) that He would be of the House of David (1 Chronicles 17:10-14), (e) that He would be born in Bethlehem (Isaiah 9:5-6: Micah 5:2), (f) that He would have to come before the destruction of the Second Temple (Daniel 9:24-27; Genesis 49:10), (g) that He would die (Isaiah 53:10; Psalm 22), (h) that He would be resurrected (Isaiah 53:10. Menachem Schneerson has failed to meet all these biblical criteria except for one; he was Jewish. He was born in Nikolaev, Ukraine, on April 18, 1902, not Bethlehem as Micah prophesied. He escaped Europe and came to New York City in March 1940. Since he has no idea what tribe he descended from, he cannot lay claim to the tribe of Judah and the House of David. He not only was born in Brooklyn, but he was born 19 centuries after the destruction of the Temple.

[32] David Berger, *The Rebbe, The Messiah and the Scandal of the Orthodox Indifference* (Portland: Littman Library of Jewish Civilization, 2001), 20-25.

[33] Because Jewish people are very sensitive about writing or speaking the name of G-d, they will often refer to Him by using the terms *Adonai* (Lord) or *HaShem* (the Name). Because of the variety of names that the *Tanakh* uses for God, it is important to be correct when referring to the Hebrew Scriptures. The reason for using these precise names is to be precise, with no intent to show insensitivity to Jewish people.

[34] **Mosaic Covenant**: God made five covenants with Israel. These covenants were divided into two groupings: conditional and unconditional covenants. *Unconditional* means that the Abrahamic, Land, Davidic, and New Covenants were made by God and cannot be broken by man. However, by *conditional* we mean that Israel had a responsibility to keep their part of the covenant to receive the blessing of God. If Israel disobeyed, God would not keep His part until they repented. Only the Mosaic covenant is conditional, based on man's performance.

people.[35] Obedience to the Law cannot save. Habakkuk 2:4 says, *The righteous will live by his faith*. There have been no offerings or sacrifices for sin because the Temple was destroyed in Jerusalem in 70 C.E. by the Romans. With the possible exception of the years between 132-135 C.E., during the second revolt against Rome led by Bar Kokhba[36] there has been no Temple or sacrifice for nearly 2,000 years. If the Law was to be the covenant to give salvation, then God has made it completely impossible for the Jewish people to bring sacrifices to Him in Jerusalem at the Temple Mount. John Johnson expresses in a very clear and understanding way the development and belief of Dual Covenant theology.[37] The basic belief came out of the Holocaust and teaches that Jewish people are saved by observance of the Law while Gentiles are saved by their belief in Jesus. In other words, Jewish people have the Mosaic Law and the Abrahamic Covenant, and Gentiles have Jesus.[38]

The purpose of the Law was to provide a redeemed people with a rule of life in the areas of civil, religious, and moral life.[39] Fruchtenbaum adds to Chafer's position by holding that the sacrificial system was also a rule of life for the Old Testament saint. Its purpose was not for securing salvation but for the time when they would fail to keep the Law. "Sacrifices were accepted as a means to restoration just as confession is for the believer today."[40] Fruchtenbaum has made two other observations. First, the 613 commandments derived from the Mosaic Law were issued as conditional. The conditional nature of the covenant is given in Exodus 15:26[41] as well as in Deuteronomy 28:15. If the commandments were obeyed, abundant blessing was promised (Deuteronomy 28:1-14). But if they disobeyed, even more abundant cursing (Deuteronomy 28:16-68) would befall them. Second, the offering on the Day of Atonement did not remove sin (Hebrews 8-10). The Day of Atonement had its shortcomings because it was a temporary answer, not the permanent answer, for sin.[42] If it had been, no further sacrifice on the Day of

---

[35] G. Jeffrey Macdonald, *Press Republican* (Plattsburgh, NY; September 13, 2002), A7.

[36] Rabbi Leibel Reznick, *The Holy Temple Revisited* (Northvale, NJ: Jason Aronson, 1993), 155-159.

[37] **Dual Covenant Theology**: This teaches that God's covenant (Mosaic Law) with the Jews hasn't been revoked and they are still in a saving covenant with God. In other words, a good Christian is saved by being obedient to the New Testament and the Jew is saved by being obedient to the Mosaic Law. However, the Mosaic Law was never a saving covenant; no one was saved by obedience to the Law but by faith alone.

[38] John J. Johnson, "A New Testament Understanding of the Jewish Rejection of Jesus: Four Theologians on the Salvation of Israel," *JETS* 43, no. 2 (2000): 229-246.

[39] Lewis Sperry Chafer, *Systematic Theology* (Dallas: Dallas Seminary, 1948) 4:159-160.

[40] Arnold G. Fruchtenbaum, *Israelology, the Missing Link in Systematic Theology* (Tustin, CA: Ariel Ministries, 1989), 376.

[41] Fruchtenbaum, *Israelology, the Missing Link in Systematic Theology*, 588.

[42] Daniel Fuchs, *Israel's Holy Days* (Neptune, N.J: Loizeaux, 1985), 64-68.

CHAPTER 1: INTRODUCTION

Atonement would have been necessary. Instead, the atonement provided only a covering for sin and restoration of fellowship but not the removal of sin.[43] The true solution for the problem of sin was fulfilled in the Person of *Yeshua ha Meshiach*[44] for He became the sin bearer (Isaiah 53) that the Mosaic Law pointed to.

In the first century, as well as today, the core belief of Judaism taught that God is one and not a unity of plurality. People need to have a good understanding of why Judaism holds that God is one (Deuteronomy 6:4), not two or three, as Jewish people understand Christianity to teach. The true biblical Church believes in the tri-unity of the Godhead and can substantiate that from the Hebrew Scriptures. But the rabbis equally believe, from the same Scriptures (and the Oral Law), that God is one and cannot be a man or God/man as is understood by believers in Messiah. How can true believers in Messiah and Jewish rabbis get two different readings from the same Scriptures? *Yeshua* was very clear on who He was, and that was clearly understood by the rabbinic leadership of Israel because *Yeshua* received a very strong, aggressive and negative response from the Pharisees and Sadducees (John 8:54-59; 10:30-31).

A clear understanding of the phrase "unity of God" is important to comprehend and needs to be defined so both Jewish and New Testament readers understand one another in this paper. New Testament believers understand that God is a unity expressed in three persons, usually referred to as the trinity: God the Father, God the Son, and God the Holy Spirit. They are indivisible (undivided) and equal in character and essence. However, the Jewish people understand that God is one, a unity, indivisible; and, therefore, they hold only to God the Father. The term "indivisible" is used because in Old Testament history the pagan gods were able to be divided into multiple locations and gods. The multiplicity of deities is explained well by Jacobs:

> There is only one God and there are no others. Allied to this is the idea that God in His essence is indivisible. A deity like Baal could be split up, as it were, into various local deities, hence the plural form Baalim and Ashterot found in the Bible when speaking of the pagan gods. God is one and indivisible. He is Lord of all. He cannot be united syncretistically with other gods.[45]

The term "indivisible" accentuates the fact that God is not divided and is outside His creation, not part of it, nor is He divided into different locations competing with Himself. True biblical believers would agree with the Jewish people in their

---

[43] Fruchtenbaum, *Israelology, the Missing Link in Systematic Theology*, 588-589.
[44] **Yeshua:** The Hebrew name for Jesus the Christ.
[45] Louis Jacobs, *A Jewish Theology* (West Orange, NJ: Behrman House, 1973), 21.

understanding of God, except they recognize the plurality of God in the New Testament as well as the multitude of references in the Hebrew Scriptures giving the foundation of the New Testament teaching of the tri-unity. Therefore, in this study, the unity of God is discussed from a New Testament viewpoint which I will refer to as *the tri-unity of God,* the concept of God being a plural unity, unless stated otherwise.

Viewing the tri-unity from a Christian perspective is not helpful for the Jewish people because of their strong monotheistic heritage. Jewish believers in Messiah *Yeshua* uphold the tri-unity, but it is not their term of preference. The problem is how to define a doctrine that has no biblical terms. "Trinity" and "tri-unity" are not biblical terms. God is so overwhelming that He overflows or transcends our human notions of personhood. Anything beyond "one" or the "unity of God" is a problem for Jewish people. Jewish believers in *Yeshua* accept the tri-unity because they have examined the historical and biblical materials and concluded that it is correct even if the term is inadequate or gives the wrong concept to the Jewish mind. Michael Schiffman has a chapter in his book called "Messianic Jews & the Tri-Unity of God" that would be very beneficial for Jewish and Gentile believers to read, to help Gentile believers understand the frame of reference that Jewish people have.[46] Jewish people do not use creeds or councils like the Nicene Council in 325 C.E. Instead of creeds, they used "testimonia" or "the quotation of Scriptures that supported their views."[47] Dwight Pryor further illustrates that there was no creedal usage of this doctrine when first-century believers spoke of *Yeshua:*

> How do they explain theologically this devotion to a man and their veneration of him with God? They don't – to the frustration of our western minds! These Jewish believers expressed their monotheism in the same manner Israel had done from the beginning – in their worship. Not abstractly with theological speculations, but with actions demonstrating loyalty, veneration and service; not with propositional truths so much as with liturgical exclamations. For them the relationship of Jesus and God focused more on identity than divinity, and the truth was framed in textual associations more than theological affirmations. For example, scriptures that apply to *YHVH* are now, prerogatives of *Adonai*, such as creation and kingship are now extended to Jesus – not as some external, albeit divine agent, but as someone within the very identity and oneness of God himself. This is a crucial point. This veneration of *Yeshua* with and connected

---
[46] Michael Schiffman, *Return of the Remnant* (Baltimore: Lederer Publications, 1992), 93-103.
[47] Fischer, "*Yeshua:* The Deity Debate," 20.

CHAPTER 1: INTRODUCTION

> to *YHVH* is permissible only if he in some way is within the *echad* of God. Otherwise such attributions of scriptures, functions, authority, power, and identity to him that apply exclusively to the God of Israel would violate the *Shema's* monotheism.[48]

That gives some idea of the Jewish frame of reference to the tri-unity and also how the early believers affirmed their belief in *Yeshua ha Mashiach*.[49]

Some Christian authors give little attention in showing the tremendous weight of Scripture the *Tanakh* provides not only in the oneness of God but His unity and plurality. Clearly, there is a need to synthesize and clarify in one book the foundations of the unity and plurality of the Godhead. This plurality also will be shown to be anchored to the *Torah*,[50] *Nevi'im*,[51] and *Ketuvim*[52] just as the oneness of God is anchored to the Hebrew Scriptures. Authors like Hodge[53] and Berkhof[54] add nothing or very little to the subject at hand. One reason is because they have not made it the emphasis or premise of their books or articles. Paul House in his *Old Testament Theology*, "summarizes its content and shows its theological significance in relationship to the whole of Old Testament Canon."[55] His theme is God and how He expresses Himself to Israel through the Hebrew Scriptures. Even though there are places where he speaks about the plural form for God, it is not the thrust of his book.[56] David Hinson's book, *Theology of the Old Testament*, deals with the oneness of God and quotes the *Shema* of Deuteronomy 6:4 without an adequate explanation of the word "one" or *echad*. In fact he says,

---

[48] Dwight A. Pryor, "One God and Lord," *Mishkan* (issue 39 2003), 56.

[49] ***Yeshua Ha Meshiach:*** This is the Hebrew words meaning Jesus the Messiah. When it goes from Hebrew to Greek to English it becomes Jesus the Christ.

[50] ***The Torah:*** Also known as the Pentateuch, the first five books of the Bible. Meaning literally "teaching" or "instruction" or "guidance." Often translated as "the Law" in English Bibles, as in "the Law of the LORD is perfect" (Psalm 19:7 [v. 8 in Hebrew]). Torah in Judaism is an elastic term, which can also mean a single point of teaching to the whole of the Hebrew Bible, and the Oral Law.

[51] ***Nevi'im***: This is the second division of the Hebrew Scriptures, called the Prophets (Joshua, Judges, 1 & 2, Samuel, 1 & 2 Kings, Isaiah, Jeremiah, Ezekiel, Hosea, Joel, Amos, Obadiah, Jonah, Micah, Nahum, Habakkuk, Zephaniah, Haggai, Zechariah, and Malachi).

[52] ***Ketuvim***: This is the third division of the Hebrew Scriptures, called the Writings (Psalms, Proverbs, Job, Song of Songs, Ruth, Lamentations, Ecclesiastes, Esther, Daniel, Ezra, Nehemiah, and 1 & 2 Chronicles).

[53] Charles Hodge, *Systematic Theology* (Grand Rapids: Eerdmans, 1970), 1:442-482.

[54] L. Berkhof, *Systematic Theology* (Grand Rapids: Eerdmans, 1941), 82-99.

[55] Paul House, *Old Testament Theology* (Downers Grove, Ill: InterVarsity, 1998), front cover.

[56] House, *Old Testament Theology,* 61-62.

> It is the ordinary word used in counting, and fails to provide any single explanation of what the Jews meant when they said that "the LORD our God is one LORD."[57]

He later speaks of "the angel of the LORD" (*Yahweh*) without any reference to the fact that the "angel of *Yahweh*" is *Yahweh* and yet distinct from the LORD (*Yahweh*). He does state "that the angel is the LORD himself."[58] He does reference Genesis 16:7-14 in connection with Hagar, but he makes no use of examples to illustrate this from Genesis 19:24 or Judges 2:1, which show that the Angel of *Yahweh* is the LORD, yet distinct from God. Walter Brueggemann's *Theology of the Old Testament* deals with Israel's relationship to *Yahweh*. He makes good observations and statements on the Hebrew Scriptures but says little about the oneness or unity and plurality of the Person of God. Thus, he does not deal with the formidable weight of evidence on how God is revealed in the Hebrew Scriptures.[59]

Books such as *Theological Word Book of the Old Testament*,[60] *All the Divine Names and Titles in the Bible*,[61] *The Names of God*,[62] *Dictionary of Old Testament Theology & Exegesis*,[63] and *Names of God*[64] do reference both the oneness or unity of God and the plurality of God. They speak of the origin and meaning of such terms as *El, Eloah, Elohim, YHVH, Adonai,* and *Echad* versus *Yachid*, plus the plural descriptions of God. However, most of these books only lay out the basic facts of the unity and plurality of God and do not draw them together. They do not enable the reader to get a full prospective of these plural terms of God in the Hebrew Scriptures and their weight as they stand together.

Another example of a study on the plurality of God is J. Barton Payne.[65] He touches on the names, titles, and plurality of God; but he does not give the depth of study beneficial to the Jewish audience. He discusses how the term *Elohim* developed during the time of Abraham to Moses rather than how it is used and understood

---

[57] David Hinson, *Theology of the Old Testament* (London: Society for Promoting Christian Knowledge, 2001), 23-24.
[58] Hinson, *Theology of the Old Testament,* 60-61.
[59] Walter Brueggemann, *Theology of the Old Testament*. (Minneapolis: Fortress, 1997).
[60] R. Laird Harris, Gleason L. Archer, Jr., and Bruce K. Waltke, eds., *Theological Wordbook of the Old Testament* (2 vols; Chicago: Moody, 1980).
[61] Herbert Lockyer, *All the Divine Names and Titles in the Bible*, (Grand Rapids: Zondervan, 1975).
[62] Andrew Jukes, *The Names of God* (Grand Rapids: Kregel, 1980).
[63] Willem A. VanGemeren, ed., *Dictionary of Old Testament Theology & Exegesis* (Grand Rapids: Zondervan, 1997).
[64] Nathan Stone, *Names of God*.
[65] J. Barton Payne, *The Theology of the Older Testament* (Grand Rapids: Zondervan, 1962), 125-127, 144-151.

CHAPTER 1: INTRODUCTION

throughout the Hebrew Scriptures. His understanding is that Abraham was a monolatrist rather than a monotheist.[66] His example of Abraham before Abimelech is lacking because nothing else in the Genesis text gives any reason to believe that Abraham was monolatrist. Yet when coupling the biblical text together with archaeology, a better candidate for monolatry is Balaam (Numbers 22:7-13). The *Bible and Spade*, a magazine of Associates for Biblical Research, gives the discovery of Balaam's name and prophecy on a pagan temple in present day Jordan.[67] Another possible candidate for monolatry would be Jethro, Moses' father-in-law (Exodus 18:11).

Baker, in the *Dictionary of the Old Testament Pentateuch*[68] spends a considerable part of an article on the etymology of the names of God without showing how the names of God relate to each other or how the text of Scripture uses them in relation to each other. It is disappointing to see his short treatment of the plural noun *Elohim*. He does not even present the possibility of *Elohim* being anything beyond "a plurality of majesty, or royal plurals, as an intensification or claim to exclusivity, or as a honorific."[69] The "plural of majesty," when referring to *Elohim*, means that when God addresses someone, He uses the plural "we" or "royal we," much as the Queen of England would use when addressing others in her presence. Baker's thoughts on the subject indicate a presupposition that the plurality of God does not play a part in his thinking.

This lack of attention to the tri-unity in the Hebrew Scriptures is also evident in evangelical theological journals. In 210 years of *Bib Sac*, *Westminster Theological Journal*, *JETS*, *Canadian Theological Journal*, *Grace Theological Journal*, and *Master's Theological Journal*s, almost nothing can be found on the tri-unity in the *Tanakh* unless it is embedded within another subject.[70]

It is not that Payne, Alexander, and others, as mentioned above, do not speak of the issues of the names of God used in a singular and plural context, but these references are scattered throughout their books. The purpose of this study is to put the references and insights of the unity and plurality of God all together and study them

---

[66] **Monolatry** is the worship of one god while recognizing other gods that can be worshipped. **Monotheism** is the belief in one God and that no other gods exist.

[67] B. G. Wood, "Prophecy of Balaam Found in Jordan," *Bible and Spade* 6 (Autumn 1977): 121-124.

[68] Desmond Alexander and David Baker, *Dictionary of the Old Testament Pentateuch* (Downers Grove, Ill: InterVarsity, 2003).

[69] Alexander and Baker, *Dictionary of Old Testament Pentateuch*, 362.

[70] Bib Sac from 1945 to present, *Westminster Theological Journal* from 1960 to present, *JETS* from 1969 to present, *Canadian Theological Journal* form 1955 to 1970, *Grace Theological Journal* from 1960 to present, and *Masters Theological Journal* from 1990 to present.

in more depth, in one place, so that a reader can get a fuller and unhindered view of the subject.

The understanding of the unity and plurality of God is the bottom line that must be dealt with before an *uncircumcised heart* of unbelief becomes a "circumcised" Jewish heart (Deuteronomy 30:6; Jeremiah 9:25-26; Acts 3:11-19; 8:26-37; Colossians 2:11). Understanding the unity and plurality of God is foundational to understanding what Moses and the prophets wrote. Before the Jewish mind can embrace *Yeshua* as the Messiah, that mind must acknowledge God as one (a unity in plurality) and the Messiah as the God/man promised by the Hebrew Scriptures.

Scriptural and Theological Basis

This study of the unity (oneness) and plurality of God is based on how the Hebrew Scriptures treat the subject. A larger study of this issue would be to show the importance of this topic and how the rabbis have interpreted the Hebrew Scriptures by showing the background and importance of the Oral Law to that interpretation. This will have to be covered in a future study.

Robert Morey has made a very basic statement which is at the very heart of this paper. If God wanted to show that He was "multi-personal," then the student of the Word would be expected to find His plurality in the Hebrew Scriptures. The same is true, if God wanted to show that He was "only one person," then that is what He would have written. Morey makes this statement:

> If the authors of the Bible believed that God was multi-personal, then we would expect to find that they would write about God in such a way as to indicate this idea to their readers. Thus, we must ask, "What would we expect to find in the Bible, if its authors believed that God was multi-personal?"
>
> On the other hand, if the authors of the Bible believed that God was only one person, i.e., they were classic Unitarians, then they would write about God in such a way as to indicate that idea. Thus, we are also warranted to ask, "What would we expect to find in the Bible, if Unitarians wrote it?" We will at times use the term "Unitarian" in its generic sense of anyone who denies the Trinity because he believes

CHAPTER 1: INTRODUCTION

that God is only one person. This would include Jews, Muslims, Arians, and Modalists.[71]

This book will be looking at some of the names for God, such as God, Lord, LORD, and how they are used throughout the Hebrew Scriptures, as well as seeing how the authors of Scriptures reveal God to the reader. This study will also state how faithful believers view the core statement of Judaism (Deuteronomy 6:4) and how the word for "one" and the plurality of God is used throughout the Law, Prophets, and Writings. Plural descriptions of God will then be discussed (such as Joshua 24:19; Psalm 149:2; Ecclesiastes 12:1; Isaiah 54:5) followed by a chapter on the Holy Spirit, and, lastly, by passages that speak of the Messiah being divine in the *Tanakh*.

Two biblical positions underlie all discussions of the plurality and tri-unity of God in the Hebrew Scriptures as it progresses throughout this study. First is the inspiration of Scripture. Fundamental, conservative, and evangelical believers affirm the inspiration of Scripture, which refers to the "breathing out of God." Scripture is God-breathed through the Holy Spirit into men. This enabled them to receive and communicate divine truth, without error, making the speaker and/or writer infallible in the communication of God's truth. The Scriptures are God-breathed.[72] A second concept, tied very closely to inspiration, involves two other related terms: verbal and plenary inspiration. By verbal, it is meant that every word of the original manuscripts of the Bible was given by inspiration of God. By plenary it is meant that this inspiration is full, complete, entire, extending to every part. So, every part of the Hebrew Scriptures and New Covenant is inspired equally by God.[73]

Since verbal and plenary inspiration is completely valid, then the words of Jesus as He taught regarding the subject of His divinity and the plurality of God should be highly regarded. He clearly states that Moses and the prophets spoke of Him:

> *Search the* [Hebrew] *scriptures; for in them you think you have eternal life: and* **they are they which testify of Me.** (John 5:39)
>
> *For had you believed Moses, you would have believed Me;* **for he wrote of Me.** (John 5:46)
>
> [25] *Then he said unto them, O fools, and slow of heart to believe all that the prophets have spoken:* [26] *Ought not Christ to have suffered*

---

[71] Robert Morey, *The Trinity: Evidence and Issues* (Grand Rapids: World Publishing, 1996), 87.
[72] H. S. Miller, *General Biblical Introduction* (Houghton, N.Y: Word-Bearer, 1960), 17.
[73] H. S. Miller, *General Biblical Introduction*, 24.

> *these things, and to enter into His glory?* ²⁷ **And beginning at Moses and all the prophets, He expounded unto them in all the scriptures [Hebrew] the things concerning Himself.**[74]
>
> (Luke 24:25-27)

Jesus was not speaking irresponsibly by telling his disciples that Moses and the prophets bore witness of Him. Or, did He really mean that He, as the Son of God, was revealed in the Hebrew Scriptures and in order to do that He would have to be presented as God, and that God would then have to be in a plural form? The Pharisees had every right to reject Him if *Yeshua* taught in the New Testament that He was divine, and the plurality of God was not taught in the Hebrew Scriptures. But if He was in the Hebrew Scriptures as He said, then the Pharisees rejected him for reasons beyond the claim of being divine, and they have been misinterpreting some very important Scriptures that God intended them to understand and believe. God would not have presented his Son in a vacuum, but the *Tanakh* would have given evidence of His divine nature. If the Father had not given ample witness of His plurality in the *Tanakh*, then He would have been setting up the Pharisees to reject Jesus, and all Israel has suffered over the centuries as a direct result of God's silence or deception on the subject of His plurality in the Hebrew Scriptures. The words of Jesus should not have been considered blasphemous as it was by the Sanhedrin (John 10:33; Matthew 26:63-66; Luke 5:21). The strangeness of the recurrence of plural terms for God in the *Tanakh* should not have stumped Christian scholars. Instead, the plurality inherent in the names of God, with the use of the term *echad* versus *yachid,* should have been clues to them. We see the distinction in major passages regarding theophanies where plural descriptions are used, and even in the *Shema* of Deuteronomy 6:4. Have Christian theologians abandoned or abdicated the doctrine of the tri-unity of God to Rabbinic Judaism? How could Christian scholars have missed so many Old Testament clues to the tri-unity of God?

The second biblical position relates to biblical interpretation. Coupled with a belief in verbal plenary inspiration is the belief in the literal method of interpretation. If the Scriptures are God-breathed, then God meant what He said, and man's attempt to reinterpret what He said is not necessary. David Cooper gives the following definition of this literal method of interpretation:

---

[74] *The Holy Bible*, King James Version (New York: Oxford University, 1996), 1281. Unless otherwise stated, all New Testament references are cited from the King James Version, published by Oxford University Press, The Scofield Reference Bible Edition (1996). Unless otherwise noted, all Old Testament references are taken from the Jewish Study Bible (JSB), published by Oxford University Press (2004) for Jewish Publication Society. Any **bold font** is added for emphasis.

CHAPTER 1: INTRODUCTION

> When the plain sense of Scripture makes common sense, seek no other sense; therefore, take every word at its primary, ordinary, usual, literal meaning unless the facts of the immediate context, studied in the light of related passages and axiomatic and fundamental truths, indicate clearly otherwise.[75]

So when coming to the names of God, like *Elohim* (a plural term for *God*), why do scholars want to argue against what God says about Himself? If verbal plenary inspiration of the Scriptures is believed by fundamental, conservative, and evangelical believers, then why do some of them try to make it the plural of majesty rather than a literal plural reference?

Remembering clearly 50 years ago, the professors at Washington Bible College impressed upon their students when looking at Scripture to always look at the context, context, context! If a passage is not viewed within the context that God gave it, then one's study is vulnerable merely to the thoughts and intellect of man. That principle applies to a study of the relationship of *Elohim* to the plurality or tri-unity of God. Scholars and translators may allow the context to determine whether it refers to pagan gods or the true God. Why are false gods recognized in the plurality (Isaiah 36:18-20), but when the same identical word (Exodus 20:2-3) is used of the true God the vast majority of the time, they explain away the plurality of God by calling it a "plural of majesty"?

Limitations of the Research Project

The primary focus of this study is the oneness or unity and plurality of God and how the Hebrew Scriptures treat the subject. Therefore, it will not be the main purpose of this book to deal with the New Testament proofs of the tri-unity. Erickson makes the comment that the *Tanakh* will lead us to a monotheistic belief, but as he said, what led the Church to move beyond the monotheistic belief was additional biblical witness (New Testament).[76] However, the *Tanakh* did not need additional New Testament revelation to substantiate the plurality or tri-unity of God, and this book will validate that. Along with the New Testament references, the Oral Law and rabbinic interpretation of the Law of Moses will be mostly excluded, and only be touched upon when it is necessary to understand the purpose of this book, which focuses on the unity and plurality of God in the Hebrew Scriptures.

---

[75] David L. Cooper, *The God of Israel* (Los Angeles: Biblical Research Society, 1945), 34-35.
[76] Millard J. Erickson, *Introducing Christian Doctrine* (Grand Rapids: Baker, 1992), 98.

Organization of Study

Image and Likeness of God – Chapter 2

Chapter two deals with a question that many people have desired to know over the centuries: What is the meaning of the *image* and *likeness* of God? Many have tried to understand just how mankind was created in His image. Countless authors have made good observations on how mankind is like God and also how mankind is not like God. The complete answer to this subject is probably unknowable. However, God did give man some parameters to work within. This chapter is focused on how mankind was created in the *image* and *likeness* of God in relationship to the plural unity of His Person.

Names of God – Chapter 3

Chapter three deals with the understanding and usage of the terms *El*, *Elim*, *Elohim*, and *Eloah* and why *Elohim* is applied to two divine beings as in Psalm 45:6-7. Some of these names are singular and some are plural according to how the Hebrew Scriptures use them. What does Hebrew grammar say in relation to *Elohim*, which is a plural term for one God? Consideration is also given to the usage of the term Lord, as *Adonai* and *Yahweh* (LORD) or *YHVH*, and why it is also applied to two divine beings in Genesis 19:24 and Zechariah 2:8-9.

It appears that Christian theologians and scholars have abandoned or abdicated the tri-unity of God in the Hebrew Scriptures to Rabbinic Judaism's interpretation of God, which has been in complete control of the Jewish people for 2,000 years. The difference is as great as day and night between biblical Judaism and Rabbinic Judaism. One leads to truth and one to falsehood in relation to how the subject of the tri-unity is treated and understood. God, who is one, chose to reveal Himself with a multitude of plural references to Himself. Why, if God chose that course to reveal Himself, do Christian scholars who believe in the tri-unity in the New Covenant, constantly force those plural references into singular interpretation in the Hebrew Scriptures? The outcome of how this subject is treated and understood by Christians from the Hebrew Scriptures determines the eternal fate of Jewish souls.

Theophanies – Chapter 4

Chapter four will deal with understanding the term *theophany* in the Hebrew Scriptures and how it is used. Jewish rabbis insist that God will not, has not, and did not, appear as a man in human history. Yet, throughout the *Tanakh*, God did appear to Abraham, Jacob, Joshua, and others in the form of a man. Jewish rabbis have that narrow, unbiblical view because if the incarnation of God is entertained at all, Rabbinic Judaism is finished. Understanding the term *theophany* involves examining such terms as *the angel of the Lord* and/or *the Captain of the Lord's Host* (Joshua 5:15), where God appeared in the form of a man with those titles. *Yahweh* also said that He would send *My angel* (Exodus 23:23) to lead them as they traveled through the wilderness. The second part of understanding *theophany* is the *Shechinah* of God, which designates God's presence.[77] The presence of God, which appeared to Moses and Israel as the Glory of God, dwelt with Israel on Mount Sinai and then in the Holy of Holies of the Tabernacle and later in the Temple of Solomon. If the theophanies of God are God, Himself, then God is a plurality and the whole of Jewish understanding is at odds with the *Tanakh*, because in those theophanies God has chosen to show Himself as one God but as a plurality within His oneness.

Shema – Chapter 5

Chapter five deals with the cornerstone and affirmation of the Jewish faith, the *Shema* of Deuteronomy 6:4. As far as Judaism is concerned, this verse puts to rest, forever, the whole subject of the plurality or tri-unity of God. It specifically puts to rest the whole subject of the Incarnation of the Messiah in the Jewish mind because "*Yahweh* is one." This chapter focuses particularly on the words *Echad* and *Yachid* and the meaning of both. Maimonides, who is called the second Moses and who lived in the eleventh century C.E., changed the reading of the *Shema* in his second of Thirteen Articles from *Echad* to *Yachid*. It is necessary to understand why these two Hebrew words in his Thirteen Articles are so very important to the Jewish understanding of the *Shema* of Deuteronomy 6:4.

Once again, Christian theologians and scholars bypass studies on exactly how that word is used throughout the Hebrew Scriptures. Is God making a statement beyond His desire for Israel to love Him and commit to Him alone? Jewish rabbis say no. However, in the *Shema*, did God have the unity or plurality of Himself in mind?

Plural Terms – Chapter 6

Chapter six will deal with the plural pronouns used of God, and other plural descriptions, showing how they apply to the unity and plurality of God. God, in

---

[77] Jacob Neusner and William Scott Green, *Dictionary of Judaism in the Biblical Period* (Peabody, Mass: Hendrickson, 1999), 577.

numerous places, used plural terms for Himself beyond the terms *Elohim*, Angel of *Yahweh*, and other combinations of terms for God, both plural and singular. The plural personal pronoun *us*, as in Genesis 1:26, that God uses of Himself seven times in the Hebrew Scriptures, will be studied. The four references in the *Tanakh* where these are found will make a strong statement toward understanding His Person and the plural emphasis that God makes.

There are other descriptive terms that God uses to further strengthen His plurality, such as the plural attribute of *Creator* in Ecclesiastes 12:1. Other descriptive plural words for God (such as *Elohim*) are located in Genesis 20:13; 35:7; 2 Samuel 7:23; and Psalm 58:11.

Holy Spirit – Chapter 7

This chapter will deal with the neglected term *spirit of the LORD* in the Hebrew Scriptures. While there are many references to God's personal character in the New Testament, the same is not as plentiful in the *Tanakh*. God did not just become a tri-unity in the New Testament; He always was a tri-unity. We will examine how the *spirit of the LORD* and God as Spirit are distinct in the *Tanakh*. The purpose of this chapter will be to substantiate that the Holy Spirit is active in the *Tanakh* and that He is represented often by His deeds or actions rather than always showing His personhood, as is usually presented in the New Testament.

Christian cults and the Jewish people reject the personhood of the Holy Spirit. To them He is merely the extension of God, or the presence of God, but not a separate distinct person. In Judaism there is no belief in a tri-unity of God. The Person of Messiah usually takes center stage on the discussion of the plurality or tri-unity of God, and not the Person of the *Ruach HaKodesh* (Holy Spirit). The absence of the argument of the Holy Spirit does not remove the importance of the ministry of the Holy Spirit in the Hebrew Scriptures.

Messiah Is Divine – Chapter 8

The purpose of this chapter, along with the background of the rest of this study, is to show that the Messiah is God. This is contrary to everything that Judaism stands for. Here the specific purpose is to show the eternality of the Messiah. The terms for *eternity* and *everlasting* are not as understood in the English language today. A complete understanding of the terms and how they were used is the first area to be discussed. The second area is to show how the term *eternal* relates to the Messiah. Passages like 1 Chronicles 17:11-14, 2 Samuel 7:10-14, Isaiah 9:6-7,

CHAPTER 1: INTRODUCTION

Micah 5:2, and Jeremiah 23:5-6 prove His divinity. Also there are other verses with the main speaker being God or *Yahweh*, and with His own words describing what happened to Him. Those descriptions of Himself can only point to one Person, the incarnation of God in the Person of *Yeshua*.

Summary and Conclusion

Chapter nine provides summary and conclusion. God revealed Himself to man through His Word, in a progressive manner. That revelation of Himself to man in Genesis 1 makes a statement of Himself as the pages, chapters, and books of the Scripture unfold His plurality before the reader until that final revelation is given in the incarnation of the Messiah to Israel. Both the plurality and the tri-unity of God can be proven in the Hebrew Scriptures. However, the tri-unity is not as well developed in the *Tanakh* as it is in the New Testament. The *Tanakh*, as it adds one teaching point upon another throughout the Law, Prophets, and Writings,[78] becomes a very formidable weight of evidence to prove the plurality of God. When all is examined, the tri-unity, and not only a plurality, comes into focus.

The knowledge and understanding of the Jewishness of the tri-unity of God is very important in reaching Jewish people (as well as the people lost in various cults). Today, the Jewish people are listed as one of the least reached groups in the United States of America.[79] Only 0.3 of one percent of Jewish people embrace *Yeshua ha Meshiach* as their Redeemer, Savior, and Lord.[80] This study will be devoted to understanding the oneness, or the unity, of God, and plurality of God as set forth in the Hebrew Scriptures by biblical, not rabbinic, interpretation.

---

[78] **Law, Prophets and Writings**: This is the Jewish designation for the three divisions of the *Tanakh*, or the Hebrew Scriptures.
[79] Patrick Johnston and Jason Mandryk. *Operation World* (Waynesboro, GA: Paternoster USA, 2001), 662.
[80] Abe Sandler, "God's Chosen People," *The Alliance Life,* Christian & Missionary Alliance, (Vol. 153, issue 2, March/April 2018).

CHAPTER 2:
IN THE IMAGE AND LIKENESS OF GOD

The topic of how man is created in reference to the *image and likeness* of Elohim could fill a book. The focus of this chapter is to show how the *image and likeness* that God used to shape mankind reflects the plurality of His Person in Elohim. This is a limited subject in relation to the doctrine of God, but a much needed one to help mankind understand this aspect of the Person, nature, and essence of Elohim. There is a need to first study these two words *image* and *likeness* which first appear in Genesis 1:26.

צֶלֶם – *Tzelem* - IMAGE

The Hebrew word צֶלֶם (tzelem or selem), meaning "image," is used in numerous places throughout the *Tanakh*.[81] Defined from a strictly human perspective, the word *image* refers to an image as a representation of a deity, such as an idol.[82] The ordinary use of *"selem"* (image) indicates a three-dimensional figure or relief like a statue, whether resembling a man or a god.[83] An *image* is a *likeness* or model of something. Examples of idols which illustrate this are the pagan gods found in 2 Kings 11:18 and Amos 5:26. Ezekiel 16:17 and 23:14 speak of images of humans, while 1 Samuel 6:5 makes reference to images of mice. The truth of that fact is that God calls them idols, and we are commanded not to make graven images of God (Exodus 20:3-4). Even when Moses, Aaron, and the 70 elders of Israel saw God, there was no description given of what they saw (Exodus 24:9-11). The following author describes God as being spirit, which is beyond our ability to completely comprehend, for He is not a physical being:

> Theologically, when the OT [Old Testament] forbids making images of God, speaks of God's mediated appearance or formlessness, or

---

[81] **Selem (tzelem)** is used 17 times: Genesis 1:26; 5:1-3; 9:6; Numbers 33:52; 1 Samuel 6:5, 11; 2 Kings 11:18; 2 Chronicles 23:17; Ezekiel 7:20; 16:17; 23:14; (used in Aramaic 17 times in Daniel 2:31, 32, 34, 35; 3:1-3, 5, 7, 10, 12, 14, 15, 18, 19); Amos 5:26.
[82] Harris, Archer, and Waltke, *Theological Wordbook of the Old Testament*, 2:767.
[83] VanGemeren, ed., *New International Dictionary of Old Testament Theology & Exegesis*, 4:645-646.

declares that humans cannot see God and live, its language communicates the transcendence and incomparability of God. In himself God is beyond human comprehension and depiction. He is known only as he makes himself known, and that necessarily occurs in mediated fashion.[84]

If God is formless and beyond human comprehension and depiction, how are we made in His image? Christianity and Judaism stand in stark contrast to Mormonism that teaches that their gods have physical bodies.[85] However, the word *image* as used by *Elohim* of Himself reflects His Person but does not reflect a physical image of Himself. What is obviously seen is that God's image does not consist of, nor is it representative of man's body, which was formed from the earth. What becomes obvious is that *Elohim* is speaking of His Person and character. Man is spiritual, intellectual, and moral in his likeness of God, but only so because of the breath of life that God breathed (Genesis 2:7) into him.[86] When man became a living soul by the breath of God, he was made in the *image* of *Elohim*, and that fact can be difficult to comprehend. We are completely dependent on God for our understanding of this great truth. Our understanding only occurs when we study the complete revelation God gave to mankind so that we could comprehend Him and how we are created in His *image*.

The conclusion is that mankind being made in the image of God is difficult to comprehend. We only know God by the revelation He makes about Himself through the Scriptures, and some of His revelations are beyond our comprehension. Yes, we are created in the image of God's Person and character, but only in a limited respect.

---

[84] VanGemeren, ed., *New International Dictionary of Old Testament Theology & Exegesis*, 4:647.

[85] Anthony A. Hoekema, *The Four Major Cults* (Grand Rapids: Eerdmans, 1965), 34-53. The Mormon book *The Articles of Faith* states that the Trinity is "three separate individuals, physically distinct from each other." It states further that "the Father is a personal being, possessing a definite form, with bodily parts and spiritual passions." It states later in the paragraph concerning Christ that He "was in the express image of His Father, after which image man also has been created." (James E. Talmage, *A Study of the Articles of Faith, Salt Lake City: The Church of Jesus Christ of Latter-day Saints*, 1982, pgs 39, 41-42.) The following is stated in the Doctrines of Covenants concerning the Mormon belief of God being a corporeal physical being: "The Father has a body of flesh and bones as tangible as man's; the Son also; but the Holy Ghost has not a body of flesh and bones, but is a personage of Spirit. Were it not so, the Holy Ghost could not dwell in us." (Doctrines and Covenants, 130:22, published by The Church of Jesus Christ of Latter-day Saints in Salt Lake City, UT.)

[86] Harris, Archer, and Waltke, *Theological Wordbook of the Old Testament*, 2:768.

CHAPTER 2: IN THE IMAGE AND LIKENESS OF GOD

דְּמוּת - *Demut* - LIKENESS

The Hebrew word דְּמוּת (*demut*) or *likeness* comes from the root word דָּמָה (*damah*) and has been defined as a pattern, form, shape, or image[87] and is used in numerous places within the pages of the *Tanakh*.[88] The technical information on the usage of the word *likeness* is as follows:

> *Damah* appears 13 times in the *qal*, where it is intransitive and should be rendered "to be like, look like" (Isaiah 1:9; 46:5; Ezekiel 31:2, 8 [twice], 18; Psalm 89:7[6]; 102:7[6]; 144:4). We may add to this two occurrences in the Aramaic *piel* in Daniel 3:25; 7:5. LXX [Septuagint] usually translates the *qal* by *homoioun*, "to be like" (9 times), and rarely also by *homoios*, "like," or *homoios einai*, "to be like." *Damah* also occurs 13 times in the *piel* (Numbers 33:56; Judges 20:5; 2 Samuel 21:5; Isaiah 10:7; 14:24; 40:18, 25; 46:5; Psalm 48:10 [9]; 50:21; Lamentations 2:13). It has in this case a "declarative-estimative" meaning (to declare or consider something or someone to be in the condition suggested by the verb), i.e., the *piel* of *damah* should be translated "to compare, to consider suitable or appropriate."[89]

John Phillips expresses the relationship between *tselem* [image] and *demut* [likeness] in Genesis 1:26 by giving a more practical expression of these two words:

> Nowhere else in the OT do these two nouns appear in parallelism or in connection with each other. The more important word of the two is "image" but to avoid the implication that man is a precise copy of God, albeit in miniature. *Demut* [or likeness] then defines and limits the meaning of selem [image]. No distinction is to be sought between these two words. They are totally interchangeable. The word "likeness" rather than diminishing the word "image" actually amplifies it and specifies its meaning. Man is not just an image but a likeness-image. He is not simply representative but representational. Man is the visible, corporeal representative of the invisible, bodiless

---

[87] VanGemeren, ed., New *International Dictionary of Old Testament Theology & Exegesis*, 1:967.

[88] Genesis 1:26; 5:1-3; Exodus 20:4; 25:9; Deuteronomy 5:8; 2 Kings 16:10; 2 Chronicles 4:3; Psalm 58:4; Isaiah 13:4; 40:18; Ezekiel 1:5, 10, 13, 16, 22, 26, 28; 8:2; 10:1, 21, 22; 23:15; Daniel 10:16.

[89] G. Johannes Botterweck, Helmer Ringgren and Heinz-Josef Fabry, *Theological Dictionary of the Old Testament* (14 vols. Grand Rapids: Eerdmans, 1978), 3:250-251.

God. *Demut* guarantees that man is an adequate and faithful representative of God on earth.[90]

Others agree. In speaking personally with Dr. Arnold Fruchtenbaum on this issue, he also agrees that "image" and "likeness" are the same in meaning and that "likeness" simply qualifies the first term, *image*.[91] Charles Feinberg states the same thing in Bib Sac (a theological journal) when he writes: "In short, use reveals the words [*tselem* and *demuth* – literally *image* and *likeness*] are used interchangeably."[92]

Distinction Between Man and Animals

Even though many authors say much about how mankind is in the *image* and *likeness* of *Elohim*, they still do not give a complete answer. Perhaps there is not a complete answer. But there is a distinct uniqueness in man that some authors capture in writing as they reference man who stands between the animal creation of *Elohim* and *Elohim* Himself. John Phillips provides outstanding insights into the differences between man and the animal kingdom; the creation of mankind reflects man's likeness to *Elohim* and not to animals:

> Man is in no way related to the beasts. What animal can transmit accumulated achievements from one generation to another? What animal experiences a true sense of guilt when it does wrong or has a developed consciousness of judgment to come? What animal shows any desire to worship? What animal has hope of immortality beyond the grave? What beast can exercise abstract moral judgment or show appreciation of the beauties of nature? (When did we ever see a dog admiring a sunset or a horse standing breathless before the rugged grandeur of a mountain range?) What animal ever learned to read and write, to act with deliberate purpose, and set goals and achieve long-range objectives? What animal ever learned to cook its food, to cut cloth and make clothes, or invent elaborate tools? What animal ever enjoyed a hearty laugh? What animal has the gift for speech? Even the most primitive human tribe possesses linguistics of a subtle, complex and eloquent nature. Man stands alone. *Physically*, he alone of all the creatures on the globe, walks upright; *mentally*, he alone

---

[90] Harris, Archer, and Waltke, *Theological Wordbook of the Old Testament*, 1:192.
[91] Arnold Fruchtenbaum, *Personal Communication*, July of 2006.
[92] Charles L. Feinberg, "The Image of God," *Bib Sac* 129:515 (July 1972): 237.

CHAPTER 2: IN THE IMAGE AND LIKENESS OF GOD

has the ability to communicate in a sophisticated manner; *spiritually*, he alone has the capacity to know the mind and will of God.[93]

Phillips expresses the chasm between man and animal. The qualities of man are the same as those of *Elohim*. *Elohim* gave these qualities to man uniquely as the image bearer of Himself.

Another aspect of mankind's uniqueness in the creation account of Genesis 1 is to see the formula that God used. The formula that *Elohim* gives shows a complete uniqueness in God's created order. On the creative days one through five and on the beginning of the sixth day, in Genesis 1 verses 3, 6, 9, 11, 14, 20, and 24, *Elohim* states *let there be*. In verse 26, the formula for the creation of mankind is unique to the other days because He states *let us* rather than *let there be*. When *Elohim* created living things He used the word מִין [*min*] meaning "kind or species." The word *min* would be similar to the modern taxonomical idea of species, making certain that all living creatures must be understood in terms of categories, or species. The creation of mankind is clearly distinct from the animal kingdom or of any other form of life that precedes it, because the human race does not belong to a category called *min*. So mankind is a unique creation and cannot be compared to creatures of any other kind, a concept that evolution has overlooked. Evolution is a destructive doctrine because it teaches mankind to compare humans to the animal kingdom, rather than to *Elohim*, their Creator. Mankind's humanity is in the *image* and *likeness* of *Elohim*, not an evolutionary process from lower life forms.

Comparisons of God in Man

Mankind is not connected to the animal kingdom, but is representative of *Elohim*, for mankind is made in His *image* and *likeness* and not like animals. The difficulty with comparing God and man in relationship to God's *image* and *likeness* in Genesis 1:26-27 is that there is no description of the likeness of *Elohim* provided.[94] What is learned comes from the progressive revelation of Scripture. That is how mankind learns of the meaning of *image* and *likeness* and how mankind represents the presence of *Elohim* on this earth:

> The likeness does not consist of the physical form at all; rather, the likeness is in the function of that form to represent the presence of

---

[93] John Phillips, *Exploring Genesis* (Chicago: Moody, 1980), 45.
[94] VanGemeren, ed., *New International Dictionary of Old Testament Theology & Exegesis*, 1:969.

God in the world; the divine presence is represented through the creation of humans, who exercise dominion (Psalm 8:5-8 [6-9]).[95]

One of the keys to understanding the *image* and *likeness* in the Person of *Elohim* that mankind represents is to grasp the meaning of Genesis 1:26-27. But this may not be completely possible. God is unknowable except as He revealed Himself to mankind in the *Tanakh*. The likelihood is that what *Elohim* revealed of Himself through His Word is only a fraction of His Person, essence, and nature, although He has revealed what man needs to know about Him, or perhaps what mankind can grasp of His Person.

Moses stated that mankind is made in the *image* and *likeness* of *Elohim* in Genesis 1:26-27. Moses does not state what *Elohim* means by *image* and *likeness*. Mankind has no way of making a full proof examination of what is intended in the Genesis account.

In the revelation that man has been given through the Scriptures, he learns that he is not part of the animal kingdom. Mankind can learn dimly through the same Scriptures how God created him in His [*Elohim*'s] likeness. Mankind is somewhat at a disadvantage because God does not give an explanation in this verse; He just makes this declaration. This much can be observed: Genesis 1:26-27 gives the only credible evidence of who *Elohim* is, and mankind is that evidence. All other passages where the terms *image* and *likeness* are used, with the exception of Genesis 5:1-3 and 9:6, are in connection with idols and other likenesses of man or animals.[96] One author has given a brief observation on the difficulty of grasping this concept:

> The passage is unique in the OT, if one disregards echoes in Genesis 5 and 9....Precisely because Genesis 1:26 stands in such isolation, it has given free rein to theological speculation.[97]

---

[95] VanGemeren, ed., *New International Dictionary of Old Testament Theology & Exegesis*, 1:969.

[96] **Image**: In the New Covenant the word "image" is used in connection with Messiah. Paul states in Colossians 1:15 that Messiah *"is the image of the invisible God"* which has a direct relationship to the tri-unity of God in the *Tanakh*. What is clearly recognized is that God created mankind in His image, and mankind is male and female as well as being individually made up of body, soul, and spirit, a tri-unity. God in His wisdom created mankind to reflect who He is in mankind, and in that wisdom God chose the Messiah to be the very image of the invisible God. As will be clearly seen in the *Tanakh*, the second member of the tri-unity of God became visible in the theophanies of the Hebrew Scriptures; but in the New Covenant, through the Incarnation of God, the invisible God became visible.

[97] Ernest Jenni and Claus Westermann, *Theological Lexicon of the Old Testament* (Peabody, MA: Hendrickson, 1997), 3:1082.

CHAPTER 2: IN THE IMAGE AND LIKENESS OF GOD

Indeed, Genesis 1:26 is unique within Scripture. Understanding just how the *image* and *likeness* of *Elohim* are revealed through mankind is difficult, but it is this image that mankind bears. All of man's life is taken up with getting to know *Elohim* well enough to understand what His *image* and *likeness* are. There is no shortage of writings on the subject of how mankind is in the *image* and *likeness* of *Elohim*. In order to continue in the quest to understand *Elohim* and the words *image* and *likeness*, we will continue to analyze them.

The words *image* and *likeness,* as stated earlier, are used synonymously and interchangeably and do not refer to two different things.[98] These two words reflect in mankind the plural (triune) personhood of an indivisible *Elohim*. Man is unique, a personal entity that at conception is created by God (Malachi 2:10)[99] and is immediately and forever joined to one's propagated human nature (body, soul, and spirit).[100] In contrast to the lower animals, which are made each after its kind or type, man is made in the *image of God*.[101] That distinction must not be missed. The following author reflects his understanding of being created in the *image of God* by saying:

> To be made in the image of God thus means that man is a creative, rational, moral being. He has creative emotions, a rational intellect, and a moral volition. These three correspond to what under the great commandment are called his soul, his mind and his heart respectively.[102]

Mankind is a spiritual being that in some way reflects the image of *Elohim*. Mankind's bodily nature does not reflect the Person of God, but mankind does reflect the Person of God through his spiritual nature. As has been stated, mankind is a reflection of *Elohim*'s invisible, incorporeal Person. Mankind is unique in all of God's creation in that he reflects the *image of God* in a way that mankind finds hard to grasp. It also needs to be clearly understood that mankind is not like *Elohim* in every dimension; he only reflects certain aspects of God's *image* and *likeness*. To illustrate, man is not immutable (changeless), nor is he omnipresent (everywhere present), nor is he omniscient (all knowing), nor is he omnipotent (all powerful), nor did mankind exist in eternity past. What mankind shares with *Elohim* are qualities

---

[98] Louis Berkhof, *Systematic Theology*, 203.
[99] In the Hebrew it is אֵל or *El*, which just happens to be in the singular.
[100] Floyd H. Barackman, *Practical Christian Theology: Examining the Great Doctrines of the Faith* (4th Ed. Grand Rapids: Kregel, 2001), 256.
[101] John Skinner, *The International Critical Commentary: A Critical and Exegetical Commentary on Genesis* (Edinburgh: T & T Clark, 1969), 30.
[102] Basil R. C. Atkinson, *The Pocket Commentary of the Bible: Genesis* (Chicago: Moody, 1957), 22.

such as personality, will, and sensibility. That is, humanity's resemblance to *Elohim* is analogous[103] but not ontologically[104] identical. To be like *Elohim* is to be patterned after Him while inferior to Him. This *image* and *likeness* are further supported by understanding that image exists in the Creation narratives by the use of the first person pronouns (I, we, us) that God used of Himself. In Genesis chapters 1 and 2, the personality and rulership of God are observed; but there are differences that quickly become apparent as the following author expresses:

> [When] both God and humans speak, [they] are referred to by personal pronouns, [they] exercise authority over lesser beings and have the capacity to make choices (Genesis 2:17). On the other hand, God has always existed (Genesis 1:1), whereas humanity was created (Genesis 1:27); humankind is under the dominion of God and is therefore not equal to him (Genesis 2:16); humankind is physical and corporeal (Genesis 2:7), but God is spirit (Exodus 33:17-23; cf. John 4:24); humans are mortal (Genesis 2:17), but God is eternal. To be in the image of God cannot mean equivalence between deity and humanity, then, but only an analogous [likeness] or corresponding relationship between the two.[105]

Elohim and mankind share some things in common, namely *Elohim*'s *image* and *likeness*. At the same time, however, that *image* and *likeness* have limitations. Mankind is created in the *image* and *likeness* of *Elohim;* not everything in mankind is equal with Him. It is in the personhood of God that we are created in His *image* and *likeness*.

How Mankind Is Like Elohim in His Person

Pastors and teachers offer to explain the tri-unity and the *image* and *likeness* of *Elohim* in order to help their congregations and students by stating that the tri-unity is like an egg with three parts, or the three components of water, or even using a tree with its roots, trunk, and branches. But all of these are inadequate to explain the tri-unity, as author E. Charles Heinze expresses:

> …common analogies of the Trinity – the egg (yoke, albumen, shell), a man (employee, husband, citizen), and water (liquid, ice, vapor) –

---

[103] **Analogous**: Showing an analogy or a likeness, permitting one to draw an analogy.
[104] **Ontology**: A study of conceptions of reality and the nature of being. It is the study of being or existence and forms the basic subject matter of metaphysics.
[105] Alexander and Baker, *Dictionary of the Old Testament Pentateuch,* 443.

CHAPTER 2: IN THE IMAGE AND LIKENESS OF GOD

have serious shortcomings which do more to hinder and mislead than to aid understanding.[106]

Heinze is exactly correct in his observation. However, he goes on to say that the three aspects of "space" (height, width, and length) come closer to explaining the tri-unity of God. I, even though viewing Heinze's statement with interest, still believe that none of the above symbolisms define the triune nature of a personal God. God intended people to understand something very special about His Person. What was it that He wanted readers of Scripture to understand?

Elohim is a plural noun for the word *God* which has given rise to many statements, both positive and negative, by Jewish and Christian scholars as to its precise meaning. The difficulty lies in the fact that *Elohim* is a plural noun. Jewish scholars reject the tri-unity of *Elohim* because in Hebrew grammar, as in English, you would have a plural noun following a plural verb. The word *created* in Genesis 1:1 is a singular verb, not a plural verb, which is the case in most instances throughout the *Tanakh*. So Jewish scholars interpret *Elohim* as one [*echad*] or as a "plural of majesty."[107] It is odd that Moses had two other Hebrew words to express the absolute oneness of *Elohim;* however, he did not use them often. The two words are אֵל or *El* and אֱלוֹהַ or *Eloah*, which are singular expressions for God and not plural as is *Elohim*. This subject will be dealt with in depth in chapter three.

After extensive research on this subject, I have found that most authors do have some good insights pertaining to the *image* and *likeness* of *Elohim*. They adequately describe the character and attributes of God; however, they miss the personal nature of Him. Gordon Talbot defines the differences between man who is made in the *image* and *likeness* of God, and animals, which are not. He states:

> Human beings were to be different from all other creatures in two distinct ways. First, they were to be made in God's image or likeness. Man would have an intelligence superior to that of animals, the ability to communicate freely by language, sensitive emotional capacities, sophisticated social relationships with others, personal consciences, and immortal souls designed to have fellowship with

---

[106] E. Charles Heinze, *Trinity & Triunity* (Dale City, VA: Epaphras Press, 1995), 6.

[107] **Plural of Majesty**: This term is used to represent God speaking in the plural as referencing Himself with the heavenly hosts (angels). Many state that the plural of majesty does not represent a true plural, or that it is an abstract plural and is not meant to represent a numeric plural. It is also referred to as a "royal we" as the Queen of England would use. This will be dealt with in detail in chapter 3.

God. Second, they were to have dominion over all the earth's resources.[108]

As man has an "intelligence superior to that of animals," God has an intelligence superior to that of man. God and man have "the ability to communicate freely by language, sensitive emotional capacities, sophisticated social relationships with others, and personal consciences." God designed us with immortal souls to have fellowship with Him. God gave man dominion over the earth's resources and the animal kingdom in reflection of God's dominion over the heavens and earth. Talbot expresses how man reflects the *image* and *likeness* of *Elohim*, yet he does not fully express the essence of the personal nature of God as is described in the tri-unity of God.

While I was attending the 2006 Messianic Jewish Alliance of America (MJAA), Messianic Rabbi David Rosenberg presented a workshop called "The Mystery of the Godhead and the Divinity of *Yeshua*." Some of the insights he presented will be reflected in the next section on the plurality of God in its relationship to mankind.

Background for the Plurality of God that Mankind Reflects

One can ask how God can be a plurality in one. How can monotheism and the triune concept of God be harmonized? The answer lies in Genesis 1:26 and within humanity. When *Elohim* and man are introduced in Genesis 1, they are both introduced in the singular and plural forms, as Thomas A. Kaizer describes:

> One feature of the text which seems to have been completely overlooked in the discussion of the divine plural is that as soon as Elohim is associated with a plurality, humankind is presented in the same way. Throughout the creation account, third person singular verbs describe God's actions, clearly presenting Him in the singular. But when the divine plural appears, thereby introducing the idea of plurality, it occurs along with the presentation of humanity as both singular and plural ("Let Us create man...so that they...." [v. 26], and "God created man in His own image, in the image of God created He him, male and female created He them" [v. 27]). Thus

---

[108] Gordon Talbot, *A Study of the Book of Genesis* (Harrisburg, PA: Christian Publications, 1981), 18.

CHAPTER 2: IN THE IMAGE AND LIKENESS OF GOD

both Deity and humanity are simultaneously presented as both singular and plural.[109]

Genesis 1:26-27 gives the only credible evidence of who *Elohim* is.[110] We are that evidence. So the focus is placed on Genesis 1:26-27. There are only two other related passages found, in Genesis 5:1-3 and 9:6. To aid in our understanding of the use of the plural and singular words as they relate to *Elohim*, the Creator, and to man, the created, I will quote Genesis 1:26-27 with the plural and singular words pointed out:

> ^{26} *And God* [Elohim – **pl**ural] *said, "Let us make man* [**S**ingular] *in our* [pl] *image* [s], *after our* [pl] *likeness* [s]. *They* [pl] *shall rule the fish of the sea, the birds of the sky, the cattle, the whole earth, and all the creeping things that creep on earth."* ^{27} *And God* [Elohim – pl] *created man* [s] *in His* [s] *image, in the image* [s] *of God* [Elohim - pl] *He* [s] *created him* [s]; *male* [s] *and female* [s] *He created them* [pl]. [Emphasis mine][111]   [Jewish Study Bible (JSB)]

In Genesis 1:27, twice God stresses that man (mankind - singular) was *created* in His image, and He uses singular pronouns for Himself here. Then a third time He states that He *created* them (mankind - plural) male and female. Sailhamer points to the plurality of God in whose image man, both singular and plural, was made:

> Verse 27 stated twice that humankind was created in God's image and a third time that humankind was created "male and female." The same pattern is found in Genesis 5:1-2a: When God created humankind..."male and female he created them." The singular,

---

[109] Thomas A. Keiser, "The Divine Plural Contextual Presentation of Plurality in the Godhead" (A paper presented March 24, 2006 to Evangelical Theological Society, Southwest Region), 2.

[110] Only two other passages use the terms "image" and "likeness" in the *Tanakh*: Genesis 5:1-3 and 9:6. All other times those two terms are used in connection with idols and other likenesses of man or animals. In the New Covenant the word "image" is used in connection with Messiah. Paul states in Colossians 1:15 that Messiah *"is the image of the invisible God"* which has a direct relationship to the tri-unity of God in the *Tanakh*. What is clearly recognized is that God created mankind in His image, God in His wisdom created mankind to reflect who He is in mankind, and in that wisdom God chose the Messiah to be the very image of the invisible God. As will be clearly seen in the *Tanakh*, the second member of the tri-unity of God became visible in the theophanies of the Hebrew Scriptures, but in the New Covenant, through the Incarnation of God, the invisible God became visible.

[111] All passages in **boldface** font in this book are mine unless otherwise indicated.

"human being," is created as a plurality, "male and female." In a similar way, the one God created humanity through an expression of his plurality.[112]

Throughout chapter one of Genesis, Sailhamer states that God is speaking and acting in the singular while using *Elohim,* a plural noun. However, in verses 26 and 27, God or *Elohim* presents Himself in the plural when He is about to create mankind, singular. In verse 27 *Elohim* again returns to the singular with the act of creating mankind, showing unity; but now, in that creative act, He creates mankind singular as plural male and female. You need to review Sailhamer's statement because it is so important to understand. Now let me finish Sailhamer's quote:

> Following this clue, one may see the divine plurality expressed in verse 26 as an anticipation of the human plurality of man and woman, thus casting the human relationship between man and woman in the role of reflecting God's own personal relationship with himself.[113]

Re-read Sailhamer's full quotation thoughtfully and slowly to grasp his statement concerning the singular-plurality of mankind, man and woman, and how we reflect "God's own personal relationship with Himself." Something that has been missed by most scholars is the fact that *Elohim* speaks in the plural and creates in the singular only in verses 26-27; He generates life; and, in that generation of life, He creates (singular) mankind, and, in particular, that life is presented as male and female, plural. Thus when man and woman generate life, they give birth to male and female images or likenesses of themselves (Genesis 5:1-3). The picture becomes clear that *Elohim* in the context of plurality creates (singular) a plural being known as humanity, male and female. Mankind then procreates and gives birth to sons and daughters, plural, in the image and likenesses of humanity. Yet in their procreation, male and female act as one (singular) to procreate that life (Genesis 2:24; 4:1), even as *Elohim* in the plural creates life acting in the singular.[114] There is a very strong

---

[112] John H. Sailhamer, *The Pentateuch as Narrative: A Biblical-Theological Commentary* (Grand Rapids: Zondervan, 1992), 95-96.

[113] Sailhamer, *The Pentateuch as Narrative: A Biblical-Theological Commentary,* 95-96.

[114] Hoekema, *The Four Major Cults,* 36. Mormonism also teaches that God is a corporeal being having flesh and bones as stated in the Doctrine and Covenants: "The Father has a body of flesh and bones as tangible as man's; the Son also; but the Holy Ghost has not a body of flesh and bones, but is a personage of Spirit." *The Book of Mormon; The Doctrine and Covenants; The Pearl of Great Price,* (Salt Lake City: The Church of Jesus Christ of Latter-day Saints, 1982), 130:22. Note: God does not procreate or have a wife as taught in Mormon theology. This concept is completely foreign to the Scripture, both in the *Tanakh* and New Covenant.

CHAPTER 2: IN THE IMAGE AND LIKENESS OF GOD

parallel in what God is saying about Himself, His personhood (plural), and about mankind (plural). Thomas Keiser presents this picture but in a more technical way in the following statement, which is only a portion of his total argument:

> A review of the expression זָכָר וּנְקֵבָה ("male and female"), occurring only in Genesis 1:27; 5:2; 6:19; and 7:3, 9, 16, reveals that the context is always one of generation of life....It is notable that the divine plural is introduced with a similar nuance to that of humankind. That is, the transition from singular to plural with reference to God is also made in the context of the generation of life ("let us make man"). Thus, not only are both the divine and human singular-plurals introduced together, they are both presented in connection with the same concept, namely, generation of life. Perhaps one can say that in both cases the text presents a cooperation of a plurality of individuals, who are simultaneously seen as a unity, in the production of life.[115]

Elohim in the plural creates (in the singular) mankind; in turn, mankind (singular) then procreates and produces images of themselves by acting together as a plural with a singular act. In order to understand just how mankind is created in His *image* and *likeness*, there needs to be a clearer and more practical, understandable presentation as to how mankind is like God.

Man and Woman, a Plurality and Tri-Unity in One

How is this possible? Now observe two known but unused examples of just how mankind is in the *image* and *likeness* of God. **First**, *Elohim*, who is a plural unity, stated, *let us make man*. The Hebrew word אָדָם or *aw-dawm`* (adam) means "mankind." *Elohim* made mankind, according to Genesis 1:27, by splitting mankind into *male and female*. Sailhamer states that *Elohim* created mankind as a plural representation of Himself, not as a single representation. *Elohim*, who said *let us*, created mankind as a plural reflection of His *image* and *likeness*:

> The singular man (Adam) is created as a plurality, "male and female." In a similar way the one God created man through an expression of His plurality. Following this clue the divine plurality expressed in v. 26 is seen as an anticipation of the human plurality of the man and woman, thus casting the human relationship between

---

[115] Keiser, "The Divine Plural Contextual Presentation of Plurality in the Godhead," 3.

man and woman in the role of reflecting God's own personal relationship with himself.[116]

The plural relationship is a significant insight and should not be missed. Man and woman were created to reflect the personal relationship that the plural unity of *Elohim* experienced from eternity past. That relationship was to be pictured as a harmonious relationship that the first man and woman were to have with each other. Man and woman were equals, yet *Elohim* gave the man headship. Woman was to submit to man as a reflection of the Son and the Holy Spirit in voluntary submission to the Father.[117] Man and woman were to reflect the harmonious relationship that existed between the members of the Godhead. So, both man and woman were created to function in the *image* and *likeness* of God:

> It is as both male and female that humankind is to function as the image of God (Genesis 1:28). Animals thus relate to one another within their own subhuman category, but in some grand and mysterious sense humankind resembles God.[118]

Together both man and woman would be responsible to have dominion over the earth and the animal world just as *Elohim* in His plural unity has dominion over the heavens and the earth as stated below:

> Male and female human members are image-bearers who both are responsible for governing the world.[119]

Here is a good picture of man and woman who bear the *image* and *likeness* of *Elohim* together. *Elohim* is a triune unity of one (*echad*). Each member of that unity has different responsibilities and functions as they relate to human experience. In their unity, *Elohim* the Father has taken the leadership role; whereas, *Elohim* the Son

---

[116] John H. Sailhamer, *The Expositor's Bible Commentary: Genesis,* 12 volumes (Grand Rapids: Zondervan), 2:38.

[117] The harmonious relationship that man and woman were to exhibit as a reflection of *Elohim* was marred by the fall of mankind into sin. What is interesting is that in the New Testament, that relationship is re-instated because we are a "new creation" (2 Corinthians 5:17) in Messiah. That which was lost in the fall to a large degree has been reinstated through the indwelling of the Holy Spirit. For once again the man has the headship and is to be a servant leader in the home where the wife who, as his equal, submits to his leadership (Ephesians 5:18-6:4; Colossians 3:1-4:6). It can be a reality IF both the husband and the wife actively walk in Messiah and do not serve selfish interests.

[118] Alexander and Baker, *Dictionary of the Old Testament Pentateuch*, 443.

[119] Kenneth A. Mathews, *The New American Commentary: Genesis 1 – 11:26,* (Nashville: Broadman & Holman, 2002), 173.

CHAPTER 2: IN THE IMAGE AND LIKENESS OF GOD

and *Elohim* the Holy Spirit have taken subordinate roles and responsibilities to the Father, yet they are equal in all respects. The Son and the Holy Spirit voluntarily submit to the Father as they carry out their responsibilities in their interaction with humans on earth. When *Elohim* created mankind and split them into male and female, they were to reflect the image of *Elohim*, who harmoniously worked together in relationship to one another in the universe. In the same way, mankind was to work harmoniously together in their relationship to one another as they exercised dominion over the earth together. As two of the equal triune members of the unity of *Elohim* submit to the Father, so woman is to submit to man, working harmoniously together as equals. I use the word "triune" which relates to three; however in the Genesis 1 account only a plurality is referenced. We know from the rest of the *Tanakh* that that plurality is a tri-unity. Male and female are equals on earth as the triune members of *Elohim* are equal in the universe; but each, whether mankind or *Elohim*, carries out different responsibilities and functions. Male and female were created in the very *image* and *likeness* of *Elohim* as reflected in this statement by Grudem:

> Just as the Father and the Son are equal in deity and equal in all their attributes, but different in role, so husband and wife are equal in personhood and value, but they are different in the roles God has given to them. Just as God the Son is eternally subject to the authority of God the Father, so God has planned that wives be subject to the authority of their husbands.[120]

In his summary statement Keiser gives a brief statement on the picture that *Elohim* gives in His creative act:

> In summary, a contextual analysis of the divine plural in Genesis 1 reveals that it is directly associated with a human plural, resulting in both Deity and humanity simultaneously presented as both singular and plural. Additionally, the presentation of each singular-plural is associated with the generation of life which, in some respect, is related to those who generate life. A comparison of the common interpretations of the divine plural with this contextual review reveals that it is best understood as plurality in the Godhead.[121]

Before we move on to the second point, it is extremely important to clarify another fact to men and women in the twenty-first century. Historically men have frequently been abusive, domineering, and have suppressed and belittled women as

---

[120] Wayne Grudem, *Evangelical Feminism & Biblical Truth* (Sisters, OR: Multnomah Publishers, 2004), 46.
[121] Keiser, "The Divine Plural Contextual Presentation of Plurality in the Godhead," 5.

though they are inferior to them. Today women have reacted to the male dominance and abuse in the feminist movement. Two wrongs do not make a right. The feminist movement is as unbiblical as the male dominance of the past and present. They both ignore God's design and plan in creating male and female in His image and likeness. A quote from Wayne Grudem will illustrate the unbiblical problem and the unwillingness to recognize God's purpose and plan:

> The Bible thus corrects the errors of male dominance and male superiority that have come as the result of sin and that have been seen in nearly all cultures in the history of the world. Wherever men are thought to be better than women, wherever husbands act as selfish "dictators," wherever wives are forbidden to have their own jobs outside the home or to vote or to own property or to be educated, wherever women are treated as inferior, wherever there is abuse or violence against women or rape or female infanticide or polygamy or harems, the biblical truth of equality in the image of God is being denied. To all societies and cultures where these things occur, we must proclaim that the very first page of God's Word bears a fundamental and irrefutable witness against these evils.[122]

Lay down this book for a minute and pick up your Bible and read Proverbs 31:10-31 about the virtuous woman. In this passage women are not presented as inferior, but as intelligent, wise, thrifty, hard working, industrious and equal partners with man. However, because of sin, man's dismissive or dominating attitude towards women exists; and the feminist movement today when it dismisses or dominates men is equally guilty of sin. Men and women are equals serving together, both with differing functions and responsibilities, but equals. Two other brief quotes by Grudem re-emphasize the point:

> Every time we talk to each other as men and women, we should remember that the person we are talking to is a creature of God who is more like God than anything else in the universe, and men and women share that status equally. Therefore we should treat men and women with equal dignity and we should think of men and women as having equal value. If men and women are equally in the image of God, then we are equally important and equally valuable to God. We have equal worth before Him for all eternity, for this is how we were created.[123]

---

[122] Grudem, *Evangelical Feminism & Biblical Truth*, 26.
[123] Grudem, *Evangelical Feminism & Biblical Truth*, 26-27.

CHAPTER 2: IN THE IMAGE AND LIKENESS OF GOD

This biblical truth is absent from Islam, which treats women as being created as inferior, deficient in intelligence, described as animals or toys for the pleasure of men. Women in Islam are a thing to be ashamed of, which is one of the reasons for the veil, forcing them to stay or remain in their homes and on it goes.[124] The concept of equality is easier to understand theologically than it is for men and women to live and practice. Why? Because humanity willfully became a fallen creation of God in overt rebellion to the Creator whose image and likeness mankind still bears. Thus, there is a need to restore that which was lost to mankind. Thus you have the allusion to the first sacrifice for sin in Genesis 3:21 and the need for a future Redeemer to mediate between fallen sinful mankind and their Creator.

Second, not only did God create man and woman to reflect His plurality, He further reflected His plurality and tri-unity by creating man and woman in three dimensions: body, soul, and spirit. Men and women in themselves are a tri-unity made up in one [*echad*] person, each of us individually are body, soul, and spirit. That designation of body, soul, and spirit is completely different from the created animal world. Of those three dimensions in the *image* and *likeness* of *Elohim*, one is visible, the body. The remaining two dimensions, being soul and spirit, are invisible. Who has seen man's soul or spirit? No one! Who has seen man's body? Everyone! Equally so, *Elohim*, in His plurality in unity, has three dimensions or persons. One of those dimensions or Persons of the plural unity of *Elohim* became visible when He chose to reveal Himself to mankind, while the other two Persons of the plural unity of *Elohim* have remained invisible. These two points on the image and likeness of *Elohim* that mankind bears give us the best insight and picture to begin to understand the mystery of the unity of God.

As will be demonstrated throughout this book, *Elohim* revealed Himself to mankind as an indivisible plurality in unity. One Person of the plural unity of *Elohim* would become visible and use physical or audible revelations of Himself to mankind. He did so through what is known theologically as a theophany, where He revealed Himself as the *angel of the LORD* or the *Shechinah* glory of God. This member of the plural unity of *Elohim* became visible on a consistent basis while the other two persons of the tri-unity of *Elohim* remained invisible. Yet when the triune *Elohim* spoke, He almost always spoke in the first person to avoid confusing mankind. The whole concept as to why *Elohim* spoke in the singular becomes very clear, and why He did not speak in a plurality is also very apparent. Mankind, after they fell into sin, worshipped many gods in their pantheon of gods. *Elohim* spoke as one [*echad*] so that mankind would not be confused as to His nature, character, and essence. It was a critical issue for *Elohim* to reveal Himself as one [*echad*] God, yet it was also

---

[124] John Ankerberg and John Weldon, *Fast Facts on Islam* (Eugene, OR: Harvest House Publishers, 2001), 55-61.

necessary to be true to His plurality of persons within Himself that He revealed Himself as a plural unity.

Anthropomorphism

The Bible often speaks of God with anthropomorphisms as if comparing Him with man, not only by using images that describe Him as a king, a shepherd, a father, and a judge, but also by speaking of *Yahweh* and/or *Elohim* as engaging in such human actions as walking (Genesis 3:8), smelling an aroma (Genesis 8:21), etc. Scripture also, through anthropomorphisms, ascribes body parts to God, including arms (Numbers 11:23), hands (Psalm 111:7), a mouth (Deuteronomy 8:3), and eyes (Deuteronomy 11:12).

Rabbinic Judaism, however, had problems with Moses and the prophets of God using these terms to describe God. The prophets sometimes describe something that God does, and God, Himself, used human terms that correspond to God having human body parts such as arms, hands, mouth, and eyes. So Judaism "softens" the Scriptures to reflect their sensitivity to God being equated with humanity by the use of anthropomorphic terms. The Jewish sages of the past have removed the wording from the translated biblical text or have substituted other words to get away from God having any identity with man as the following statements from Goldberg clearly express:

> In personal references to God, all anthropomorphic expressions are avoided and other expressions are substituted. All human traits ascribed to deity are toned down or avoided so as not to create false impressions among the unlearned, namely, that Yahweh was not like any pagan deity. The expressions of Memra and Shekinah are used freely in substitutions.[125]

Goldberg expresses that the Jewish translators of both the Greek Septuagint (LXX)[126] and the Aramaic Targums (paraphrase) did not like the anthropomorphism of the *Tanakh* and thus would change the words to reflect God's glory or presence rather than allow the biblical text to stand as written with terms like *the hand of God* or *The LORD stood by* [Abraham]. One of the reasons they did not like the language

---

[125] Louis Goldberg, "The Deviation of Jewish Thought from an Old Testament Theology in the Intertestamental Period." Doctor of Theology. diss., Winona Lake, IN: Grace Theological Seminary, 1963, 53.

[126] **Septuagint** is the name of the oldest Greek translation of Scriptures undertaken by 70 sages in Alexandria beginning in the third century B.C.E.

was and is that God is a pure spirit and does not have arms, legs, feet, or such; whereas, the pagans made images of gods that Israel worshipped before the captivity, images which had those human characteristics.

Another author references Maimonides who correctly viewed that for God to have a body or form was irrational but also deadly heresy.[127] With that concept, biblical Christianity would have to be in complete agreement. The confusion comes because biblical Christianity without hesitation stands on the fact that God is spirit, indivisible, and does not have a body, period. However, biblical Christianity also embraces the fact that God can and did take on human form for the benefit of communicating with human beings by the use of theophanies. The Bible literally teaches that God, who is spirit, can and did take on flesh as the Messiah, to be the sin-bearer to fulfill the promises to Abraham and David in the future. The incarnation has two major purposes given in Scripture: The Messiah first took on a physical body to deal with sin and to fulfill God's promises to Israel through Himself; and He will physically return to fulfill His promises to the fathers (Abraham, Isaac, and Jacob). But Rabbinic Judaism has misunderstood biblical faith, and Goldberg continues to state just how they attempted to get away from the literal meaning of these anthropomorphisms:

> Anthropomorphisms are rendered in such a way in translation as to avoid any possible misconception. Thus God does not smell an offering but accepts it; He does not go before the people but He leads them. Instead of God hearing or seeing, it is said it was revealed or heard before Him. God's feet are His glorious throne (Targum Isaiah 38:5; 60:13)....Shekinah is another word used as a substitute for personal references to God. In this instance, anthropomorphic references to God in the Isaiah text are attributed in the Targum to the Shekinah or the glory of the Shekinah, e.g., hiding the eyes is removing the presence of His Shekinah, to see the King is to see the glory of the Shekinah (1:15; 6:5).[128]

What is interesting is that God, as He revealed Himself to mankind, had no problem with anthropomorphic terms in describing Himself. God chose language, human language, to help man understand Him in terms that mankind could identify with:

---

[127] George Foot Moore, "Intermediaries in Jewish Theology: Memra, Shekinah, Metatron," *Harvard Theological Review*, vol. 15 (1922), 41.
[128] Goldberg, Doctoral Thesis, 20-21.

All Scripture is written in human language, not some divine language. God's revelation is "accommodated," as Calvin liked to say, to human understanding. Scripture takes abstract attributes of God, no less than concrete images of him, from human life – words that have uses in our conversation about earthly things. This is the only kind of revelation there is. The purpose of revelation is communication, and so the very purpose of revelation is to get God's message into human terms. Granted that God is not a physical being, we are rightly inclined to say that He does not really have hands, though human hands appropriately symbolize the means of God's workmanship.[129]

God not only chose to use anthropomorphic terms to relate to mankind in a manner that mankind would understand, but He also used many word pictures to describe Himself. A partial list follows:

- God pictured as the Father.

- God as also related to His people as a husband (Isaiah 54:5).

- God as a shepherd (Numbers 27:17; Psalm 77:20).

- God the potter (Isaiah 64:8; Jeremiah 18 - 19).

- God as a farmer (Isaiah 5).

- God as a refiner (Psalm 12:6; Proverbs 17:3; Malachi 3:2).

- God as a landowner (Matthew 20:1-16).

- God as like a lion, a leopard, or a bear, who will devour His wicked people (Hosea 13:7-8).

- God as the Rock (Deuteronomy 32; 1 Samuel 2:2; 2 Samuel 22:2-3, 32, 47).[130]

These anthropomorphic word pictures present a further interesting facet of how God chose to reveal Himself. It does need to be clearly and emphatically stated that God is spirit and not human. God does not have body parts as humans; He is pure spirit. The rabbis, in attempting to "protect" God by using alternate terms, have over-reacted to God's using human terms of Himself in speaking to men and have

---

[129] John M. Frame, *The Doctrine of God* (Phillipsburg, NJ: P & R Publishers, 2002), 367.
[130] Frame, *The Doctrine of God*, 366-377.

CHAPTER 2: IN THE IMAGE AND LIKENESS OF GOD

distorted the Word of God. God in His Word is completely capable of protecting His own Person and character without the help of well-intentioned rabbis.

To move beyond this, God throughout the pages of the *Tanakh* used multiple male images, and He always spoke in the masculine. God in His wisdom also chose, at times, to use feminine references to Himself, a practice which bothers some people. As previously stated, however, when *Elohim* created mankind; He created both male and female to reflect His *image* and *likeness*. He reflected His plural Person; there is nothing in Scripture to indicate that God is sexually a male. However, the female characteristics of woman came from the creative mind and hand of *Elohim*. He created the female as an equal partner for man. Below is the first of three rare references that illustrates God referring to Himself in the feminine:

> *You neglected the Rock that begot you, Forgot the God* [El] *who brought you forth* (Jewish Publication Society JPS).
> (Deuteronomy 32:18)

In Deuteronomy 32:18, Moses gives both the masculine and the feminine as he speaks to Israel about their God. Kohlenberger translates the Hebrew word יְלָדְךָ in the masculine as "he fathered you,"[131] which corresponds with the English word "begot you" in the Jewish Study Bible (JSB) quoted above. Then Gramcord[132] referenced Brown, Driver, and Briggs, who identify מְחֹלְלֶךָ as "in pain as childbirth" which is a feminine characteristic.[133] Kohlenberger translates the phrase as "one bearing you," or as in the King James, the one that "formed thee." Moses, in speaking of God, uses feminine characteristics to illustrate His relationship with Israel. Moses is speaking to God about the burden of Israel that he [Moses] is carrying:

> *Did I conceive all this people, did I bear them, that You should say to me, Carry them in your bosom as a nurse carries an infant....?*
> (Numbers 11:12a JSB)

Does Moses' using feminine language to describe his relationship to Israel mean that Moses was feminine? Hardly. The following author expresses this issue well:

---

[131] John Kohlenberger, *The Interlinear NIV Hebrew-English Old Testament* (Grand Rapids: Zondervan, 1987), 579.
[132] Paul A. Miller, *Gramcord* (Vancouver, WA: Gramcord Institute, 1999), www.Gramcord.org.
[133] Francis Brown, S. R. Driver, ands Charles A. Briggs, *A Hebrew and English Lexicon of the Old Testament,* (Oxford: Clarendon, n.d.).

In this image, God plays both male and female roles in Israel's origin. In Numbers 11:12, Moses, frustrated by the grumbling of the Israelites, denies before God that he (Moses) conceived these people and brought them forth. So he asks, "Why do you tell me to carry them in my arms, as a nurse carries an infant?"[134]

Moses, as he speaks to God, says in paraphrase: "Did I conceive or become pregnant? Did I give birth? Am I to carry them as a nurse carries an infant?" Jewish translators clearly saw and translated the female references that Moses was comparing to God in relation to the people. Another reference of God given by Isaiah where *Yahweh* uses feminine characteristics of childbirth in connection to Himself is found in Isaiah 42:14:

> *I have kept silent for too long, kept still and restrained Myself; Now I will scream like a woman in labor, I will pant and I will gasp.* (JSB)

The King James Version states, *now will I cry like a travailing woman*. They both say the same thing using different words. The travailing woman or the woman in labor is in the feminine as *Yahweh* refers to Himself in relation to Israel. As Frame states:

> But "now, like a woman in childbirth, I cry out, I gasp and pant." Feminine nouns do not necessarily denote female persons.[135]

Frame is absolutely correct. The usage of feminine characteristics does not necessarily denote female persons. God used the expression to illustrate to Israel the agony and pain that He experienced as Israel served and worshipped other gods.

In the three examples above, the Scriptures refer to God in the feminine. The purpose of recording all this is to get a better understanding of God's attitude toward woman. God created woman as co-equal with man, each having individual responsibilities, with *Elohim* giving the headship to man. All of these feminine and masculine anthropomorphisms were to be an earthly reflection of a heavenly reality of the Godhead. *Elohim*, in His plural unity, chose to reflect this aspect of His image to mankind in the creation of mankind, male and female.

Elohim further expresses His plural unity in making mankind a tri-unity, having a body, soul, and spirit. Mankind, being of a triune nature, reflects *Elohim*, even as each member of the tri-unity of *Elohim* is co-equal yet voluntarily submitted to one member in the plural unity of *Elohim* for the purpose of ministering to

---

[134] Frame, *The Doctrine of God*, 380.
[135] Frame, *The Doctrine of God*, 380-382.

CHAPTER 2: IN THE IMAGE AND LIKENESS OF GOD

mankind. God created mankind in His *image* and *likeness*. But that does not make mankind divine nor does it give him a "spark of divinity":

> While both "image" and "likeness" express correspondence to God, "likeness" indicates that this correspondence is one of similarity, not identicalness. That the image of God in humans is not one of identical correspondence is supported by the fact that this image was created while God Himself is uncreated. Also, it is very likely that God's image has unrevealed features that the divine image in people does not have. Keep in mind that this divine image in humans is not essentially their having God's divine nature. This would make them to be God. To my mind, it means that humans have a created feature, apart from their propagated human nature, that is like something that belongs to God's makeup and distinguishes them from lower creatures. This correspondence gives humans a sacredness, dignity, and value that animals do not have (Genesis 9:6; James 3:9; cp. 2 Peter 2:12).[136]

Man was created in the *image* and *likeness* of God. The writers of Scripture as well as God Himself used anthropomorphisms to help humanity understand His Person, nature, character, and essence. However, in the use of these anthropomorphisms, let it be understood that God DOES NOT have a wife and God is NOT feminine! Nothing in Scripture supports such conclusions. God created the sexes so men and women could share companionship and propagate the earth. In other words, God is not anti-woman; He created her as co-equal with man but with different responsibilities and functions than He gave to man. In this twenty-first century, liberal Jewish and Christian scholars attempt to feminize God or to make Him gender neutral. This is absolutely ludicrous and shows the complete depravity of mankind in trying to bring God down to their level, as in Mormon theology. That concept of God cannot, in any way, be supported by the Scriptures. God was not made in man's image and likeness, for then God would not be God at all. It is sin in the world that obscures the *image* and *likeness* that mankind is made in, and it is sin that has given birth to the suppression of woman by the physically stronger male. Man, in his sin, has distorted the *image* and *likeness* of *Elohim* that male and female are to model.

It is a common teaching among rabbis that Christianity took on the teachings of the Trinity, which was accepted officially at the Council of Nicea in 325 C.E. They

---

[136] Barackman, *Practical Christian Theology: Examining the Great Doctrines of the Faith*, 256.

add that it was to accommodate the pagans who had been worshipping Greek and Roman gods, as the following two quotes state:

> If belief in the Trinity is idolatry, then from the Jewish point of view, this concept is perhaps even more objectionable. The pagan gods came down in human form, copulated with mortals, and bore human children. Many Christian historians attribute it to the early Christians who were attempting to win over pagans to their new religion, and therefore adopted this pagan concept.[137]

> Jews could make a counter-charge that the Christian Scripture [sic], with their pagan doctrines of Incarnation and a god co-habiting with a human, are an unwarranted addition to Scripture.[138]

Rabbinic Judaism wants to charge biblical faith with incorporating the pagan Greek and Roman world where the gods co-habited with women and had offspring. They attempt to place the incarnation in this category. One thing where even biblical believers will agree with Judaism is in understanding that after Constantine, the Roman Catholic Church did compromise the Christian faith to entice pagans to Christianity. However, one very big point is purposely overlooked by Rabbinic Judaism. The doctrine of the incarnation was well established in the Jerusalem Church long before the pagans were even evangelized. Remember that all the books of the New Testament were written before the fall of Jerusalem in 70 C.E., except the writings of the Apostle John.

In summary, the purpose of this section was not to try to explain every facet of how mankind was created in the *image* and *likeness* of *Elohim*. The purpose was to get a better understanding of the triune nature of *Elohim* and to realize that He created mankind to reflect Himself. God created mankind as male and female with the intent to lessen the natural doubt that *Elohim* Himself is a plural unity. He created mankind with a body which is visible, and a soul and spirit which are invisible. Because mankind reflects His *image* and *likeness*, it is not so hard to believe that He Himself chose to have one Person of His plural unity reveal Himself visibly, while the other two persons remain invisible. *Elohim* gave to male and female total equality but with different functions and responsibilities with man given headship. Because of the way He created man and woman, it is not hard to believe that the persons of the triune *Elohim*, being completely equal, chose within Themselves to voluntarily

---

[137] Aryeh Kaplan, *The Real Messiah? A Jewish Response to Missionaries* (New York: National Conference of Synagogues, 1985), 17.
[138] Chaim Picker, "Make Us a God!" *A Jewish Response to Hebrew Christianity; A Survival Manual for Jews* (New York: iUniverse Press, 2005), 12.

CHAPTER 2: IN THE IMAGE AND LIKENESS OF GOD

submit Themselves to the First Person of the plural unity as the head. As the following chapters in this book unfold, the plurality and tri-unity of God will be clearly seen and understood. Throughout the *Tanakh,* God did present Himself as a plural unity of one [*echad*]. When the Messiah came as the visible Person of the invisible plural unity of *Elohim,* He came as Moses and the prophets said He would: Messiah was and is God, indivisible in the fullest sense of the word.

In reading through this book, keep this discussion on the *image* and *likeness* of God at the center of your thinking. In Genesis 1:26, with *Elohim* making man and woman in His image as a reflection of His plurality, He chose to make Himself – the invisible, indivisible God – visible in revealing His Person, essence, and attributes through the revelation of Himself through His written Word to mankind.

CHAPTER 3:
NAMES FOR GOD

The nature and essence of God, as it relates to the revelation of the plurality or tri-unity of God in the Hebrew Scriptures, is an area of controversy between liberal theologians and Jewish rabbis[139] on one side, and fundamental and evangelical theologians on the other. Even among conservative theologians, there seems to be a tendency not to follow through on their beliefs from the New Testament to the Hebrew Scriptures. The primary, authoritative source material that the New Testament writers used was the Hebrew Scriptures. God did not just reveal Himself as the triune God out of a vacuum in the New Testament. Rather, He started in Genesis 1 using clear statements of Himself in such terms as *Elohim* and *us*. Geisler makes the following statements on these two terms:

> It is true that the very word for God in the Old Testament (*Elohim*) is plural in form; indeed, it can be translated "gods" (Psalm 82:6). However, when used of God, it is plural grammatically, not ontologically. It is plural in literary form, but not in actual reality.
>
> The use of "we" or "us" of God is another literary form known as a royal or regal plural. It is used of royalty and of God in Semitic cultures.[140]

Geisler (quoted above), though not seeing the plurality of God in the term *Elohim*, does see the tri-unity of God throughout the *Tanakh*. It is regrettable that an apologist like Geisler would make such an erroneous statement. However, many of his references are looking back from the New Testament to the *Tanakh*.[141] That is a questionable practice and yet an easy thing to do. Scholars must not read New Testament truth back into the Hebrew Scriptures. The Scriptures are inspired by God; every word, in every part of Scripture, is equally inspired. Man's logic and wisdom cannot reinterpret what God, Himself, said. As was said before, the New Testament was not written in a vacuum. The theological foundations and principles of all

---

[139] **Jewish rabbis**: By placing rabbis together with liberals, this does not mean to imply that rabbis are liberal. Liberals and rabbis may have the same conclusions, but they both arrive at them from totally different perspectives.

[140] Norman Geisler, *Systematic Theology* (Minneapolis: Bethany House, 2003), 2:277.

[141] Geisler, *Systematic Theology*, 278-290.

THE TRI-UNITY OF GOD IS JEWISH

Church doctrines are rooted and anchored in the Hebrew Scriptures. The difficulty of dealing with the plurality or tri-unity of God in the Hebrew Scriptures is determining how much, or if there is anything on it, found in the *Tanakh*. There is seemingly endless insistence by Jewish rabbis that the plurality of God in the *Tanakh* does not exist. They must insist that the plurality of God is non-existent or else, in their minds, Rabbinic Judaism is finished.

The disconnect in assessing the references to the plurality of God in the Hebrew Scriptures lies with Christian scholars who appear to follow the rabbis' lead. This chapter demonstrates the same basic argument that the rabbis make, which minimizes the impact that the doctrine of the plurality or tri-unity of God could have in the *Tanakh*. The Hebrew Scriptures are more than just the foundation of Judaism. They are also the foundation for all doctrines that the apostles taught in the New Testament. Corroboration of this lies in the statements made by the Apostles Paul and Peter in 2 Timothy 3:16 and 2 Peter 1:20-21, respectively:

> [20] *All scripture is given by inspiration of God, and is profitable for doctrine, for reproof, for correction, for instruction in righteousness.*
>
> [21] *Knowing this first, that no prophecy of the scripture is of any private interpretation. For the prophecy came not in old time by the will of man: but holy men of God spoke as they were moved by the Holy Ghost* [Spirit].

These verses are directly referencing the Hebrew Scriptures. Paul and Peter, under the guidance and inspiration of the Holy Spirit (*Ruach haKodesh*), penned these words (2 Timothy 3:16; 2 Peter 1:21) to express the fact that the Hebrew Scriptures were the foundational document for themselves, as well as for Luke, John, and the other authors of the New Testament.

אֵל *El*

El is used in the Hebrew Scriptures as a singular form for God about 238 times and is a very ancient Semitic term that was widely used.[142] In fact, it is said by Friedrich Oehler to be the oldest Semitic name for God.[143] In the Ugaritic Canaanite

---

[142] Harris, Archer, and Waltke, *Theological Wordbook of the Old Testament*, 1:42.
[143] Gustave Friedrich Oehler, *Theology of the Old Testament*, (Grand Rapids: Zondervan, 1883), 87.

culture "*El*, the pagan god, was the proper name of the titular head of the hierarchy of deities."[144]

Preuss explains that *El* was "connected with the conception of a heavenly council. His titles include bull, ancient one, hero, king, and creator."[145] Although a particular definition of *El* may not be derived from Hebrew Scriptures, it contains material aids in understanding and has a direct relationship to Israel:

> *El* was considered the chief among the Canaanitic deities. Likened to a bull in a herd of cows, the people referred to him as "father bull" and regarded him as creator. *Asherah* was the wife of *El*.
>
> Chief among the seventy gods and goddesses that were considered offspring of *El* and *Asherah* was *Hadad*, more commonly known as *Baal*, meaning Lord.[146]

The etymology of *El*, when tracing all known historical information, makes it very difficult to come up with an original meaning. David Baker gives the following: (1) "The derivation or etymology of *El* and its related forms is unclear." He further adds that the term has to do with power.[147] James Smith also concurs with Baker in saying that (2) "Most frequently mentioned suggestions for the original meaning are 'power' or 'fear,' but these are widely challenged and much disputed."[148]

The Hebrew Scriptures predominantly use *El* as a generic term for God.[149] *El* is rarely used by itself. More often, it is used in combination with other words that further describe Him. An example would be Genesis 16:13 where Hagar spoke of God as "*El* who sees."[150] Throughout the Torah (Law), Prophets, and Writings of the Hebrew Scriptures, in both prose and poetry,[151] writers used *El* in at least three different ways. The following are some samples of how the authors of Scripture used this term.

El is used as a designation for *Elohim*. *El* is personal, showing His character of holiness, justice, and might and that He is to be feared. The term *El* can be used by

---

[144] Alexander and Baker, *Dictionary of the Old Testament Pentateuch*, 360.
[145] Horst Dietrich Preuss, *Old Testament Theology* (Trans. Leo G. Perdue: 2 vols.; Louisville: Westminster John Knox), 1:149.
[146] Samuel J. Schultz, *The Old Testament Speaks* (New York: Harper & Row), 92.
[147] Alexander and Baker, *Dictionary of the Old Testament Pentateuch*, 360.
[148] Harris, Archer, and Waltke, *Theological Wordbook of the Old Testament*, 1:42.
[149] Harris, Archer, and Waltke, *Theological Wordbook of the Old Testament*, 1:41.
[150] Payne, *The Theology of the Older Testament*, 145.
[151] John R. Kohlenberger, III, and James A Swanson, *The Hebrew English Concordance to the Old Testament* (Grand Rapids: Zondervan, 1998), 95-96.

itself, without being combined with other terms, as is illustrated in the following examples.

- First, *El* is not a man (Numbers 23:19).

- Secondly, *El* brought Israel out of Egypt (Numbers 23:22).

- Thirdly, *El* made covenant promises both to Abraham (Genesis 17:1) and to Jacob (Genesis 35:11).

- Fourthly, Moses pleads to *El* who is also identified as *Yahweh* for Miriam's healing from leprosy (Numbers 12:13).

- Fifthly, according to Deuteronomy 32:18, *El* is the one who birthed Israel.

- Lastly, when Jesus cried out to the Father on the cross, *My El, my El why hast Thou forsaken Me*, He was quoting from Psalm 22:1.

The following combination of names shows *El* to be the same God as *Elohim* or *Yahweh*. *El* is combined with other terms to represent God in His various attributes such as *El Elyon*, The Highest God that Melchizedek refers to in Genesis 14:18. *El Gibbor* or *Mighty God* is used as one of the names of the Messiah in Isaiah 9:6-7. *El Roe* means the "Lord that sees" in Genesis 16:13-14. Moses refers to *El Olam* in Psalm 90:2 meaning "God of Eternity." When speaking to Abraham God refers to Himself as *El Shaddai* or God Almighty, the All Sufficient God as in Genesis 17:1.

The Hebrew Scriptures use numerous adjectives with *El*, showing the personal character of God, such as *El* of heaven (Psalm 136:26) and the Most High *El* used by both Abraham and Melchizedek in Genesis 14:18-20, 22. *El* is faithful in all that He says (Deuteronomy 7:9) and He also hides Himself (Isaiah 45:15). Jonah refers to God as a gracious *El* (Jonah 4:2) who can also be a great and dreadful *El* as is referenced in Daniel 11:36. *El* is the God of Jacob (Psalm 146:5) and the *El* of Israel (Psalm 68:35). *El*, when used with LORD (*Yahweh*) and God (*Elohim*), shows that *El* in the Scriptures is the God of Israel, the God of the Bible (Deuteronomy 4:31; Joshua 22:22).

This word for God (*El*) is always used in the singular form. Most often it is used of the true God of Israel and is used of God by itself and with other descriptive words. The different words for God relate to each other. This word for God reveals a personal God, a mighty God, a God to be feared, and a covenant-making God.[152]

---

[152] Harris, Archer and Waltke, *Theological Wordbook of the Old Testament,* 1:42-43.

CHAPTER 3: NAMES FOR GOD

Liddon observes that God used the words for Himself, with the singular verbs and plural nouns and pronouns. He says the following:

> When Moses is describing the primal creative act of God, he joins a singular verb to a plural noun. Language, it would seem, thus submits to a violent anomaly, that she may the better hint at the mystery of several Powers or Persons who not merely act together but who constitute a single Agent. The Hebrew language could have described God by singular forms, such as *El, Eloah*, and no question would have been raised as to the strictly Monotheistic force of those words. The Hebrew language might have amplified the idea of God thus conveyed by less dangerous processes than the employment of a plural form. Would it not have done so unless the plural form had been really necessary, in order to hint at the complex mystery of God's inner life, until that mystery should be more clearly unveiled by the explicit Revelations of a later day.[153]

This statement could be repeated under the sections of *Eloah* and *Elohim* a little latter in this book. God, through the pen of Moses, wanted to teach monotheism to Israel as an absolute truth, but He also wanted to give reference to His plurality. Moses had the words for God available to express the oneness of God only, but he did not choose to use them often.

אֵלִים *Elim*

Elim is the plural form of *El* but is used only four times in the Hebrew Scriptures (Exodus 15:11; Psalm 29:1; 89:6[7][154]; Daniel 11:36).[155] This word seems to bear no special significance. In fact, most books referred to do not even acknowledge the word. One text refers to the Exodus 15:11 passage as it relates to pagan gods.[156] *Elim* is called, along with *Elohim*, a plural form of *El*.[157] However, others have taken the Psalm references of *Elim* and applied them to angels and sons

---

[153] J. Glentworth Butler, *Butler's Bible Works* (6 vols. New York: Funk & Wagnalls, 1889), 1:92.

[154] When a Scripture reference appears as in Psalm 89:6[7], verse 7 in brackets means that in English translations, it is found in verse 6; but in Hebrew Scriptures, it would be found in verse 7.

[155] Botterweck, Ringgren and Fabry. *Theological Dictionary of the Old Testament*, 1:254.

[156] Alexander and Baker, *Dictionary of the Old Testament Pentateuch*, 361.

[157] Jenni and Westermann, *Theological Lexicon of the Old Testament*, 1:115.

of God or as heavenly beings.[158] Keil and Delitzsch also use the Psalm references and render them as sons of God or angelic beings.[159]

Elim seems to have no bearing on the subject of this study. Even though *Elim* is the plural of *El*, it is never used of the true God, thus making it a moot issue for the subject.

אֱלָהּ *Elah*

Elah is used 89 times in the Hebrew Scriptures. All but one of them (in Jeremiah) are used during the time of the exile (Daniel) or post-exilic period (Ezra). Of those 89 references, at least 15 of them are to false gods.[160] *Elah* is the Aramaic form of *Eloah*, which is known as a verbal noun, "and is associated with the Hebrew verb *alah*, meaning to fear, to worship, to adore."[161] *Elah* indicates that the living and true God is identified with His people in captivity. It also carries a meaning of an oak, a tree symbolizing durability, a virtue characteristic of Him as being the Everlasting God.[162] It is also a singular word for God, and it is used in the same context as *Yahweh* (Ezra 6:18, 21-22).[163]

Elah is the same God as *El*, *Eloah*, *Elohim,* and *Yahweh*. This word was used exclusively during the exile and post-exilic period, when the oneness of God needed to be taught and reaffirmed to Israel, after their displacement from the land by God for worshipping other gods. As Israel was once again being instructed under the leadership of Nehemiah and Ezra, the concept of monotheism was of utmost importance. The following question must be asked even though the answer cannot be known this side of life, but the observations and questions remain, drawing the student of the Scriptures to this unanswerable question. If, as the rabbis say, God is one alone with no plurality, how is it that an all-knowing God could not see down through the corridor of time and prevent this problem in the beginning?

- First, why isn't the singular form of God, Elah, used exclusively by Haggai, Malachi, Zephaniah, Zechariah or Ezekiel, exile or post-

---

[158] H. C. Leupold, *Exposition of the Psalms* (Grand Rapids: Baker, 1959), 250.
[159] C. F. Keil and F. Delitzsch, *Commentary on the Old Testament* (trans. James Martin; 10 vols.; Grand Rapids: Eerdmans, 1973). 5:368.
[160] George V. Wigram, *The Englishman's Hebrew Concordance of the Old Testament* (Peabody, Mass: Hendrickson, 1996), 78-79.
[161] Lockyer, *All the Divine Names and Titles in the Bible*, 8.
[162] Lockyer, *All the Divine Names and Titles in the Bible*, 8-9.
[163] Samuel Prideaux Tregelles, *Gesenius' Hebrew and Chaldee Lexicon to the Old Testament Scriptures*(Grand Rapids: Eerdmans, 1957), 48.

exilic writers, and not just in Ezra, and Daniel? Israel's worship of other gods was one of the major reasons for their displacement. If the urgency of teaching monotheism was so important, the observation once again is present.

- The second question is, since *Elah* is used to affirm monotheism to exiled and post-exilic Israel, why did Daniel and Ezra also use *Elohim*?

- The third question is, if God is one alone, a unity, why didn't the writers of Scripture, during that era, only use singular terms to remove all doubt and prevent future controversy?

These questions are an argument from silence, to be sure, yet why the Hebrews used these words still remains a haunting question.

אֱלוֹהַ *Eloah*

Eloah occurs 57 times in the Hebrew Scriptures and may be the singular form of plural *Elohim*. Most of those references (41) occur in the book of Job.[164] The others are scattered mostly in the poetic portions of the Scriptures. *Eloah* first appears in Deuteronomy 32:15-17, then 2 Kings, 2 Chronicles, Nehemiah, Psalms, Proverbs, Isaiah, Daniel, and Habakkuk. Its use stretches from Job, believed by some to be the oldest book in the Hebrew Scriptures, to the post-exilic time of Nehemiah. In Job, there are two references where God uses the term *Eloah* of Himself: In 39:17, He uses it to relate to His providence; and in 40:2 to His attribute of being Almighty.[165] *Eloah* is unique in that it does not occur in combination with other divine names. *Eloah* is reaffirmed as God, in the singular, by this following observation:

> This term for God was usually clearly used for Israel's God, the true God. This is evident from the fact that the Levites in the post-exilic period used the term in quoting the descriptive revelation of God given in Exodus 34:6-7, where the original revelation to Moses had used *El* and *Yahweh* (Neh. 9:17).[166]

---

[164] VanGemeren, ed., *Dictionary of Old Testament Theology & Exegesis*, 1:405.
[165] Harris, Archer, and Waltke, *Theological Wordbook of the Old Testament*, 1:43.
[166] Harris, Archer, and Waltke, *Theological Wordbook of the Old Testament*, 1:43.

VanGemeren says that the terms *Eloah*, *El* and *Yahweh* are interchangeable names of God.[167]

Eloah is used throughout the time period of the Hebrew Scriptures, along with *El*, as being singular for the name of God. But the writers of the Scriptures chose to use these names sparingly in relation to the term *Elohim*. Noam Hendren speaks to the point when he says:

> The first hints of plurality are found in the terms used to designate God – "*Elohim*" and "*Adonai*" – both of which are plural forms of existing singular nouns. Had the biblical authors intended to assert the absolute (rather than compound) unity of the Godhead, they had readily available singular terms (*Eloah*, *Adoni*, as well as *El*) which would have avoided any confusion on this crucial point.[168]

Hendren points out that if the Hebrew writers wanted to show monotheism throughout the Scriptures, thus leaving no doors open for a plurality of God, they could have used *El, Elah,* or *Eloah* in the place of *Elohim*, but they chose not to do that. Instead they chose to use a plural word for God the vast majority of the time rather than the singular form of God (*El, Elah, Eloah*), showing the plural nature of God. This reality is brought out by Barackman when he specifically says that "*Elohim*, the plural form, indicates the plurality of Persons within the divine Trinity."[169] The authors of Scripture left the door open for the New Testament's teaching of the tri-unity.

אֱלֹהִים *Elohim*

What is true of singular words for God (*El, Elah, Eloah*) is also true of the plural word *Elohim*. The etymology is, at best, uncertain.[170] Jack Scott presents three possibilities on the root of *Elohim*. First, he takes for granted that *jlh* is the assumed root of *El, Eloah* and *Elohim*, meaning "gods" or "God." Next, he says "The view that the three Hebrew words come from one root is much disputed, and a final verdict is lacking." His third statement is: "More probable is the view that *Elohim* comes

---

[167] Willem A. VanGemeren, ed., Dictionary of *Old Testament Theology and Exegesis* (Grand Rapids: MI: Zondervan, 1997), 1:405.
[168] Noam Hendren, "The Divine Unity and the Deity of Messiah," *Mishkan* (issue 39, 2003): 38.
[169] Barackman. *Practical Christian Theology*, 66.
[170] Alexander and Baker, *Dictionary of the Old Testament Pentateuch,* 360.

from *Eloah* as a unique development of the Hebrew Scriptures."[171] Yet Payne makes further statements:

> *El*, seems to have arisen from the root *jul*, the probable meaning of which is to be strong (cf. Genesis 31:29 "power").[172]

There is just no solid consistent information as to the etymology of *Elohim*. The words being used: "assumed," "much disputed," "lacking," and "probable" indicate that there is nothing much here that is solid. There are words such as *Elohim* that scholars do not have enough information about to draw a strong conclusion. Since there is no consensus on the etymology of *Elohim*, the only alternative to help in understanding *El, Eloah,* and *Elohim* is to see how the Hebrew Scriptures use them and in what context they are used; but that is beyond the scope of this book. What is known and recognized is that *El, Elah, Eloah,* and *Elohim* are all nouns translated as "God" in the singular, except for *elohim* when it references pagan "gods" in the plural. However, when *Elohim* is translated as singular in the English text, there ought to be a note stating that *Elohim*, though used as a singular when translated, is in fact a plural noun.

It is very important to see how *Elohim*, in particular, is used within the Hebrew text in relationship to *El, Eloah, Yahweh,* and the Angel of *Yahweh*. First, *Elohim* is used 2,600 times and is the second most frequent substantive in the Hebrew Scriptures following *ben* (son).[173] *Elohim* is introduced exclusively throughout the creation account of Genesis 1:1-2:3 as the God of creation. *Elohim* is not a personal name but the general Hebrew word for deity.[174] Also, *Elohim* is often paired with *Yahweh* (יהוה) as in Genesis 2:4-5; Exodus 34:23; Psalm 68:18 [19] .[175] In fact, *Elohim* and *Yahweh* are combined together 930 times throughout the Hebrew Scriptures in one of the following translated forms: LORD thy God, LORD God, LORD our God, LORD my God, LORD your God, LORD their God, and LORD his God.[176] God, through the writers of Scripture, chose to use the plural form of Himself instead of using the singular form exclusively. He was teaching that He was a plurality. However, Rabbinic Judaism wants to substantiate monotheism without plurality by trying to ignore the fact that God chose to use a plural description of Himself for one particular reason: He is a plurality (tri-unity).

---

[171] Harris, Archer, and Waltke, *Theological Wordbook of the Old Testament*, 1:41.
[172] Payne, *The Theology of the Older Testament*, 145.
[173] Jenni and Westermann, *Theological Lexicon of the Old Testament*, 1:116.
[174] Nahum M. Sarna, *The JPS Torah Commentary, Genesis* (Philadelphia: The Jewish Publication Society, 1989), 5.
[175] Harris, Archer, and Waltke, *Theological Wordbook of the Old Testament*, 1:44.
[176] Robert Young, *Young's Analytical Concordance to the Bible* (Grand Rapids: Eerdmans), 411-418.

God was revealing Himself to Israel by showing His indivisible oneness and at the same time showing His complex unity, being also a plurality. This is not acceptable to the Jewish mind because it is an antithesis and appears to go against the strict monotheism of Judaism.[177] *Yahweh* is combined with *El*, which is the singular form; and it is combined 21 times out of 258.[178] *Elah*, the singular form, is never once used out of a possible 95 times.[179] *Eloah* is used only once in Psalm 68:31 out of 58 times.[180] All of these combinations are in the singular, which would show absolute monotheism. But the fact that *Elohim* is used in combination with *Yahweh* over 930 times is a significant amount more than the aforementioned group. God is showing to Israel that, indeed, He is one and that He is a unity and that unity is a plurality.

Alexander and Baker describe *Elohim* as a plurality, a person involved in the lives of His created beings. *Elohim* shows His personhood in a plural context. He is not distant, unconcerned, or detached from human need. *Elohim* is used of God as the Creator (Genesis 1:1, 27; 2:3-4, 5:1). He interacts with humans (Genesis 18; Deuteronomy 34:10 with Numbers 12:6-8), and walks with man (Genesis 3:8; 5:24). He speaks to people (Genesis 8:15; 9:8, 12, 17; 17:3, 23; 21:2; 35:15; 46:2) and listens to them (Genesis 21:17; 30:17, 22; Exodus 2:24). He provides for them (Genesis 1:29, 2:8-9, 15; 4:25; 9:27; 22:8; 28:4; 30:18, 20) and protects them (Genesis 31:7, 9, 16; 45:5, 7). He also makes covenants (Genesis 9:16) and promises (Genesis 17:9) to man. *Elohim* is gracious and does good (Genesis 50:20; Exodus 1:20); but at the same time, He obligates man to keep certain responsibilities and commandments (Genesis 2:16; 3:1, 3; 6:22; 7:9, 16; 17:9, 16; 21:4, 12; 31:16, 24; 35:1, 11; Exodus 18:23).[181]

According to Jack B. Scott, as quoted by Harris, Archer, and Waltke, titles are attached to the noun *Elohim* that pertain to His work of Creation (Isaiah 45:18), His sovereignty (Isaiah 54:5), as well as focusing around His majesty or glory. Yet a far more frequent title is found in those passages that pertain to the Savior God.[182] In *Elohim*, the plurality of God is expressed in ways which would minimally show the activity of God the Father and God the Son in a salvation context.

Elohim is also mighty, terrible, and executes judgment, as Deuteronomy 10:17-18 speaks of Him:

---

[177] Schiffman, *Return of the Remnant*, 95.
[178] Robert Young, *Young's Analytical Concordance to the Bible*, 411.
[179] Robert Young, *Young's Analytical Concordance to the Bible*, 411.
[180] Robert Young, *Young's Analytical Concordance to the Bible*, 418.
[181] Alexander and Baker, *Dictionary of the Old Testament Pentateuch*, 362.
[182] Harris, Archer, and Waltke, *Theological Wordbook of the Old Testament*, 1:44.

> *For the Lord your God is God supreme, and Lord supreme, the great, the mighty, and the awesome God, who shows no favor and takes no bribes, but upholds the cause of the fatherless and the widow, and befriends the stranger, providing him with food and clothing.*[183]

Elohim shows Himself in a multitude of ways. Unlike *El*, *Elah*, or *Eloah*, *Elohim* always appears as a plural, not in the singular, in the Hebrew Scriptures. This word for God is used of both God, as the true God predominantly, and of false pagan gods of the lands around Israel. Although a plural noun, associated verbs, and descriptive terms are usually in the singular.[184] Since *Elohim* is plural, the term presents a paradox and attracts attention because the monotheistic God of Israel is representing Himself as a plurality. *Elohim* is used in the Hebrew text over 2,600 times as a plural (of these, 2,350 are in reference to the God of Israel), which is many more times than the singular usages of *El* (258), *Elah* (95), and *Eloah* (58) combined. *Elohim*, with singular nouns, verbs, and descriptive terms, definitely shows monotheism; but its use also can encourage an argument in favor of plurality, rather than against it.[185]

Arguments Against a Literal Understanding of Elohim

Neither Jewish nor Christian scholars object to the scriptural term *Elohim* that is used for God. The problem lies with how biblical scholars interpret *Elohim* in the context where *Elohim* is used by God of Himself or where others refer to Him as God in His revealed Word. There is no conscious effort, on the part of conservative Christian scholars, to undermine a doctrine of Scripture. In respect to Jewish scholars, Paul says in Romans there is a spiritual blindness upon the hearts of Jewish people resulting in not being able to see the plurality of God (Amos 8:11-12). Paul, in Romans 11:10, is very clear as he quotes David in Psalm 69:23: *Let their eyes be darkened, that they may not see, and bend down their back always.*

---

[183] Adele Berlin and Marc Zvi Brettler, *The Jewish Study Bible* (New York: Jewish Publication Society, *Tanakh* Translation, 2004), 388. (All Old Testament references are cited from this translation unless otherwise noted.) Three other translations are cited here but not quoted . (1) Alexander Harkavy, *The Twenty-Four Books of the Old Testament* (2 vols., New York, N.Y: Hebrew Publishing, 1916), (2) Isaac Leeser, *The Twenty-Four Books of the Holy Bible* (New York: Hebrew Publishing, n.d.), (3) *The Holy Bible, The Orthodox Jewish Bible* (3rd edition, New York: Artists For Israel International, 2002).

[184] Sarna, *The Jewish Publication Society Torah Commentary: Genesis*, 5.

[185] Arnold A Fruchtenbaum, *Messianic Christology* (Tustin, CA: Ariel Ministries, 1998), 103.

Most of the authors (Jewish and Christian) cited agree that *Elohim* is plural and that it should be looked upon as a "plural of majesty" or an intensified form of the word. They, for the most part, do not think there is enough contextual evidence to warrant understanding *Elohim* as a plural reference to God. However, they say that it is a foundation from which the New Testament builds its doctrine of the trinity or tri-unity. Mathews states the following:

> Why the plural was also used of the one God of Israel is uncertain, though most ascribe it to the use of the Hebrew plural that indicates honor or majesty. As a plural it is a literary convention that reflects special reverence.[186]

In the judgment of this author, this statement does not reflect a verbal plenary view of inspiration. Mathews states that its interpretation is uncertain and most scholars ascribe that there is not enough biblical evidence to support plurality. He continues:

> Since its plurality does not designate more than one entity, its morphological shape does not necessarily refer to the plurality of the Godhead. It is unreasonable to burden this one word *Elohim* with a developed view of the Christian Trinity. It is fair to say, however, that the creation account (1:2, 26-27) implies that there is a plurality within God (cf. 3:22; 11:7; 18:1ff.). But it is not until the era of the church that the Trinity is clearly articulated. New Testament tradition ascribes to Christ a role in creation (John 1:1-3; Colossians 1:15-17; Hebrews 1:2), but it is less clear about the role of the Spirit.[187]

Mathews hedges on the implications of *Elohim's* plurality and in the process explains away what God was intending readers to understand about Himself in the *Tanakh*. This researcher sees two things: First, the "burden" of a full-blown development of the tri-unity is not being laid on one word. However, something is going on throughout the pages of the *Tanakh*. God, by His choice of terms, is saying that He, *Elohim*, is a plurality. Second, this whole argument has given this author a strong impression that Christian theologians have conceded the subject to Rabbinic Judaism.

Statements have been made by various authors on the plural aspect of *Elohim*. Louis Jacobs, a Jewish author, makes an honest statement when he says that the plural form of God has long been a puzzle to the rabbis. They are obliged, by Judaism, to defend it against "sectarians" (Christians) who say that the plural form is

---

[186] Mathews, *The New American Commentary*, 1a:127.
[187] Matthews, *The New American Commentary*, 1a:127.

CHAPTER 3: NAMES FOR GOD

proof of more than one god.[188] Arnold Fruchtenbaum, a Jewish believer in Messiah *Yeshua*, says that the Hebrew grammar requires that when the plural form is used, as is the case with *Elohim*, the verbs agree with the associated nouns in both gender and number.[189] *Elohim* is plural and is used of the true God and the false gods as seen in Exodus 20:2-3. When it is used of false gods, the verbs will also be plural, which is correct Hebrew grammar. When *Elohim* is used of the true God, the verbs, as in Genesis 1:1 (*Elohim* created), are singular which shows the unity and oneness of God. But that singular construction can also imply that, even though *Elohim* is one, He is also a plurality in that oneness. Youngblood identifies the oneness and plurality of God in Genesis 1:

> The first verse of Genesis itself provides us with a helpful cue. It tells us that "God created" (Genesis 1:1). The noun "God" is plural in the Hebrew text, but the verb "created" is singular in the Hebrew text. The Bible clearly teaches that God is one being, a unity (Deuteronomy 6:4; 1 Corinthians 8:4). At the same time, the Bible just as clearly teaches that the one God exists in three persons and is therefore also a trinity.[190]

Youngblood clearly sees and understands that God in His omniscience chose to reveal Himself as one being and yet at the same time a unity of three Persons. In reference to the oneness of *Elohim*, Hebrew grammar also demonstrates the plurality of *Elohim* as in Exodus 20:3 and Deuteronomy 13:2. In both cases, when referring to *elohim* as false gods, it is correctly translated as "gods" by both Jewish and Christian scholars.

Numerous authors affirm the view that *Elohim* is to be understood as a "plural of majesty" and not as a reference to the plurality of God:

> The plural ending is usually described as a plural of majesty and not intended as a true plural when used of God. This is seen in the fact that the noun *Elohim* is consistently used with singular verb forms and with adjectives and pronouns in the singular.[191]

---

[188] Louis Jacobs, *A Jewish Theology*, 138.
[189] Fruchtenbaum, *Messianic Christology*, 103.
[190] Ronald Youngblood, *The Book of Genesis*, 2nd ed. (Eugene, OR: Wipf and Stock Publishers, 1991), 23.
[191] Harris, Archer, and Waltke, *Theological Wordbook of the Old Testament*, 1:44.

> The grammatical form of Elohim is that of an abstract plural of greatness or majesty, and not a true numeric plural.[192]

> The divine name, *Elohim* probably describes a plural of intensity or plural of majesty (simply "God" – an abstract plural).[193]

> The plural form may signify majesty or serve to intensify the basic idea. The preference for the use of *Elohim* in this chapter, rather than the sacred divine name *YHVH*, may well be conditioned by theological considerations; the term *Elohim*, connoting universalism and abstraction, is most appropriate for the transcendent God of creation.[194]

> Though morphologically plural, the word is regularly used as a singular when referring to Israel's God. This is shown by the regular use of singular verbs and adjectives in conjunction with the term. The purpose and meaning of the plural form is debated, with some seeing it as a plural of majesty, or royal plural as an intensification or claim to exclusivity, or as an honorific.[195]

> Some scholars have held that the plural represents an intensified form for the supreme God; others believe it describes the supreme God and His heavenly court of created being[s]. Still others hold that the plural form refers to the triune God of Genesis 1:1-3, who works through Word and Spirit in the creation of the world. In any event, *Elohim* conveys the idea that the one Supreme Being, who is the only true God, is in some sense plural.[196]

Collectively, the consensus of these scholars is that the term *Elohim* is not a true plural, and it does not represent the plurality of God in the *Tanakh*. Their arguments are centered around these thoughts: *Elohim* is a "plural of majesty," and secondly, Hebrew grammar of the plural noun is followed by a singular verb when speaking of the true God, showing that God is one alone. They are reaffirming the belief, by the use of Hebrew grammar, that false gods, which always have plural verbs, show only the plural concept of pagan gods, such as Baal. This is a Jewish rabbinic argument

---

[192] Payne, *The Theology of the Older Testament*, 145.
[193] Preuss, *Old Testament Theology*, 1:149.
[194] Sarna, *The Jewish Publication Society Torah Commentary: Genesis*, 5.
[195] Alexander and Baker, *Dictionary of the Old Testament Pentateuch*, 362.
[196] Ronald F. Youngblood, *New Illustrated Bible Dictionary* (Nashville: Thomas Nelson, 1995), 504.

whose views are different on inspiration[197] from that which is held by fundamental and evangelical scholars. Also, they generally do not use the literal interpretation of the Scriptures, or as Renald Showers calls it, the historical-grammatical method.[198]

Arguments for a Literal Understanding of Elohim

In the preceding section, no flexibility was shown toward the proposition that God could be revealing Himself by using the same Hebrew grammar to show exceptions in the language. God is affirming His oneness and plurality while protecting the teaching of the Hebrew Scriptures against polytheism. Israel was surrounded by polytheistic Canaanite nations, as well as the Amorites, Moabites, and the Egyptians.

When *Elohim* is modified by a singular word, both Jewish and Christian translators want it to be understood as God, when God meant it to be understood as a plural representation of Himself with the singular modifier to show His oneness. Cooper expresses the same thing when he asks:

> Why should the grammar be ignored and the word be translated as if it were a singular noun when it refers to Israel's God, since the facts are that it is a plural noun and means more than one?[199]

According to Hebrew grammar, if *Elohim* is plural, it is not grammatically correct for singular verbs to follow. So the Hebrew construction breaks down with the pattern of Hebrew grammar. However, there are several instances where plural verbs follow *Elohim*, the true God, which is grammatically correct as in 2 Samuel 7:23:

> *And who is like Your people Israel, a unique nation on earth, whom God went and redeemed as His people, winning renown for* **Himself?**

---

[197] **Jewish Inspiration**: Based on Numbers 12:5-8, there are three tiers of Inspiration. First, because God spoke to Moses face to face in the Torah (Law), that is the most inspired. Secondly, God spoke to Prophets in visions and dreams, so they are less inspired than the Law. Thirdly, the least inspired are the Writings.

[198] Renald E. Showers, *There Really is a Difference!* (Bellmawr, NJ: Friends of Israel Gospel Ministry, 1990), 53.

[199] David L. Cooper, *The God of Israel*, 24-25.

Literally it says:

> *And what one nation on the earth is like Thy people Israel, whom God [Elohim]* **they** *went to redeem for* **themselves.**[200]

Robert Morris, a Jewish believer in *Yeshua*, speaks to the fact that Jews for Judaism[201] teaches that the Doctrine of the Trinity is a pagan concept.[202] Yet 2 Samuel 7:23 says that more than one *Elohim* redeemed Israel.

In dealing with arguments for *Elohim* being a unity, the first concept to consider is a complex unity. God did introduce Himself as a plurality and tri-unity in the *Tanakh*. An example can be given from Genesis 2:24 of a complex unity when God took two separate identities (man and woman) and put them together as a complex unity of one. This concept is difficult for Jewish people to comprehend in relation to *Elohim*. Stan Rosenthal, a Jewish believer in Messiah *Yeshua*, tells how they view it:

> Jewish people often object to the tri-unity of God because of what they believe is taught in the *Shema*...The accepted premise among Jewish people views this as saying that God is indivisibly one. Consequently, the objection is raised: I cannot believe in this person, Jesus, whom Christians claim to be God. For them the *Shema* appears to have silenced forever the argument which embraces the historic Christian belief in the deity of Jesus.[203]

Rosenthal is simply saying that the *Shema*, to the Jewish people, teaches that God is indivisible, and because of that, Jesus is another god. Hence, they reject Jesus as God, as well as God's substitutionary sacrifice for sin. The *Shema* has become the watchword in Judaism, and they use it to show that *Elohim* (God) is indivisible, one. In this section, the object is to show that God is indivisible, one, and yet plural. The argument that *Elohim* represents a "plural of majesty" is a foreign concept in the *Tanakh*. The Hebrew kings never spoke of themselves as a "plural of majesty," so there is no background for this concept in the Hebrew Scriptures, which the following statement expresses:

---

[200] Fruchtenbaum, *Messianic Christology*, 104.

[201] **Jews for Judaism**: Jews for Judaism is an anti-missionary organization that works against Christian missionaries to Jewish people; these anti-missionaries strongly try to reconvert new Jewish believers in Messiah back to Rabbinic Judaism.

[202] Robert Morris, *Anti-Missionary Arguments: The Trinity* (Irvine, CA: HaDavar Messianic Ministries), 1.

[203] Stanley Rosenthal, *One God or Three?* (Bellmawr, NJ: Friends of Israel Gospel Ministry, 1978), 17-18.

CHAPTER 3: NAMES FOR GOD

But that is to read into Hebrew speech a modern mode of address. So far as our biblical records can help us, the kings of Judah and Israel are all addressed in the singular.[204]

So in the Hebrew text the kings of Judah and Israel never used a "plural of majesty" in speaking of themselves. This is echoed by Grudem when he says:

> In Old Testament Hebrew there are no other examples of a monarch using plural verbs or plural pronouns of himself in such a "plural of majesty," so this suggestion has no evidence to support it.[205]

The closest thing to the idea of "plural of majesty" is in Isaiah 7:13-14 when God speaks of the House of David. However, that is a collective statement about the House of David, not a "plural of majesty." Nathan Stone echoes the fact that the term "plural of majesty" is an expression unknown to the kings of Israel:

> They say that the plural is only a plural of majesty such as used by rulers and kings. But such use of the plural was not known then. We find no king of Israel speaking of himself as "we" and "us."[206]

Although the Queen of England uses the "plural of majesty," England is a western Gentile nation; whereas, Israel is a Middle Eastern Semitic nation, now twenty centuries removed from modern England. This has been observed and answered by Stuart Briscoe:

> Some commentators suggest that the plural words are used to give a sense of intensity and majesty to God (in much the same way that the Queen in her official pronouncements uses the "royal we"). But a clear statement about the Trinity becomes apparent when the "Us" and "Our" and the plural *Elohim* are considered alongside the statement about the "Spirit of God" being active in creation.[207]

Henry Smith says that the "plural of majesty" cannot be accepted today because "such plurals of majesty…are without parallel in Hebrew."[208] Then he draws an inaccurate conclusion by saying that the only plausible view is that the word originally was narrowed down to apply to One and that vestiges of a belief in a group

---

[204] George A. F. Knight, *A Christian Theology of the Old Testament* (Carlisle, UK: Paternoster Publishing, 1998), 54.
[205] Wayne Grudem, *Systematic Theology* (Grand Rapids: Zondervan, 1994), 227.
[206] Stone, *Names of God*, 16.
[207] Stuart Briscoe, *The Communicator's Commentary* (vol. 1. Waco, TX: Word, 1987), 34.
[208] Henry Smith, *The Religion of Israel* (New York: Charles Scribner's Sons, 1914), 14.

of divine beings have survived even in our present Bible. He then cites Genesis 1:26: *Let us make man in our image* and 3:22 where God takes counsel with His associates, or as in 6:2 with the *sons of God*. Smith uses human logic instead of letting Scripture interpret Scripture. It appears that since he does not accept a high view of Scripture, he attempts to find some natural human answer rather than accepting the plurality of God. Towner uses similar logic by stating that "plural of majesty" is not likely, but then goes on to state that because the plural personal pronoun is used rarely by God, it must be a heavenly council:

> Is God using the "plural of majesty," and speaking in the manner of the queen of England or the pope? Not likely! If anyone has the right to make self-references in the plural (especially considering that God is, at least from a Christian point of view, a Holy Trinity), it would surely be God. However, this plural usage happens again only very rarely (Genesis 3:22; 11:7; Isaiah 6:8). Surely, if God were thinking majestically, the plural would be used more consistently than that. We are left, then, with the heavenly council as the only likely way of explaining this use of the plural in verse 1:26.[209]

The fact is that God did use first person plural pronouns only in four passages. But to conclude that it must be a heavenly council merely on that basis, is ignoring the abundance of other plural references that not only show Him to be a plurality but also a tri-unity.

Interpreting Scripture must always be done within its immediate and distant context, whether in the *Tanakh* or the New Testament. If the Hebrew Scriptures do not use a "plural of majesty," why do scholars force a reading into the text? The Scriptures, as a whole, are the writings of God, Himself, to reveal Himself to mankind. The only viable way to develop that concept, when studying the Scriptures, is to let God reveal Himself rather than reading into the text what God never intended. God is intending man to understand from Genesis 1, that He is a plural compound One. This concept of a complex unity is not "plural of majesty" or intensity but a complex unity of the tri-unity of God. Complex unity is expressed well by Robert Morris:

> Philosophically, the idea of a complex, indivisible unity is not foreign to the Bible. The nation of Israel is a complex indivisible unity (one nation made up of 12 tribes), the Law of Moses is a complex, indivisible unity (one law made up of 613

---

[209] W. Sibley Towner, *Westminster Bible Companion: Genesis* (Louisville, KY: Westminster John Knox Press, 2001), 24-25

commandments), and marriage is a complex, indivisible unity (a one flesh relationship consisting of man and woman). Is it inconsistent if the God of the Universe is a complex, indivisible unity as well?[210]

Is God a complex unity? Yes. Can he reveal Himself in a tri-unity? Yes. To force the fully developed doctrine of the tri-unity from the New Testament into Genesis 1 or the word *Elohim,* is completely exegetically improper. What can be seen is that God is a plurality, not a "plural of majesty," which is a foreign term to the *Tanakh*. It can also be seen that God is a complex-compound unity. It is the strong opinion of this author that God has given ample evidences of His unity, as well as His plurality.

It's not that Israelite people did not know how to use the word "we"; they did use it, but kings didn't use it when they were functioning as kings. There is only one consistent use of the "we" that so many scholars want to see as plural of majesty. But it is just not present in the Hebrew text in relation to the kings of Judah or Israel. One predominant way that the word "we" is used is in prayers of confession before God. Some of the great men of God confessed their sins and the sins of the nation before God using *we*. They have used the plural *we* but not as a plural of majesty as seen in the following references from Isaiah, Daniel, and Nehemiah:

Isaiah

> 53:2 He had no form or beauty that *we* should look at Him.
>
> 53:3 No charm, that *we* should find Him pleasing.
>
> 53:4 Yet it was our sickness that He was bearing, Our suffering that He endured. *We* accounted Him plagued, smitten, and afflicted by God.
>
> 53:5 But He was wounded because of our sins, crushed because of our iniquities. He bore the chastisement that made us whole, and by His bruises *we* were healed.

Daniel

> 9:5 *We* have sinned; *we* have gone astray; *we* have acted wickedly; *we* have been rebellious and have deviated from Your commandments.

---

[210] Robert Morris, *Anti-Missionary Arguments: The Trinity*, 3.

9:8   The shame, O LORD, is on us, on our kings, our officers, and our fathers, because *we* have sinned against You.

9:9   To the Lord our God belong mercy and forgiveness, for *we* rebelled against Him.

9:11   All Israel has violated Your teaching and gone astray, disobeying You; so the curse and the oath written in the Teaching of Moses, the servant of God, have been poured down upon us, for *we* have sinned against Him.

9:13   All that calamity, just as is written in the Teaching of Moses, came upon us, yet *we* did not supplicate the LORD our God, did not repent of our iniquity or become wise through Your truth.

9:14   Hence the LORD was intent upon bringing calamity upon us, for the LORD our God is in the right in all that He has done, but *we* have not obeyed Him.

9:15   Now, O Lord our God, You who brought Your people out of the land of Egypt with a mighty hand, winning fame for Yourself to this very day, *we* have sinned, *we* have acted wickedly.

9:18   Not because of any merit of ours do *we* lay our plea before You but because of Your abundant mercies.

Nehemiah

1:6   Let Your ear be attentive and Your eyes open to receive the prayer of Your servant that I am praying to You now, day and night, on behalf of the Israelites, Your servants, confessing the sins that *we* Israelites have committed against You, sins that I and my father's house have committed.

1:7   *We* have offended You by not keeping the commandments, the laws, and the rules that You gave to Your servant Moses.

We is used in the confession of sin, but it is never used in the context of a king speaking in reference to himself and his court. Nor do you find the king

CHAPTER 3: NAMES FOR GOD

speaking of himself and the people as "we." When he speaks it is within the context of "I am the king."

Getting back to the plural word *Elohim*, Cooper states that the regular ending for a plural noun in the masculine gender and plural number is ים (*im*) and that with this grammatical structure no one would disagree.

> Since this word has the plural ending and is listed by all lexicographers and grammarians as a noun in the plural number, we must accept this connotation in every instance unless there are facts in the context showing a departure from the ordinary, usual literal meaning.[211]

Previously cited authors say that *Elohim* is not a true plural word. Yet when the plural Hebrew ending is present, it is consistently treated as a plural until God describes Himself. This is an observation anyone can make. Observe in either the *Tanakh* or an Hebrew/English interlinear, אֱלֹהִים (*Elohim*) is consistently translated as God in the singular. The plural Hebrew ending is ים (*im*), as in *Cherubim, Seraphim,* or *Shedhim* (demons). Whenever the ending *im* is used, it is translated in the plural, except for *Elohim*. It is the view of this author that many of the previously cited authors want to explain away the plural '*im*' ending rather than accept it for what it is, a plural.

The plural personal pronouns of God which will be covered under a later chapter are relevant here. What does God say about Himself? *Elohim* is making a statement early in human history (3 of the 4 times in Genesis) that He is a plurality by using the plural personal pronoun *us* before the time of Abraham. The references are: *Let US make man* (Genesis 1:26). When Adam and Eve sinned, God said: *They have become one of US* (Genesis 3:22). Also, at the tower of Babel God said, *Let US go down* (Genesis 11:7). The other plural pronoun reference is found in the call of Isaiah when God said, *Who will go for US?* (Isaiah 6:6). Isaiah hears pronouns in the singular and plural, simultaneously, from the very "lips" of God.[212]

The argument of what God has written cannot be expressed too strongly. He was revealing Himself to His people. Why do scholars explain the plurality of *Elohim* in ways that do not seem to be in harmony with the context of how God has chosen to reveal Himself to His people? Jack Scott, in *Theological Wordbook of the Old Testament*, states that the word *Elohim* is not to be understood as a true plural:

---

[211] David L. Cooper, *The God of Israel*, 34.
[212] Knight, *A Christian Theology of the Old Testament*, 55.

The plural ending is usually described as a plural of majesty and not intended as a true plural when used of God. This is seen in the fact that the noun *Elohim* is consistently used with singular verb forms and with adjectives and pronouns in the singular.[213]

In agreement with Scott, Page Kelley says that "אֱלֹהִים (*Elohim*) is plural in form but normally functions as a singular noun."[214] Contrary to Scott's and Kelley's statements, if they base their view on verbal plenary inspiration and the literal method of interpretation of the Scriptures, it is impossible to arrive at that conclusion. This author believes that if *Elohim* is viewed by verbal plenary inspiration, using the literal method of interpretation, the conclusion must be that God is using the term *Elohim* of Himself to strongly state that He, as God, is presenting Himself in a plural context. Not only must scholars be consistent in their view of inspiration, but they must also be consistent in using the literal method of interpretation. Otherwise scholars become the authority, and God is reduced to just a point of argument.

Jesus (*Yeshua*) expected the Pharisees to know and understand the plurality of *Elohim* when He equated Himself with God, the Father, as in John 10:30. The fact that Hebrew grammar is broken when a singular verb is used with the plural noun [*Elohim*] should immediately attract the attention of the reader. It can be argued that God is revealing Himself as a plural God who is, in essence, one. Why turn and explain away the conclusion that *Yeshua* expected the Pharisees to see?

Another important observation is that often *Elohim* and *Yahweh* are used together denoting the same God, as was previously mentioned at the beginning of the section entitled *Elohim*. *Yahweh* and *Elohim* are combined showing unity and plurality, and *Elohim* and *Yahweh* are both individually applied to two divine personalities, distinct and separate from each other, yet a unity of one, a compound unity. *Yahweh* in Hosea 1:2, 7 is applied to two separate and distinct *Yahweh*s who are their *Elohim*s. It is pointed out by Fruchtenbaum that Hosea is saying there are two *Yahweh*s which are separate and distinct from each other, yet a unity:

> When the LORD first spoke to Hosea, and the LORD said to Hosea, Go, get yourself a wife of whoredom....But I will have compassion on the house of Judah. And I will give them victory through the LORD their God [*Elohim*], I will not give them victory with bow, and sword and battle, by horses and riders.[215]

---

[213] Harris, Archer, and Waltke, *Theological Wordbook of the Old Testament*, 1:44.
[214] Page H. Kelley, *Biblical Hebrew: An Introductory Grammar* (Grand Rapids: Eerdmans, 1992), 32.
[215] Fruchtenbaum, *Messianic Christology*, 105.

Fruchtenbaum says that the speaker is *Elohim* who will save them by *Yahweh*, their *Elohim*. Fruchtenbaum is correct, except for the fact that *Elohim* is not the speaker. *Yahweh* is the speaker. Here the speaker is the LORD, or *Yahweh*, communicating to Hosea rather than *Elohim* saying that He will send another LORD, or *Yahweh*, who is their *Elohim*, to save them. So *Yahweh*, the speaker, the personal God of Israel, is going to send another *Yahweh*, who is their *Elohim*, to save them. Here the text is dealing with two *Yahwehs* rather than two *Elohims*, and the one being sent is their *Elohim*. A second example of two *Elohims*[216] is found in Psalm 45:6-7[7-8] where *Elohim* is applied to two separate and distinct *Elohims*:

> *Your throne, O God, is forever and ever: A scepter of righteousness is the scepter of Your kingdom. You love righteousness, and hate wickedness: Therefore God, Your God, has anointed You with the oil of gladness above Your fellows.* (NKJV)

Dr. Arnold Fruchtenbaum has noted that in Psalm 45:6-7, the first *Elohim* is being addressed; and the second *Elohim* in the passage is the God of the first *Elohim* mentioned. Here are two distinct *Elohims*. *Elohim's Elohim* has set *Elohim* above His fellows and Has anointed Him with the oil of joy or gladness.[217]

Another source of evidence to show the plurality of *Elohim* are the plural verbs and modifiers that follow *Elohim*. Normal Hebrew grammar says that following the plural *Elohim* with a plural verb or modifier is correct grammar:

> אֱלֹהִים [*Elohim*] is plural in form, but normally functions as a singular noun. However, it may also function as a plural noun, accompanied by plural modifiers and plural verb forms. This usually occurs when reference is being made to the "gods" of the nations.[218]

In most places throughout Scripture, *Elohim* is followed by a singular verb or modifier, which is the expected Hebrew grammatical construction. Yet there are four verses with *Elohim* and four plural verbs, or modifiers, that apply to the true *Elohim*. This usage also coincides with normal Hebrew grammatical construction. The impact of this wording is that *Elohim* is a true plurality of God, and these four examples help to further show that plurality.

---

[216] Grudem, *Systematic Theology*, 227.
[217] Fruchtenbaum, *Messianic Christology*, 104.
[218] Kelley, *Biblical Hebrew: An Introductory Grammar*, 32.

- First, in Genesis 20:13, Abraham says, *When God (Elohim) caused me to wander from my father's house.* Literally, it says, "God (*Elohim*) They caused me to wander."

- Second, in Genesis 35:7, Jacob says, *And he built there an altar and called the place El-beth-el: because there God appeared unto him, when he fled from the face of his brother.* Again, it literally says, the God (*Elohim*) revealed Themselves.

- The third is in 2 Samuel 7:23. David said, *And what one nation in the earth is like Your people, even like Israel, whom God went to redeem for a people to Himself?* Literally, again David said, "whom God (*Elohim*) They went to redeem for Themselves."

- Lastly, in Psalm 58:11[12], the psalmist says, *So that a man shall say, truly there is a reward for the righteous: truly there is a God that judges in the earth.* Literally it means, "God (*Elohim*) They judge on earth"! So here the testimonies of Abraham, Jacob, David, and the Psalmist refer to God in the plural.

Sadly, in their separate systematic theologies, Hodge,[219] Bancroft,[220] Buswell,[221] Barackman,[222] Grudem,[223] Berkhof,[224] and Erickson[225] do not cover or recognize these four passages (Genesis 20:13, 35:7, 2 Samuel 7:23, and Psalm 58:11). Only *Strong's Systematic Theology* refers to Genesis 20:13 and 35:7 as plural descriptions of *Elohim* the true God.[226] In these systematic theologies that pastors, theological students and lay people refer to, they find a completely inadequate treatment of the plurality and tri-unity of God in the Hebrew Scriptures.

Lastly, none of the preceding arguments for the plurality or tri-unity of *Elohim* in the Hebrew Scriptures is new to the New Testament. When embracing the concept of God as a trinity, the Church is not witnessing the birth of something new. Plurality has been firmly established and reflected throughout the pages of the *Tanakh*. The *Tanakh* and New Testament are Trinitarian to the very heart. This tri-unity of God in the New Testament has its foundations clearly in the *Tanakh*. This

---

[219] Hodge, *Systematic Theology*, 1:442-482.
[220] Emery H. Bancroft, *Christian Theology* (Grand Rapids: Zondervan, 1964), 71-73, 83-85.
[221] James Oliver Buswell, *A Systematic Theology of the Christian Religion* (Grand Rapids: Zondervan, 1962), 1:102-129.
[222] Barackman, *Practical Christian Theology*, 60-68.
[223] Grudem, *Systematic Theology*, 226-261.
[224] Berkhof, *Systematic Theology*, 82-99.
[225] Erickson, *Introducing Christian Doctrine,* 96-105.
[226] Augustus H Strong, *Systematic Theology* (Westwood, N.J: Fleming H. Revell, 1965), 318.

doctrine is not *in the making* in the New Testament, it has already been made.[227] Warfield gives a very logical argument for the foundation of the tri-unity in the word *Elohim* as he introduced it to us in the following statement:

> It was the task of the Old Testament revelation to fix firmly in the minds and hearts of the people of God the great fundamental truth of the unity of the God-head; and it would have been dangerous to speak to them of the plurality within this unity until this task had been fully accomplished. The real reason for the delay in the revelation of the Trinity, however, is grounded in the secular development of the redemptive purpose of God: the times were not ripe for the revelation of the Trinity in the unity of the Godhead until the fullness of the time had come for God to send forth His Son unto redemption, and His Spirit unto sanctification."[228]

Warfield is saying that in Genesis 1, or even in the Torah, God did not present a full-blown revelation of Himself because of the rampant polytheism in the ancient world. He was a triune God from the beginning, but used progressive revelation to unfold His tri-unity until the full revelation was given in the New Testament. That does not eradicate the fact that His plurality (and tri-unity) is presented in the *Tanakh* through numerous avenues. David L. Cooper also expresses why God revealed Himself, both as a unity (one) and as a plurality:

> What is the reason for the use of this plural noun referring to the Divine Being with the verb in the singular number? There can be but one true explanation which is that, while emphasizing the distinct personalities of the God-head, the ancient writers were anxious to refute polytheism and to assert the unity and the oneness of these divine personalities. Thus this peculiar grammatical usage is an affirmation of both the unity and plurality of the Divine Being.[229]

Schiffman, a Jewish believer, expresses why the tri-unity of God is not fully revealed in the Hebrew Scriptures:

> The reason a formal trinitarian concept does not exist in the Old Testament is not because it is borrowed from Hellenism, as some suggest, but because as the revelation of God is progressive, so as

---

[227] Warfield, *Biblical and Theological Studies*, 32.
[228] Warfield, *Biblical and Theological Studies*, 33-34.
[229] David L Cooper, *God's Gracious Provision for Man* (Los Angeles: Biblical Research Society, 1953), 114.

with the nature of the Messiah Himself, a full enough revelation did not exist in Jewish scripture until the New Covenant.[230]

Due to the fact that the singular verbs or modifiers follow *Elohim*, God was showing the Jewish people the plurality of Himself and the fact that the combination of the plural and singular lends support to the plurality of God. In the Soncino Commentaries, rabbis try to say the opposite, that it can only mean the unity of God:

> The Hebrew has the plural form, the plural of majesty; but no idea of plurality is to be read into the word, because the verb created is in the singular.[231]

As illustrated, *Elohim* denotes the oneness of God, the fact that He is indivisible, but is at the same time plural. "Plural of majesty" does not apply because "plural of majesty" is not used by Hebrew kings as the leadership in Israel within the *Tanakh*. Contrary to Abraham Ibn Ezra's above quote, the plurality can be read into *Elohim* because God used it in revealing Himself. David L. Cooper further states that writers of the *Tanakh* used all three names of God: *El, Elah, Eloah* in the singular and *Elohim* in the plural. Cooper demonstrates that the writers of the *Tanakh* had ample words to express the singular, absolute oneness of God; but, in the majority of cases, chose the plural *Elohim* instead:

> The English word which is translated "God" in the Hebrew Scriptures in the majority of cases is אֱלֹהִים *Elohim*. This term is in the plural number, as everyone who knows Hebrew admits. Moses and the prophets referring to...idols in the plural...invariably used this same form. Since it connoted a plurality of idols, it certainly indicates a plurality of the divine personalities subsisting in the one divine essence when applied to the true God. Frequently, however, Moses and the prophets used אֵל *El*, in referring to the Divine Being, which is in the singular number and means only one. Occasionally they used אֱלוֹהַ *Eloah*. Beyond controversy this also is in the singular number. If the Divine Being were simply a single personality, the sacred writers could have used either of these words in the singular to convey that idea. In Joshua 22:22 however appear both the singular and plural forms, which combination amounts to an affirmation regarding the unity of the divine personalities

---

[230] Schiffman, *Return of the Remnant*, 94.
[231] A. Cohen, *The Soncino Chumash, the Five Books of Moses with Haphtaro*th (London: Soncino, 1993), 1.

constituting the one God: אֵל אֱלֹהִים יְהוָה אֵל אֱלֹהִים יְהוָה "God, Gods, Jehovah, God Gods, Jehovah."[232]

Cooper's argument on the names of God is well done, and his reference to Joshua 22:22 is quite convincing. In this text, Joshua repeats, twice for emphasis, that *El* (singular), *Elohim* (plural), and *Yahweh* (singular) are both singular and plural terms for God. In this verse, the God of Israel is called by all three names; and one of them is in the plural. When the *Ruach haKodesh* [Holy Spirit] of God wrote the Scriptures, every word was inspired (verbal plenary), because He knew exactly what He wanted to say.

The authors of Scripture use the plural forms of *Elohim* that denote pagan gods only in the context that Israel does not worship plural gods as the heathen do. They worship a plural God who is a complete, complex unity, indivisibly one, and completely equal in nature, character, and essence. The greater portion of the 2,600 uses of *Elohim* in the Bible refers to the God of Israel; only about 250 of these uses refer to pagan gods. The writers of Scripture use the term as a contrast between plural pagan gods and the plural indivisible God of Israel.

Moses from Genesis through Deuteronomy was God's human author who composed the whole of the Pentateuch. Moses used the term *Elohim* throughout his writings of the true God. *Elohim* met with Abraham, Isaac, Jacob, and Moses and was the One who guided the children of Israel through the wilderness to the Promised Land.[233] The Creator God of Genesis 1 is the same God throughout the Torah who does refer to Himself in the plural. Throughout the Torah, God is identified as not just *Elohim*, but as *Yahweh*, *Adonai*, the Messenger (Angel) of the LORD, and the *Shechinah* of God. Psalm 96:5, in reference to the Creator God, calls Him LORD.

Dual Plurality

Hebrew nouns have another quality that impacts the study, and that quality is *number*. *Number* is the singular and plural aspect as it relates to nouns. Another expression of *number* used in Hebrew is the *dual*, which indicates plurality, but only in the sense of "a pair or two." Ross, in his Hebrew grammar, clarifies that "Hebrew nouns have three numbers, singular, plural and dual. Dual is a special kind of plural ending used to indicate a pair, or two of something."[234] Examples of dual nouns are:

---

[232] David L. Cooper, *What Men Must Believe* (Los Angeles: Biblical Research Society, 1953), 105.
[233] Sailhamer, *The Expositor's Bible Commentary*, 2:20.
[234] Allen P. Ross, *Introducing Biblical Hebrew* (Grand Rapids: Baker Academic, 2001), 71.

two ears (אָזְנַיִם), two days (יוֹמַיִם), two horses (סוּסַיִם), two mares (סוּסָתַיִם), two hands (יָדַיִם), two feet (רַגְלַיִם), and two horns (קַרְנַיִם). Rendsburg states:

> Although most grammars have not recognized them, dual forms are not as rare in Hebrew as one might expect.[235]

He goes on in his article to illustrate that the dual is used more often than normally seen, such as in Ruth 1:22, when the text says concerning Ruth and Naomi "and they (c. dual) came to Bethlehem."[236] D. L. Cooper adds insight that the dual is never used of God, which would simply mean that if *Elohim* is a plurality; He must be more than two.

> Usually this form of noun was employed when a pair of objects was mentioned. When, for instance, a Hebrew wished to speak of a person's hands, he put the noun in the dual number. The same thing was true with reference to eyes and feet. By the use of this form the writer indicated that there were but two. If there had been only two personalities in the Divine Being and the prophets had wished to emphasize that fact, they could have put the word of God in the dual number. But not one time did they resort to any such method. On the contrary, as we have already seen, they used a word for God in the singular and another in the plural number, which facts show that there were at least three personalities constituting the Divine Being. The noun in the singular number doubtless stressed the unity of God, whereas the one in the plural laid emphasis upon the plurality of the Almighty. In the original the plural word for God is used with a verb in the plural number in Genesis 20:13 and 35:7. Evidently, since the Scriptures are infallibly inspired, there was a very definite reason why the noun for God, *Elohim*, is used here with a plural verb."[237]

Observations and insights such as these should not be ignored and minimized, because the *Tanakh* is God's book; and He is revealing Himself to Israel and mankind. A Christian Arab from the West Bank area of Israel drew a parallel between Arabic and Hebrew in relation to dual plurality:

> Our Arabic verbs and pronouns are very different from many other languages. The Old Testament, written in Hebrew, has similar verbs

---

[235] Gary Rendsburg, "Dual Personal Pronouns and Dual Verbs in Hebrew" *JQR* 73, no. 1 (1982):38-58.
[236] Rendsburg, "Dual Personal Pronouns and Dual Verbs in Hebrew," 40.
[237] David L. Cooper, *What Men Must Believe*, 105-106.

and pronouns. Arabic has a singular, a dual, and then a plural verb. "He ate" would be *Akal*. "They (two) ate" would be *Akalou*. In the Semitic language, the verb frequently identifies the number of persons involved in the action. "You" in English can refer to one, two, or a million, but not so in Arabic or Hebrew.[238]

Shorrosh affirms that the tri-unity is assumed in the very first chapter in Genesis (1:26 and 3:22) in the Hebrew Scriptures. Barackman states that God is one (6:4) but that *Elohim* indicates a plurality of persons (Genesis 1:1) coupled with the *us* passages (Genesis 1:26).[239] From Barackman's perspective, *Elohim* clearly indicates more than two because it always has a plural ending and never has a dual ending. He also says that God is a tri-unity because of passages such as Isaiah 48:16, which is a representation of three persons.[240]

Special uses of *Elohim*, in a plural sense, serve as a powerful argument for His plurality. In Genesis 3:5, Satan says to Eve, "You shall be as *Elohim* (plural), knowing good and evil." Why would Satan be using that plural descriptive word so early in human history? There were no other gods or idols at that point to be worshipped. There was nothing! Adam and Eve were in innocence of paradise at that stage of history; no sin was yet in the world. Could it be that Satan used *Elohim* because, as one of the *cherubim*, he served in the immediate presence of God and knew God to be a plurality? Charles Baker expressed the impact of *Elohim* in relation to Adam and Eve:

> Satan told Eve that she and her husband would be as gods, knowing good and evil[;] it would appear that Eve at this time could not have known of any false gods or others who could be called gods, and it would therefore make better sense to make *Elohim* here refer to the one true God. There is nothing in this verse to make the first occurrence of *Elohim* (translated "God" in verses 1 and 3) to be a different person from the *Elohim* (translated "gods") at the end of the verse.[241]

Baker's observation has merit and sheds insight into understanding the probable situation in the temptation scene of Genesis 3.

---

[238] Anis A. Shorrosh, *Islam Revealed: A Christian Arab's View of Islam* (Nashville: Nelson, 1988), 239.
[239] Barackman, *Practical Christian Theology*, 63.
[240] Barackman, *Practical Christian Theology*, 66.
[241] Charles F. Baker, *A Dispensational Theology* (Grand Rapids: Grace Bible College, 1971), 143.

In Psalm 138:1, David says that before the gods he will sing praise "unto You" ("God"). David was not a polytheist, and yet David praised God before the *Elohims*; and *Elohim* is translated from the Hebrew Scripture as gods![242] Why do all these translations (ASV 1901, NASV, KJV, NKJV, NIV, RSV, and ESV) use "gods"? How is this to be understood? Did David praise *Elohim* because he understood something about the plural nature of *Elohim*? Or is David praising *Elohim* before the judges in Israel (Exodus 21:6; 22:8, 9, 28)? Both are real possibilities, but the second one is more likely. *Elohim* is translated as "God" with a marginal note saying "to the judges" in the *Tanakh* of the Jewish Publication Society (JPS).[243] Obviously, David was praising *Elohim* in the "Holy Temple," not before false gods, but before the judges. Baker makes the following observation:

> Of course, David could have had in mind praising God before some great ones in the earth, but it is unlikely that he was thinking about standing in an idol temple to praise God. It seems more likely that he was simply reiterating what he had said in the first part of the verse; "I will praise thee with my whole heart: before *Elohim* will I sing praise unto thee."[244]

Since Adam and Eve knew nothing of polytheism, understanding the Genesis 3:5 reference as a plurality of God would fit into their frame of reference. David was a monotheist in his worship of God, and the Psalm's reference that he was worshipping God in His Holy Temple "before the judges" makes more sense. It is hard to believe that God would move the writers of the *Tanakh* to select a name for God from polytheistic terminology, since that same Hebrew Scripture completely condemns polytheism. If God did breathe His Word through Moses, David, and the prophets, it seems more logical to believe that He led them to use the plural noun with singular verbs and adjectives to reveal something of His true nature as a tri-unity. This truth would only be fully revealed after the incarnation of His Son, the Messiah of Israel.[245]

The translation of Exodus 21:5-6, below, illustrates how the Scriptural text can be translated correctly to reflect the context of the passage:

---

[242] The following translations all use "gods": ASV 1901, NASV, KJV, NKJV, NIV, RSV.
[243] *Tanakh: The Holy Scriptures*, (Philadelphia: The Jewish Publication Society, 1985), 117.
[244] Baker, *A Dispensational Theology*, 143.
[245] Baker, *A Dispensational Theology*, 142.

CHAPTER 3: NAMES FOR GOD

And if the servant shall plainly say, I love my master, my wife, and my children; I will not go out free: Then his master shall bring him unto the judges [elohims].[246]

The New American Standard Bible (NASB) uses the word "God" in this verse, but in the footnotes it says "or judges." Clearly *Elohim* is translated in the plural when it refers to God's representatives, the judges, but that is not the case when it is translated pertaining to the true God. In Psalm 97:7 *Elohim* is used again and translated "gods," but the text is referring to angels who are called to worship God.[247] So *Elohim* is made plural when the text demands it, but when it is used of God, authors switch to the "plural of majesty" to explain away the plural aspect. Attempting to change the meaning by interpreting plural as singular is not *rightly dividing the word of truth* (2 Timothy. 2:15). Have Christian theologians conceded or abdicated the tri-unity of God to Rabbinic Judaism?

Clearly, scriptural usages of *Elohim* indicate that the plurality of God, as well as the tri-unity of God, was present in the beginning of God's revelation of Himself. Over the years of interacting with this world's perspective, there seems to be the consensus that religion evolved from polytheism to monotheism. Some authors, like Jacobs,[248] allude to the fact that monotheism developed in an evolutionary manner from polytheism[249] over the centuries, to henotheism,[250] and then to monotheism,[251] which Israel embraced. He further states that this is a matter for biblical scholarship, contrasted to Payne who says:

> Historically, however, this truth was only progressively revealed by God and grasped by fallen man. Before the fall Adam knew God, but most of his descendants became polytheists (Josh 24:2).[252]

Dyrness references Payne's statement as well, saying that Israel had no clear understanding of monotheism.[253] Israel, as a group, may have lost that concept because of the idolatry in Egypt, but not everyone in Israel lost monotheism. Niehaus, in his book, *God At Sinai*, reflects on the Apostle Paul's statement

---

[246] Alexander Harkavy, *The Twenty-Four Books of the Old Testament*, 123.
[247] David L. Cooper, *The God of Israel*, 35.
[248] Jacobs, *A Jewish Theology*, 22
[249] **Polytheism**: The belief in many gods.
[250] **Henotheism**: The worship of one god without denying the existence of other gods.
[251] **Monotheism**: The belief that there is but one God.
[252] Payne, *The Theology of the Older Testament*, 125.
[252] William Dyrness, *Themes in Old Testament Theology* (Downers Grove: InterVarsity, 1977), 125.
[253] William Dyrness, *Themes in Old Testament Theology*, 48.

(Romans 1:18-32), which is the reverse of Jacob's premise. God had revealed Himself to mankind from the beginning. But man chose, from the beginning, to turn his back on God and worship images of mortal man, birds, animals and reptiles:

> Those pagan religions – characterized by polytheism (or henotheism at best) and idolatry – represent a *weltanschauung* that is degraded from the truth. The [A]postle Paul put pagan religion in perspective when he portrayed it as a result of the Fall. According to Paul, humanity knew God from the beginning but chose not to glorify him or give thanks to him, and as a result, "their foolish hearts were darkened" and "they became fools and exchanged the glory of the immortal God for images made to look like mortal man and birds and animals and reptiles (Romans 1:21-23)."[254]

The concept that *Elohim* revealed Himself, from the beginning, is continued by Henry Thiessen: "We assert that monotheism was the original religion of mankind."[255] The concept of God did not evolve from polytheism to monotheism but rather degenerated from monotheism to polytheism. What better reason and convincing proof can be given than these scriptural uses of *Elohim* where God revealed Himself to Adam and Eve as one God in a plurality of unity? This is further suggested by Jack Scott:

> However, a better reason can be seen in Scripture itself where, in the very first chapter of Genesis, the necessity of a term conveying both the unity of the one God and yet allowing for a plurality of persons is found (Genesis 1:2, 26).[256]

So *Elohim* opens the door for God's revelation of Himself in a plural manner. He is one God. He has revealed Himself to mankind as a plurality of unity, indivisible. He is revealed as a tri-unity, which the Hebrew word *Elohim* represents by being translated as a plurality. The rabbinic argument affirms the oneness of God, which preserves their rejection of Jesus as the God/man, who is equal, in essence, with the Father, who is *Elohim* a plurality, yet one.

From the time of Moses through the exile, Israel struggled with worshipping *Elohim*, alone, as God. Joshua, at the end of his life, challenged Israel to choose who they were going to serve (Joshua 24:14-15). He told them to put away the gods (*elohim*) which their fathers served. In Judges 2, where the cycle of sin is given, the

---

[254] Jeffrey J. Niehaus, *God at Sinai* (Grand Rapids: Zondervan, 1995), 82.
[255] Henry C. Thiessen, *Lectures in Systematic Theology* (Grand Rapids: Eerdmans, 1979), 38.
[256] Harris, Archer, and Waltke, *Theological Wordbook of the Old Testament,* 1:44.

first step to bondage was the worship of Baal (v. 11). The worship of other gods (*elohim*) was Israel's stumbling block throughout the pages of the *Tanakh*, but Israel knew that their God was *Elohim*, *Yahweh*, and that He demanded complete, exclusive worship. As Isaiah 44 points out so clearly, the other gods (*elohim*) were not gods (*elohim*) at all but mere objects of wood and stone or heavenly bodies, all lifeless, created by the imagination of man's mind and with his hands.

אֲדוֹן *Adonai*

The word *adonai*, translated "Lord," is the plural of *adon* (lord) in the Hebrew Scriptures and is consistently in the plural when used of God.[257] The word is used by itself 134 times and connected to *Yahweh* 315 times.[258] That is an additional 449 plural references with *Elohim* and other plural descriptions (discussed later) to show the plurality of God. However, Jenni calls *adonai* a majestic plural as seen with *Elohim*.[259] Robert I. Alden (quoted by Harris, Archer, and Waltke) affirms *adonai* as a plural usage in his statement, "It always refers to God," as is true with *Elohim*; but he also equates it with "plural of majesty" as is often done with *Elohim*.[260] This is the same argument used with *Elohim* in trying to make it a "plural of majesty" instead of accepting it as God used it. The Scripture, God's revelation of Himself, speaks for itself. If He chose to use the plural *adonai* for Lord as He spoke of Himself, who are scholars to say that He cannot speak of Himself in that manner? Barackman also says of *Adonai*, that "the plural form indicates the plurality of Persons."[261] Even more significant is the statement from a Jewish dictionary:

> *Adon* means lord, master when applied to persons in authority (Genesis 45:8-9; Deuteronomy 10:17; Judges 19:26-27; 1 Samuel 29:8), and is occasionally used for God (Exodus 23:17; 34:23; Joshua 3:11, 13). *Adonai*, on the other hand, is a plural form based on *Adon*, but is used exclusively for God and is often used as a parallel to *YHVH* (Genesis 15:2, 8; Joshua 7:7; Isaiah 25:8) or as a substitute for it (Isaiah 13:17; Amos 7:7-8, 9:1; Ezekiel 18:25).[262]

---

[257] Fruchtenbaum, *Messianic Christology*, 105.
[258] Botterweck, Ringgren, and Fabry. *Theological Dictionary of the Old Testament*, 1:62.
[259] Jenni and Westermann, *Theological Lexicon of the Old Testament*, 1:24.
[260] Harris, Archer, and Waltke, *Theological Wordbook of the Old Testament*, 1:13.
[261] Barackman, *Practical Christian Theology*, 66.
[262] Neusner and Green, *Dictionary of Judaism in the Biblical Period*, 389.

The plural usage of *Adonai* in connection with, or in place of, *Yahweh*, which further makes the point that *Yahweh* is "one" and within that oneness is plurality, adding more weight to the usage of plurality for God in the *Tanakh*.

Adonai and *Yahweh* were equally used of God as divine names before 300 B.C.E.; after that period of time, *adonai* gradually came into use more than *Yahweh*. Finally, around the time of Christ, *adonai* completely replaced *Yahweh* in the spoken language.

יהוה *Yahweh*

Although *Yahweh* is Israel's personal name for God, during the late Second Temple period, this name had come to be regarded as unspeakably holy and therefore unsuitable for use in public, although it was used privately in the synagogue and Temple.[263] By the Middle Ages, its pronunciation was lost.[264] *Yahweh* was replaced by the word *Adonai* for Lord sometime before the end of the Second Temple period.

Yahweh is made up of the Hebrew consonants hwhy or [yhwh], which taken together is called the Tetragrammaton.[265] No consensus exists in relation to the structure and etymology of *Yahweh*. The name is generally thought to be a verbal form derived from the root *hwy*, later *hyh*. The meaning of the word is not completely certain, but the general consensus is "to be, happen, become" or "be at hand, exist, come to pass."[266] *Yahweh* seems to be native to Hebrew, since there seem to be no references to the word among the other nations before the time of Moses.[267] The primary explanation of *Yahweh* occurs in Exodus 3:13-15, where God reveals His name to Moses. Those verses state that He is the one who exists (Exodus 3:14); He is with His people; (v.12), and He wants to be known by them (v. 15).[268] In Exodus 6:3, God told Moses that Abraham, Isaac, and Jacob knew Him as *El Shaddai* (God Almighty), but *Yahweh* was His name even in the times of the patriarchs. Moses, as he records the history of man and the call of Abraham and his descendents in Genesis, starts using God's name (*Yahweh*) in chapter 2:4. *Yahweh*, which is used

---

[263] Neusner and Green, *Dictionary of Judaism in the Biblical Period*, 259.
[264] Stone, *Names of God*, 25.
[265] Botterweck, Ringgren, and Fabry, *Theological Dictionary of the Old Testament*, 1:71.
[266] Botterweck, Ringgren, and Fabry. *Theological Dictionary of the Old Testament*, 5:500.
[267] Alexander and Baker, *Dictionary of the Old Testament Pentateuch*, 363.
[268] Alexander and Baker, *Dictionary of the Old Testament Pentateuch*, 363.

6,828 times, is the second most used word in the Hebrew language[269] in the singular form,[270] which lays a very strong foundation for monotheism in the Scriptures.

Genesis 21:33 clearly identifies *Yahweh*, who is called upon and is connected with *El*, the God of eternity who is everlasting. *Yahweh* is identified with *Elohim* in Leviticus 19:2, where the people are to be *holy, for I, the LORD (Yahweh) your God (Elohim) am holy*. *Yahweh* in combination with *Elohim* is significant because the two are equated with each other. The difference in meaning, with the combination of these names, is that *Yahweh* is their personal God and *Elohim* is more removed from the creation as expressed here:

> In the Pentateuch…The name *Yahweh* is employed when God is presented to us in His personal character and in direct relationship to people or nature; and *Elohim*, when the Deity is alluded to as a Transcendental Being who exists completely outside and above the physical universe.[271]

While *Yahweh* and *Elohim* are called holy in Leviticus 19:2, holy is a very special statement which only applies to *Yahweh*. In Isaiah 6:3, *Yahweh* is addressed this way: *Holy, Holy, Holy is Yahweh of hosts*. In Deuteronomy 5:9, Moses also spells out that *Yahweh*, *El*, and *Elohim* all pertain to a jealous God. *For I, the LORD (Yahweh) your God (Elohim), am a jealous God (El)*. These three words are used as synonyms for the same God.

Yahweh's name is also combined with other words, making compound forms of His name to describe certain aspects of His Person. Such as *Yahweh-jireh*: "The LORD will provide" (Genesis 22:14) and *Yahweh-Nissi*: "The LORD our banner" (Exodus 17:15). Other compound forms are *Yahweh-Shalom*: "The LORD is peace" (Judges 6:24) and *Yahweh-Sabbaoth*: "The LORD of hosts" (1 Samuel 1:3). The last compound forms are *Yahweh-M'Kaddesh*, meaning "The LORD thy sanctifier" (Exodus 31:13), a reference to the Messiah, *Yahweh-Tsidkenu*: "The LORD our righteousness" (Jeremiah 23:6). The only question concerning the name *Yahweh* is the root word for the name of God. Everything else seems to be in agreement in relationship to His singularity and oneness.

Yahweh is singular in the Hebrew text, yet plural terms of God are connected with His name. *Yahweh and El* (both singular) and *Elohim* (plural) are used together as the same God, both plural and singular designations of God. There are plural

---

[269] Enns, *The Moody Handbook of Theology*, 197.
[270] Chafer, *Systematic Theology*, 6:17.
[271] Walter A Elwell, *Evangelical Dictionary of Theology* (Grand Rapids: Baker, 1986), 466.

references to *Yahweh* (LORD) in the English text that are not always recognized by the casual reader of the Scriptures.

Two Yahwehs in the *Tanakh*

Yahweh is the name of Israel's personal God, and the word substantiates that God is one alone. His oneness is borne out in many passages of the Hebrew text (Genesis 21:33; Exodus 20:2; Leviticus 19:2; 20:26; 21:8; Deuteronomy 4:24; 5:9; 6:4; Isaiah 41:4, 44:6, 45:5, 14, 18, 21; 48:12; Jeremiah 2:5, 11). Yet God, in His revelation of Himself, continues to identify Himself (*Yahweh*) with plurality, as presented in the following Scriptures.

GENESIS 19:24

In Genesis 18-19, three men visit Abraham; and he recognizes them simply as men. The promise is given of Isaac's birth in Genesis 18:9, but the text does not begin to identify the men until Genesis 18:13, where the one man identifies Himself as *Yahweh*. The other two men are identified as angels going to Sodom (Genesis 19:1). The focus of this section of Scriptures is not the two men who left but the one who identified Himself to Abraham as *Yahweh*. In Genesis 19:13-23 Abraham is having a dialogue with *Yahweh*, the LORD. Rabbis say that God cannot become a man in human form; yet here *Yahweh* appeared in human form, and He even had a meal with Abraham. This passage of Scripture goes against what Rabbinic Judaism teaches about the nature of God as seen in this quote by Weiss-Rosmarin:

> The Unity of God, sacred to Judaism beyond all else, is utterly irreconcilable with the Christian idea of the divisibility of the Divine Being and, above all, with the belief in incarnation. According to Jewish belief God is pure spirit, eternally transcendent and divorced from even the slightest vestige of corporeality. Christianity, on the other hand, asserts that God became man in Jesus, a teaching which is contrary to the very spirit of Judaism.[272]

Weiss-Rosmarin says that Judaism is "irreconcilable" to what Christians believe about *Yeshua* and the incarnation. To him, God is pure spirit and in no way can He be placed in a corporal body. Yet in Genesis 18, God did come in a corporal body and even ate a meal with Abraham. Weiss-Rosmarin's statement is in complete

---

[272] Trude Weiss-Rosmarin, *Judaism and Christianity, the Differences* (Middle Village, NY: Jonathan David, 1997), 21.

conflict with the statements of Moses, who records what Abraham saw and heard. Weiss-Rosmarin continues with two short statements:

> Is not this contrary to all Jewish teachings of God which emphasize and stress that God is not like man and can never become man or even resemble man? Judaism has always fought, and with all weapons at its disposal, against the Christian idea of incarnation, that is to say, of God's coming into human life. The thought that "God was made man" is shocking beyond words to the Jew who believes that God is One and Unique, and that this Uniqueness consists also in His utter difference from anything and everything in existence and anything and everything man can possibly fashion in his mind to label "God." Christian Trinity [inexplicably]...divides the Unity of God into three, namely, God the Father, Jesus the Son and the Holy Spirit...[273]

One must ask, "Where in the *Tanakh* does God say He cannot become a man or even resemble man?" Christianity does not teach that God can be divided into three, nor does it teach tri-theism, which is what Rabbinic Judaism teaches concerning Christianity but not biblical Judaism. Weiss-Rosmarin continues:

> Jewish monotheism is not only the negation of the many gods but also the Rejection of the personification of God on the one hand and of the deification of human beings on the other. Judaism's refusal to worship Jesus is therefore not only due to its repudiation of the doctrine of incarnation, the belief that God became a person, but equally so to its defiant resistance to all and any attempts of according Divine qualities and honors to mere mortals.[274]

Weiss-Rosmarin's perspective is tainted by the writings of Rabbinic Judaism. If Rabbinic Judaism were to acknowledge even the possibility of the plurality of God, then Rabbinic Judaism would fall like a sandcastle on the seashore. Yet, contradictory to what Weiss-Rosmarin said, *Yahweh* did appear in human form as a man to Abraham, the Father of the Jewish people, and to Jacob as he wrestled with the Angel of *Yahweh* (Genesis 32:24-30; Hosea 12:3-5) and to Joshua before the attack of Jericho (Joshua 5:13-15). In Genesis 18, the one man who identifies Himself eight times between verses 13 and 33 is *Yahweh*. In this section of Scripture *Yahweh* is in human form and eating a meal with Abraham after he had washed the visitors' feet. Fruchtenbaum comments on Genesis 19:24 by saying that *Yahweh*, the

---

[273] Weiss-Rosmarin, *Judaism and Christianity, the Differences*, 21-22.
[274] Weiss-Rosmarin, *Judaism and Christianity, the Differences*, 21-23.

one who was talking with Abraham, rains down fire from *Yahweh* in heaven. Clearly there are two distinct *Yahwehs* showing plurality:

> The first *YHVH* is on earth and is said to be raining down fire from a Second *YHVH* who is in heaven. Two distinct persons are called *YHVH* in the same text.[275]

So not only are there two *Yahwehs*, but one of them is in a human form and is called the Angel of the LORD.

ZECHARIAH 2:8-9

In this passage one *Yahweh* will be sent to Israel, and Israel will recognize that He was sent by another *Yahweh*. Bob Morris, a Jewish believer in Messiah, says *Yahweh* is presented as two distinct *Yahwehs*, one sending the other:

> In verse 12 of the *Tanakh* (verse 8 in English), *YHVH* #1 is the speaker. He speaks about the value of Israel using the word picture of the pupil of the eye. Israel is personal and valuable and protected by God as the eye of a man is personal, valuable and protected by him. He is extremely personal here using the term "My eye." Then in verse 9, *YHVH* #1 says that He is being sent to accomplish a task by *YHVH* #2. One *YHVH* is sending another *YHVH* to perform a task.[276]

Walter Kaiser, also referring this passage of Scripture, sees the same thing as Morris noted above: "Mystery of mysteries, *Yahweh* is Lord, yet He was also sent."[277]

HOSEA 1:1-7

In Hosea 1:1-7, not only are there two *Yahwehs*,[278] but an additional factor is added in verse 7. *Yahweh*, who spoke in verses 2, 4, and 6, will deliver Israel by sending another *Yahweh* who is Israel's *Elohim*. This passage is even more interesting because of that additional factor.[279] Not only are there two *Yahwehs*, but the second *Yahweh* that is being sent is their *Elohim*, plural God.

---

[275] Fruchtenbaum, *Messianic Christology*, 105.
[276] Robert Morris, *Anti-Missionary Arguments: The Trinity*, 6.
[277] Walter C. Kaiser, Jr., *The Communicator's Commentary: Micah – Malachi* (21vols. Waco, Tex: Word, 1992), 21:315.
[278] Grudem, *Systematic Theology*, 228.
[279] David L. Cooper, *The God of Israel*, 27.

CHAPTER 3: NAMES FOR GOD

Isaiah 44:6

In this passage of Isaiah there is another reference to two distinct *Yahwehs*. One called Himself "*Yahweh* the King of Israel," and then refers to a second as "His Redeemer, the *Yahweh* of hosts.*"* It can be clearly seen in this verse that there are two distinct *Yahweh*'s. God throughout the *Tanakh,* shows His plurality, but it is especially seen in the book of Isaiah.

What is clearly seen is that *Yahweh* speaks of Himself and then of another *Yahweh,* but at the end of the verse He states: *and beside me there is no God* (KJV) or *Elohim.* *Yahweh* refers to two *Yahwehs* and then states there is no other *Elohim*. *Yahweh* emphasizes His oneness and unity, and *Elohim* emphasizes His plurality in unity. There is one additional point concerning the Angel of *Yahweh*, which also shows His plurality; however, this will be developed in the next chapter, entitled "Theophanies." *Theophany* is the theological term used to describe instances when God revealed Himself visibly or by audible means. That chapter will be dedicated to showing God's plurality through two kinds of theophanies, the Angel of *Yahweh* and the *Shechinah* glory of God.

In Scripture *Yahweh*, though singular, is also seen as a plurality, but in that plurality He is never combined with a female counterpart, such as *Asherah* (1 Kings 15:13; 2 Kings 17:10; 2 Chronicles 19:3; 33:19; Micah 5:14), a female counterpart of the *Baal*, the pagan gods of Canaan. One author says:

> The fact that *Yahweh* never had a female counterpart is of great fundamental value. The Hebrew language does not even have a native word for goddess![280]

Yahweh expresses God's oneness and unity as well as two equal beings called *Yahweh*. Even the plurality of *Yahweh* is evident as it is clearly presented from the above-mentioned Scriptures.

This chapter examined the names of God (*El, Elah, Eloah, Elohim,* Lord, and LORD), and concluded that God used both singular and plural names for Himself. God also used singular verbs or adjectives with the plural noun *Elohim* to draw attention to Himself as the monotheistic God who in essence is plural. Particular attention was given to *Elohim* and *Yahweh* (LORD), which shows that God did reveal Himself as a plurality in unity.

---

[280] Th. C. Vriezen, *An Outline of Old Testament Theology* (Newton, Mass: Charles T. Branford Company, 1970), 327.

CHAPTER 4: THEOPHANIES

Theophany is not a biblical term.[281] It is a theological term used to refer to visible or auditory (or both) manifestations of God.[282] In other words, a theophany is a manifestation of God to the physical senses.[283] God becomes visible or audible so that man can actually interact with Him. *Theophany* is a Greek word that is derived "from two Greek terms, *theos* (God) and *phaino* (shine, give light), but in the passive, the verb means "to appear" or "to be revealed.""[284] Hence, the appearance of the "captain of the host of the LORD" before Joshua, or as the glory (*Shechinah*) of God that appeared before all Israel on Mount Sinai was a theophany of God.

The theophanies of God, the instances where He made Himself visible or audible (or both) according to Scripture, further affirm the plurality of God. Each theophany, or visible appearance of God, shows God's manifestation as *Yahweh*, yet at the same time the theophany is also distinct from *Yahweh*. The term *theophany* applies both to the appearance of God in human form and the appearance of His glory, two instances that are of interest in studying the concept of God's tri-unity in Scripture.

God always takes the initiative in revealing Himself. He never reveals Himself completely, only in a temporary way. There is only one permanent manifestation of God, and this was the incarnation of Messiah when He dwelt on the earth for approximately 36 years.[285] The following is an example of a theophany, found in Exodus.

In Exodus 24:9-11, there is a unique appearance of *Yahweh* before Moses, Aaron, and his two sons, as well as the 70 elders of Israel. At this point, seventy-four men literally "saw" the God of Israel in a human form. Morey points out that not only

---

[281] Merrill C. Tenney, *The Zondervan Pictorial Encyclopedia of the Bible,* 5 vols. (Grand Rapids: Zondervan Publishing House, 1975), 388.
[282] Elwell, *Evangelical Dictionary of Theology,* 1087.
[283] Enns, *The Moody Handbook of Theology,* 258.
[284] Geoffrey W. Bromiley, *The International Standard Bible Encyclopedia* (Grand Rapids: Eerdmans, 1988), 4:827.
[285] Elwell, *Evangelical Dictionary of Theology,* 1087.

did they see the God of Israel (v. 10), but they stared at God (v. 11). Morey makes the following observations:

> That the men saw God in human form is clear from the fact that, in verse 10, the form had "feet" (Heb. רַגְלָיו and Gk. πόδας) and God was "standing before them as opposed to "sitting" on the throne before them (cf. Isaiah 6:1).
>
> It is impossible to escape the fact that the appearance which they saw had feet and, if God had feet, then He had legs. And if He had legs, then He had a torso, etc.
>
> This passage cannot be dismissed on the basis that it was a dream. What happened to these seventy-four men was not a dream because, (1) the men were not asleep and, (2) dreams are never group events. Throughout the Bible, only individuals had dreams (Genesis 20:3; 31:10; 37:5; Judges 7:13; Daniel 2:3).
>
> Neither can we dismiss this passage as a vision. The biblical authors had no problem identifying when visions took place (Genesis 15:1; Numbers 12:6; Ezekiel 1:1).[286]

What the seventy-four men saw and stared at was the God/man standing before them identified both as the God of Israel and *Yahweh*. What they saw was a theophany of God.

This discussion on theophany is divided into two sections. First is the Angel of *Yahweh* where He speaks audibly and appears in human form. The second appearance is the *Shechinah* glory of God where He appears in His glory with fire, cloud, and smoke, as on Mount Sinai.

Theophany – The Angel of the LORD

Theophanies, in the Hebrew Scriptures, could appear to men in one of four forms so that God could magnify and authenticate His revelation of Himself to His servants.[287] The term is used to indicate how God appeared in these four different forms with four basic purposes, as described in the four examples below.

---

[286] Morey, *The Trinity: Evidence and Issues*, 123.
[287] Tenney, *Zondervan Pictorial Encyclopedia of the Bible*, 5:720.

CHAPTER 4: THEOPHANIES

1. He appeared in *human form* to Abraham (Genesis 18) and to Joshua (Joshua 5).

2. He appeared in a *non-human form* in Exodus 3.

3. He appeared as *an angel* in Exodus 23:20-23.

4. He *spoke audibly* in Genesis 3:8; 1 Kings 19:12, and Matthew 3:17.

Theophanies had four basic purposes:

5. God appeared to initiate/ratify a covenant with Abraham (Genesis 15) and later with Moses and the Israelite nation at large (Exodus).

6. God appeared to instruct, or correct, His covenant partner, Israel (Joshua 5:13-15; 1 Kings 18:20-40).

7. God appeared to commission or encourage prophets (Isaiah 6; Ezekiel 1; 1 Kings 18:9-18).

8. God appeared to the nation to bring covenantal judgment on His rebellious subjects (Leviticus 9:23-10:2; Numbers 11:1-2; 12:2).[288]

Theophany is viewed by Christians and by the Jewish people differently. What is quite clear according to Morey is that:

> As a man, God walked, talked, ate and fellowshipped with other men. During these times God could be seen by the human eye, touched by the human hand, and heard by the human ear. God was literally manifested in the flesh and dwelt among us. The Invisible became Visible and the Immaterial became Material without ceasing, at any time, to be true deity.[289]

Christians often look at the passages that deal only with the Angel of *Yahweh*. For example, Chafer seems to focus on that narrow view of theophany:

---

[288] Alexander and Baker, *Dictionary of the Old Testament Pentateuch*, 860.
[289] Morey, *The Trinity: Evidence and Issues*, 106.

Theophany usually is limited to appearances of God in the form of man or angels, other phenomena such as *shekhinah* glory not being considered a theophany.[290]

However, the Scriptures indicate a broader view, which includes the above mentioned four categories.

The Angel of *Yahweh*

There are numerous times in the Hebrew Scriptures that *Yahweh* is associated with, and is distinguished from, the Angel of *Yahweh* (LORD – *YHVH*). A careful study of the Hebrew Scriptures will clearly show that God and the Angel of the LORD are two different persons and that they both differentiate Themselves from each other as Reymond expresses:

> A careful analysis of the relevant passages will disclose that God differentiates himself from this Angel by the very title itself as by the fact that he refers to him in the third person and may even address him in the second person in 2 Samuel 24:16, and yet the Angel in his speeches, while also often distinguishing himself from God, lays claim to divine attributes and prerogatives, indeed, to identity with God.[291]

These distinctions between the Angel of *Yahweh* and the LORD will be examined, but before these examples from Genesis 22, Judges 2:1 and Zechariah 3:1-10 are viewed, another matter in the *Tanakh* needs to be cleared up.

Before describing the appearances of the Angel of the LORD, the term *angel* needs clarification due to the unbiblical imagery that has been attached to the term *angel* from the Middle Ages to the present time. Today, when people think of angels, they picture in their mind angels as created beings with wings, wearing a halo, both male and female, and sitting on a cloud playing harps. These mental pictures are not biblical and give an incorrect picture of angels, and, in particular, of the Angel of the LORD.

The word מַלְאָךְ is the Hebrew word meaning "*a messenger.*" The word, when translated correctly, is *messenger* and not *angel*. Anyone who took a message to someone else and delivered that message is called a מַלְאָךְ in Hebrew, or

---
[290] Chafer, *Systematic Theology*, 5:31.
[291] Robert L. Reymond, *Jesus: Divine Messiah* (Ross-shire, Scotland: Mentor Imprint, 2003), 72.

CHAPTER 4: THEOPHANIES

messenger. It would include both a human messenger, such as a prophet who delivers a message from God to an individual, king, or nation and also a heavenly messenger (angel) that God sends to bear messages to His earthly servants. There are both human and heavenly messengers, and each is very distinct. Man is man, and heavenly spirits (angels) are not human beings. This Hebrew word מַלְאָךְ is used hundreds of times in the Hebrew Scriptures and is understood as "messenger." There is nothing mystical or magical about the word.[292]

How did the Hebrew word "messenger" become "angel" in our Bibles today? Morey gives a brief history or evolution of the word:

> If the word מַלְאָךְ simply meant "messenger," then where did we get the word "angel?" The mistake was made during the Middle Ages. The Greek word ἄγγελος was used in the Septuagint (LXX) for מַלְאָךְ because it also meant messenger. It was a real and proper translation from Hebrew to Greek.
>
> This is in contrast to the Latin Bible where the Greek word ἄγγελος is merely transliterated into Latin and becomes *angelus*. Thus, instead of translating the words and ἄγγελος as "messenger," the Latin Bible transliterated the Greek word ἄγγελος into the Latin word *angelus*.
>
> This error was further compounded when the Latin Bible was translated into English. Instead of translating the Latin word *angelus* as "messengers," it was transliterated into the English word "angel." They did not translate it most of the time, but simply retained the Latin transliteration.[293]

Morey continues by illustrating Matthew 11:10, where the Greek word ἄγγελος is translated "messenger" and not angel. This meant that the English translators knew the difference but most of the time chose to transliterate instead of translate the Hebrew (מַלְאָךְ) and Greek (ἄγγελος) words.[294] In order to be consistent with the Scriptures throughout the rest of this book, the term *messenger* will be used instead of *angel*. Now we will return to our study of the use of the Angel of Yahweh in Scripture.

---

[292] Morey, *The Trinity: Evidence and Issues*, 138.
[293] Morey, *The Trinity: Evidence and Issues*, 139.
[294] Morey, *The Trinity: Evidence and Issues*, 139.

THE TRI-UNITY OF GOD IS JEWISH

GENESIS 22

The first example of Messenger (Angel) of *Yahweh* in Scriptures comes from Genesis 22:11-12 with the broader context in verses 1-19.

Genesis 22:1-2

¹ And it came to pass after these things, that God [Elohim] did tempt Abraham, and said unto him, Abraham: and he said, Behold, here I am. ² And He said, Take now your son, your only son Isaac, whom you love, and go into the land of Moriah; and offer him there for a burnt-offering upon one of the mountains which I will tell you of.

Genesis 22:11-12

¹¹ And the angel of the LORD called unto him out of heaven, and said, Abraham, Abraham: and he said, Here am I. ¹² And He [the angel of the LORD] said, lay not your hand upon the lad, neither do any thing unto him: for now I know that you fear God [Elohim], seeing you have not withheld your son, your only son from Me.

Genesis 22:15-16

¹⁵ And the angel of the LORD called to Abraham out of heaven the second time. ¹⁶ and said, by Myself have I sworn, says the LORD [Yahweh], for because you have done this thing, and have not withheld your son, your only son: (KJV)

In Genesis 22:1, *Elohim* gave Abraham instructions for offering his son as a sacrifice to Him. When Abraham was about to offer his son, the Messenger (Angel) of *Yahweh* stopped him in Genesis 22:11-12. Then the Messenger of *Yahweh* said *for now I know that you fear God* [Elohim], referring back to who initially instructed Abraham. But here in verse 12 the Messenger of *Yahweh* uses the personal pronoun *Me*, which refers back to *Elohim* in verse 1. The Messenger (Angel) of *Yahweh* equates Himself with *Elohim* by using the personal pronoun *Me* to refer to Himself.

In this section of Scripture, God identifies Himself four ways: first, as *Elohim* (Genesis 22:1); second, as the Messenger (Angel) of *Yahweh*

CHAPTER 4: THEOPHANIES

(Genesis 22:11); third as *Me* (Genesis 22:12), referring back to the first two terms for God; and fourth, as *Yahweh* (Genesis 22:16).

In this latter text (Genesis 22:15-16), *Elohim* (plural) the Godhead is speaking and then one of the Godhead speaks separately, as the Messenger (Angel) of *Yahweh*, who also represents Himself as *Yahweh* in verse 16. This Messenger (Angel) of *Yahweh* identifies Himself as the one who swore to Abraham earlier, which reflects back on the Abrahamic Covenant of Genesis 12 and 15. Here the Messenger (Angel) of *Yahweh* has identified Himself with *Elohim* and also spoke as *Yahweh*, yet He is distinct from *Elohim*.

JUDGES 2:1

The second example of the Messenger (Angel) of *Yahweh* is found in Judges 2:1, which is a fascinating reflection of the distinctiveness of the Messenger (Angel) of *Yahweh* from *Yahweh*.

> *And an angel of the LORD came up from Gilgal to Bochim, and said, I made you to go up out of Egypt, and have brought you unto the land which I swore unto your fathers: and I said, I will never break My covenant with you.*

The person speaking in Judges 2:1 is the Messenger (Angel) of *Yahweh* who makes reference to four things: (1) delivering them from Egypt, (2) bringing them into the Promised Land, (3) promising an oath unto Abraham (the Abrahamic Covenant), and (4) promising to never break His covenant with them.

Notice, first of all, that the Messenger does not introduce His speech to the nation of Israel by saying, *Thus says Yahweh*, which was the practice of the prophets as in Judges 6:8. Here the Messenger (Angel) of *Yahweh* speaks in the first person as God, Himself, the One who brought them out of Egypt into the land that was promised to their fathers.[295] According to Morey some Jewish commentaries, such as "*Targum of Jonathan,*" have the words, "Thus says *Yahweh,*" but the phrase does not appear in any Hebrew manuscripts or the Septuagint.[296] Second, the Messenger of *Yahweh* makes the reference that He brought them into the Promised Land. Exodus 33:2-3 expresses the same thing as Judges 2:1. Third, the Messenger of Yahweh makes the statement in Judges 2:1 that *I had promised an oath to your fathers*. That is a direct reference to the Abrahamic Covenant in Genesis 15 as the same one that walked between the cut animals. The Messenger of *Yahweh* made the

---

[295] Morey, *The Trinity: Evidence and Issues,* 156.
[296] Morey, *The Trinity: Evidence and Issues,* 157.

Covenant with Abraham. Fourth, the Messenger of Yahweh says *I will never break My covenant with you*. So in Judges 2:1 the Messenger (Angel) of *Yahweh* is clearly distinct from *Yahweh*, yet He is equal to Him and He speaks as God.

Let us take another look at where in Judges 2:1 the Messenger of Yahweh says that He brought Israel out of Egypt. Notice a connection with *Yahweh* and His reference to this messenger, reflected in Exodus 23:20-23:

> [20] *I am sending an angel before you to guard you on the way and to bring you to the place that I have made ready.* [21] *Pay heed to him and obey him. Do not defy him, for he will not pardon your offenses, since My Name is in him;* [22] *but if you obey him and do all that I say, I will be an enemy to your enemies and a foe to your foes.* [23] *When My Angel goes before you and brings you to the Amorites, the Hittites, the Perizzites, and Canaanites, the Hivites and the Jebusites, and I will annihilate them.*

In these verses *Yahweh* speaks of *an (Messenger) angel* in (verse 20) and *My (messenger) angel* in (verse 23), and He equates Him as one with Him when He says, *My Name is in Him.*

In Isaiah 42:8 and 48:11 *Yahweh* makes these statements:

> [42:8 1] *I am the LORD, that is My name; I will not yield My glory to another, nor My renown to idols.*

> [48:11] *For My sake, My own sake, do I act – lest My name be dishonored! I will not give My glory to another.*

Vine connects God's glory with the name of God (*Yahweh*):

> This is a ratification of the significance of His Name. His glory is the manifestation of His nature, attributes and power.[297]

Yahweh makes this connection. He, *Yahweh*, will not give or yield His glory (*Shechinah*) to another. Yet in Exodus 23:20-23, *Yahweh* says that His name is in the Angel. The Messenger of *Yahweh* appears numerous times as He leads them to the Promised Land as the *Shechinah* of God. So who is the messenger? In Exodus 32:34 and 33:2-3, *Yahweh* adds more information on the messenger:

---

[297] V. E. Vine, *Isaiah* (Grand Rapids: Zondervan, 1946), 108.

CHAPTER 4: THEOPHANIES

Exodus 32:34
Go now, lead the people where I told you. See, My angel shall go before you. But when I make an accounting, I will bring them to account for their sins.

Exodus 33:2-3
I will send an angel before you, and I will drive out the Canaanites, the Amorites, the Hittites, the Perizzites, the Hivites, and the Jebusites – a land flowing with milk and honey. But I will not go in your midst, since you are a stiffnecked people, lest I destroy you on the way.

Twice *Yahweh* says that He will send *My* (messenger) *angel* or *an angel* (messenger) before Israel to lead them into the Land. *Yahweh* clearly states that He will not go up with them. So who is that Messenger? Exodus 33:14-16 seems to contradict the other passages that say He didn't go with them. In this dialog between Moses and the LORD (*Yahweh*), Moses requested that the *Yahweh*s' presence go with them, and *Yahweh* consented because Moses had found favor and knew His name. According to verse 11, it is Yahweh that is speaking here. Now Yahweh is a singular term, yet we see from Genesis 19:24 and Hosea 1 that there are two Yahwehs, even though *Yahweh* itself a singular word. The word "presence" in the Hebrew used here is פָּנֶי (*panim*) meaning "face," which is also a plural.[298]

It is the view of this author that the Messenger of *Yahweh* (Judges 2:1) is also called the "messenger of His Presence" in Isaiah 63:9, who would be the Second Person of the Godhead, rather than God the Father, going up with them. It is also interesting to note that the *Jewish Study Bible* recognizes the messenger as divine. 2:1 clearly answers that question by stating the *Angel* (Messenger) *of Yahweh* brought them up from Egypt. In verses 4 and 5, notice the response of the people: *The people broke into weeping. So they named that place Bochim, and they offered sacrifices there to the LORD.* Their response was that the Messenger of *Yahweh* was equal to and yet distinct from *Yahweh*.

ZECHARIAH 3:1-10

¹ And he showed me Joshua the high priest standing before the angel of the LORD, and Satan standing at his right hand to resist him. ² And the LORD said unto Satan, The LORD rebuke you, O Satan, even the LORD that has chosen Jerusalem rebuke you: is not this a brand plucked out of the fire? ³ Now Joshua was clothed with filthy garments, and stood before the angel. ⁴ And he [the angel] answered

---

[298] Harris, Archer, and Waltke, *Theological Wordbook of the Old Testament*, 2:727.

and spoke unto those that stood before him, saying, take away the filthy garments from him, and unto him he said, behold, I have caused your iniquity to pass from you, and I will clothe you in costly garments. ⁵ And I said, let them set a fair mitre [turban] upon his head. So they set a fair mitre upon his head, and clothed him with garments. And the angel of the LORD stood by.

⁶ And the angel of the LORD warned Joshua, saying, ⁷ Thus says the LORD of hosts; if you wilt walk in My ways, and if you will keep My charge, then you shall also judge My house, and shall also keep My courts, and I will give you places to walk among these that stand by. ⁸ Hear now, O Joshua the high priest, you, and your fellows that sit before you: for they are men of distinction: for, behold, I will bring forth My servant the Sprout of David. ⁹ For behold the stone that I have laid before Joshua; upon one stone shall be seven eyes: behold, I will engrave the graving thereof, says the LORD of hosts, and I will remove the iniquity of that land in one day. ¹⁰ In that day, says the LORD of hosts, shall you call every man his neighbour under the vine and under the fig-tree.

This third and last example of Messenger (Angel) of *Yahweh* comes from Zechariah 3:1-10. This is the last reference to the Messenger (Angel) of *Yahweh* in the *Tanakh*. In verse 1, the Messenger (Angel) of the *Yahweh* is introduced. In verse 2, the NASB uses the name *Yahweh*, but in the Jewish Publication Society Version (JPS), it has in brackets "the (Messenger) angel of" *Yahweh*.[299] In verse 4, this Messenger (Angel) of *Yahweh* is able to remove iniquity, which only God can do. Again, in verse 5, the JPS version interprets the messenger as the Messenger (Angel) of *Yahweh*. In verse 6, the Messenger (Angel) of *Yahweh* charges the High Priest, Joshua, and then speaks in verse 7 as the *Lord of Hosts*. Also, in verse 7, the Messenger (Angel) of *Yahweh* commands them to *walk in MY ways*.[300] Here again the Messenger of *Yahweh* speaks as *Yahweh*, showing not only that He is equal and one with *Yahweh* but also that He is distinct from *Yahweh*. Listed in the footnotes are the other passages in the *Tanakh* of the Messenger (Angel) of *Yahweh*.[301]

---

[299] Berlin and Brettler, *The Jewish Study Bible*, 1253.
[300] Charles L. Feinberg, *God Remembers, A Study of the Book of Zechariah* (New York: American Board of Missions to the Jews, 1965), 54-58
[301] Other references of the Messenger of *Yahweh* are: (a) Genesis 16:7, 13 in connection with Hagar; (b) Abraham's visitors in Genesis 18, where one of them is the Messenger of *Yahweh*; (c) Genesis 31:11-13 and 32:24-30 as two examples of dealings with Jacob; (d) Moses with his initial contact with the Messenger of *Yahweh* in Exodus 3:2-15 when he is commissioned; (e) Joshua 5:14-15, before the battle of Jericho when Joshua is confronted by the Captain of

CHAPTER 4: THEOPHANIES

Yahweh Is Distinct from The Messenger (Angel) of The LORD

Yahweh is the personal God of Israel. However, when He communicates with Israel in person, *Yahweh* does so through the Messenger (Angel) of the LORD (*Yahweh*), also called the Messenger of God (*Elohim*). As discussed in the previous section, *Yahweh* and the messenger of the LORD (*Yahweh*) spoke as God; and both are distinct personalities, yet both speak as God (Genesis 32:24-30; Exodus 3:4-5; Joshua 5:14-15; Judges 2:1; 6:11-24; 13:2-24).[302]

Hengstenberg meticulously demonstrates that *Yahweh* and the Messenger (Angel) of the LORD (*Yahweh*) are two distinct personalities.

> Sound Christian Theology has discovered the outlines of such a distinction betwixt the hidden and the revealed God, in many passages of the Old Testament, in which mention is made of the Angel or Messenger of God.[303]

> There is no substantial difference betwixt the passages in which Jehovah Himself is mentioned, and those in which the Angel of Jehovah is spoken of.[304]

Like Hengstenberg, Payne expresses the point that the Messenger (Angel) of the LORD (*Yahweh*) is distinct from God and yet is God.[305] He also maintains that in Exodus 14:9 and Numbers 20:16, the Messenger leads; while other passages say God leads.[306] In fact, Payne even lays out the possibility that there may be other appearances that have not yet been seen:

---

the Host; (f) when Gideon is confronted with the Messenger of *Yahweh* in Judges 6:11-24; and (g) regarding Manoah and his wife in Judges 13:2-24; (h) also during the time of Hezekiah as the Messenger of *Yahweh* destroys 185,000 Assyrian soldiers in 2 Kings 19:35; and (i) the last occurrence, in Zechariah 1:12-14, 3:6-8.

[302] Buswell, *A Systematic Theology of the Christian Religion*, 122.
[303] E. W. Hengstenberg, *Christology of the Old Testament*, 4 Vol., (Grand Rapids: Kregel, 1956), 1:116.
[304] Hengstenberg, *Christology of the Old Testament*, 1:119.
[305] Payne, *The Theology of the Older Testament*, 167-168.
[306] Payne, *The Theology of the Older Testament*, 168.

It is indeed possible that when visible appearances of God occur elsewhere in the Scriptures the actual subject may again be the *Malakh Yahwe*,[307] even though the term itself may not be used.[308]

Notice in the above statement that Payne said it was possible that *Elohim* or *Yahweh* have revealed Themselves in other passages not yet known or understood at this point. It is an open question. Payne sums up his argument about the Messenger (Angel) of the LORD (*Yahweh*) by saying that:

> Old Testament revelations of the unique angel of the Testament can be appreciated only when understood as pre-incarnate appearances of Jesus Christ the Second Person of the Trinity and the one Savior of mankind.[309]

Chafer argues for two distinct personalities since God, at times, spoke as the Messenger (Angel) of *Yahweh* and at other times as *Yahweh* Himself:

> The fact is that the Angel of Jehovah is at times One other than Jehovah, and at other times He is Jehovah Himself.[310]

Clearly, the Messenger (Angel) of the LORD (*Yahweh*) is recognized as the Second Person of the tri-unity of God. He is distinct from the Father and yet one in unity with God. Both being distinctive Hebrew terms, the Messenger (Angel) of the LORD (*Yahweh*) and *Elohim* give very strong evidence that the plurality, or tri-unity of God, is indeed in the Hebrew Scriptures. In other words, the Messenger (Angel) of the LORD (*Yahweh*) was clearly God Himself.[311]

Throughout the *Tanakh*, both *Yahweh* and the Messenger (Angel) of *Yahweh* are in the singular form for God. The Messenger (Angel) of *Yahweh* and *Yahweh* both, without question, teach the oneness of God because they are always in the singular form. What must be identified is that the Messenger (Angel) of *Yahweh*, who is distinct from *Yahweh*, speaks as *Yahweh*. This is an inescapable fact when these passages are studied. These facts also show plurality within *Yahweh* because the Messenger (Angel) of *Yahweh* is distinct from *Yahweh*. In both cases, the Messenger (Angel) of *Yahweh* and *Yahweh* relate to Israel as a monotheist God. Yet in the revelation of Themselves, they do so in a compound or complex unity as the *Shema* in Deuteronomy 6:4 will confirm in the next chapter.

---

[307] The Hebrew noun **malakh** means "messenger" or "angel."
[308] Payne, *The Theology of the Older Testament,* 168.
[309] Payne, *The Theology of the Older Testament,* 170.
[310] Chafer, *Systematic Theology,* 1:299.
[311] Tenney, *The Zondervan Pictorial Encyclopedia of the Bible,* 5:389.

CHAPTER 4: THEOPHANIES

Shechinah

Theophanies may be divided into two sections: the Messenger (Angel) of the *Yahweh* and the *Shechinah* or glory of God's presence. The Hebrew word for *Shechinah* is שכינה, which literally means "the dwelling," as in Genesis 9:27. The definition is "the majestic presence or manifestation of God which has descended to 'dwell' among men."[312] Rabbi Nahmanides (1194-1270) considered it the essence of God as manifested in a distinct form.[313] The *Shechinah* as a theophany includes the non-human appearances of God through fire, cloud, and smoke. The Jewish people called that revelation of Himself the *Shechinah* of God or the glory of God.

According to VanGemeren the word *Shechinah* does not occur in the *Tanakh*. VanGemeren continues by stating that:

> The root *skn* occurs not only in the verb ("dwell"), but also in the noun *miskan* ("dwelling place," "tabernacle") and the name Shecaniah ("*Yahweh* dwells"; e.g., 1 Chronicles 3:21f.).[314]

Fruchtenbaum concurs with VanGemeren and adds some practicality to the above statement:

> The usual title found in the Scriptures for the *Shechinah* Glory is the glory of Jehovah, or the glory of the Lord. The Hebrew form is *Kvod Adonai*, which means "the glory of Jehovah" and describes what the *Shechinah* Glory is.
>
> Other titles give it the sense of "dwelling," which portrays what the *Shechinah* Glory does. The Hebrew word *Shechinah*, from the root *shachan*, means "to dwell." The Greek word *Skeinei*, which is similar in sound as the Hebrew *Shechinah* (Greek has no "sh" sound), means "to tabernacle."[315]

The Hebrew word for glory, כָּבוֹד (kavod), as in the *glory of the LORD filled the tabernacle* in Exodus 40:34, is not the term *Shechinah*, but glory. Over the years through Israel's contact with Hellenism, the glory of the LORD was equated with

---

[312] Isidore Singer, *The Jewish Encyclopedia* (New York: Funk and Wagnalls Co., 1906), 11:258.
[313] Singer, *The Jewish Encyclopedia*, 11:259.
[314] Bromiley, *The International Standard Bible Encyclopedia*, 4:466.
[315] Arnold G. Fruchtenbaum, *The Footsteps of the Messiah: A Study of the Sequence of Prophetic Events* (Tustin, CA: Ariel Ministries, 2003), 599.

Shechinah. Post-exilic Jews, and later Christians,[316] understood the term *Shechinah* as "to dwell" or "to reside."[317] The Apostle John picks this up in John 1:14 where he says, *The Word was made flesh, and dwelt* (tabernacled or *shekhinah*) *among us*. *Shechinah* first appears in the *Targums*[318] and rabbinic literature.

Niehaus takes the theophanies of God back to Genesis 1 to the creation account, as well as to the fall of man in Genesis 3, including the judgment account of Genesis 6, and labels them pre-Sinai theophanies.[319] The fact is that God did communicate to Adam and Noah, but it does not indicate how. God, in Genesis 3:8, did communicate directly with man in the Garden by his voice, but no further information is given about how He walked with them. With Noah, it simply says in Genesis 6:13 that God spoke to him, but it does not say how He communicated the information. In the biblical text there is not enough evidence to say, with authority, how God communicated in these instances.

Whether God reveals His presence as plurality to the nation of Israel as *Yahweh*, the Messenger (Angel) of *Yahweh*, or as *Shechinah* glory of God, that presence is the Second Person of the Godhead. That is rarely disputed among fundamental and evangelical scholars.

The first undisputed *Shechinah* is recorded in Genesis 15:9-18.[320] In these verses God made a covenant with Abraham by walking between the carcasses of slaughtered animals.

> When the sun was set and it was very dark, there appeared a smoking oven, and a flaming torch which passed between these pieces (vv. 17-18).

This pre-Sinai theophany introduces smoke (smoking oven) and fire (flaming torch), two non-human elements that are part of the Mount Sinai theophanies. These are characteristic of the *Shechinah* of God that appeared to Israel and to some of the prophets. In Judges 2:1, the Angel (Messenger) of *Yahweh* identifies Himself as the covenant maker with Abraham, which was confirmed in the pre-Sinai theophany of

---

[316] Merrill F. Unger, *Unger's Bible Dictionary* (Chicago: Moody Press, 1952), 1009.
[317] James Orr, *The International Standard Bible Encyclopedia*, 5 volumes (Grand Rapids: Eerdmans, 1939), 4:2758.
[318] **Targum**: This is an Aramaic paraphrase of the Hebrew Scriptures from the first century B.C.E. into the first century of the C.E. The "*Targums* regarded the *Shechinah* as God himself." It was first used in the *Targums* to avoid the anthropomorphic references to God as in Genesis 9:27 - "let him [God] dwell in the tents of Shem" to "may the Glory of his shekhinah dwell in the midst of the tents of Shem."
[319] Niehaus, *God at Sinai*, 142-171.
[320] Niehaus, *God at Sinai*, 172-180.

CHAPTER 4: THEOPHANIES

Genesis 15. There is little doubt that the *Shechinah* of God and the Messenger (Angel) of *Yahweh* were the same persons.

The second notable *Shechinah* was the burning bush that attracted Moses' attention when he was shepherding sheep on Mount Sinai (Exodus 3). Verse 2 makes it clear that it was the Messenger (Angel) of *Yahweh* who appeared to Moses in a blazing fire from a bush that was not consumed. This Messenger (Angel) told Moses to remove his shoes because he was standing on holy ground, in the presence of God. Then, He referred to the Abrahamic Covenant (Genesis 15:12-18) and the predicted deliverance that was going to take place. Moses was to deliver the Israelites. When asked His name, the Messenger (Angel) of *Yahweh* responded, *I AM WHO I AM*. This *I AM* is undoubtedly the same Person as the Messenger (Angel) of *Yahweh*, the *Shechinah* of God, in the burning bush. This appearance to Moses led to a personal relationship between Israel and their God.

In the third notable *Shechinah*, God traveled with Israel by giving them a pillar of cloud by day and a pillar of fire by night (Exodus 13:21-22). As the Egyptian army advanced against Israel at the shore of the Red Sea (Sea of Aquaba),[321] that evidence of God's glory became a wall between the Egyptian army and the Israelites. According to Exodus 40:36-38, this cloud and fire led them throughout the wilderness wanderings. Up to this point, God had appeared only to individual patriarchs and Moses. Now He was appearing to the nation of Israel at large. However, God could not completely reveal Himself because the holiness of His very nature required that He conceal Himself from the presence of man in the form of a thick, dark cloud.[322]

In this appearance of the *Shechinah* of God, the pillar of cloud and fire moved between the Egyptian army and the Israelites. Exodus 14:19 says, *The Angel (Messenger) of God, who had been going ahead of the Israelite army*. Here the *Shechinah* is identified as the Messenger of *Elohim*.[323] The use of *Elohim* is significant in that it identifies the *Shechinah* of God, or the theophany of God, within a plural context. It does so in the plural form of *Elohim* rather than as *El, Elah,* or *Eloah* in the singular. Then, as if such proofs were insufficient, verse 24 declares that this Messenger (Angel) of *Elohim* was *Yahweh* looking down from the pillar of cloud and fire. Clearly, the plural *Elohim* and the singular *Yahweh* were the same persons.

---

[321] Campus Crusade for Christ, *The Exodus Revealed, Search for the Red Sea Crossing* (Irvine CA: Discovery Media Productions, 2001), videotape.
[322] Alexander and Baker, *Dictionary of the Old Testament Pentateuch*, 861.
[323] Arthur W. Kac, *The Messiahship of Jesus* (Grand Rapids: Baker Book House, 1986), 200-201.

It is also noted that the phrase *Angel* (Messenger) *of God* is used (seven times) alternately with the *Angel (Messenger) of Yahweh.*[324]

The fourth notable *Shechinah* is God's appearance before the whole nation of Israel at the foot of Mount Sinai. The human reaction to the *Shechinah* of God that appeared before Israel was one of fear and terror.[325] Deuteronomy 18:16 expresses the fear and terror of the people as they heard and saw His glory or *Shechinah*. The *Shechinah* of God rested on Mount Sinai, and a cloud covered it (Exodus 24:16) to conceal His full glory. As *Yahweh* spoke from the midst of the fire and cloud, Israel *heard the sound of words, but saw no form, only a voice* (Deuteronomy 4:12). Deuteronomy 5:22 adds that the Lord spoke *from the midst of the fire, of the cloud and of the thick gloom, with a great voice*. Exodus 19:16-20 adds more descriptive words: *thunder and lightning flashes, thick cloud, very loud trumpet sound, so that all the people...trembled, smoke because the Yahweh descended upon it in fire, its smoke ascended like the smoke of a furnace, and the whole mountain quaked violently,...sound of the trumpet grew louder and louder*. The *Shechinah* of God, the Second Person of the Godhead, was the pre-incarnate Messiah as He established the Mosaic Covenant with Israel.

The fifth notable *Shechinah* appearance was when God took his place in the Holy of Holies in the Tabernacle. Since the Glory of God cannot be seen by man, God covered His glory, or *Shechinah*, with a thick dark cloud that filled the Tabernacle as He took up residence there (Exodus 40:34-35).[326]

The sixth notable *Shechinah* appearance was the pillar of fire by night and the cloud by day that followed Israel as they traveled for 40 years through part of the Sinai Peninsula and part of western Arabia. The *Shechinah* of God appeared at numerous times as He met with Moses, but also as He appeared to judge individuals or the nation. The following are six examples of individual and corporate judgments that were given to Israel for their rebellion in the wilderness. These judgments (Exodus 23:23; 32:34; 33:3) were not carried out by *Yahweh* because He did not go with them; rather, the Messenger carried out these judgments as He took Israel through the wilderness and into the Land. So all of the following examples are the Messenger (Angel) of *Yahweh*, equal to yet distinct from *Yahweh*, showing plurality:

> (1) Nadab and Abihu offered strange fire before the Lord[327] in Leviticus 10:1-2, and fire came from the presence of *Yahweh* and

---

[324] Botterweck, Ringgren, and Fabry. *Theological Dictionary of the Old Testament*, 1:281.
[325] Alexander and Baker, *Dictionary of the Old Testament Pentateuch*, 863.
[326] Elwell, *Evangelical Dictionary of Theology*, 1010.
[327] Niehaus, *God at Sinai*, 208.

consumed them. Leviticus 9:23-24 shows that it was the glory of *Yahweh* that was present and that fire proceeded from *Yahweh*.

(2) In Numbers 11:1-2, at Taberah, Israel murmured before God, and He responded to their sin: *The fire of the LORD burned among them and consumed some of the outskirts of the camp.*[328]

(3) In Numbers 12:2-5 the *Shechinah* of God appeared at the *doorway of the tent of meeting* in judgment of Aaron and Miriam for their sin against Moses, their brother, and condemned their sin and caused Miriam to be leprous.[329]

(4) Numbers 14:10 says that the *Shechinah* of God appeared before Israel *in the tent of meeting* to quell the riot against Moses after the report of the ten unbelieving spies. Verse 23 gave the verdict that Israel would not *see the land which I swore to their fathers*. This act of rebellion, their refusal to believe *by faith* in Him, was an unpardonable sin (Numbers 14:11). This was an *evil congregation* (vv. 27, 35; cf. Matthew 12:31-45), and, as a result, He condemned them to wander in the wilderness for 38 years until they all died.

(5) Later Korah, a Levitical family, not of the family of Aaron, rebelled against Moses and Aaron as they gathered the congregation against Moses and Aaron at the door of the tent of meeting. There the glory of the *Yahweh* appeared to the congregation. He opened the earth and swallowed up all the families of Korah, Dathan, and Abiram and sent fire to consume 250 men offering incense (Numbers 16:1-40). This was not their God-given responsibility.[330] They were usurping responsibilities reserved for the Aaronic priests.

(6) Even after such a devastating judgment, Israel grumbled against Moses and Aaron saying that they were the cause of the death of these men. Again, the *Shechinah* of God appeared with a plague upon the people so that 14,700 died (Numbers 16:42, 49). As mentioned earlier in this section, the *Shechinah* of God was the pre-incarnate Messiah of Israel.

---

[328] Niehaus, *God at Sinai*, 210.
[329] Niehaus, *God at Sinai*, 211.
[330] Niehaus, *God at Sinai*, 214-215.

Each one of these six examples of the *Shechinah* glory of God shows that these persons are one, yet distinct. Exodus 23:20-23 clearly states that *Yahweh* did not go with Israel, but that He sent His Messenger (Angel), which establishes the fact that *Yahweh* and His Messenger in these *Shechinah* glory references are equal and distinct. Clearly, these *Shechinah* references establish the plurality of God.

The seventh notable *Shechinah* appearance occurred when the presence of God filled the new Solomonic Temple in Jerusalem.[331] In 1 Kings 8:10-11; 9:3, and 2 Chronicles 7:1, the *Shechinah* of God (the glory of *Yahweh*) filled the Temple. As in the Mount Sinai appearance, His presence was manifest as a cloud. Solomon (1 Kings 8:12) refers to the cloud as a thick cloud. Not only did the *Shechinah* of God fill the Temple, but fire came down from heaven and consumed the burnt offerings and sacrifices.

The eighth notable *Shechinah* appearances that could be called post-Sinai appearances, occurred when Isaiah and Ezekiel each received their commissions as prophets.[332] In chapter 6, Isaiah saw the Lord sitting on His throne. Verses 1-3 give a description of God that very few have seen. Verse 4 has two examples of a theophany: *The foundations of the thresholds trembled at the voice of Him...the temple was filling with smoke*. This theophany marks God's call of Isaiah into his prophetic ministry, recalling to memory Israel's Mount Sinai experience and the consecration of Solomon's Temple.[333]

While Isaiah's vision was awesome, Ezekiel's vision was indescribable. Certain theophanic pictures are seen in Ezekiel 1, such as *a great cloud with lightning flashing continually* (v. 4). The first chapter of Ezekiel is filled with things like nothing else in the Hebrew Scriptures. This theophany is also associated with Ezekiel's call found in chapter 2:3.[334]

Ezekiel chapters 8-11 describe the sin of the religious and political leaders of Israel in their worship of pagan deities in the Temple. Not only is Israel's sin described in these chapters, but the *Shechinah* of God is in the process of leaving the Temple of God to return to heaven (Hosea 5:15; Matthew 23:37-39). Niehaus, in giving a rabbinic Jewish response, says that in 70 C.E. the *Shechinah* of God went into exile with the captives.[335] Passages in Ezekiel document that the *Shechinah* of God left the Temple in 592 B.C.E. (Ezekiel 8:1) in several stages (Ezekiel 9:3; 10:18; 11:23). Singer also states that the *Shechinah* of God was one of five things missing in

---

[331] Niehaus, *God at Sinai*, 243.
[332] Isidore Singer, *The Jewish Encyclopedia*, 12:137.
[333] Niehaus, *God at Sinai*, 249-254.
[334] Niehaus, *God at Sinai*, 254-279.
[335] Niehaus, *God at Sinai*, 577.

the Second Temple.[336] Also, according to Josephus, neither the Ark of God nor the *Shechinah* was present in 63 B.C.E. when Pompey, the conquering Roman general, entered the Temple and the Holy of Holies.[337] So the *Shechinah* did not go into exile with the captives but left the Temple and the nation over 600 years earlier and returned to heaven. Proof of the absence of God's tangible glory from the Temple is that Pompey was not struck dead upon penetrating the veil as Jewish authors like Singer,[338] and Schurer[339] attest. Christian authors also validate those Jewish authors, such as Pfeiffer,[340] Moeller,[341] Sloan,[342] and Sacchi.[343]

The last possible reference to the theophany of God is found in Daniel 5:5 when the hand of God wrote on the wall in the banquet hall in Belshazzar's palace. Some background information must be given to lead up to the Daniel reference. Deuteronomy 9:10 (cp. Exodus 31:18; 32:15-16; 34:1) refers to the *Shechinah* of God who wrote the Ten Commandments with *the finger of God*. This event was part of the *Shechinah* of God's activities on Mount Sinai. In the New Testament, *Jesus stooped down and with His finger wrote on the ground* (John 8:6). Jesus, the Messiah of Israel, and the *Shechinah* of God, was the pre-incarnate Messiah, who now, with His *Shechinah* glory veiled in flesh, does not speak immediately but wrote with His finger, the *finger of God* (Deuteronomy 9:10), in the ground. Did He stoop and write the seventh commandment as He wrote with His finger on Mount Sinai? That will never be known, but the John 8:6 text does have strong implications.

The fingers of God are mentioned in three other places. One is found in Psalm 8:3 (not a theophany), where David says, *When I consider Your heavens, the work of Your fingers*. The second reference is a metaphor used for God by Pharaoh's magician as they reacted to the plagues in Exodus 8:19. The third reference is the one now under consideration. More evidence for a theophany is found in Daniel 5:5, where *suddenly the fingers of a man's hand* appeared before Belshazzar on the banquet hall wall. This was a theophany, and the reason for that conclusion is because it was a supernatural event. The context involves the Temple vessels being defiled by a proud and obstinate king who evidently learned little from his

---

[336] Singer, *The Jewish Encyclopedia*, 11:260.
[337] Flavius Josephus, *Josephus Complete Works* (trans. William Whiston. Grand Rapids: Kregel, 1978), 436.
[338] Singer, *The Jewish Encyclopedia*, 10:123.
[339] Emil Schurer, *A History of the Jewish People in the Time of Jesus Christ*, 1:322.
[340] Charles F. Pfeiffer, *Old Testament History* (Grand Rapids: Baker, 1973), 586.
[341] Henry Moeller, *The Legacy of Zion: Intertestamental Texts related to the New Testament* (Grand Rapids: Baker, 1977), 126.
[342] W. W. Sloan, *Between the Testaments* (Paterson, NJ: Littlefield, Adams & Co., 1964), 58.
[343] Paolo Sacchi, *The History of the Second Temple Period* (Sheffield, England: Sheffield Academic Press, 2000), 270.

grandfather, Nebuchadnezzar. This was the hand of God, not a lesser being, who wrote with His fingers.

In summary, all of the aforementioned references of the *Shechinah* glory of God reflect the conclusion that the *Shechinah* and the Messenger (Angel) of *Yahweh* are equal to, and yet distinct from, *Yahweh*. God appeared as a man (Genesis 18) and in the burning bush (Exodus 3) as the Messenger (Angel) of *Yahweh*. These two points are important, but the main emphasis is that God's personal presence was revealed. In other words, as the passages are examined, the terms for *Yahweh* and the theophanies of God are distinct from each other.

The big question is: "Who is the Angel (Messenger) of *Yahweh*?" If God appeared in a localized place, then who was He? Christian scholars maintain that the Messenger (Angel) of *Yahweh* and other disclosures of God were the Second Person of the Godhead, God the Son, Jesus Christ. For example, Walvoord points out four reasons why the Messenger (Angel) of *Yahweh* is Messiah *Yeshua* and not the Father or the Holy Spirit:

1. The Second Person is the visible God of the New Testament (John 10:30).

2. The Angel of *Yahweh* no longer appears after the incarnation (John 5:36-38).[344]

3. Both the Angel of *Yahweh* and Messiah are sent by the Father.

4. In the process of elimination, it could not be the Father; for the Father is the sender. The Angel of *Yahweh* appears in a bodily form, usually in human form: the Holy Spirit never has appeared in human or bodily form.[345]

When observing the theophanies of God, the words of John the Baptist in John 1:18 come to remembrance in relation to who has seen the Father:

No man has seen God at any time, the only begotten Son, which is in the bosom of the Father, He hath declared Him.

---

[344] Isaiah 48:16 and Zechariah 2:8-9 say that Angel of *Yahweh* is sent by *Yahweh*. In John's gospel *Yeshua* clarifies that the Father sent Him; 3:34; 4:34; 5:23-24,30, 36-38; 6:29, 38-39, 44, 57; 7:16, 18, 28-29, 33; 8:16, 18, 26, 29, 42; 9:4; 10:36; 11:42; 12:44-45, 49; 13:20; 14;24; 15:21; 16:5, 27; 17:3, 8, 18, 21, 23, 25. These 40 references document that the Father sent Messiah into the world.
[345] John F. Walvoord, *Jesus Christ our Lord.* (Chicago: Moody, 1969), 44-46.

CHAPTER 4: THEOPHANIES

The words of *Yeshua* in John 14:9-11 declare that He is the exact representation of the Father, which parallels the author of Hebrews (1:1-3) who states that God has spoken through His Son. Because He was the Son being equal to the Father, on the Mount of Transfiguration, His glory was veiled in flesh at the time of His incarnation (Matthew 17:1-8).

The *Tanakh*, through the theophanies, is a rich source of information on the plurality of God. Minimally, with this rich source of biblical information from the *Tanakh*, the rabbis should have recognized the plurality of *Yahweh* as He presented Himself as different persons, equal, indivisible, yet a plurality.

When the character and essence of God is examined in light of Luke 24:25-27, 44-48, it is clear that *Yeshua*, when speaking to the two disciples on the Emmaus Road, taught that the Law, Prophets, and Writings referred to Him:

> *And beginning at Moses and all the prophets, He expounded unto them in all the scriptures the things concerning Himself* (v. 27, KJV).

> *...These are the words which I spoke unto you, while I was yet with you, that all things must be fulfilled, which were written in the law of Moses, and in the prophets, and in the psalms, concerning Me. Then He opened their understanding, that they might understand the scriptures* (vv. 44-45, NASB).

Perhaps today, in this intellectual age, scholars have retreated from what *Yeshua* taught to His disciples on that eventful day. These verses apply to all that was said of *Yeshua* in the Law, Prophets, and Writings. One of the many things that *Yeshua* would have related from the *Tanakh* was to show the disciples that He was the Messenger (Angel) of *Yahweh*, the *Shechinah* of God, as well as *Yahweh* and *Elohim*, the Creator and covenant-making God with Israel. What an awesome view of *Yeshua* in the Hebrew Scriptures that must have been. Based on the New Testament, these persons in the theophanies, in the form of man – Messenger (Angel) of *Yahweh* and *Shechinah* of God – are the pre-incarnate Messiah of Israel.[346]

All of the references of the *Shechinah* Glory of God, together with the Messenger (Angel) of *Yahweh* references, amount to a heavy weight in substantiating the plurality or tri-unity of God. The Father and the Holy Spirit are never revealed in a physical form anywhere in the Scriptures. Only the Second Person of the tri-unity appeared in human form as a theophany or as the *Shechinah* Glory of God.

---

[346] Enns, *The Moody Handbook of Theology*, 216.

CHAPTER 5:
SHEMA

> *⁴ Hear, O Israel! The LORD is our God, the LORD alone. ⁵ You shall love the LORD your God with all your heart and with all your soul and with all your might. ⁶ Take to heart these instructions with which I charge you this day. ⁷ Impress them upon your children. Recite them when you stay at home and when you are away, when you lie down and when you get up. ⁸ Bind them as a sign on your hand and let them serve as a symbol on your forehead; ⁹ inscribe them on the doorposts of your house and on your gates.* (Deuteronomy 6:4-9)

The *Shema* provides a statement of unity to both Jewish and Christian believers. God is one, indivisible; He is Israel's God and their full attention and worship is to be directed to Him alone. Our focus of attention is verse 4, *Hear, O Israel! The LORD is our God, the LORD alone* [is one]. However, on occasion, the *Shema* of Deuteronomy 6:4 presents conflict and disagreements on the nature of God. Whether *Yahweh* is "one" alone as Judaism believes, or whether *Yahweh* is a tri-unity as Christianity believes, there is much contention in relation to the Hebrew word *echad*. Even though Christianity accepts the belief in the tri-unity of God, many scholars as documented in this chapter, do not see the plurality or tri-unity of God in Deuteronomy 6:4.

Resolving the difficulty of this text calls for a five-fold analysis: (1) the Jewish view of God and how Judaism views the *Shema* compared to Christian viewpoints; (2) Christianity's struggles with the proper meaning of *echad*; (3) comments by Christian authors as to why or why not *echad* should be taken as "one alone" or as a "tri-unity"; (4) the significance of the Hebrew term *yachid* in relationship to *echad*; and (5) this writer's conclusions and observations on *echad*.

Judaism

The *Shema* of Deuteronomy 6:4-9 is the cornerstone of the Jewish faith. In studying the *Shema*, verse 4 in particular, the word translated "one" from the Hebrew

אֶחָד (*echad*) must be analyzed. The Jewish concept of the unity of God is grounded on a particular understanding of this word *echad* in the *Shema*.

Judaism is emphatic about the unity and oneness of God. God is pure spirit, a corporeal being, and cannot, in any way, become a man as they see it. They see Christians as Tri-theists, dividing God into three Persons. The incarnation of God as a man is irreconcilable in their minds. For example, Jacobs, a Jewish author, states:

> There is only one God and there are no others. Allied to this is the idea that God in His essence is indivisible. A deity like Baal could be split up, as it were, into various local deities, hence the plural form Baalim and Ashterot found in the Bible when speaking of the pagan gods.[347]

> The polytheistic deities were thought of as separate beings, frequently in conflict with one another, each having a part of the universe for his or her domain. Monotheism denies the existence of such beings.[348]

Gerald Root comments that pagan mythology portrays each god as doing his or her own thing. However, there is no such conflict when there is one God. If there were many gods, there would be no uniformity in the universe; whereas, with *Yahweh*, there is no such conflict. For example, think of it this way. If *Yahweh* was in charge today, and He made light to travel at 186,000 miles per second; but tomorrow, another god gained control and wanted light to travel at 50,000 miles per second, the whole universe would be in complete chaos. That is only one example of untold myriads of possible illustrations. From the Jewish perspective, God must be God with no rivals.[349]

Jacobs continues to state along with Weiss-Rosmarin the perception of Jewish scholars:

> For many of them the idea of God's unity embraced the further idea that there is no multiplicity in His Being, that, as they expressed it, His was an "absolute simplicity."[350] The Unity of God, sacred to Judaism beyond all else, is utterly irreconcilable with the Christian idea of the divisibility of the Divine Being and above all, with the

---

[347] Jacobs, *A Jewish Theology*, 21.
[348] Jacobs, *A Jewish Theology*, 22.
[349] Gerald Root, "*A Critical Investigation of Deuteronomy 6:4*" (B.D. thesis, Grace Theological Seminary, 1964), 42.
[350] Jacobs, A Jewish Theology, 27.

belief in incarnation. According to Jewish belief God is pure spirit, eternally transcendent and divorced from even the slightest vestige of corporeality. Christianity, on the other hand, asserts that God became man in Jesus, a teaching which is contrary to the very spirit of Judaism.[351]

Is not this contrary to all Jewish teachings of God which emphasize and stress that God is not like man and can never become man or even resemble man?[352]

How, then, can the Jewish and Christian ideas of God be reconciled, or how can it be said that the "two religions are truly, basically one"? Is the One and Unique God, the absolute Unity – unknowable, indefinable – really the same as the Christian Trinity which divides the Unity of God into three, namely, God the Father, Jesus the Son and the Holy Spirit? Is the Jewish transcendent and purely spiritual belief in a God in Whom there is no trace of matter and Who can never become corporeal really the same as Christian belief which glories in God "who made man?"[353]

Sometimes Christian authors like Erickson, make confusing statements that appear to support the Jewish concept of Christianity that God is divisible, a plurality. Erickson says that, "He (God) is an organism, that is, a unity of distinct parts."[354] True New Testament believers have never embraced God as being three parts of a whole. Judaism cannot accept God becoming man, and equally Judaism cannot accept placing upon man divine qualities. This is reflected in Weiss-Rosmarin's statements:

> Jewish Monotheism is not only the negation of the many gods but also the rejection of the personification of God on the one hand and of the deification of human beings on the other. Judaism's refusal to worship Jesus is therefore not only due to its repudiation of the doctrine of incarnation, the belief that God became a person, but equally so to its defiant resistance to all and any attempts of according Divine qualities and honors to mere mortals.[355]

---

[351] Weiss-Rosmarin, *Judaism and Christianity*, 21.
[352] Weiss-Rosmarin, *Judaism and Christianity*, 21.
[353] Weiss-Rosmarin, *Judaism and Christianity*, 21-22.
[354] Erickson, *Introducing Christian Doctrine*, 100.
[355] Weiss-Rosmarin, *Judaism and Christianity*, 23.

> Catholicism as well as Protestantism worships persons and the images of persons. However,...Catholicism venerates in addition to Jesus a large and still expanding pantheon of Saints and their relics, besides devoting a special cult to the worship of the "Mother of God."[356]

Generally speaking, Jewish people view Christianity from the theological background of Roman Catholicism because it was the Church, under Roman leadership, that they primarily had to deal with in the past. It is primarily the corrupt teaching of the Catholic Church and the Church Fathers before them that has resulted in treacherous anti-Semitism over the centuries, but Protestants share guilt in the negative treatment of Jewish people. To Judaism, God is a pure spirit-being; and it is inconceivable that a man could be God or that God would become man. Judaism holds, with unwavering dogmatism, that man is nothing more than man. Christians would completely agree with the Jewish assessment of man but differ in the believing that God did become a man.

The Jewish sentiments about the incarnation are stated again by Weiss-Rosmarin:

> To Judaism man is man and God is God and shall remain God in unequalled and eternal majesty.[357]

> The man Moses has been its watchword through the ages; thus it has warded off all attempts to enthrone any mortal as God. With equal consistency it has refused to admit the possibility of any man's sharing in God's perfection, or the incarnation of God in any human being.[358]

> During the Middle Ages the Jewish assertion of God's unity became an explicit denial of the Christian dogma of the Trinity, a total disavowal of the thesis that God, though one, is somehow at the same time three persons, "co-eternal and co-equal."[359]

These statements reveal the antagonism of Judaism towards the Christian teaching on the Trinity. One reason for drawing a distinct line in the sand is because of the unbiblical, anti-Semitic positions that the Church has held. The Church, through the

---

[356] Weiss-Rosmarin, *Judaism and Christianity*, 24.
[357] Weiss-Rosmarin, *Judaism and Christianity*, 26.
[358] Weiss-Rosmarin, *Judaism and Christianity*, 27.
[359] Milton Steinberg, *Basic Judaism* (New York: A Harvest/HBJ Book, 1947), 45.

Church Fathers, laid the foundation for the anti-Semitism that was practiced against the Jews for 1,500 years.[360] One long quote suffices to reflect the hatred of the Jew by the Church, and even by great men of the Reformation. Martin Luther's quote is enough to point out the anti-Semitism that infiltrated Christendom:

> First, he urged, "their synagogues should be set on fire, and whatever is left should be buried in dirt so that no one may ever be able to see a stone or cinder of it." Jewish prayer-books should be destroyed and rabbis forbidden to preach. Then the Jewish people should be dealt with, their homes "smashed and destroyed and their inmates put under one roof or in a stable like gypsies, to teach them they are not master in our land." Jews should be banned from the roads and markets, their property seized and then these "poisonous envenomed worms" should be drafted into forced labour and made to earn their bread "by the sweat of their noses."[361]

This kind of unbiblical rhetoric influenced the attitudes and actions of the Church for centuries. More could be written, but that is not the purpose of this book. The Jewish position, which was firm to begin with, became a granite rock. In summary, God is one to the Jewish people, period! To them, belief in the incarnation is inconceivable.

Christianity

Judaism views Paul, the Hellenized Pharisee, rather than *Yeshua* as the founder of Christianity. Pryor points out that the New Testament letters provide impressive evidence that the early first-century believers in the (Jewish) church had the highest Christology.[362] Peter was very clear in his letters that *Yeshua* is God (1 Peter 1:1-25; 2:21-24; 4:11; 2 Peter 1:16, 18) the Savior, Redeemer, and resurrected Lord. James spoke of himself as the *bond-servant* of *Yeshua* (1:1, NASB) and challenged his readers to correctly *hold your faith in our glorious Lord Jesus Christ* (2:1, NASB) without favoritism. Jude is clear that *Yeshua* is Savior: *be glory, majesty, dominion and authority, before all time and now and forever* (v. 25, NASB). John, in the first chapter of both his Gospel and in his First Epistle, clearly states that *Yeshua* is God. The theme of the writer of Hebrews is that *Yeshua* is better than the angels, Moses, the priesthood, and sacrifices. We know that James, Peter, Jude, John, and the writer of Hebrews, who knew Paul, did not just copy Paul's theology because they rarely saw each other. The early Jewish Church knew who *Yeshua* was by

---

[360] Stan Telchin, *Abandoned* (Grand Rapids, Baker Book House, 1997), 51-72.
[361] Paul Johnson, *A History of the Jews* (New York, HarperCollins, 1987), 242.
[362] Pryor, "One God and Lord," 55.

living, teaching, and dying for their belief that *Yeshua* was the Messiah of Israel, the God/man.

Just as Judaism has its own view of the New Testament, Christians bring their own perspective to their understanding of Deuteronomy 6:4. The meaning that one takes away through the eyes of Christianity will differ depending on how one views the tri-unity of God in the Hebrew Scriptures. *Echad* has become somewhat of a difficult word for many to interpret. I believe it has a rich meaning, but has been given a narrow, restricted definition by Judaism because of the negative impact of Christian witness.

First, in considering verse 4 in the Hebrew, the *Shema* revolves around four words – יְהוָה אֱלֹהֵינוּ יְהוָה אֶחָד (*LORD* our God, *LORD* is One). There is no problem in belief or interpretation with *Shema Israel* (*Hear O Israel*.) Nor is there a problem in belief or interpretation with יְהוָה אֱלֹהֵינוּ (*LORD our God*) except the way *Elohenu* is viewed (*our Gods* or *God*). *Yahweh* is Israel's personal name for their God *Elohim*, who is the Creator and the covenant maker! The major problem lies with יְהוָה אֶחָד (*LORD is one,*) that God is "one" in regard to interpretation, which will affect belief. *Yahweh* is One, but the difficulty is what is meant by "one."

Although Herbert Wolf, a contributing author to *Theological Wordbook of the Old Testament*, suggests that the lexical and syntactical difficulties of יְהוָה אֶחָד ("LORD is one") are evident in numerous translations, all aspects of the challenge can be represented by four common translations. The *LORD is one* is translated four different ways, which incorporate each specific aspect of the particular interpretation. The first view of Deuteronomy 6:4 is "the LORD is our God, the LORD alone."[363] Herbert Wolf's explanation of his option above is that it has in its favor both the broad and immediate context of the book of Deuteronomy. The *Shema* serves as the introduction to motivate Israel to keep the command to love the LORD (v. 5). This notion suits this command in verse 5 very well because the LORD is Israel's unique God who stands alone, along with Israel's obligation to love that God.

The second view of Deuteronomy 6:4 expresses the interpretation as LORD our God: LORD is unique (only one).[364] Lohfink and Bergmann state that *echad* should be understood as "only one," or "unique one." This is one God who led them, loved them (Deuteronomy 5:10), and gave them the Law. God did it without the help of foreign gods (Deuteronomy 32:12). The *Shema* saw Israel's obligation to respond to this unique God in love by being obedient to the Law or Decalogue. Points one and two seem to be very close in their views.

---

[363] Herbert M. Wolf in Harris, Archer, and Waltke, *Theological Wordbook of the Old Testament,* 1:30.
[364] Botterweck, Ringgren, and Fabry. *Theological Dictionary of the Old Testament*, 1:196.

CHAPTER 5: SHEMA

The third view of Deuteronomy 6:4 of looking at the *Shema* is "the LORD our God, the LORD is one." Jenson points out that:

> The syntax of the verbless sentence is disputed, but analogy with other uses of "LORD our God" in Deuteronomy suggests that the traditional syntax should be retained ("The LORD our God, the LORD is One").[365]

He points out further that "one" is not a title or name of God but an adjective of quality. The correlation between the two halves of Deuteronomy 6:4 suggests that the interpretation of *Shema* is not pointed against the polytheism of the day or to a non-abstract monotheism, but it is a claim to Israel's total obedience to their God to the exclusion of all others.

The last view of Deuteronomy 6:4 says, the LORD our God, the LORD is a unity of one.[366] The essence of oneness is linked to the *Shema*, and the *echad* is a compound or complex unity, a united one. This view not only includes the uniqueness and oneness of God but also the unity of God expressed in three Persons. This oneness, yet a compound unity, possesses the summation of all divine attributes which in their essence are undivided. These three Persons of the tri-unity do not act independently of one another.

All four of the above positions hold to a basic truth that God is "one alone," "unique one," the only one to be loved and worshipped. The last one agrees with the other three but adds the dimension that all that was said of the other three is true. It adds that God is a compound or complex unity, and the word *echad* expresses that interpretation (Genesis 1:5; 2:24).

McConville gives the same points for possible interpretation but says nothing concerning the unity of God about how the word *echad* is used. However, he does give two additional helpful points in determining how the word is used but again with no conclusions:

> Between the other renderings the chief difference concerns whether to translate *echad* as an adjective, "one," or an adverb "alone."

---

[365] VanGemeren, ed., *Dictionary of Old Testament Theology and Exegesis,* 1:350.
[366] Enns, *The Moody Handbook of Theology,* 199-200.

> It differs from the First Commandment (Deuteronomy 5:7) in that the emphasis falls heavily on the word "one."[367]

He states that the problem of how *echad* is to be translated, whether as an adjective or as an adverb, is at the center of the question; but he gives no conclusion. Further, he also admits that the emphasis, the thrust, the focus of the verse, is on *echad*. This does not conclude the unity of God and plurality, but he does reinforce the fact that this word *echad* is the focus of attention by Moses. This author believes the key to understanding the verse is to see just how this word *echad* is used first by Moses and then by the rest of the *Tanakh*. (See appendix two concerning the usage of *echad* in the Torah.)

In the preceding paragraphs, it was observed that *echad* is interpreted four ways. *Echad* is used 970 times throughout the Hebrew Scriptures.[368] What is meant by this word? Does the word indicate one of unity, one alone, or one of uniqueness? Smith says that the precise meaning is unclear.[369] That is seen from the previous paragraph with the four possible usages of *echad*. Do those who believe in the tri-unity read too much into *echad*? The immediate context of the word in the book of Deuteronomy requires that *Yahweh* is the one and only God and Israel's personal God.[370] Both Judaism and Christianity would agree with this view.

Evans has noted that *echad*, which expresses the unity of the Godhead, is not simple but compound and is always used to describe a divine unity.[371]

According to Payne the *Shema* teaches that God is a divine unity of singularity:

> This passage does not primarily concern a divine unity of simplicity; that God constitutes a unity within Himself, in contrast, for example, with Baal, who was splintered up so as to exist separately in countless individual plots of ground (hence the plural, the Baalim). It concerns rather the divine unity of singularity; that God constitutes the sole deity, as opposed to others, which is the essence of monotheism.[372]

---

[367] J. G. McConville, *Apollos Old Testament Commentary: Deuteronomy* (Downer Grove, IL: InterVarsity, 2002), 140-142.

[368] Jenni and Westermann, *Theological Lexicon of the Old Testament*, 1:79.

[369] Ralph L. Smith, *Old Testament Theology Its History, Method, and Message* (Nashville: Broadman and Holman, 1993), 226-227.

[370] Botterweck, Ringgren, and Fabry. *Theological Dictionary of the Old Testament*, 1:196.

[371] William Evans, *The Great Doctrines of the Bible*. (Chicago: Moody, 1974), 26-27.

[372] Payne, *The Theology of the Older Testament*, 126.

CHAPTER 5: SHEMA

Deuteronomy 6:5, which says to *Love the LORD your God with all your heart*, is only relevant because God is the only one.[373] The *Tanakh*, as it recorded the Prophets and the Writings, affirms the fact of Moses' monotheism. The people, however, as a whole, did not love the Lord because they worshipped other gods and did not worship God alone.

Usages of *Echad*

TWO BECOMING ONE

Janzen's article on the "most important word" in the *Shema* is devoted to the *Shema* but fails to show the importance of *echad* in the *Shema*. The *Shema* is the most significant verse where *echad* appears, and the question is how it is interpreted in the *Shema*. Other references to *echad* throughout the *Tanakh* should be analyzed in relation to the immediate context so that the Deuteronomy 6:4 passage can be clearly understood as to whether it refers to one or a compound unity. Upon reading Janzen's article, this most important word (*echad*) is not dealt with in relation to the issue of oneness and/or compound unity as it relates to the *Shema*. He refers to *echad* in several passages in the *Tanakh* without any relationship to the immediate context (Deuteronomy 6:4). He does seem to embrace *echad* as being one "alone." He consistently refers to the broader context of Deuteronomy 6:4-5. Janzen's article lacks evidence of a biblical study of the word *echad* and how it is used in the *Tanakh* and in the *Shema* and elsewhere.[374]

An analysis of the Hebrew Scriptures uncovers three distinct usages of the term *echad*. The word *echad* is first used as a compound unity.[375] It is two separate persons becoming an *echad*, a unity, in Genesis 2:24 which says, *Therefore shall a man leave his father and his mother, and shall cleave unto his wife; and they shall be one [echad] flesh*. Genesis 11:1 applies the same concept to language: *And the whole earth was of one [echad] language, and of one speech*. All humanity had *echad* speech. The spies, upon returning from Canaan in Numbers 13:23, brought with them a cluster (*echad*) of grapes. Exodus 24:3, Judges 20:1, and Ezra 3:1 picture the nation of Israel answering God with one (*echad*) voice and gathering before the Lord as one (*echad*) man. In Ezekiel 37:17, 19, 22, Ezekiel is told by God to put together two sticks as an *echad* stick, *And join them one to another into one [echad] stick...even with the stick of Judah, and make them one [echad] stick,...and I will make them one*

---

[373] Payne, *The Theology of the Older Testament,* 126.
[374] J. Gerald Janzen, "On the Most Important Word in the *Shema* (Deuteronomy VI 4-5)," *Vetus Testamentum* 37, 3 (1987): 280-300.
[375] Harris, Archer, and Waltke, *Theological Wordbook of the Old Testament,* 1:30.

[*echad*] *nation in the land.* The two sticks represented the houses of Israel and Judah being joined together, in the future, as one *echad* nation.

Other references to *echad* that support two separate units becoming one are found in Genesis 34:22; Exodus 25:36; Numbers 14:15; Joshua 10:42; 1 Samuel 11:7b; 1 Kings 22:13b; 2 Chronicles 5:13, 30:12; Nehemiah 8:1; Proverbs 1:14; Jeremiah 32:39; and Malachi 2:10. Although this "unity" concept of *echad,* of two becoming one is used the least in number of all three divisions mentioned at the beginning of the paragraph, yet the unity aspect has become the focal point in discussions of Deuteronomy 6:4.

PLURALITY WITHOUT UNITY

A second way *echad* is used is to show things or persons in relationships that do not require a compound unity (the first category considered).[376] However, this usage is still within a plural context, as in Exodus 17:12:

> *But Moses' hands were heavy; and they took a stone and put it under him, and he sat thereon; and Aaron and Hur stayed up his hands, the one* [*echad*] *on the one side, and the other* [*echad*] *on the other side and his hands were steady until the going down of the sun.*

The same *echad* is also applied to offerings. In Leviticus 12:8, for example, sacrificial animals are considered *echad*:

> *And if she be not able to bring a lamb, then she shall bring two turtledoves, or two young pigeons; the one* [*echad*] *for the burnt offering and the other* [*echad*] *for a sin offering.*

Samson, in Judges 16:29, also uses the context of plurality where it says he:

> *...took hold of the two middle pillars upon which the house stood, and on which it was borne up of the one* [*echad*] *with his right hand, and the other* [*echad*] *with his left.*

After David's sin with Bathsheba, Nathan comes before David with the story in 2 Samuel 12:1 of two men in a city, where *one* [*echad*] *was rich and other* [*echad*] *poor.*

These usages of *echad* are in the context of plurality but not in a compound unity. Other references show the same concept (Genesis 21:15; Exodus 25:19;

---

[376] VanGemeren, ed., *Dictionary of Old Testament Theology and Exegesis,* 1:349.

Numbers 6:11; Deuteronomy 21:15; Joshua 4:2; 1 Samuel 1:2; 1 Kings 3:25; 2 Kings 6:5; 1 Chronicles 29:1 and 2 Chronicles 3:17). This usage of e*chad* is used more frequently than the other two (the two becoming one or separateness).

The third way *echad* is used is to indicate the separateness or individuality of a thing or person. This division will be reflected in three parts, and the first denotes one standing by itself.[377] The second, as in Joshua, demonstrates a cardinal "one" as Joshua enumerates the kings one by one (Joshua 12:9-24 [32 times]). The third is used as an ordinal (first or first one) number as seen in Exodus 40:17 when the Tabernacle was set up on the *echad* or first day of the first month.[378]

Additional passages that demonstrate this third type of *echad* include: (Genesis 33:13; Exodus 23:29; Leviticus 23:18; Numbers 7:13-82 [85 times]; Deuteronomy 17:6; Joshua 12:9-24 [32 times]; Judges 9:53; 1 Samuel 26:8; 2 Samuel 12:3; 1 Kings 2:16; 11:13; 2 Kings 8:26; 2 Chronicles 18:7). An interesting factor is that even when *echad* is used as an *individual one*, its context often is dealing with two or more of something.

The term is usually referring to a singular object, but it is also used in the context of many. In the three passages of Numbers 7:11-82 (85 times), 29:1-38 (24 times), and Joshua 12:9-24 (32 times), the *cardinal one* is mentioned a total of 141 times in an individual sense.

With these three factors in mind, how do scholars interpret *echad* in Deuteronomy 6:4? It seems that the oneness of God is not the question; instead, the discussion surrounds the compound unity and plurality of God.

Comments by Christian Authors on *Echad*

This section is divided into two parts: those who do not see and those who do see the plurality (or tri-unity) of God in Hebrew Scriptures, in particular, in Deuteronomy 6:4. Christian authors are divided over the interpretation of the term *echad*, except they agree that Moses is affirming the oneness, uniqueness, and the unity of God. Only with a passing notice do they say that *echad* may mean a compound one of unity. Herbert Wolf states that *echad* is singular, but the usage of the word *echad* in the *Shema* allows for the New Testament teaching of the Trinity. The doctrine of the Trinity is foreshadowed in the Hebrew Scriptures, but this verse concentrates on the fact that God is one and that Israel owes its exclusive loyalty to

---

[377] Herbert Wolf as a contributor to Harris, Archer, and Waltke, *Theological Wordbook of the Old Testament,* 1:30.
[378] VanGemeren, ed., *Dictionary of Old Testament Theology and Exegesis,* 1:349.

Him (Deuteronomy 5:9; 6:5).[379] Wolf merely speaks of compound unity, along with other possible usages of the word.

Echad Not Seen as Compound Unity

Lohfink and Bergman basically say that Deuteronomy 6:4 is to be regarded as a reiteration of the love motif in Deuteronomy 5:10 which states, *but showing kindness to the thousandth generation of those who love Me and keep My commandments:*

> The demand for love is itself one of the many formulations of the fundamental demand made on Israel to worship *Yahweh* alone and not any of the other gods.[380]

These two scholars continue by saying that Deuteronomy 6:4 can be interpreted as two nominative sentences in sequence. This means that "*Yahweh our God*," is taken and pressed to mean that God, though plural, is to be taken as singular, and the second half of the passage, "*Yahweh is one*" is used to express this God as being one. They also mention that it could be taken as one nominative sentence, with three different possibilities, as to subject and predicate:

> That Deuteronomy 6:4 contains a "mono-Yahwistic" statement: a statement made in opposition to dividing *Yahweh* into many local individual *Yahwehs*.[381]

Lohfink and Bergman do not even discuss the possibility of a compound unity. They emphasize only the oneness, uniqueness, and unity of God.

Philip Jenson refers to five usages of *echad* in the Hebrew text. He claims that the *Shema* is not intended to do three things as referenced in the statement below, but that it does affirm monotheism. However, no hint is even given to the placement of the *Shema* into the category of a compound unity in his summary statement:

> The correlation between the two halves of the sentence and the following verses suggests that this is not so much an abstract monotheism as a claim to Israel's total obedience and the exclusion of any other (cf. 5:7). The immediate context does not suggest that it

---

[379] Herbert Wolf as a contributor to Harris, Archer, and Waltke, *Theological Wordbook of the Old Testament*, 1:30.
[380] Botterweck, Ringgren and Fabry. *Theological Dictionary of the Old Testament*, 1:196.
[381] Botterweck, Ringgren and Fabry. *Theological Dictionary of the Old Testament*, 1:197.

is directed against polytheism or different ideas of *Yahweh* found in local cults. Nor is this idea used to support the Deuteronomy program of the centralization of worship. However, in the broader context of Deuteronomy and the OT [Old Testament] it can imply unity, uniqueness, and monotheism.[382]

Sauer, in *Theological Lexicon of the Old Testament*, says that Deuteronomy 6:4 may refer to God as a *cardinal one*. He gives two possible translations to the last phrase: "*is one Yahweh*" or "*Yahweh is one* [alone]." His summary statement says that this passage "most clearly expresses *Yahweh's* unity and exclusivity" and that the statement "is embedded in the commandment to love this unique LORD."[383]

While the authors have helpful information, they do not interact with the relationship between *Yahweh* and *Elohim* or *echad* when used of *Yahweh* and *Elohim*. They look at *echad* within the larger context of the Hebrew Scriptures to determine its possible usage in Deuteronomy 6:4. They all affirm the unity, oneness, and uniqueness of God. However, in the opinion of this author; they do not even give *echad* a look as to the possibility of the plurality of God within their interpretations.

Other authors say little, either pro or con. Enns, as an example, simply states that the essence of God is linked to Deuteronomy 6:4 with *echad* being a compound unity or united one. There is no real explanation of how he arrived at that position.[384]

Peter Craigie speaks to the fact that *echad* can be rendered in a number of different ways, stating that one could be a title or name of God. He affirms the uniqueness and unity of God but says nothing about the possibility of *echad* being a *compound one*.[385]

Eugene Merrill does not deal with *echad* as a compound unity. But he makes this interesting observation of the text:

> The Divine Name should be construed as a nominative in each case and the terms "our God" and "one" as parallel predicate nominatives.[386]

---

[382] VanGemeren, ed., *Dictionary of Old Testament Theology and Exegesis,* 1:349-350.

[383] Jenni and Westermann, *Theological Lexicon of the Old Testament,* 1:79.

[384] Enns, *The Moody Handbook of Theology,* 199-200.

[385] P. C. Craigie, *The New International Commentary on the Old Testament: The Book of Deuteronomy;* Grand Rapids: Eerdmans, 1976), 168-169.

[386] Eugene H. Merrill, *The New American Commentary*. (vol. 4. Nashville: Broadman & Holman, 1994), 4:163.

This statement is saying that "LORD," in both cases, is nominative and "our God" and "one" is the predicate. The predicate describes the LORD as (1) *Elohim* and (2) as one. The two words describe, or are reflective of, the nominative. He drops the statement at that point and does not explain what he was trying to establish. This subject and explanation is again discussed at the end of this chapter.

David Hinson does not deal with *echad* as a compound unity. He simply affirms the concept of God being a unity. However, Hinson raises an interesting question:

> But is there any evidence that people of Old Testament times began to share in thoughts which would gradually lead to the New Testament doctrine of the Trinity? Did God provide them with experiences which would prepare the way for belief in the Trinity? Were they, without full realization, experiencing God the Trinity?[387]

Hinson follows up the previous remarks with three sections on wisdom, the Word of God, and the Spirit of God, which is helpful information. But it was also very disappointing because he does not deal with *Elohim, El, Eloah, Yahweh,* and Lord in their relationship to each other. His defining statement is:

> Some readers may ask why God's revelation of Himself in Old Testament times omitted the idea of the Trinity. The answer seems to be that the Jews needed first to grasp the truth about the Unity of God.[388]

On the contrary, the whole point as we move through this book is that the *Tanakh* written by God did not omit the idea of the plurality and tri-unity from the pages of the Hebrew Scriptures.

Reginald Fuller clearly reveals his mockery and unbelief in relationship to the Scriptures. However, he does make one very helpful statement concerning Judaism moving toward recognizing distinction within the Godhead:

> But already the Judaic tradition was moving to the direction of recognizing distinctions within the activity of God. These activities included creation, revelation/redemption, and indwelling presence. It was also moving in the direction of distinctions within the being of God, distinctions corresponding to these activities, ascribing them to the Wisdom of Word (logos) and the Spirit of God. Judaism did not

---

[387] Hinson, *Theology of the Old Testament*, 50.
[388] Hinson, *Theology of the Old Testament*, 49.

go very far in this direction, but the direction was certainly established. The Christian community was impelled to move much further, though still in the same direction. Thus it eventually developed the doctrine of the Trinity. This development was not a deviation from the Hebrew Scriptures but a continuation of a process already begun. On the other hand, those who remained under the first covenant backtracked from this line of development.[389]

Fuller's comments on Judaic tradition moving in the direction of recognizing distinctions within the activity of God would be an extremely interesting subject to follow through. What did Fuller see in his research that prompted his remarks? That will have to be a future study. The first-century believers in Messiah did clearly see the distinctions in the Godhead.

Marvin Wilson gives some valuable information on the *Shema* and its background from the Intertestament period and during the life and times of *Yeshua*. Wilson is strong on the unity of God but not on the compound unity. His defining statement is:

> In the Old Testament *echad* usually refers to a single unit, such as a person. Certain interpreters have insisted, however, that *echad* may also be used to designate a collective unit (Genesis 1:5; 2:24; Numbers 13:23), a diversity with unity. Thus some Christian scholars have found room for trinitarian monotheism in the *echad* of Deuteronomy 6:4. So interpreted, God is seen as a complex unity, not simply as numerically one. It must be remembered, however, that the main focus of the *Shema* in its original setting – ancient Near Eastern polytheism – is clearly upon the fact that there is one God.[390]

It is true that the original setting was clearly to promote monotheism, but to say that it rules out the possibility of a compound or complex unity is unwarranted.

Although Paul House states that *Yahweh* is unique and possesses a unified character, he makes no mention of God being a compound one.[391]

---

[389] Reginald H. Fuller, "The *Vestigia Trinitatis* in the Old Testament," in *The Quest for Context and Meaning* (ed. Craig A. Evans and Shemaryahu Talmon (Leiden, Netherlands: Brill, 1997), 507.
[390] Marvin R. Wilson, *Our Father Abraham* (Grand Rapids: Eerdmans, 1989), 125.
[391] House, *Old Testament Theology*, 178.

Ernest Wright, in the *Interpreter's Bible*, holds the *Shema* to be a statement of "Israel's exclusive attention, affection, and worship and is not diffused, but single."[392] He affirms the unity and oneness of God.

The *Shema* is of great importance, not just for the Jewish people and the whole discussion of the oneness and unity of God, but also for Christians discussing the theological impact of this verse, *Hear, O Israel! The LORD is our God, the LORD alone*. It is surprising that many Christian scholars do not generally acknowledge as a legitimate argument that *echad* is a compound or complex unity of God. Apparently these scholars deem the idea that the term *echad* may reflect the truth of God being a compound or complex unity to be unimportant, based on their concept of how *Elohim* and the tri-unity of God is treated, in general, by many Christian scholars.

Echad Seen as Compound Unity

Some authors do acknowledge that the *Shema* presents God simultaneously as both "one" and a compound unity. A select group of scholars openly acknowledge the reference to God's compound unity in the usage of *echad* and even state it emphatically, but it is often without support. Gerald Root, in his thesis on Deuteronomy 6:4, makes several statements that only deal with the unity of God.

> The answer is this: the verse emphasizes the unity of God rather than the Trinity, but it does not deny God's Triunity. The verse does not concern itself with the question and neither affirms nor denies the Trinity.[393]

> If God is One, in what sense is He One? He is one (אֶחָד) God but three Persons. The normal usage of this word allows such an interpretation.[394]

In referring to Genesis 2:24; 11:6; and Exodus 24:3, which all deal with *echad* as being a compound unity, he says:

> It is evident that that word cannot be restricted to the sense of only or alone.[395]

---

[392] George Arthur Buttrick, *The Interpreter's Bible*. (Nashville: Abingdon, 1953), 2:372-373.
[393] Root, "A Critical Investigation of Deuteronomy 6:4," 38.
[394] Root, "A Critical Investigation of Deuteronomy 6:4," 38.
[395] Root, "A Critical Investigation of Deuteronomy 6:4," 39.

Root is not avoiding the compound unity of God, but he does not come out strongly for it, even though he goes much further than the previous texts cited above. Here is his statement of summary for his position:

> It was God's choice of the word to lead Israel away from idolatry and emphasize His unity, and yet elastic enough to permit a far greater revelation of Himself at a later time. Nor could the argument be used that this word has not as of this time obtained this particular meaning, for it was used long before and after God's revelation in Deuteronomy 6:4.[396]

Root presents the oneness of God very strongly and the compound unity of God in an open, meaningful manner, but without commitment.

When speaking of *echad*, Thomas A. Thomas strongly presents not just the unity of God, but the compound unity of God. He points out that there are two ways to look at *echad*:

> There are at least two senses in which the word one can be used; namely, first of all, in the sense of a compound unity, or, in the second place, in the sense of a single unit; that is, either more than one object composing a whole, or the whole being made up of only a single object. The question, then, is, in which of these two senses is the word אֶחָד to be taken?[397]

He discusses Genesis 2:24, Numbers 13:23, and Judges 20:1 as examples to support a compound unity. His defining statement is:

> It is clearly the term used to express compound unity. Consequently, then, it is quite possible that when Moses declares in Deuteronomy 6:4 "Hear, O Israel: the Lord our God is one (אֶחָד) Lord" he is using the term in this sense. God is one, it is true, but why not in the sense that a man and his wife are one, and the cluster of grapes is one, or as the whole congregation of Israel is one? There is no internal reason why it could not be so used.[398]

Lewis Sperry Chafer clearly raises the two possible views of *echad*. First, he states that God is One and there is no other. Secondly, he cites Genesis 1:5 and 2:24

---

[396] Root, "A Critical Investigation of Deuteronomy 6:4," 40.
[397] Thomas A. Thomas, "The Trinity in the Old Testament" (Th. M. thesis., Dallas Theological Seminary, 1952), 4-5.
[398] Thomas, "The Trinity in the Old Testament," 7.

as showing the possibility that *echad* is a compound unity.[399] Chafer simply raises the issue and then drops it, without further explanation.

Jim Nixon points out that Deuteronomy 6:4 allows for the plurality of God. He further says that it does not teach the tri-unity of God but the plurality of God.[400] His position is that the *Shema* teaches exclusive monotheism, the total denial of any other view, as well as denial of God being plural, regarding Deuteronomy 6:4.[401] Nixon has picked up the rabbinic response of Judaism. Now Deuteronomy 6:4 does teach monotheism but not exclusive monotheism. He has not researched the Hebrew word *echad* used 382 times by Moses and he never referenced *echad* as an absolute monotheism. If only scholars would do biblical research instead of copying the teachings of the sages like Maimonides. Maimonides completely understood what *echad* meant, which is why he changed it to *yachid* which is an absolute one. He was attempting to get away from the biblical teaching in the Hebrew Scriptures of the oneness of God in a plural context in order to distance Judaism from the concept of Yeshua as God's deliverer.

Henry Heydt, former president of Lancaster School of the Bible, states very clearly his position on the *Shema* by affirming the oneness and compound oneness with *echad* in the following statement:

> The Jew does not understand the Christian doctrine of the Trinity (tri-unity) because he does not understand the teaching of his own Scriptures on unity. There are two kinds of oneness, absolute oneness and compound oneness, and the Hebrew has two words to express these. The word for absolute oneness is *yachid*.[402] (Genesis 22:2, 12, 16)

Messianic Jewish scholars Stan Rosenthal,[403] Lewis Goldberg,[404] Arnold Fruchtenbaum,[405] and Robert Morris[406] show the usage of *echad* in Deuteronomy 6:4 as a compound unity of God in the Hebrew Scriptures. They see *Elohim* as a plurality of God and *echad* as a complex or compound unity of God.

---

[399] Chafer, *Systematic Theology*, 1:266-267.
[400] Jim Nixon, "The Doctrine of the Trinity in the Old Testament" (Th. M. thesis., Dallas Theological Seminary, 1974), 11-12.
[401] Nixon, "The Doctrine of the Trinity in the Old Testament," 22-23.
[402] Henry Heydt, *Studies in Jewish Evangelism* (New York: American Board to the Jews, 1951), 124.
[403] Rosenthal, *One God or Three?* 17-26.
[404] Goldberg, *Our Jewish Friends*, 80-83.
[405] Fruchtenbaum, *Messianic Christology*, 108.
[406] Robert Morris, *Anti-Missionary Arguments: The Trinity*, 14-16.

CHAPTER 5: SHEMA

The next three authors (Brown, Cooper, and Morey) were the only three men who dealt with the issue of the plurality of God in a concrete, detailed manner. The others said either nothing, merely eluded to a compound unity, or made strong statements in its favor. Yet even those who made strong statements of belief did not give a comprehensive study of *echad*.

In dealing with two Jewish objections to the tri-unity of God, Michael Brown presented Deuteronomy 6:4 in a detailed apologetic format on the plurality and tri-unity of God in conjunction with *echad*.[407] One example shows some of the interpretative problems that come with absolute oneness, which is the rabbinic approach:

> The rabbis spoke much about the *shekhina*, the Divine Presence, corresponding also to the feminine, motherly aspects of God. They taught that the *Shekhina* went into exile with the Jewish people, suffering with "Her" children in foreign lands. According to this concept, God cannot be "whole" again until His people return from their physical and spiritual wanderings and the Temple is rebuilt. The rabbis based this idea on verses that spoke of God being with His people (corporately or individually) in their trouble, distress, and exile.[408]

This explanation of the Jewish people says that God is divisible and will not be whole again until Israel, as a nation, is regathered from every nation on earth and reestablished in the Land. So much for God being a unity and indivisible! If God is not a complex unity, how can He be one when He is divided?

David L. Cooper presents a strong, detailed and comprehensive case for the tri-unity of God in the Hebrew Scriptures and for *echad* being a compound unity. He begins with his belief in verbal plenary inspiration. Therefore, he deals with the Hebrew text by letting Scripture interpret Scripture, thereby letting God reveal Himself as He chose. In Cooper's book, *What Men Must Believe*, the chapter on "The Unity of the Divine Personalities," gives a biblical argument for the tri-unity of God, as well as the *Shema*, not only proving monotheism but compound unity as well. Cooper illustrates that with the usage of *Elohim*, one of the other words used in Deuteronomy 6:4. Moses knew that *Elohim* was plural, so why didn't he use *El* or

---

[407] Michael L. Brown, *Answering Jewish Objections to Jesus, Vol. 2 of Answering Jewish Objections* (Grand Rapids: Baker Books, 2000), 2:3-37.
[408] Michael L. Brown, *Answering Jewish Objections,* 2:12.

Eloah instead of *Elohenu* (אֱלֹהֵינוּ), "our Gods?" *Elohim* is grammatically incorrect as it is in many places when it is followed by singular verbs.[409]

Robert Morey compares the Unitarian and Trinitarian viewpoints of the Scriptures in relationship to God. He observes that if God is one, a solitary person, then it would be expected that the authors of Scripture would use the Hebrew word יָחִיד (*yachid*). If that were the case, it would be very damaging to the Trinitarian view. However, what is found is that the word for God is never used with יָחִיד.[410] Instead, what is found is that אֶחָד (*echad*) is used in connection with God. Morey states that אֶחָד is the only available Hebrew word they could use to express the idea of a compound or complex *one*.[411] So, once again, if the authors of Scripture believed God was a plurality or tri-unity, then one would expect to find the usage of אֶחָד to express a multi-Personal God over against a God who was *one alone*.

If, in the *Shema*, Moses was teaching monotheism alone, as Judaism states, then why didn't Moses do one of the following in his presentation of God? Why didn't he use correct grammar by using the correct singular forms for God by using *Yahweh* our *El* or *Eloah*? Was the use of *Elohim* a mistake, or was Moses guided by the *Ruach haKodesh* (Holy Spirit) as he penned the *Shema*? Finally, why did Moses choose to use a plural concept for *one* rather than a singular concept of God?

Yachid - יָחִיד

The differences between *echad* and *yachid* are significant in the *Tanakh*. *Echad* minimally means unity, a unity involving a plurality; whereas, the meaning of *yachid* is to express absolute oneness, *one* standing by itself, alone. *Yachid* suits that purpose very well. *Yachid* יָחִיד appears 12 times in the Law, Prophets, and Writings of the Hebrew text. It is used five times in reference to an only son (Zechariah 12:10), three times in reference to a child (Judges 11:34), twice in reference to being "lonely" (Psalm 68:6), and twice in reference to *your precious life* (Psalm 22:20).[412] Paul Gilchrist says that this word "basically refers to an only child," and its basic meaning is "only begotten son, beloved, with secondary meanings of isolated and lonely."[413] In reference to life, Brown, Driver, and Briggs say:

---

[409] David L. Cooper, *What Men Must Believe*, 113.
[410] Morey, *The Trinity: Evidence and Issues*, 88.
[411] Morey, *The Trinity: Evidence and Issues*, 89.
[412] Kohlenberger and James A. Swanson, *The Hebrew English Concordance to the Old Testament*, 697.
[413] Harris, Archer, and Waltke, *Theological Wordbook of the Old Testament*, 372.

CHAPTER 5: SHEMA

> My only one, for my life, as the one unique and priceless possession which cannot be replaced.[414]

The word *yachid* comes into play because of Moses Maimonides (1135-1204 C.E.), also known as Ramban. He was a philosopher, a Torah and *Talmud* scholar who wrote many commentaries as well as practiced medicine. One of the things that Maimonides wrote was the 13 principles of the Jewish faith.[415] The second principle is as follows:

> I believe with perfect faith that God is one. There is no unity that is in any way like His. He alone is our God – He was, He is, and He will be.[416]

As Maimonides (Ramban) wrote the second principle of faith, he substituted *yachid* for *echad* in his translation of Deuteronomy 6:4 of the Hebrew text. He clearly recognized that *yachid* contradicted the Christians use of *echad* that could possibly be used to prove the tri-unity of God.

A Jewish believer in Israel reflects on Ramban's thoughts and why he replaced *echad* with *yachid*:

> For Ramban, the term *echad* allowed for elements of personal complexity within the Godhead which he had excluded *a priori* for philosophical reasons. As used in the *Tanakh*, *echad* is the word of choice to express the unification of two or more elements to form one entity. Whether it is "the evening and the morning" combining to form "one day" (Genesis 1:5), male and female becoming "one flesh" (Genesis 2:24), or Ezekiel's two sticks becoming "one stick" in his hand (37:17), a compound unity is the result.
>
> Thus, by describing the Lord as *echad*, the *Shema* does not exclude complexity within the essential divine unity. As Ramban understood, the term falls far short of asserting an absolute philosophical unity.[417]

It is also important to note the comment by Robinson "that his (Maimonides') attempts to unite Aristotle and Torah had a profound influence on his Christian contemporaries."[418] Did men like Maimonides and Rashi (1040–

---

[414] Brown, Driver, and Briggs, *A Hebrew and English Lexicon of the Old Testament*, 402.
[415] Robinson, *Essential Judaism*, 415-421.
[416] Robinson, *Essential Judaism*, 416.
[417] Hendren, "The Divine Unity and the Deity of the Messiah," 38.
[418] Robinson, *Essential Judaism*, 420.

THE TRI-UNITY OF GOD IS JEWISH

1105 C.E.)[419] have an impact on Christianity by obscuring the full significance of *Elohim* and *echad*? It is known that Rashi did teach a modified interpretation of the Suffering Servant and His relationship to the Jewish understanding of Isaiah 53. His teaching on Israel being the servant of the LORD is today taught by every rabbi in every synagogue to purposely deflect the reader away from understanding the biblical intent of Isaiah 53 regarding the Messiah. Today the Jewish position on Deuteronomy 6:4 is that God is *yachid*, an absolute one. If Moses was teaching complete, absolute monotheism, then Deuteronomy 6:4 should have the following reading: (1) *Yahweh* our *Eloah* or *El* (God), *Yahweh* is *yachid* (absolute one). Instead, he taught (2) *Yahweh* our *Elohenu* (our Gods), *Yahweh* is *echad* (a compound unity).

The first statement reflects the meaning taught by Maimonides. The second statement reflects the meaning as taught by Moses. There is quite a difference. Moses was guided by the *Ruach haKodesh* (Holy Spirit) in what he wrote; Maimonides was guided by man's logic.

The consequential differences between *echad* and *yachid* are made quite clear by scholars like Chafer,[420] Rosenthal,[421] Heydt,[422] Goldberg,[423] Brown,[424] Fruchtenbaum,[425] Cooper,[426] Benach,[427] and Criswell.[428] As the result of studying the Hebrew language and making *aliyah* to Israel, Moshe Golden shared the invaluable insight that in Modern Hebrew, *yachid* is a compound *one* and *echad* is an absolute *one*, which is just the opposite of the Hebrew Scriptures. So the true meaning of Scripture is once again obscured from the modern Jewish reader.

---

[419] **Rashi** (Rabbi Shelomo Yitzkhaki): was an extraordinary Torah and Talmudic scholar. He was fluent in many languages, an accomplished poet, and a skilled philologist. He wrote many commentaries on the Torah. Today his commentaries are part of the Talmud itself.
[420] Chafer, *Systematic Theology*, 1:267.
[421] Rosenthal, *One God or Three?* 21.
[422] Heydt, *Studies in Jewish Evangelism*, 125.
[423] Goldberg, *Our Jewish Friends*, 81-82.
[424] Michael L. Brown, *Answering Jewish Objections*, 2:4.
[425] Arnold A. Fruchtenbaum, *The Trinity – Manuscript #50*, (Tustin, Cal: Ariel Ministries, 1983), 11-12.
[426] David L. Cooper, *The God of Israel*, 44-57.
[427] Henry Benach, *Go To Learn* (Chattanooga: International Board of Jewish Missions, 1997), 20-22, 48-50.
[428] W. A. Criswell, *The Criswell Study Bible* (Nashville: Nelson, 1979), 233.

CHAPTER 5: SHEMA

Author's Position on *Echad*

A careful analysis of *echad* in the Hebrew Scriptures clarifies that the term signifies unity in the context of plurality. The context of Deuteronomy and the Torah, as a whole, is to present God as *one*. Yet sprinkled throughout the text of the Torah and the *Tanakh*, monotheism is conceptualized as a unity of Persons equal in nature and essence but with differing activities. Interwoven throughout the *Tanakh* are clear instances with abundant evidence of the plurality of God. Abundant evidence of that plurality is found in repeated instances of the plural word *Elohim*, as well as theophanies, and the appearances of the Messenger (Angel) of *Yahweh* and the *Shechinah* of God. Included are personal pronouns and plural descriptions that God uses of Himself, which are discussed in the next chapter.

Walter Zimmerli confirms the use of plural unity of the verb *echad* in Ezekiel 21[16)] by stating that the only way this word makes any sense in the context of Ezekiel 21:21 is to see it as a plural compound of unity.[429] He simply says that it "gives no satisfactory sense unless understood from אֶחָד (*echad*)."[430] It was noted earlier in this chapter that one possible way of interpreting *Shema* is to see *Yahweh* in Deuteronomy 6:4 as a nominative, while *Elohim* and *echad* are predicates of the nominative or descriptive of the nominative.[431] If *Elohim* is a plural description of God, then it makes complete sense that *echad*, being a compound unity, also expresses a plurality. The text of Deuteronomy 6:4 would look like this:

Singular (*Yahweh*) our plurality (*Elohim*), Plural

Singular (*Yahweh*) is a compound one (*echad*), Plural

The term *Elohim* reflects back to *Yahweh*, and *echad* reflects back to *Yahweh*. Thus, the God of Israel is a compound unity. This author believes that the *echad* of the *Shema* is a compound unity, but recognizes that there is far stronger evidence to show that *echad* is minimally a plurality. (See appendix two.) Because *Elohim* is never presented as a dual personality, yet still as a plurality, He has to be more than two. By examining the Scriptures clearly, we learn that God expressed Himself in three Persons.

In the Hebrew Scriptures the Father speaks to the Son (Psalm 2:7), and the Son speaks to the Father (Zechariah 1:12).[432] We also recognize occasions when the

---

[429] There is a discrepancy with some translations between finding it in verse 16 or verse 21.
[430] Walter Zimmerli, *Ezekiel 1* (Philadelphia: Fortress Press, 1979), 430.
[431] Merrill, *The New American Commentary*, 4:162-163.
[432] Geisler, *Systematic Theology*, 2:288-289.

Holy Spirit acts. For example, the Holy Spirit came upon and filled Bezaleel (Exodus 35:30-31), the spirit of wisdom filled Joshua (Deuteronomy 34:9), the spirit came upon Saul (1 Samuel 11:6) and left him (1 Samuel 16:14), as well as came upon David when he was anointed by Samuel (1 Samuel 16:13). The Hebrew Scriptures and the New Testament, together or separately, never present more than three Persons. Although the tri-unity is not explicitly presented in the Hebrew Scriptures, yet it is present.[433] Otherwise, Jesus was making false claims of His divinity to the Jewish nation to whom He was presenting Himself as the Messiah and God.

Lewis Goldberg sums up this issue of the plurality of God in relation to Deuteronomy 6:4 by saying:

> We need to be scriptural even though we may never completely understand the scriptural concept. We never completely understand the scriptural concept. We see from the wording of Deuteronomy 6:4 that it was not Moses' intent to avoid a composite description of God. Rather, he was led to express God's nature in this way to allow for the future unfolding of the truth it contains.[434]

The problem with interpreting the *Shema* is that scholars attempt to understand the word *echad* in the context of Deuteronomy. Normally, when studying the immediate context has not been fruitful, the larger context is sought; but this has not been the usual response so far. I have not observed many scholars studying the word *echad* to see how the word was used by Moses all 382 times in the Torah (the books of Moses) and beyond. What becomes very clear in studying the use of the word by Moses and other Bible authors is a profound revelation. *Echad* is used consistently in a plural context not only in the writings of Moses but throughout the *Tanakh* as a whole. (See appendix two.)

---

[433] Geisler, *Systematic Theology*, 2:289-290.
[434] Goldberg, *Our Jewish Friends*, 82.

CHAPTER 6:
PLURAL DESCRIPTIONS

This chapter focuses on the personal pronouns attributed to God, and other plural descriptions of God, a significant area of debate and controversy between Christian and Jewish scholars. The initial discussion involves four passages where God refers to Himself by using plural pronouns (Genesis 1:26, 3:22, 11:7; Isaiah 6:8).

Pronouns

In the Hebrew text, the plural term for God is *Elohim*. From Genesis 1 through Genesis 2:3, *Elohim* is the only one identified and the only one doing the action of creating. God (*Elohim*) chose to reveal Himself by not predominantly using the singular forms for God (*El, Elah, Eloah*) which were available for His use. Those who subscribe to verbal plenary inspiration must also affirm the literal meaning of the words in the text. The text (Genesis 1 – Genesis 2:3) makes use of a plural descriptive term referring to God as a plural compound-complex unity. Therefore, at least two persons were involved in the creation of the world. This fact, if accepted, makes null and void such counter-arguments as "plural of majesty," or "plural of deliberation," remnants of polytheism, "heavenly court," and "angels" as alternate explanations of the term *echad* in this context. It is the view of this author that these counter arguments that Jewish and Christian theologians force unnaturally upon the text do an injustice to God and how He chose to reveal Himself. Jamieson, Fausset, and Brown make clear that all such counter-arguments are "contrary to the whole tenor of Scripture."[435] Understanding the plurality of reference in the following passages from Genesis and Isaiah requires a clear grasp of the significance of the seven plural Hebrew pronouns found in these passages.

All the verbs are first person common plural forms in the Qal Imperfect tense. The suffixes attached to the prepositions are also first person common plural forms. They indicate a plurality of persons acting and making decisions.

---

[435] Robert A. Jamieson, A. R. Fausset, and David Brown, *A Commentary: Critical, Experimental and Practical on the Old and New Testaments* (6 vols. Grand Rapids: Eerdmans, 1945), 1:8.

THE TRI-UNITY OF GOD IS JEWISH

Genesis 1:26 נַעֲשֶׂה אָדָם בְּצַלְמֵנוּ כִּדְמוּתֵנוּ

Let Us make man – Verb Qal Impf 1 c p

In image of Us – Prep ncms const suffix 1 c p

In likeness of Us – Prep ncfs const suffix 1 c p

Genesis 3:22 כְּאַחַד מִמֶּנּוּ

Like one of

From Us – Prep + 1 c p suffix

Genesis 11:7 נֵרְדָה וְנָבְלָה

Let Us go down – Verb Qal Impf 1 c p

And let Us confuse – Verb Qal Impf 1 c p

Isaiah 6:8 יֵלֶךְ־לָנוּ

He will go – for Us - Prep + 1 c p suffix[436]

To illustrate, in 1:26 the verb *make* is an imperfect first person common plural with the pronoun *us* which is also a first person common plural. In this passage the person speaking is plural and the verb of action is in agreement. From this point on, *us* and *our,* the English equivalents to the Hebrew plural pronouns, will be used.

Genesis 1:26

And God said, Let Us make man in Our image, after Our likeness. They shall rule the fish of the sea, the birds of the sky, the cattle, the whole earth, and all the creeping things that creep on the earth.

In this verse, *Elohim* makes a clear statement of intent: *Let Us make man.* This is a unique statement in two ways. First, throughout this chapter, *Elohim* said,

---

[436] Taken from Gramcord software and Owens, *Analytical Key to the Old Testament* (Grand Rapids: Baker Book House, 1989), 5, 13, 41; Kohlenberger, *The Interlinear NIV Hebrew-English Old Testament,* 1:3, 8, 24, 4:13.

CHAPTER 6: PLURAL DESCRIPTIONS

Let there be (verses 3, 6, 9, 14, 20). Then in verse 26, with the creation of mankind, He says, *Let Us make man*. Hamilton relates these two phrases this way:

> The shift from the consistent use of the verb in the jussive (e.g., "Let there be") to a cohortative ("Let us make") is enough to prepare the reader for something momentous on this sixth day.[437]

There is a significant difference when the verb on the other days of creation is, *Let there be;* but on the sixth day, the verb *make* is grammatically plural.[438] Indeed, *Elohim* is not going to just create man. He is going to create man uniquely by doing and saying, *Let Us make man in Our image, after Our likeness*. *Elohim* used the personal, plural pronoun *Us*, which obviously references two or more persons. The pronoun *Us* describes *Elohim* when about to create man, in *Our image* and *Our likeness*.

According to Owens, the two Hebrew words בְּצַלְמֵנוּ – כִּדְמוּתֵנוּ translated *in Our image – in Our likeness*, have plural suffixes.[439] Miller states that the words *image* (*selem*) and *likeness* (*demut*) are in the singular.[440] Clearly, the uniqueness of the plural personal pronouns in Genesis 1:26 draws attention to *Elohim*'s choice of specific words to indicate specific actions. For example, in Genesis 1:1, it is *Elohim* who creates. Because the term *Elohim* is plural, it declares God as plural. At the same time, the usage of the singular verb *created* shows *Elohim*'s unity. In verse 26, the pronoun *Our* is tied to two singular words *image* and *likeness* showing the one speaking as being plural while at the same time confirming His unity. The above observation is important because there is no justification for forcing onto the text interpretations like consulting with a "heavenly court" or "angels," which Loewen and Towner do in their articles in relation to Genesis 1:26:

> The example that is sometimes given, "let us make man in our image," probably does not refer to a plurality of Gods, but rather to some kind of "heavenly council" with which God is represented as being in consultation.[441]

We are left, then, with the heavenly council as the only likely way of explaining this use of the plural in verse 1:26. Even in the latest hand

---

[437] Victor P. Hamilton, *The New International Commentary on the Old Testament: The Book of Genesis,* Chapters 1-17 (Grand Rapids: Eerdmans, 1990), 134.
[438] Mathews, *The New American Commentary*, 1a:161.
[439] Owens, *Analytical Key to the Old Testament*, 1:5.
[440] Paul A. Miller, *Gramcord, www.Gramcord.org*.
[441] Jacob A. Loewen, "The Names of God in the Old Testament," *The Bible Translator* 35, no. 2 (1984): 201- 207.

to contribute to the final form of the Pentateuch – the Priestly writer – we come smack up against the feeble remnants of polytheism. God is speaking for the entire divine court.[442]

One thing becomes very clear. Mankind was not created in the image of angels. *Elohim* is omnipotent, omnipresent, and omniscient. He does not need to consult angels. The *Our* is not *Elohim* speaking to angels but *Elohim* speaking to equal partners in the Godhead.[443] Clearly, there is a consultation with a divine council, but that divine council is the tri-unity of God, which at this point is only reflective of God's plurality. Mathews makes a good observation that the first hearers did not understand tri-unity but did understand plurality:

> The first audience could not have understood it in the sense of a trinitarian reference. Although the Christian Trinity cannot be derived solely from the use of the plural, a plurality within the unity of the Godhead may be derived from the passage.[444]

Mathews' position on the plurality of God is visible in his comments on Genesis 1, but the tri-unity is not visible to him there. However, he leaves the door open for the plurality of God for the progression of revelation to the tri-unity of God.

While Morris does not see Genesis 1 showing the tri-unity of God, there are other passages in the Hebrew Scriptures, such as Psalm 2:7, 45:7, 110:1, and Isaiah 48:16, that record members of the Godhead speaking to each other.[445] Cassuto also gives three valued points on why *Elohim* has no reason to consult angels. He says:

> Against this interpretation it can be contended: (1) that it conflicts with the central thought of the section that God alone created the entire world; (2) that the expression 'Let us make' is not one of consultation; (3) that if the intention was to tell us that God took counsel, the Bible would have explicitly stated whom He consulted, as we are told in the other passages that are usually cited in support of this theory (1 Kings 22:19; Isaiah 6:2-8; Job 1 and 2).[446]

Cassuto's three points make it evident that *Elohim* did not consult anyone besides Himself. However, Cassuto is not consistent with the Genesis 1:26 text because he

---

[442] Towner, *Westminster Bible Companion: Genesis*, 25.
[443] Henry M. Morris, *The Genesis Record* (Grand Rapids, MI: Baker, 1976), 72.
[444] Mathews, *The New American Commentary,* 163.
[445] Henry Morris, *The Genesis Record,* 72.
[446] U. Cassuto, *A Commentary on the Book of Genesis: Part One* (Jerusalem: Magnes Press, 1961), 54.

improperly applies "plural of exhortation." For example, when a person exhorts himself to do a given task, he uses the plural: "Let us go!" "Let us rise up!" "Let us sit!" and the like.[447] Again, the explanation ignores the plain sense of what *Elohim* said. Leupold dogmatically sees the tri-unity in the Genesis 1 account,[448] but some insist only because he has read tri-unity into the text. For example, Youngblood claims the tri-unity is not revealed in the Genesis 1 account.[449] Morris holds that *Elohim* did consult with Himself, equal partners of the Godhead before time:

> The Lamb had, in the determination of these councils, been slain before the foundation of the world; the names of the redeemed had been written in His book of life before the foundation of the world; and God called those who were to be saved by His grace, before the world began. (1 Peter 1:20; Revelation 17:8; 2 Timothy 1:9)[450]

Kac observes that the plural verb *let us make* and the two nouns with plural suffixes make it obligatory to translate the text as saying: *And Elohim said, Let Us make man in Our images and Our likenesses.* Kac points out that up to verse 26, *Elohim* alone is the Creator; then in verse 26, with the creation of mankind, a double plural appears.[451] There is no need to stretch both the word *Elohim* and other personal pronouns to say something *Elohim* did not intend.

Another aspect of the plurality and unity of *Elohim* is evident in verse 27. Although *Elohim* makes a statement of intent in verse 26, He immediately follows that through with projected action in verse 27. He uses several singular words in verse 27 to express and emphasize His unity in the creation of man. *Elohim* used "created" three times, which is singular in expressing His creation of mankind. This emphasizes His oneness and unity by stating that *in His* [singular] *image, the image of God* [*Elohim*] *He created him* [man]." While verse 26 clearly pinpoints the plurality of *Elohim*, the singularity of *Elohim* in verse 27 further demonstrates that *Elohim* is a unity of one and a plurality. Mathews confirms that view:

> Our passage describes the result of God's creative act by both plural and singular pronoun "his image" in v. 27. Here the unity and plurality of God are in view. The plural indicates an intradivine

---

[447] Cassuto, *A Commentary on the Book of Genesis: Part One*, 54.
[448] H. C. Leupold, *Exposition of Genesis* (Grand Rapids: Baker Book House, 1942), 86.
[449] Ronald Youngblood, *The Genesis Debate* (Nashville: Nelsons, 1986), 123.
[450] Henry Morris, *The Genesis Record*, 73.
[451] Kac, *The Messiahship of Jesus*, 165.

conversation, a plurality in the Godhead, between God and His Spirit.[452]

Taking into account all that has been said, it is not difficult to understand that God chose to reveal Himself as *Elohim*, who is plural. He engaged with the other members of the Godhead to create man in Their image. The other lines of reasoning such as "plural of majesty," "plural of deliberation," and "heavenly courts or councils" that Christians and Jewish scholars use to interpret the Hebrew Scripture fall short of the context that God, in His wisdom, gave to reveal Himself to mankind. Youngblood clearly and precisely states what the human finite mind on the issue of the triune God will not grasp and yet is taught:

> Though a mystery, the uniplurality of God's nature is taught consistently throughout Scripture.[453]

Genesis 3:22

In Genesis 3:22 God again uses the personal plural pronoun *Us* in the biblical text. First observe the verse:

> *And the LORD God said, "Now that the man has become like one of Us knowing good and bad, what if he should stretch out his hand and take also from the tree of life and eat, and live forever!"*

In the first half of this verse, the words LORD God (*Yahweh Elohim*), and the phrase *man has become like one of Us*, God used name distinctions to focus attention on His personal name, essence, and plurality. *Yahweh* (singular) and *Elohim* (plural) use the personal plural pronoun *Us* to designate who is doing the talking. It is God, Himself, a singular/plural one. Morris adds some further insight by saying that there is a "heavenly council," so to speak, as was also observed in Genesis 1:26; however, that heavenly council is the inner council of the tri-unity of God:

> Verse 22 gives a brief insight into the inner councils of the triune Godhead as in Genesis 1:26, [sic] such a council was recorded relative to the decision to create man, so now the council decrees his expulsion from the garden and the tree of life. In both passages, the

---

[452] Mathews, *The New American Commentary*, 1a:163.
[453] Youngblood, *The Book of Genesis*, 30.

divine unity is stressed ("And the LORD God said") and also the divine plurality ("Us").[454]

God, in His tri-unity, says that man is like one of *Us*. How did man become like God? It was only in the sense that now man can know good and evil, not as some who indicate that man was upgraded to become like a divine being or angel. Merrill makes the point that in some way man is becoming like God:

> That is, man in some sense has become like God. Surely the divine lament is not that man has become like an angel or some other creature.[455]

Only in one regard did man become like God. After the fall, man knew good and evil.[456] Man is not and cannot be like divine beings or angels. It would be a promotion to be like an angel. Instead, man became degenerate and enslaved to sin. Merrill continues his statement with a contrast. The Creator of the universe does not need the assistance of lesser beings:

> Again, it is hardly conceivable that the Lord is invoking the assistance of the angels or anyone else. It is He alone who creates, commands, and judges His creation. It is He alone who speaks and who does so on occasion as a subject described by grammatically plural terminology.[457]

Merrill is correct. It is inconceivable that God would be comparing man with divine beings like angels. As the great I AM, He does not need the assistance of any creature in judging man that He, Himself, had created to serve Him.

In Genesis 3:22 and 1:26 *Elohim* was showing His plurality, along with His unity. However, in Genesis 3:22, there is one difference. *Yahweh*, which is singular, shows oneness; while *Elohim* is showing plurality in oneness.

One further observation on this passage which continues to show plurality is in these words from Genesis 3:22:

> *And the LORD God said, Now that the man has become like one of Us, knowing good and evil.*

---

[454] Henry Morris, *The Genesis Record,* 131.
[455] Youngblood, *The Genesis Debate,* 122.
[456] David A. Hubbard and Glenn W. Barker, *World Biblical Commentary: Genesis 1-15* (52 vols.; Waco, TX: Word Books, 1987), 85.
[457] Youngblood, *The Genesis Debate,* 122.

In appendix two, a detailed chart is given on the word *echad*, meaning "one," and how it is used in the Torah or the Five Books of Moses. The overwhelming conclusion of the study is that *echad* is used by Moses within a plural context exclusively. In Genesis 3:22, God stated that man has become like *echad*, "one" of *Us*. Here God uses a plural word (*echad*) to represent Himself, along with the plural personal pronoun *Us*. The plurality of God is very strong in Genesis 3:22 in the following three words: *LORD God* (*elohim*, a plural), *one* (*echad*, a plural unity) and *Us* (a plurality). You have both the singular and plural words for God, but in this sentence the plurality is represented in the three terms *Elohim*, *echad* and *Us* rather than the absolute oneness that Judaism presents. If verbal plenary inspiration is believed, then the only conclusion to this passage is that God is revealing Himself as a plurality.

Genesis 11:7

> *Let Us, then, go down and confound their speech there, so that they shall not understand one another's speech.*

In Genesis 11:7, *Yahweh*, not *Elohim*, says, *Let Us go down* to confuse the language of the people. The point in Genesis 1:26 is that *Elohim* says, *Let Us make man*, but in Genesis 3:22 it is *Yahweh Elohim* saying that man has become one of *Us*. In Genesis 1:26 *Elohim* (plural) says *let Us;* whereas, in 3:22 Israel's personal name for God, *Yahweh*, is combined with *Elohim* to indicate that these names for God are interchangeable. The name *Yahweh*, which emphasizes unity and oneness, is combined with *Elohim*, which is a plurality. Observe the progression of the names of God in Genesis 11:7; here God simply uses His personal name, *Yahweh*, when saying, *Let Us go down*. The significant shifts in the nouns from *Elohim* to *Yahweh Elohim* to *Yahweh* are significant because the plural personal pronoun *Us* is used each time to designate the plurality of God. Whether God uses *Elohim*, *Yahweh Elohim*, or *Yahweh*, it points to the same reality, that God is a unity of one, yet plural.

Speiser's argument on "grammatical plural" states that the phrase *Let Us go down* in 11:7 is "grammatically plural; or this may be a plural of majesty."[458] According to Speiser, though emphasizing the fact that this is grammatically plural, he suggests that it is to be interpreted in reality as a singular statement. Speiser also uses the same explanation of the *let Us* in Genesis 1:26. This view raises the question of one's priority and methods of interpretation of Scripture. If the term *let Us* is grammatically plural, what reason is there to change it to mean "singular" other than that *"plurality"* does not fit a certain theological perspective. Although God, by

---

[458] E. A. Speiser, *The Anchor Bible: Genesis* (Garden City, NY: Doubleday, 1964), 75.

inspiration, did not give the names of the tri-unity in the very first chapter of His revelation to mankind, there is no reason to remove, delete, or discount the use of the plural noun and plural pronouns to describe His personhood. Speiser makes this statement to defend his view on the grammatical plural being changed, in his assessment, to a singular meaning:

> For the singulars "my image, my likeness" [sic] Heb. employs here plural possessives, which most translations reproduce. Yet no other divine being has been mentioned; and the very next verse used the singular throughout. The point at issue, therefore [sic] is one of grammar alone, without direct bearing on the meaning.[459]

Thus, Speiser argues that although *Elohim* is a grammatical plural, because He used singular modifiers, the plurality should be ignored.[460] Thus, the singular aspect of grammar would take precedence over the literal interpretation when God chose to use a personal plural pronoun. If that is Speiser's implication, then the word *Elohim* would simply translate as a singular, which is what all translations do. If that argument be the case, God is a very poor communicator, being completely ineffective with language to convey His essence to mankind.

The standard interpretation of the text in Genesis 11:3-4 also shows the inconsistency of scholars. When man uses *let us*, the phrase is considered plural, but when *Yahweh* uses *let Us*, the same phrase is considered singular. The people at Babel said *Let us make bricks* and *let us build for ourselves,* and they used plural personal pronouns. This observation about the people in the land of Shinar is never argued. Yet when *Yahweh* uses *Let Us go down*, all of a sudden scholars, like Speiser, take the same *let Us* and then attempt to say that *Yahweh* is not speaking in a plural. The grammar in verses 3-4 is the same as verse 7. All of the usages of *let us make* or *let us go down* are first person common plural (1 c p), yet Speiser would make the reference to God (verse 7), which he says is a grammatical plural, to be taken as a singular while the references to the people are to be taken literally:

Genesis 11:3 נִלְבְּנָה לְבֵנִים וְנִשְׂרְפָה

    Let us make bricks – Verb Qal Cohortative 1 p
    and **let us** bake – Verb Qal Impf 1 c p

Genesis 11:4 וְנַעֲשֶׂה־לָּנוּ

---

[459] Speiser, *The Anchor Bible: Genesis*, 7.
[460] See chapter two, section under *Elohim*.

THE TRI-UNITY OF GOD IS JEWISH

So **let us** make – Verb Qal Impf 1 c p

For **us** – Prep 1 c p

Genesis 11:7 נֵרְדָה וְנָבְלָה

Let Us go down – Verb Qal Cohortative 1 p

And **let Us** confuse – Verb Qal Cohortative 1 p

Morris so aptly gives his contrast between Nimrod and God. Nimrod's council meets, saying *let us* and God's "council" meets saying *let Us*. God's council is the equal members of the triune God:

> But as Nimrod and his cohorts had held a council of conspiracy and aggression on earth, so God now called a "council," as it were, in heaven, to institute formal action to prevent the accomplishment of Nimrod's plans. Such a divine council is indicated by the plural pronoun in verse 7, "let Us."[461]

Yahweh uses the plural personal pronoun *Us*, as He refers to His divine council of the Godhead, when They went down and confused the language of the people. One other observation deserves attention in Genesis 11:1, 6. As was discussed in chapter four (and appendix two), *echad* in the *Shema* of Deuteronomy 6:4 minimally has to be viewed within a plural context. In verses 1 and 6, *echad* is used not only in a plural context but also in the context of a unity:

> *¹ Everyone on earth had the same [echad] language and the same [echad] words.*
>
> *⁶ And the LORD said, If as one [echad] people with one [echad] language for all, this is how they have begun to act.*

The whole context of this passage is dealing with plurality, whether it is the plurality of man acting together because they have one language so that they can accomplish their act of rebellion against God, or whether it was God, Himself, referring to Himself in plurality. When Scripture is taken literally, as God intended it to be, there is only one conclusion a student of the Scriptures can come to: God who is one is also a plurality.

---

[461] Henry Morris, *The Genesis Record*, 273.

CHAPTER 6: PLURAL DESCRIPTIONS

Isaiah 6:8

Then I heard the voice of my Lord saying, "Whom shall I send? Who will go for Us?" And I said, "Here am I; send me."

In this passage *Adonai* uses two personal pronouns (*I* and *Us*) as He invites Isaiah to his prophetic ministry by saying, *Whom shall I send? Who will go for Us?* First, Isaiah says that he *beheld my Lord [Adonai] seated on a high and lofty throne.* Obviously, *Adonai* in verse 1 is God Almighty. Leading up to this in Isaiah 6:3, the Seraphim who minister before God continuously say, *Holy, Holy, Holy, is the LORD [Yahweh] of hosts.* Then *the House* (heavenly Temple) *kept filling with smoke*, which is a reference to the *Shechinah* of God (6:4) filling the Temple. After that, Isaiah speaks of his sinfulness and says, *My own eyes have beheld the King LORD [Yahweh] of Hosts* (6:5). Then Isaiah heard the voice of *Adonai* saying, *Whom shall I send? Who will go for Us?* (v. 8). *Yahweh* and *Adonai* are used interchangeably with one notable distinction. *Yahweh* is singular; and *Adonai*, when used of God, is plural.[462]

From the time of Isaiah to the time of *Yeshua*, about 700 years, the word *Adonai* (plural) slowly began to replace *Yahweh* (singular) as the name of God; and that is significant. That actually occurred sometime before the end of the Second Temple period. *Yahweh* and *Adonai* are the same Person, and even though the Seraphim are in the context serving *Yahweh*, it is *Adonai* (plural) who asks the question (v. 8) for the triune God in Isaiah's presence. The major names of God are all used with the personal plural pronoun *Us*. This usage plural pronoun *Us* occurs with *Elohim* (Genesis 1:26), *Yahweh Elohim* (Genesis 3:22), *Yahweh* (Genesis 11:7), and *Adonai* (Isaiah 6:8).

Opposition to Plural Pronouns

God is one alone and yet a plurality, for He refers to Himself in the context of plurality by using plural pronouns. God is one; with that no one would disagree. While the Hebrew Scriptures give a plural description, many Jewish and Christian theologians do not see these plural pronouns as referring to the plurality of God. Hasel, in his article, clarifies the extent of the disagreement:

> What does the plural "us" in this enigmatic phrase indicate? Should it be changed to the singular or does it indeed have a plural meaning?

---

[462] Neusner and Green, *Dictionary of Judaism in the Biblical Period*, 389. See chapter two, section under Adonai.

If it has a plural meaning, is its intention to express an address between gods, or between God and heavenly beings, or between God and the earth or earthly elements? Is it a plural of majesty, a plural of deliberation, or a plural of fullness? These suggestions and their supporting arguments will receive critical consideration with an attempt to evaluate their cogency.[463]

Liberal Christian and Jewish scholars agree with one another that the *Us* cannot represent plurality. Their views express how the plural *Us* should be treated. In the following paragraphs, their views will be discussed briefly.

In the Hebrew Scriptures, there are four references to plural personal pronouns where God uses them of Himself to indicate plurality. Of these four references, three of them are found in Genesis: in the creation account (Genesis 1:26), the Fall of man (Genesis 3:22), and the confusing of the language at the tower of Babel (Genesis 11:7). The remaining plural pronoun is found in Isaiah 6:8. These four references to the personal plural pronouns support the plurality of God. Of these four, the greatest controversy swirls around disagreement about the plural pronouns in Genesis 1:26. Often authors refer back to the Genesis 1:26 passage when dealing with the other three passages on plural pronouns. These four passages on the plural pronouns will be examined in two ways: (1) from the perspective of Jewish and Christian scholars who oppose them as references to the plurality of God, and (2) from Christian authors who affirm the plurality of God in these passages.

Four common proposals surface to be discussed. A number of Jewish and Christian scholars seek to discredit the plural personal pronouns by using one or more of the four different lines of argument:

(1) The first line of argument states that when *Elohim* used the words *Us* and *Our*, He was referring to His "heavenly court," which included angels, sons of God, and Seraphim.

(2) This second line of argument states that the usage is one of "plural of majesty."

(3) The third line of reasoning is that the usage points to a "plural of deliberation."

(4) The fourth line of argument is that *Elohim* is referencing the earth, which He had just created, to assist Him.

---

[463] Gerhard F. Hasel, "The Meaning of 'Let Us' in Genesis 1:26," *AUSS* 13 (1975): 58-66.

CHAPTER 6: PLURAL DESCRIPTIONS

The Heavenly Court Argument

The following comments reflect the Jewish interpretation of the plural personal pronoun *Us* in the *Tanakh* presented by Sarna and Slotki. Sarna refers to *Elohim* and the pronoun *Us* by saying:

> This is an Israelite version of the polytheistic assemblies of the pantheon monotheized and depaganized.[464]

Sarna gives his resistance to the plural personal pronouns by saying:

> *Elohim* is a comprehensive term for supernatural beings and is often employed for angels.[465]

Sarna asserts that in Genesis 35:7 angels are seen as divine beings.[466] Another Jewish response is by Slotki, in the Soncino series, whose sources of authority are Rabbis Abraham Ibn Ezra (1092-1167) and David Kimchi (1160-1235).[467] He states that the *Us* (Isaiah 6:8) represents the angelic host. These interpretations are widely held views in Judaism from both modern and ancient scholars as represented by Sarna and Slotki on how the plural personal pronouns that God uses of Himself are interpreted by the Jewish scholars.

Christian authors refer to other Jewish writers to understand their claims, and this is true when it comes to the plural personal pronouns of God. Driver asserts that Jewish thought is that these reflect God and His "heavenly court" whom He is consulting:

> General Jewish interpretation and some Christians (notably Delitzsch) [sic] is that God is represented as including with Himself His celestial court (1 Kings 22:19), and consulting with them before creating the highest of His works, man.[468]

Fruchtenbaum, a Jewish believer, explains another Jewish point of view. He illustrates from Rashi concerning the activity of angels in the creation of mankind that man was not created by angels but was created in the image of angels. According

---

[464] Sarna, *The JPS Torah Commentary on Genesis*, 12.
[465] Sarna, *The JPS Torah Commentary on Genesis*, 25.
[466] Sarna, *The JPS Torah Commentary on Genesis*, 241.
[467] I. W. Slotki, *The Soncino Books of the Bible, Isaiah* (New York: Soncino Press (1983), 30.
[468] S. R. Driver, *Westminster Commentaries, the Book of Genesis*, (London: Methuen & Co, 1911), 14.

to Rashi, God was being polite, or showing good manners and humility, by asking permission of the lower beings, angels, to create man in their image.[469] Merrill also references Rashi in a journal article concerning the *let Us* of Genesis 1:26 in the following quote from Rashi:

> We will make man – Although they did not assist Him in forming him and although this [use of the plural] may give the heretics an occasion to rebel, yet the passage does not refrain from teaching proper conduct and the virtue of humbleness, namely, that the greater should consult, and take permission from the smaller; for had it been written, "I shall make man," we could not, then, have learned that He spoke to His judicial council but to Himself. And as a refutation of the heretics it is written immediately after this verse "And God created the man," and it is not written "and they created."[470]

Rashi's whole statement is an assumption that he makes with absolutely no precedent in the *Tanakh* of *Elohim* showing humbleness by consulting the lesser (angels) before He creates man. Ryle, who also references the Jewish explanation that God was addressing the inhabitants of heaven, adds this statement in connection to Genesis 1:26 by saying:

> [This is the] old Jewish explanation that God is here addressing the inhabitants of heaven. In the thought of the devout Israelite, God was one, but not isolated. He was surrounded by the heavenly host (1 Kings 22:19), attended by the Seraphim (Isaiah 6:1-6), holding His court with "the sons of God (Job 1:6)."[471]

Ryle also points out the same thing just quoted in relation to the Jewish interpretation of Genesis 3:22.[472]

Among Christian scholars, Hamilton replicates the Jewish argument that the pantheon of gods was replaced by the heavenly court concept:

---

[469] Arnold A. Fruchtenbaum, *Genesis* (27 tapes, Tustin, CA: Ariel Ministries, n.d.), tape 1, chapter 1:26.
[470] Eugene H. Merrill, "Rashi, Nicholas De Lyra, and the Christian Exegesis," *WTJ* 38 (1975): 66-79.
[471] Herbert E. Ryle, *Cambridge Bible: the Book of Genesis* (London: Cambridge University, 1914), 19.
[472] Ryle, *Cambridge Bible: the Book of Genesis,* 19.

CHAPTER 6: PLURAL DESCRIPTIONS

In the biblical adaptation of the story the pantheon concept was replaced with the heavenly court concept. Thus, it is not other gods, but to the angelic host, the "sons of God," that God speaks.[473]

Westermann, within a discussion speaking of Genesis 3:22, states that many modern scholars refer to the heavenly court as polytheistic in intent:

> ...whether the phrase "like one of us" means "the higher spiritual beings," **or the heavenly court (H. Gunkel and the majority of recent interpreters)**, or whether God includes the other gods with himself, the phrase being actually polytheistic in intent....[474] [Emphasis mine]

Driver uses ancient Babylonian accounts to support his argument that the biblical account arose out of a pantheon of gods in a pre-Israelite background:

> There is force in these considerations; and probably the ultimate explanation has to be sought in a pre-Israelite stage of the tradition (such as is represented by the Babylonian account; where a polytheistic view of man's origin found expression). This would naturally be replaced in a Heb. recession by the idea of a heavenly council of angels, as in 1 Kings 22; Job 1:38; Daniel 4:14; 7:10.[475]

> It has been regarded as a survival of polytheism, and has been compared with "*Elohim*," a plural word for "God" which some regard as a relic of polytheism.[476]

Some Christian scholars such as Davidson are very clear in their meaning that God's plurality is not represented by pagan polytheism. They argue that God is representing Himself as a true plurality in unity as Isaiah 6:8 and Genesis 1:26 affirm:

> There is no vagueness or obscurity in either of the passages referred to. If God, who speaks in these passages, uses the word "us" of

---

[473] Hamilton, *The New International Commentary on the Old Testament: The Book of Genesis*, Chapters 1-17, 133.
[474] Claus Westermann, *Genesis 1-11, A Continental Commentary* (trans. John J. Scullion: Minneapolis, MN: Fortress Press, 1994), 272-273.
[475] S. R. Driver et al., eds., *The International Critical Commentary: Genesis* (Edinburgh: T & T Clark, 1930), 31.
[476] Ryle, *Cambridge Bible: The Book of Genesis*, 18.

Himself, there is a perfectly clear statement to the effect that the Godhead is a Plurality.[477]

Davidson is open to the idea that *Adonai* did include the plurality of *Elohim*. However, he also opens the door to the angels being included:

> The point, however, is whether the Divine speaker uses the word "us" of Himself, i.e. of the Godhead alone, or whether He does not rather include others, e.g. His heavenly council along with Him. The opinion of most expositors is to the latter effect.[478]

Clearly, Jewish scholars will avoid the plural personal pronouns by referring to polytheism, the pantheon of gods, which were monotheized and depaganized at a later time. Jewish scholars will also assert the argument of *heavenly court* and *angels* being involved in the *Us* passages. Driver suggests that the Genesis 1:26 account refers back to ancient pagan Babylonian accounts of a pantheon of gods. According to this line of argument, the *heavenly host* are one and the same thing with polytheistic relics of gods that have remained in the biblical text. It will also be noted that some authors intertwine the *heavenly court* and *angels* with pagan origins so that the phrase *let Us* becomes a relic of polytheism carried over from paganism[479] rather than a clear presentation of God's plurality.

It is clear, to this author, that when the plain sense of Scripture is used and left to speak for itself, there is no problem understanding these texts. The danger of perverting the text arises whenever a person has a preconceived belief and cannot see the plurality of God. As Creator of the universe, God was always a plurality and is understood in the New Testament as a tri-unity. Scholars, both Jewish and Christian, may be taking liberties with the Scripture in an attempt to understand it, but in reality they are perverting it. It stands to reason that God, in the presentation of His Son to Israel as their Messiah and to mankind as the Savior from sin, would not present a new doctrine of plurality or tri-unity. God would not, in the middle of His redemptive plan for Israel and the world, present the central figure of Scripture without a foundation being laid in the *Tanakh*. While the *Tanakh* minimally presents the plurality of God in only select instances, the concept is planted well before Messiah undertakes His earthly ministry of salvation.

---

[477] A. B. Davidson, *The Theology of the Old Testament* (New York: Scribner's, 1928), 129.
[478] Davidson, *The Theology of the Old Testament*, 129.
[479] G. Herbert Livingston, *The Pentateuch in Its Cultural Environment* (2nd ed. Grand Rapids: Baker Book House, 1987), 140.

CHAPTER 6: PLURAL DESCRIPTIONS

The Plural of Majesty Argument

The second line of argument is the view of "plural of majesty." The "plural of majesty" argument given by both Jewish and Christian scholars contends that God was speaking as a Western monarch, as the Queen of England would speak to her subjects.[480] Rabbi Hertz, editor of the Haftorah, in speaking of Genesis 3:22 refers to the *Us* as a "plural of majesty." This usage supposedly comes as a consequence of the Fall, when man became *as one of the angels;* or by interpreting *Us* as a "plural of majesty."[481] Rabbi Hertz follows the logic to its natural conclusion:

> Man is become as God – omniscient. Man, having through disobedience secured the faculty of unlimited knowledge, there was real danger that his knowledge would outstrip his sense of obedience to Divine Law.[482]

Unfortunately, that interpretation of *Us* making it a "plural of majesty" puts *Elohim* in the same class of beings that are ministering spirits (angels) and to man. The "plural of majesty" is echoed again by Sarna in his commentary on Genesis 11:7.[483] The rabbis say that *Elohim* is speaking like a Western monarch who uses the royal "we."[484] Authors, such as Ryle, Hamilton, Westermann, and Skinner advocate or have cited others who raise the possibility that these arguments of "plural of majesty" or "heavenly court" could be a reference to a pantheon of gods with a polytheistic reference to God. What is notable is that frequently "plural of majesty" and "heavenly court" are linked to a pantheon of gods or a survival of polytheism, as it relates to these four plural personal pronoun texts.

> On the plural, "we will go down," cf. comments on [Genesis] 1:26 and 3:22, one is not to assume as background remnants of polytheistic talk or the idea of the heavenly court (as do many modern exegetes, like G.A. Cooke, F.M. Cross, H. Schmidt).[485]

Westermann points out clearly that these plural personal pronouns in Genesis are not to be understood from a background of polytheism as some modern exegetes have done.

---

[480] Briscoe, *The Communicator's Commentary: Genesis,* 1:34.
[481] Sarna, *The JPS Torah Commentary on Genesis,* 13.
[482] J. H. Hertz, *The Pentateuch and Haftorahs* (London: Soncino Press, 1952), 13.
[483] Sarna, *The JPS Torah Commentary on Genesi*s, 39.
[484] For more information on "plural of majesty" refer back to *Elohim* in chapter two.
[485] Westermann, *Genesis 1-11, A Continental Commentary,* 552.

The Plural of Deliberation Argument

The third line of reasoning is the argument of "plural of deliberation," or God thinking something through within Himself, as if saying, *Let Me or I will make man*. *Plural of deliberation* means that the speaker is conferring or consulting with himself. Reyburn and McG. Fry refer to Isaiah 6:8 as an example of God consulting Himself before acting.[486] Westermann uses grammar to further his argument in pressing for "plural of deliberation:"

> The grammatical construction is a plural of deliberation. In favor of a plural of deliberation in 1:26 is the fact that in Isaiah 6:8 the plural and the singular are used in the same sentence with the same meaning; similarly in 2 Samuel 24:14 where it is a question of one and the same conclusion: "...Let us fall into the hand of the Lord...but let me not fall into the hand of man."...A clear example of this type of deliberation occurs in Genesis 11:7; "Come let us go down...," has shown that this usage perseveres right down to the present day.[487]

But Westermann misses the point of his own examples. When David say "us" he means the nation, but when *Yahweh* (singular) says *let Us go down,* it is the one God who is expressing His plurality. Turner, in his book on Genesis, is in agreement and refers to Westermann that this passage should be treated as a "plural of deliberation."[488]

Ryle points out that in Genesis 11:7, God is either announcing His purpose by using a deliberative first person plural, or that He is addressing the powers of heaven that attend to and minister to Him.[489]

The Haftorah, which references Genesis 1:26, states: "Scripture represents God as deliberating over the making of the human species." The phrase *let Us make man* is a "Hebrew idiomatic way of expressing deliberation as in 11:7; or, it is the 'plural of majesty,' royal commands, being conveyed in the first person plural."[490]

Then Hamilton also states that these plural personal pronouns are *Elohim* deliberating with Himself:

---

[486] William D. Reyburn and Euan McG. Fry, *A Handbook on Genesis* (New York: United Bible Societies, 1997), 50.
[487] Westermann, *Genesis 1-11, A Continental Commentary,* 145.
[488] Laurence A. Turner, *Genesis* (Sheffield, England: Sheffield Academic Press, 2000), 23.
[489] Ryle, *Cambridge Bible, the Book of Genesis,* 148.
[490] Hertz, *The Pentateuch and Haftorahs,* 5.

CHAPTER 6: PLURAL DESCRIPTIONS

This verse is a deliberation. God dialogues with Himself and observes that man has become "like one of Us" in "knowing good and evil."[491]

It is highly improbable that an all-knowing and all-powerful *Yahweh Elohim* would talk with Himself; rather *Elohim* is to be understood minimally as a plurality. Christian scholars seem to be forcing an interpretation on the text that is not there. God is not deliberating with Himself. There is no need to because He is plural yet a unity of one, indivisible.

The fourth line of argument is that *Elohim* is referencing the earth that He had just created. Rabbi Ramban or Nachmainides, a thirteenth-century rabbi, says of Genesis 1:26 that the phrase *let Us make* in *our image* refers to "the aforementioned earth."[492] Payne Smith refers to twelfth-century rabbi Maimonide's view that God took counsel with the earth; for the earth supplied the body of man, and *Elohim* provided the soul of man.[493] This point does not show up as a Christian argument, even though the earth is in the context of Genesis 1. Rabbi Moshe Ben Nachman (1195–1270) gives the following reason for the usage of the earth in the creation of man:

> The correct explanation of *na'aseh* (let us make) [which is in the plural form when it should have been in the singular] is as follows: It has been shown to you that G-d created something from nothing only on the first day, and afterwards He formed and made things from those created elements. Thus when He gave the water the power of bringing forth a living soul, the command concerning them was *Let the water swarm*. The command concerning cattle was Let the earth bring forth. But in the case of man he said, Let us make, that is, I and the aforementioned earth, let us make man, the earth to bring forth the body from its elements as it did with the cattle and beasts, as it is written, and the Eternal G-d formed man of the dust of the ground, and He, blessed be He, to give the spirit from His mouth, the Supreme One, as it is written, And He breathed into his nostrils the breath of life. And He said, In our image, and after our likeness, as man will then be similar to both. In the capacity of his body, he

---

[491] Hamilton, *The New International Commentary on the Old Testament: Genesis* chapters 1-17, 208.
[492] Moshe ben Nachman, *Ramban (Nachmanides), Commentary on the Torah – Genesis* (trans. Charles B. Chavel: New York: Shilo Publishing House, Inc. 1999), 52.
[493] Payne Smith, *The Handy Commentary, Genesis, ed.* Charles John Ellicott (London: Cassell & Company, n.d.), 79.

will be similar to the earth from which he was taken, and in spirit he will be similar to the higher beings, because it [the spirit] is not a body and will not die. In the second verse, He says, In the image of G-d He created them, in order to relate the distinction by which man is distinguished from the rest of created beings.[494]

The only problem with his interpretation is that in verses 3, 6, 9, 14, 20, and 24 there is not a plural personal pronoun in connection to the "Let the" or "Let there" as on the other days of creation. Only in verse 26 with the creation of man is there a plural personal pronoun. Nachmanides uses a logical argument except when he includes the earth as a partner in the creation of man; that is not a rational statement. Material things do not have intelligence to understand or emotion to feel, let alone a will to make a choice. The earth simply is there because God placed it there. The only thing that the rabbis can point to is the statement that, if they do not obey the Law (Deuteronomy 4:26; 30:19; 31:28), God promises to call heaven and earth to witness against them. In conclusion, Isaiah 40:13 is quite clear that God does not have to be informed by any counselor, whether it be the material earth or with created beings.

In summary, arguments are given for both the reality of the plurality of God in the plural personal pronouns in the *Tanakh* and the arguments against these pronouns being understood as plural statements by God. Alan Hauser, who does believe in the tri-unity in the New Testament, claims that both Genesis 1 and the *Tanakh*, as a whole, do not present the plurality of God. Youngsblood quoted Hauser as saying:

> The issue of whether the doctrine of the Trinity is implied in Genesis 1 does not have any substantive impact on the broader issue of the validity of the doctrine.[495]

On the contrary, the plurality of God does have an impact on witnessing to Jewish people. Mankind and Jewish people, according to Romans 1, stand before God in judgment, condemned. However, the Jewish people as a whole were worshipping the one true God, not idols, at the time of Messiah's First Coming; but they still missed their Messiah (God incarnate) because they didn't recognize the plurality of God in the *Tanakh*.

Hauser, again as quoted by Youngblood, makes a strong statement to totally discredit the tri-unity in the *Tanakh*:

---

[494] Nachman, *Commentary on the Torah – Genesis*, 52-53.
[495] Youngblood, *The Genesis Debate*, 110.

CHAPTER 6: PLURAL DESCRIPTIONS

Furthermore, when one looks at the Old Testament it becomes clear that there are no discernible references to the Trinity. Claimed allusions to the Trinity became perceptible by hindsight only after the Church councils had defined the doctrine. Without perspective of the Church councils and the Church Fathers who formulated the creeds, it is inconceivable that we could even speak of a doctrine of the Trinity in the Old Testament. In other words, it would not be possible to state the doctrine even in skeleton form on the basis of passages chosen only from the Old Testament.[496]

God did give ample testimony of His plurality in Genesis 1 of the Torah (the five books of Moses), as well as throughout the rest of the *Tanakh* (the entirety of the Hebrew Scriptures). Every Jewish person who had contact with *Yeshua* in that day was responsible for rejecting or accepting Him as the God/man. The fact is that Israel, as a nation, rejected Him (Matthew 12:22-42) and turned Him over to the Romans for crucifixion. The nation also stands condemned because God did reaffirm His plurality in the *Tanakh*. Contrary to the above quote, the doctrine of the tri-unity does have substantive impact on the broader issue of the doctrine of salvation. If the plurality of God was not given in the *Tanakh*, then *Yeshua* would also have been taking unjustified liberties with the *Tanakh* when He insisted that the Law, Prophets, and Writings spoke of Him.

Hauser contends that the development of the doctrine of the tri-unity, after the Church councils, was an act of hindsight. There is one major problem with Hauser's view. Almost 300 years before the council of Nicea in 325 C.E., the tri-unity of God had already been recognized and was being taught by the first-century Church. The first-century believers, such as Matthew, Mark, Luke, John, Paul, James, Peter, Jude, and the author of Hebrews, did not need the councils to make creeds (which were made because of error in the Church) to have and hold to the tri-unity of God. They were eyewitnesses of the Glory of God. As John says, *our hands have handled, of the Word of life* (1 John 1:1). As stated earlier in this paper, God did not present Messiah in a vacuum.

Hauser sums up his writing with this summary of the doctrine of the tri-unity:

Thus we conclude that these plurals can be understood to refer to the different persons of the Trinity only if that concept is read into the passage and only if the plurals are made to carry meanings and

---

[496] Youngblood, *The Genesis Debate*, 111-112.

implications that run counter to similar usages elsewhere in the Old Testament.[497]

The author's opinion is that if believers only had the *Tanakh* to study, the conclusion minimally would be that God is one, but is somehow more complex than the word *one* normally conveys. He is a plurality. Even without any exposure to the New Testament, that belief would be a minimal understanding of the Hebrew Scriptures. Let us continue our investigation.

Plural Verbs Used With *Elohim*

There are other passages in the Scriptures (Genesis 20:13; 35:7; 2 Samuel 7:23; Psalm 58:11) that throw light on the plurality of God in the *Tanakh*. Hebrew grammar requires that verbs agree with associated nouns in both gender and number. When *Elohim* is used of the true God, these rules are normally broken because the plural noun is almost always followed by a singular verb except in the four verses cited above. When used with the plural noun *Elohim*, the use of a singular verb should attract attention. Likewise, the plural verbs that follow *Elohim* should equally attract attention. Even though the grammar is normal, this is an unusual combination because of its infrequent use in the *Tanakh*. Fruchtenbaum expresses the significance well:

> It is also said that while *Elohim* is plural, the verbs used with it are always singular when applied to the true God, and plural for false gods. The rules of Hebrew grammar require that verbs agree with the associated nouns in both gender and number. When *Elohim* is used for pagan gods, these rules are always followed and a plural verb is always used. When *Elohim* is used of the one true God, however, these rules are normally broken – the plural noun *Elohim* is usually followed by a singular verb. While it is true that this is most often the case, it is not always the case. There are several places in the Hebrew text where *Elohim*, speaking of the God of Israel, is followed by a plural verb.[498]

The following passages are four rare incidents where the noun *Elohim* and the verb are plural in reference to the true God.

---

[497] Youngblood, *The Genesis Debate*, 123.
[498] Fruchtenbaum, *Messianic Christology*, 103-104.

CHAPTER 6: PLURAL DESCRIPTIONS

Genesis 20:13

> *So when God [Elohim, plural] made [caused] me [to] wander from my father's house, I said to her Let this be the kindness that you shall do me: whatever place we come to, say there of me: He is my brother.*

Because the plural noun *Elohim* with plural verb "cause (me) to wander" is so unusual in connection to *Elohim*, Reyburn, Driver, as well as the Haftorah attempt to explain away the plural reference to the true God. For example, Driver asserts that when Abraham made this statement, he was accommodating Abimelech's polytheistic outlook, as Abimelech believed in many gods. Driver states the following:

> The verb is plural, perhaps, in conversation with a heathen, from accommodation to a polytheistic point of view. *Elohim*, even when used of the true God, is occasionally construed with a plural, for reasons which cannot always be definitely assigned.[499]

This is also the same argument given in the Haftorah.[500] Reyburn's own argument contends that with the plural noun *Elohim* and the plural verb *wander*, it "is probably best to take the plural usage in a singular sense, since this usage occurs elsewhere."[501] Wenham says that this verse speaks of the true God, but because of the plural verb as seen by Reyburn, *Elohim* should be rendered "gods they caused me to wander" instead of "(*Elohim* or God) they caused me to wander," because the interpretation "gods" better accommodates Abimelech's polytheistic outlook.[502] However, because this is considered an anomaly,[503] many scholars want it to read as *Elohim He*. If this plural verb with the plural noun *Elohim* is an anomaly, how is it that in Hebrew grammar it is the norm? The plural noun *Elohim* and the singular verb are the exception and not the grammatical rule. The rule is that all plural Hebrew nouns have plural verbs.[504] The fact that Christian scholars consider the plural noun, *Elohim*, and plural verb as correct usage, is an anomaly of its own according to Hebrew grammar. God chose to give this representation of Himself, and it does not need to be changed.

---

[499] Driver, *Westminster Commentaries, the Book of Genesis,* 208.
[500] Hertz, *The Pentateuch and Haftorah,* 71.
[501] Reyburn and McG. Fry, *A Handbook on Genesis,* 455.
[502] Gordon Wenham, *Word Biblical Commentary: Genesis 16-50* (Waco, Tex: Word, 1987), 72.
[503] **Anomaly**: a deviation from the common rule, irregular.
[504] There are two other words that would also have this in common with *Elohim*, there are "waters" and "heavens."

The reason for changing its interpretation is because it does not meet a prescribed view that God can use a plural verb to affirm His plurality if He chooses to do so.

Westermann indicates that it is quite unlikely that Abraham adapted to Abimelech's polytheism, because the God of Abraham also spoke to Abimelech and gave him instructions.[505] The context of this passage does not warrant Abraham accommodating a heathen (Genesis 20:1, 17).[506]

Simply stated, according to the biblical text, *Elohim* (they) caused me to wander is the literal rendering. Because God chose the wording through inspiration, there is no reason to alter the meaning as Reyburn, Driver, and the Haftorah prescribe should be done.

Genesis 35:7

> *There he built an altar and named the site El-bethel, for it was there that God [Elohim] had revealed [plural verb] Himself [Themselves] to him when he was fleeing from his brother.*

This passage clarifies that upon Jacob's return to Canaan, *Elohim* revealed Themselves to Jacob after he built the altar. True to Hebrew grammar, the plural *Elohim* is followed by a plural verb *revealed*, which carries the interpretation that *Elohim* revealed Themselves, and that is God demonstrating His plurality. Westermann uses the same argument as in Genesis 20:13, that even though *revealed* is plural, it should be treated as a singular.[507] Speiser says that the verb *revealed* is plural but that the term *Elohim* should be rendered "divine beings."[508] Reyburn discusses the text and includes nothing about a plural verb. Driver points out that the plural verb (revealed) "suggests that the sentence preserves a more polytheist version of the Bethel-legend than Genesis 28:12."[509]

Hamilton recognizes the plural verb and sees *Elohim* referring to the true God for two reasons. First, *Elohim* should have the same meaning as in verses 1 and 5, where it clearly refers to the true God. Secondly, the text gives no evidence that the

---

[505] Westermann, *Genesis 12-36, A Continental Commentary*, 327.
[506] For additional comments on these passages (Genesis 20:13, 35:7, 2 Samuel 7:23 and Psalm 58:11), see pages 14, 42, 49-50.
[507] Westermann, *Genesis 12-36, A Continental Commentary*, 552.
[508] Speiser, *The Anchor Bible: Genesis*, 270.
[509] Driver, *Westminster Commentaries, The Book of Genesis*, 424.

messengers (angels) revealed themselves to Jacob.[510] However, since God is the actual author of the infallible, inspired Scriptures, He had Moses record the specific personal pronouns and/or verbs that convey the clear meaning of plurality and/or trinity. Therefore the more precise translation would be, *Elohim revealed Themselves to Jacob,* showing the plurality in the Godhead.

2 Samuel 7:23

> *And what one nation in the earth is like Your people, even like Israel, whom God [Elohim, plural] went to redeem for a people to Himself [Themselves], and to make Him a name, and to do for you great things and terrible, for Your land, before Your people, which You redeemed to Yourself from Egypt, from the nations and their gods?*
>
> (NASB)

This verse is the third example of God using a plural verb (redeemed) with His name (*Elohim*). Kohlenberger translates *they went out and redeemed,* as being plural.[511] He shows that the plural reference grammatically clearly refers back to *Elohim*. Gramcord also treats the phrase as a plural referring back to *Elohim*.[512] Keil and Delitzsch state that the plural phrase refers to the true God.[513] Through the use of correct grammar (using a plural noun with a plural verb), *Elohim* accomplishes the same result as when He violated correct grammar (using a plural noun with a singular verb) to bring attention to His plurality. Hence, this plural verb can literally be translated "whom *Elohim* they went to redeem for Themselves." It has been observed by all the authors investigated that the reverse is never true: A singular verb is never used in an obvious passage that deals with false gods.

Psalm 58:11(12)

> *Men will say, "There is, then, a reward for the righteous; there is, indeed, divine justice on earth."*

---

[510] Hamilton, *The New International Commentary on the Old Testament: Genesis 18-50* (Grand Rapids: Eerdmans, 1990), 377.
[511] Kohlenberger, *The Interlinear NIV Hebrew-English Old Testament,* 2:270.
[512] Paul A. Miller, *Gramcord, www.Gramcord.org.*
[513] Keil and Delitzsch, *Commentary on the Old Testament,* 2:352.

> *And men will say, "Surely there is a reward for the righteous; Surely there is a God [Elohim, plural] who judges [judge] on earth!"*
>
> (NASB)

In this verse, *Elohim* and the modifier, *judge*, are in the plural. Lange says that this is the same usage as in Genesis 20:13 and 2 Samuel 7:23.[514] Both Beale[515] and Owens[516] identify the word *judge* as being plural. There is not much discussion in commentaries on the plural aspect of the word *judge* with *Elohim*. This verse could be translated literally as "*Elohim* they judge on earth!" Thus, Fruchtenbaum states that this and other "plural verbs in reference to the true God support the idea of plurality in the Godhead."[517]

Other Plural Descriptions

The next eight additional Hebrew Scriptures describe God as plural. Each is significant, but there will only be a very brief statement about each one.

Deuteronomy 5:23

> *For what mortal ever heard the voice of the living [plural adjective] God [Elohim] speak out of the fire, as we did and lived?*

Weinfeld says that both words in the phrase *living God* are in the plural. *Elohim* is plural for God and *living* is a plural adjective (also found in 1 Samuel 17:26, 36 and Jeremiah 10:10; 23:36).[518] As a plural adjective, *living* is a description of *Elohim* that gives added weight to God's plurality. Yet according to Gerleman, there are other passages that are translated *living*, but they are in the singular (Joshua 3:10; Hosea 1:10; Psalm 42:3; 2 Kings 19:4, 16 with Isaiah 37:4, 17; 2 Samuel 22:47 with Psalm 18:47).[519] Though this term is not used in every case as a plural adjective, there are five passages cited where *Elohim* uses plural adjectives to describe Himself.

---

[514] John Peter Lange, *Lange's Commentary on the Holy Scriptures* (trans. Philip Schaff; 12 vols. Grand Rapids: Zondervan, 1960), 5:353.
[515] Todd S. Beale, William A. Banks, and Colin Smith *Old Testament Parsing Guide: Job-Malachi*, 2:45.
[516] Owens, *Analytical Key to the Old Testament*, 3:356.
[517] Fruchtenbaum, *Messianic Christology*, 104.
[518] Moshe Weinfeld, *The Anchor Bible: Deuteronomy 1-11* (New York, NY: Doubleday, 1991), 320-321.
[519] Jenni and Westermann, *Theological Lexicon of the Old Testament*, 1:415.

CHAPTER 6: PLURAL DESCRIPTIONS

Deuteronomy 10:17

> *For the Lord your God is God of gods, and Lord of lords, a great God, a mighty, and a terrible, which regards not persons, nor takes reward.*[520]

Moses uses several different names for the same God, as seen more clearly in the New American Standard Bible (NASB):

> *For the LORD [Yahweh] your God [Elohim] is the God [Elohim] of gods [Elohim] and the Lord [Adonai] of lords [Adonai], the great, the mighty, and the awesome God [El] who does not show partiality, nor take a bribe.*

This verse could be translated as, *For Yahweh* (singular) *your Elohim* (plural) *is the Elohim* (plural) *of Elohim* (plural) *and the Adonai's* (plural) *of Adonai's* (plural)[521] *the great, the mighty, and the awesome El* (singular)." Cooper comments not only on the divine personalities of God, but also on the polytheistic error that must be avoided:

> These expressions echo the plurality of divine personalities of the one Sovereign Being. But to avoid the error of polytheism, He asserts their unity using the word *El*, God, in the singular number. Then He differentiates Himself from idols by asserting His absoluteness in greatness, power and terribleness. He is the almighty sovereign.[522]

Cooper expresses the cautions that God took in giving a clear picture of His plurality while protecting His unity with the use of *El*.

Joshua 24:19

> *Joshua, however, said to the people, "You will not be able to serve the LORD, for He is a holy* [plural adjective] *God* [Elohim, plural].

---

[520] Harkavy, *The Twenty-Four Books of the Old Testament*, 1:307.
[521] David L. Cooper, *The God of Israel*, 33.
[522] David L. Cooper, *The God of Israel*, 34.

As Joshua gives an unusual speech to Israel at the end of his life, he speaks of *Elohim* as being a *holy God* as well as a jealous God. Both Kohlenberger[523] and Miller[524] acknowledge the word *holy* as a plural adjective. Lange says that it is a plural adjective and also cites 1 Samuel 17:26 with Joshua 24:19.[525] Both Cooper[526] and Fruchtenbaum[527] agree that *holy* should be translated *holy Gods*. By the inspiration of the Spirit of God, Joshua chose to use another plural descriptive adjective to further add weight in describing the plurality of God.

Ecclesiastes 12:1

> *Remember also your Creator in the days of your youth, before the evil days come and the years draw near when you will say, "I have no delight in them.* (NASB)

In this passage, without the term *Elohim* or God mentioned, Solomon makes an interesting statement: *Remember now your Creator in the days of your youth* (KJV). There is a range of views on the meaning of *Creator* in this passage. Ogden and Zogbo state:

> "Your Creator" is the object of the imperative "remember." The form here is plural (literally "those who created you").[528]

Ogden and Zogbo recognize it as a plural as does Leupold.[529]

Bore'ekha is the plural form *bore'im* plus a suffix and means literally "Creators." Along with these plural affirmations of *Creator* it is also unique because this word is also a plural adjective, which Kohlenberger translates as "Ones-Creating you."[530] Longman says the difficulty with the word *Creator* is that it is plural, meaning that the literal reading is "your Creators."[531] However, there is no difficulty

---

[523] Kohlenberger, *The Interlinear NIV Hebrew English Old Testament,* 70.
[524] Paul A. Miller, *Gramcord, www.Gramcord.org.*
[525] Lange, *Lange's Commentary on the Holy Scriptures,* 2:185.
[526] David L. Cooper, *The God of Israel,* 29.
[527] Fruchtenbaum, *Messianic Christology,* 107.
[528] Graham S. Ogden and Lynell Zogbo, *A Handbook on Ecclesiastes* (New York: United Bible Societies, 1997), 418.
[529] H. C. Leupold, *Exposition of Ecclesiastes* (Columbus, OH: Wartburg Press, 1952).
[530] Kohlenberger, *The Interlinear NIV Hebrew English Old Testament,* 588.
[531] Longman Tremper, III., *The New International Commentary on the Old Testament: Ecclesiastes* (Grand Rapids: Eerdmans, 1998), 264.

CHAPTER 6: PLURAL DESCRIPTIONS

because if inspiration of Scripture means anything, then God can represent Himself as a plural. Jamieson, Fausset, and Brown state that clearly when they say:

> The Hebrew is Creators, plural, implying the plurality of persons, as in Genesis 1:26.[532]

If grammatically *Creator* is a plural, why attempt to change what God, in His infinite wisdom, gave in His Word?

However, the Jewish Publication Society (JPS) version replaces *creator* with an alternate interpretation of this word. That version says, "So appreciate your vigor in the days of your youth."[533] The omission is significant because *creator* and not *vigor* appears in the Hebrew Scriptures. The following explanation is given:

> Some commentaries think the text as we have it may have been damaged in transmission.[534]

This means there must be alternative readings to the Masoretic Text.[535] Along these lines, three views[536] have arisen on how to interpret the word *creator* in this text; and one of these is reflected in the JPS version. The three views are first that it has a possible meaning of "your well" which is a metaphoric reference to a man's wife, a source of refreshment and a well of procreation.[537] The second possible meaning is "your grave" or "your pit," which reflects death. The third possible meaning is "your vigor" which reflects man's health and strength.

The Hebrew text tells the reader that man is to remember His *Creator* in the days of his youth. Others want to depart from this literal meaning to an alternate non-Masoretic reading. The fact remains that *Creator* here is plural; there is some support for this interpretation as often in the wisdom literature, God is referred to as Creator.

---

[532] Jamieson, Fausset, and Brown. *A Commentary: Critical, Experimental and Practical on the Old and New Testaments,* 3;541.
[533] Berlin and Brettler, *The Jewish Study Bible,* 1620.
[534] Ogden and Zogbo, *A Handbook on Ecclesiastes,* 418.
[535] Longman, III, *The New International Commentary on the Old Testament: Ecclesiastes,* 267.
[536] James L. Crenshaw, *The Old Testament Library, Ecclesiastes* (Philadelphia: Westminster Press, 1987), 184-185,
[537] Robert Gordis, *Koheleth, The Man and His World, A Study of Ecclesiastes* (New York: Schocken Books, 1968), 340.

Psalm 149:2

Let Israel rejoice in its Maker [plural adjective]; *let the children of Zion exult in their king.*

Israel is to sing a new song to *Yahweh*, and Israel is to *rejoice in its maker*. *Maker* is also a plural adjective and when literally translated this passage would say, *Let Israel be glad in its Makers*. Keil and Delitzsch refer to *Maker* as "The Creator of Israel"[538] in the plural form. Dahood also notes that *Maker* is a plural and even ties the term in with Isaiah 54:5.[539] The interesting point is that Owens[540] recognizes *Maker* as a plural adjective but refuses to acknowledge the plurality of God in this passage. Clearly, with *Elohim* and the *Let Us* personal pronouns of Genesis as well as other plural descriptive words such as *Creator* and *Maker*, God presents Himself as a plurality by the use of a variety of plural terms for God.

Isaiah 54:5 (comparing KJV with NASB)

⁵ For He who made you will espouse you – His name is "LORD [Yahweh] of Hosts." The Holy One of Israel will redeem you – He is called "God [Elohim] of all the Earth." (Jewish Study Bible)

*⁵ For your **husband** is your **Maker**, Whose name is the **LORD** [Yahweh] of hosts; and your Redeemer is the Holy One of Israel, Who is called the **God** [Elohim] of all the earth.* (NASB)

When these two verses are compared, the language is strikingly different, as if the plural words referring to God are being skirted. By changing the use of plural words to describe God, the meaning of the verse is also changed.

The plural descriptions in this verse present some very good images of God's relationship to Israel. There are four words to be noted in this verse: *Yahweh, Elohim, Husband,* and *Maker*. First, *Yahweh* is the personal name of Israel's God, in the singular. *Elohim*, being plural, is second and is used to name God and to affirm plurality. And finally, two plural adjectives, *maker* and *husband*, literally mean that Israel has "Makers" and "Husbands." Keil and Delitzsch confirm this usage and also refer to some of the same passages previously discussed in this chapter

---

[538] Keil and Delitzsch, *Commentary on the Old Testament,* 5:412.
[539] Mitchell Dahood, *The Anchor Bible: Psalms 101-150* (Garden City, NY: Doubleday, 1970), 357.
[540] Owens, *Analytical Key to the Old Testament,* 3:519.

(Joshua 24:19; 1 Samuel 17:26; Genesis 20:13; 35:7; and 2 Samuel 7:23).[541] Vine briefly combines *Maker* and *Husband* with *Elohim*[542] to affirm that *Elohim*, of Genesis 1, is the Creator (Ecclesiastes 12:1) and is Israel's *Husband* and *Maker* who made the covenant with them on Mount Sinai. Both *Husband* and *Maker* are plural adjectives describing *Yahweh*, which is in the singular. Young basically makes application of this passage to God and the Church rather than to God's relationship to Israel.[543] That raises another theological issue that will not be discussed in this book, the differences between Covenant[544] and Dispensational Theology.[545] In Isaiah 54:4-5, Young does recognize the plural adjectives but attributes them to "plural of majesty." The impact of this verse is that Israel has "Makers" and "Husbands" whose name is *Yahweh* of hosts. *Yahweh* is Israel's Redeemer, the Holy One of Israel, whose name is *Elohim*. Once again, these verses show a plural affirmation of His being.

Isaiah 50:1-6

> *Thus said the LORD: ...The Lord God gave me a skilled tongue, to know how to speak timely words to the weary. Morning by morning, He rouses, He rouses my ear to give heed like disciples. The Lord God opened my ears, and I did not disobey, I did not run away. I offered my back to the floggers, and my cheeks to those who tore out my hair. I did not hide my face from insult and spittle.*

Walter Kaiser recognizes these verses as a "Servant of the LORD" passage and along with four other passages (Isaiah 42:17; 49:1-6; 50:4-9; and 52:13-53:12) as

---

[541] Keil and Delitzsch, *Commentary on the Old Testament*, 7:344.

[542] Vine, *Isaiah*, 174.

[543] Edward J. Young, *The Book of Isaiah* (Grand Rapids: Eerdmans, 1972), 3:364.

[544] **Covenant Theology**: Covenant Theology teaches that the Church has replaced Israel and that now the Church is the Israel of God. Therefore, because God has no place for Israel in the future, the Church assumes all the promises to Israel. Israel can expect only the cursings. Covenant Theology sees only the dispensation of Grace, which involves all of time from Adam to present.

[545] **Dispensational Theology**: Acknowledges seven dispensations during which salvation is by faith alone. It recognizes Israel and the Church as two distinct groups that God has chosen to work through. During the Dispensation of Grace (Acts 2 through the Rapture of the Church) God is working with the Church, both Jewish and Gentile believers, and not the nation of Israel at this time. However, because of His covenant promises to Abraham, God will again establish Israel at the beginning of the Millennial Kingdom; and the Messiah will reign over the world from Jerusalem.

referring to the pre-incarnate Messiah.[546] There are three basic explanations as to who *the Servant of the LORD* might be in these passages.[547] First, Rashi, the renowned rabbi from the Middle Ages, taught that the servant was Israel.[548] The second is David Kimkhi, another renowned rabbi of the twelfth and thirteenth centuries taught that "the servant is said to be Isaiah himself."[549] Briggs taught that this is not a reference to the Messiah and, like Kimkhi, taught that it probably refers to Isaiah.[550] The third basic explanation is that the Servant of the LORD is the Messiah, Jesus.[551]

Arnold Fruchtenbaum observes the plurality of God in this passage; whereas. no one else seems to recognize plurality here. According to Fruchtenbaum, *Yahweh* (Isaiah 50:1) is the First Person of the plurality to be mentioned. However, in verse 4, a Second Person of the plurality is mentioned in the phrase *the Lord God hath given Me*.[552] The *Me* is the speaker identified in verse 1 as *Yahweh*. In verse 4, *Yahweh* speaks of *Adonai Elohim*, who gave Him the tongue of the learned. Who are these personalities of plurality? Verses 5 to 6 identify the person, not by name, but by the actions He voluntarily receives. The description is a preview of the flogging and mocking of the Messiah *Yeshua* [Jesus] (Matthew 27:26, 30-31).[553] In verse 6, Young gives a good insight into the volunteer beatings that the Messiah received before the crucifixion:

> There is majesty in the description, as though the servant were in full control of the situation. He sets himself forth as one who acts. Instead of saying that men beat him he declares that he himself gave his back to those who struck him. He either voluntarily yielded himself to flogging, or he offered himself thereto.[554]

---

[546] Walter C. Kaiser, Jr., *Toward an Old Testament Theology* (Grand Rapids, Zondervan, 1991), 215.

[547] There are several other authors that can be studied as to the three basic views on the Servant of the Lord passages in Isaiah: (1) Victor Buksbazen, *Isaiah's Messiah* (Bellmawr, NJ: Friends of Israel Gospel Ministry, 2002). (2) David Baron, *The Servant of Jehovah* (Jerusalem: Keren Ahvah Meshihit, 2000). (3) Michael L. Brown, *Answering Jewish Objections to Jesus* (vol. 3. Grand Rapids: Baker, 2003), 40-49.

[548] Slotki, *The Soncino Books of the Bible, Isaiah,* 247.

[549] Slotki, *The Soncino Books of the Bible, Isaiah,* 247.

[550] Charles A Briggs, *Messianic Prophecy* (Peabody, MA: Hendrickson, 1988), 356.

[551] Edward J. Young, *The Book of Isaiah,* 3:301.

[552] Fruchtenbaum, *Messianic Christology,* 50-51.

[553] Herbert Wolf, *Interpreting Isaiah* (Grand Rapids: Zondervan, 1985), 210.

[554] Edward J. Young, *The Book of Isaiah,* 3:300.

Therefore, verse 4 and following identifies the speaker as *Yahweh*, the Servant of the LORD, who refers to the "Father" as *Adonai Elohim*. Here again, there are two members of the Godhead present, God the Father and God the Son.

Zechariah 11:4-14

> *Then I said to them, "If you are satisfied, pay me my wages; if not, don't." So they weighed out my wages, thirty shekels of silver – the noble sum that I was worth in their estimation. The LORD said to me, "Deposit it in the treasury." And I took the thirty shekels and deposited it in the treasury in the House of the LORD.* (vv. 12-13)

Two observations on this verse: First, the Jewish Study Bible again deflects the intent of the Scriptures in saying that the 30 pieces of silver was a "noble sum." It was NOT; it was the price of contempt: the price to be given for a dead slave (Exodus 21:32). Secondly, although this passage shows that the speaker is *Yahweh*, yet what happened to *Yahweh* never happened to God the Father but to God the Son. Numerous scholars agree on the identity of *Yahweh* in Zechariah 11:12-13 as *Yeshua*, the Messiah of Israel, (Keil and Delitzsch;[555] Unger;[556] Merrill;[557] Baron;[558] Kaiser;[559] Smith;[560] Hengstenberg;[561] Feinberg;[562] Henderson;[563] and Laetsch.[564] It has already been noted that the *Tanakh* records two *Yahwehs* (Genesis 19:24, Isaiah 44:6, Hosea 1:4-7, and Zechariah 2:8-9).[565] In this passage (from Zechariah 11) the LORD (*Yahweh*) is presented as the good Shepherd as Zechariah acts out the symbolic action of receiving the LORD's wages from the people.[566]

One thing about the verse stands out clearly. The LORD (*Yahweh*) was speaking and used the term *I* repeatedly to reaffirm throughout this passage that it

---

[555] Keil and Delitzsch. *Commentary on the Old Testament in Ten Volumes*, 10:368.
[556] Unger, *Zechariah: Prophet of Messiah's Glory* (Grand Rapids: Zondervan, 1963), 199.
[557] Eugene H. Merrill, *An Exegetical Commentary: Haggai, Zechariah, Malachi* (Chicago: Moody, 1994), 298.
[558] Baron, *The Visions and Prophecies of Zechariah*, 380, 403-407.
[559] Kaiser, *The Communicator's Commentary: Micah – Malachi*, 394.
[560] James Smith, *The Promised Messiah*, 444.
[561] Hengstenberg, *Christology of the Old Testament*, 4:35.
[562] Charles L. Feinberg, *The Minor Prophets* (Chicago: Moody, 1952), 328.
[563] Ebenezer Henderson, *Thornapple Commentaries: The Twelve Minor Prophets* (Grand Rapids: Baker, 1980), 420.
[564] Theodore Laetsch, *The Minor Prophets* (St. Louis: Concordia, 1956), 474.
[565] See Chapter 2, section entitled *Yahweh*.
[566] Baron, *The Visions and Prophecies of Zechariah*, 380.

was He who spoke (verses 4, 6-10, 12-14). Verses 4 and 13 identified LORD (*Yahweh*) as the speaker; whereas, in the other verses, He uses the first person pronoun *I*. In Zechariah 11:12, *Yahweh* asks for His wages through Zechariah, who was acting out the role of the good Shepherd. The good Shepherd (Messiah) makes a request that is not compulsory. The wages that *Yahweh* desired was Israel's love, obedience, and devotion to God, their Shepherd.[567] However, instead of giving Him the internal or spiritual wages of their repentance, Israel gave Him a monetary wage, which was a deliberate insult.[568] Israel could have refrained from paying wages altogether but instead insulted the good Shepherd with 30 pieces of silver, which according to the Law, was the price of a dead slave (Exodus 21:32).[569] Merrill clarifies that *Yahweh*, rather than Zechariah, is the one being appraised as unworthy (Zechariah 12:13).[570] The one who was sold out for 30 pieces of silver was the LORD [*Yahweh*], the personal God of Israel, in this case, the Messiah *Yeshua*. Matthew 23:37 takes on greater meaning when it is understood that *Yeshua* is speaking as the God of the Hebrew Scriptures or as LORD (*Yahweh*), from the *Tanakh*:

> *O Jerusalem, Jerusalem, you that kill the prophets, and stone them which are sent to you, how often would I have gathered your children together, even as a hen gathers her chickens under her wings, and you were unwilling!*

Tri-Unity in Isaiah

Isaiah was an eighth-century prophet, a contemporary with Micah. His presentation of Emmanuel (Isaiah 7-12), the Servant of the LORD (Isaiah 42, 49, 50, and 53), and the future restoration of Israel (Isaiah 54, 60-66) makes the book of Isaiah one of the greatest treasures in the *Tanakh*. Isaiah prophesied the captivity of Israel and the fall of Babylon to the Medes and Persians, as well as God anointing Cyrus, who would permit Jewish people to return home, back to the land of Israel. Isaiah prophesied the birth of the Messiah, His message, His rejection, and His sufferings. Isaiah was a great prophet, a man who received an abundance of prophecies from the Lord concerning His people and His Messiah. Last of all, Isaiah brings all three members of the unity of God together in at least three chapters (Isaiah 48:12-16, 61:1, 63:7-14). These chapters provide the best evidence for the tri-unity of God in the Hebrew Scriptures.

---

[567] Charles L. Feinberg, *The Minor Prophets*, 328.
[568] Hengstenberg, *Christology of the Old Testament*, 4:35.
[569] James Smith, *The Promised Messiah*, 444.
[570] Merrill, *An Exegetical Commentary: Haggai, Zechariah, Malachi*, 298.

CHAPTER 6: PLURAL DESCRIPTIONS

Isaiah 48:12-16

> *Listen to Me, O Jacob, Israel, whom I have called: I AM He – I AM the first, and I AM the last as well. My Own hand founded the earth, My right hand spread out the skies. I call unto them, let them stand up.* (vv. 12-13)

> *Draw near to Me and hear this: From the beginning, I did not speak in secret; from the time anything existed, I was there. And now the Lord God has sent Me, endowed with His spirit.* (v. 16)

The passage begins with a familiar word, *Shema*, the same word used in Deuteronomy 6:4. It becomes obvious that God wants Israel to hear because He uses the term *listen* (*Shema*) in verses 12, 14, and 16. Yet in verse 18, *Yahweh* says that Israel did not hear or obey His commandments. In verse 12, the speaker is establishing that He called them by saying, *Listen* (*Shema*) *to Me, O Jacob, Israel, whom I called*. According to Judges 2:1, the Messenger (Angel) of *Yahweh* called Israel where He references the Abrahamic Covenant in Genesis 15. All three references reflect the same Person. *Yahweh* continues speaking by saying, *I AM He, I AM the first, I AM the last*. That phrase simply means that *Yahweh* was before time and will be after time is no more. *Yahweh* continues in verse 13, reflecting back to Genesis 1 by identifying Himself as *Elohim* the Creator whose *Own hand founded the earth, My right hand spread out the skies. I call unto them, let them stand up*. Verses 14 and 15 refer to Cyrus, the Mede, who will judge Babylon and allow Israel to return. In verse 16 it is as if *Yahweh* was calling Israel to come close and *hear* (*Shema*). He makes one point: *I did not speak in secret;* He did not hide His thoughts from them. From the time of their calling, even the calling of Cyrus, He was there. Young accurately states that from the beginning, God spoke openly and clearly to His people:

> *Beginning* refers to the time when God first began to give prophetic revelations. From the moment that God first spoke to man through the prophets He did not speak in secret but openly and clearly.[571]

Up to this point in these verses, there is general agreement among scholars that it is *Yahweh* who is speaking. However, in the last part of this verse, there is no unanimity among scholars as to who is speaking.

---

[571] Edward J. Young, *The Book of Isaiah*, 3:258.

There are two contradictory views concerning the identity of the speaker in Isaiah 48:16c, *And now the Lord God has sent Me, endowed with His spirit*. A footnote in the JPS version says that it literally reads "and His spirit."[572] Slotki says that according to Rabbi David Kimchi (1160-1235), the *sent one* is the prophet who was present, and he would be sent with His Spirit within him.[573] According to Slotki, "Bible critics" have come to the conclusion that there are three Isaiahs who wrote the book of Isaiah, and the second (Deutero-) Isaiah would be the prophet represented in verse 16.[574] Others in the same frame as Slotki say that there are two Isaiahs. These scholars want to change speakers and insert Isaiah or an anonymous "Second Isaiah."[575] Yet still others believe that the speaker is *Yahweh* Himself. Wolf summarizes the two views as to the speaker:

> The phrase the Sovereign LORD has sent me, with his Spirit, either means that God sent Isaiah to speak these words through the power of the Holy Spirit or that God would send the Servant as another of the new things He would perform (verse 16).[576]

Webb points out that the speaker in Isaiah 48:16c must be the Servant of the LORD (*Yahweh* the Messiah) due to the context in which the statement is placed. Webb gives his thoughts on the subject that *Yahweh* is speaking before and immediately following this phrase in question. So since *Yahweh* is speaking before and after the phrase, *And now the Lord God has sent Me, endowed with His spirit*, it makes no logical sense to say that someone else is speaking:

> With this issue hanging heavily in the air, the scene is set for the Servant of the LORD to take center stage again in chapter 49. In fact it is more than likely that his voice has already been heard here in chapter 48. For who else can it be who announces his presence in verse 16 with the words, *And now the Sovereign LORD has sent me, with his Spirit*?
>
> But the reference to the Spirit pointedly recalls the presentation of the Servant in 42:1, *I will put My Spirit on Him*. And the voice we hear in *the Sovereign LORD has sent me* sounds remarkably like the

---

[572] Berlin and Brettler, *The Jewish Study Bible*, 882.
[573] Slotki, *The Soncino Books of the Bible, Isaiah*, 237.
[574] Slotki, *The Soncino Books of the Bible, Isaiah*, Introduction x, 237.
[575] Barry G. Webb, *The Message of Isaiah* (Downers Grove, IL: Inter-Varsity, 1996), 192.
[576] Wolf, *Interpreting Isaiah*, 204.

CHAPTER 6: PLURAL DESCRIPTIONS

voice we are about to hear again in 49:1: *before I was born the LORD called Me.*[577]

Vine does not even make reference to the comment that there is another speaker in verse 16c. He points to the speaker as being the Messiah. He very clearly states his view:

> The close of verse 16 brings before us a striking instance of the work of the Trinity: and now the Lord God hath sent Me and His Spirit. That Christ is the Speaker, and not the prophet is to be gathered from a comparison with 61:1. His words are undoubtedly a prelude to what He is about to declare of Himself in chapter 49:5-6.[578]

In contrast, Young points out that the Lord and the speaker are two different persons:

> Who is the speaker in the third clause? Obviously it cannot be the Lord, for a distinction is made between the speaker and the Lord.
>
> The speaker is the Servant par excellence, already introduced in 42:1, and about to be brought more prominently into the picture in chapters forty-nine, fifty, and fifty-three.[579]

The point of this whole discussion is to discover who is in view in verse 16. There are two sides with completely opposing views. If the speaker is not *Yahweh*, minimally the plurality of God is still present with the *Lord God* and *His Spirit*. But if *Yahweh* (Me) is the speaker from verse 12 onward, the tri-unity of God is present. If *Yahweh* is the speaker, this is significant. The one who called Israel (to the Abrahamic Covenant) also identified Himself as the I AM (Exodus 3:14), the first and last, and in Genesis 1, the Creator. Verse 16c gives three distinct personalities in the Godhead. The reference of *Me* is distinct from the Lord God (*Adonai Elohim*) and is distinct from the Holy Spirit. Simply put, the Lord God (the Father) sends Me (the Son), and the Holy Spirit. It is not a coincidence that in the Gospel of John, *Yeshua* refers over 40 times to the fact that the Father sent Him, which collaborates with Isaiah 48:16 as well as Zechariah 2:6-11. In Isaiah 48:16, there is a very clear presentation of the tri-unity of God, which is supported by Barackman, Strong, and Berkhof. Strong's position is clear when he states that "there are three who are

---

[577] Webb, *The Message of Isaiah*, 192.
[578] Vine, *Isaiah*, 139.
[579] Edward J. Young, *The Book of Isaiah*, 3:258-259.

implicitly recognized as God."⁵⁸⁰ Berkhof, in referencing the tri-unity of God in Isaiah 48:16, says that in the Hebrew Scriptures God speaks to other members of the Godhead and the Messiah speaks of God the Spirit:

> God is the speaker, and mentions both the Messiah and the Spirit, or the Messiah is the speaker who mentions both God and the Spirit, Isa. 48:16; 61:1; 63:9, 10. Thus the Old Testament contains a clear anticipation of the fuller revelation of the Trinity in the New Testament.⁵⁸¹

Likewise, Barackman specifically states that Isaiah 48:16 is a reference to the tri-unity of God in the Hebrew Scriptures:

> [That] the Trinity consists of more than two Persons is indicated by the plural noun "God" (Heb. *Elohim* in Genesis 1:1) and the plural pronoun "us" (Genesis 1:26; 3:22; 11:7; Isaiah 6:8). The three Persons of the Trinity are seen in Isaiah 48:16 and 61:1, with the Son (the Messiah) speaking in both passages.⁵⁸²

In summary, the support is there, from numerous sources, that Isaiah 48:16 is a reference to the triune God of the Hebrew Scriptures.

Isaiah 61:1-2a

> *The Spirit of the Lord God is upon Me, because the LORD has anointed Me; He has sent Me as a herald of joy to the humble, to bind up the wounded of heart, to proclaim release to the captives, Liberation to the imprisoned; to proclaim a year of the LORD's favor.*

This passage is a well-known passage from the Hebrew Scriptures to those familiar with the New Testament because *Yeshua* quoted it when He read from the scroll of Isaiah in the synagogue in Nazareth (Luke 4:16-22). The only thing the Soncino Commentary series says about the verse is that the anointing is to be taken metaphorically because only kings and priests were anointed.⁵⁸³ However, it seems unlikely that *Yeshua* would have been anointed since He was neither an earthly king

---

⁵⁸⁰ Strong, *Systematic Theology*, 317-318.
⁵⁸¹ L. Berkhof, *Systematic Theology*, 86.
⁵⁸² Barackman, *Practical Christian Theology*, 63.
⁵⁸³ Slotki, *The Soncino Books of the Bible, Isaiah*, 237, 298.

nor a priest. So how was He anointed? According to Isaiah 11:2 and 42:1, *Yeshua*, by the Holy Spirit, will be anointed for service. Matthew 3:16 says exactly the same thing as Isaiah 61:1, that He was anointed, not with oil, but with the Holy Spirit.

The tri-unity of God is clearly enunciated in Isaiah 61:1. Kaiser speaks to the point by saying:

> *Yahweh* appoints the Servant and the Spirit anoints him, thereby making one of the earliest constructs of the doctrine of the Trinity. Rather than being anointed with oil as many [of] the priests and kings in the OT, this Servant is anointed by the Holy Spirit himself.[584]

Vine states firmly that "this passage speaks of the Trinity."[585] Young echoes that point by saying that Isaiah 61:1 is Trinitarian in content and that the speaker is the Messiah.[586] Berkhof recognizes all three passages as representing the tri-unity of God (Isaiah 48:16, 61:1, 63:7-10).

Isaiah 63:7-14

In Isaiah 48:16 and 61:1, Isaiah emphasizes the tri-unity of God. Previously, it was all in one verse, but here (in Isaiah 63:7-14) it is spread out over several verses. Isaiah himself is speaking on behalf of *Yahweh*. He refers to *Yahweh* in verse 7:

> *⁷ I will recount the kind acts of the **LORD**, The praises of the **LORD** – For all that the **LORD** has wrought for us, the vast bounty to the House of Israel that He bestowed upon them according to His mercy and His great kindness.*

In verse 9, he refers to the *Angel of His presence*, who saved Israel from their affliction (see Exodus 23:20-23); this was the same Messenger (Angel) of *Yahweh* that appeared throughout biblical history in the *Tanakh*, who led them out of Egypt, through the wilderness, and into the Promised Land of Canaan.

> *⁹ In all their troubles He was troubled, and **the angel of His Presence** delivered them. In His love and pity He Himself redeemed them, raised the, and exalted them all the days of old.*

---

[584] Walter C. Kaiser, Jr., *The Messiah in the Old Testament* (Grand Rapids: Zondervan, 1995), 183.
[585] Vine, *Isaiah*, 199.
[586] Edward J. Young, *The Book of Isaiah*, 3:459.

Then, in verses 10 and 14, Isaiah references the Holy Spirit. Once again, the tri-unity of God is present.

*[10] But they rebelled, and grieved His **holy spirit**; then He became their enemy, and Himself made war against them.*

*[14] Like a beast descending to the plain? Twas the **spirit of the LORD** gave them rest; thus did You shepherd Your people to win for Yourself a glorious name.*

CHAPTER 7:
THE HOLY SPIRIT IN THE *TANAKH*

The men who penned the New Covenant clearly perceived the Holy Spirit to be as much *God* as they did *Yeshua* (Jesus). However, understanding the nature of God is still challenging. People of a Unitarian belief see the Holy Spirit as only an impersonal power or influence of God. Once again, can it be determined from the Hebrew Scriptures alone that the Holy Spirit is indeed God, equal in His nature and essence with God the Father and God the Son? The distinctions – first, second, and Third Person – are not believed to be a reference to rank, because all three Persons are equal in power and honor.[587]

The New Testament has abundant references to the Person of the Holy Spirit, and because of this abundance, many authors rely heavily on the New Testament to prove the personality of the Holy Spirit. In dealing with progressive revelation, the relationship between the Messiah, the Son of God, and the Holy Spirit is not as clearly stated as in the *Tanakh* as in the New Testament; but the references are there, and the Holy Spirit is active in the *Tanakh*.

Difficulties with the Term "*Spirit*" רוּחַ

One of the difficulties with understanding the nature of the Holy Spirit is how to determine if He is distinct from God the Father because the Father is also Spirit. It also should be noted that the Second Person of the Godhead is also Spirit; so, how do you determine that He is distinct from the Father who is Spirit? Just as we investigated the Second Person of the Godhead, we will be looking at the Third Person of the Godhead; and we see a recurring theme, that They are all Spirit. Erickson states the problem of understanding the term "Spirit" as it relates to God:

> It is often difficult to identify the Holy Spirit within the Old Testament, for it reflects the earliest stages of progressive revelation.

---

[587] Leon J. Wood, *The Holy Spirit in the Old Testament* (Eugene, OR: Wipf and Stock Publishers, 1998), 13.

In fact, the term "Holy Spirit" is rarely employed here. Rather, the usual expression is the "the Spirit of God."[588]

Louis Goldberg, a Jewish believer in Messiah, drew attention to a basic understanding scholars must have as they deal with the distinction between God, who is a spirit, and the Holy Spirit. He states the following:

> Of course, our Jewish friends do not acknowledge the Spirit as One in the tri-unity of God; the term Spirit is recognized as a synonym for God.[589]

John S. Feinberg also expresses the difficulty of determining whether a certain text is speaking of the Father's spirit or the Holy Spirit:

> The OT also frequently refers to the Spirit of God. Though in some passages such as Genesis 6:3 ("My spirit shall not strive") and Psalm 139:7 (the psalmist asks God, "Where can I go from thy Spirit?") it is not entirely clear whether the Spirit is a distinct personage or rather a reference to God the Father's Spirit, there are many passages in which the Spirit is distinct.[590]

This study has proved the reality of Goldberg and Feinberg's observations. In verses that refer to the Spirit of God, it can be difficult to prove there is a distinction between the Father and the Holy Spirit. Hildebrandt echoes Feinberg's explanation that the Hebrew Scriptures reveal the "Spirit," but that the focus is different than in the New Testament, when he says:

> But the main difficulty in presenting the personhood of the Spirit in the OT is due to the OT focus on the deeds of the Spirit in relation to humankind. Thus, non-personal words and phrases are used to describe the Spirit as divine energy, as a wind and fire, as light and space.[591]

Some authors, such as Erickson, see clearly the Third Person of the Godhead in the Hebrew Scripture but also recognize the difficulties in distinguishing His Person. He points out that the words "Spirit" and "God" are two nouns and that many

---

[588] Millard J. Erickson, *Christian Theology*, 2nd Ed. (Grand Rapids: Baker Books, 1998), 881.
[589] Louis Goldberg, *Our Jewish Friends*, 83.
[590] John S. Feinberg, *No One Like Him* (Wheaton: Crossway Books, 2001), 454.
[591] Wilf Hildebrandt, *An Old Testament Theology of the Spirit of God* (Peabody, MA: Hendrickson, 1995), 89.

times the reader could not distinguish between the two different persons, as seen in the following quote:

> Most Old Testament references to the Third Person of the Trinity consist of the two nouns *Spirit* and *God*. It is not apparent from this construction that a separate person is involved. The expression "Spirit of God" could well be understood as being simply a reference to the will, mind, or activity of God. There are, however, some cases where the New Testament makes it clear that an Old Testament reference to the "Spirit of God" is a reference to the Holy Spirit. One of the most prominent of these New Testament passages is Acts 2:16-21, where Peter explains that what is occurring at Pentecost is the fulfillment of the prophet Joel's statement, "I will pour out my Spirit on all people" (2:17).[592]

These authors express the same concerns that this author sees on how the term "spirit" is used in connection with God. However, T. S. Caulley goes too far when he makes a definite statement that the Holy Spirit is not mentioned, as a person, in the Hebrew Scriptures. He states:

> The OT does not contain an idea of a semi-independent divine entity, the Holy Spirit. Rather, we find special expressions of God's activity with and through men. God's spirit is holy in the same way his word and his name are holy; they are all forms of his revelation and, as such, are set in antithesis to all things human or material.[593]

Caulley leaves the impression that the Holy Spirit is not a separate entity from the other members of the Godhead. Caulley further confirms that impression when he states:

> Holy Spirit: In the NT, the [T]hird [P]erson of the Trinity; in the OT, God's power. In the OT the spirit of the Lord is generally an expression for God's power, the extension of himself whereby he carries out many of his mighty deeds.[594]

Caulley seems to deny the personality of the Holy Spirit in the *Tanakh*. J. H. Raven is quoted by Erickson who reflects the same view as Caulley, when he states the following:

---

[592] Erickson, *Christian Theology*, 2nd Ed, 882.
[593] Elwell, *Evangelical Dictionary of Theology*, 521-522.
[594] Elwell, *Evangelical Dictionary of Theology*, 521.

> There is here no distinction of persons in the Godhead. The Spirit of God in the Old Testament is God himself exercising active influence.[595]

That statement is not acceptable, as will be seen later in this chapter, because the *Tanakh* does make a distinction between *God* and the *Spirit*. God, as the greatest communicator in the universe who reveals Himself as a plurality in the Hebrew Scriptures, would not reveal His nature and essence in an incomplete manner. The writers of the New Testament completely understood the concept of the plurality of God, including the Holy Spirit, as the Third Person of the Godhead. How did they come to understand that concept? It was through the *Tanakh*! Some scholars do not see the Holy Spirit and verses that speak of the spirit; and, admittedly, is sometimes difficult to determine how to interpret these references. Consequently, in this chapter, we will deal only the verses that show, without question, that the Holy Spirit is a person.

The Use of the Term "Spirit"

The basic idea of *ruach* (Gr. *Pneuma*) is "air in motion" from air which cannot come between a crocodile's scales (Job 41:16) to the blast of a storm (Isaiah 25:4; Habakkuk 1:11). The Hebrew word רוח or *ruach* is used 387 times in the Hebrew Scriptures.[596] Wood says that *ruach* is used in a noun or verb form 388 times. Wood further states that it is used in the following ways:

> It is used to designate the human spirit, God's Holy Spirit, and several other entities such as "wind," "breath," "odor," and "space." Surprisingly, its most basic meaning seems to have been "wind."[597]

Ruach is used in all portions of the *Tanakh,* and we see Hildebrandt give an account in each section of the Hebrew Scriptures. It is used 38 times in the Torah (Law) while 201 times in the Prophets (47 in former Prophets and 154 in the latter Prophets), is found 139 times in the Writings, and is used in the Aramaic portions of Daniel 11 times.[598] Of the 387 times that *ruach* is used, the term is applied 136 times

---

[595] Erickson, *Christian Theology*, 2nd Ed, 882. Erickson quotes J.H. Raven from his work called the *History of the Religion of Israel* (Grand Rapids, MI: Baker, 1979), 164.
[596] VanGemeren, ed., *Dictionary of Old Testament and Exegesis,* 3:1073.
[597] Leon J. Wood, *The Holy Spirit in the Old Testament,* 16.
[598] Hildebrandt, *An Old Testament Theology of the Spirit of God*, 2.

CHAPTER 7: HOLY SPIRIT

to God and 129 times to man or animals. The basic meaning is physical "wind" or "breath."[599]

Ruach has different uses for spirit as expressed in emotions of aggressiveness (Isaiah 25:4) or anger (Judges 8:3; Proverbs 29:11). *Ruach* or breath is further used to signify activity and life (Job 17:1), a "second wind," and he "revives" (Judges 15:19; 1 Samuel 30:12; Genesis 45:27). The breath of mankind is in the hands of God (Job 12:10; Isaiah 42:5). Also, *ruach* is used of angelic beings as in "a spirit from God."[600] Other examples of this usage of *ruach* are as follows: as the *wind* shakes the trees (Isaiah 7:2), or as in the *"cool"* of the day (Genesis 3:8), or as the *breath* which the Lord gives to the people (Isaiah 42:5), or even as bad breath (*odor*) as in Job 19:17 where the literal rendering is "my *breath* is strange to my wife."[601] In the *Dictionary of Old Testament Theology and Exegesis*, it is divided into six areas (wind, compass point, breath, disposition, seat of cognition and volition, and spirit) to help show the usage of *ruach*. Under wind:

> (1) *Ruach* is used to refer to the force of nature, commonly known as wind (Exodus 10:13; Numbers 11:31; 1 Kings 18:45; 2 Kings 3:17; Psalm 48:7 [8] ; Isaiah 7:2; 41:16; Jeremiah 18:17; Ezekiel 17:10; Hosea 13:15; Jonah 4:8).
>
> (2) *Ruach* was used as four compass points, as in "every wind" or as in "every direction" (Ezekiel 5:10-12; 12:14; 17:21; Jeremiah 49:36; Ezekiel 37:9; Zechariah 2:6[10]; Daniel 7:2).
>
> (3) *Ruach* is also rendered as "breath," which is similar to *wind*, in that both denote the movement of air. It is used to "refer to the life-sustaining function called breathing or breath. This breath is the essence of life (Genesis 6:17; Job 12:10; Isaiah 38:16; 42:5; Ezekiel 37:5-14; Malachi 2:15-16).
>
> (4) *Ruach* is used to show "a person's or group's disposition, attitude, mood, inclination, as an approximate synonym of *nepel*, appetite, disposition, person (Genesis 26:35; Exodus 6:9; 1 Kings 21:5; Job 21:4; Proverbs 14:29; Isaiah 19:3; Ezekiel 3:14)."

---

[599] Dyrness, *Themes in Old Testament Theology*, 86.
[600] Harris, Archer, and Waltke, *Theological Wordbook of the Old Testament*, 836.
[601] Dyrness, *Themes in Old Testament Theology*, 86.

(5) *Ruach* denotes the seat of cognition and volition, those activities involved in thinking, aptitude, and decision-making. The knowledge and ability to perform a particular task is one clear example of this use of *ruach* (1 Chronicles 28:12; Isaiah 29:24; Ezekiel 11:5-6; 20:32; 38:10).

(6) Lastly, in the *Tanakh* the most significant usage of *ruach* involves its representation of the metaphysical or numinous, specifically the "Spirit of God/the LORD." The expression "Spirit of God" actually appears only 11 times (Genesis 1:2; Psalm 104:29; Job 33:4), "Spirit of the LORD" 25 times (Judges 9:23; 1 Samuel 16:14-16, 23; 18:10; 19:9), and Holy Spirit 3 times (Psalm 51:11 [13] ; Isaiah 63:10-11).[602]

Personality and Work of the Holy Spirit in the *Tanakh*

Many Scriptures deal with *ruach* in a non-personal manner, but the focus of this paper is on the ways in which the term reflects the personality of the Holy Spirit and how He is distinct from the Father and the Son. The Holy Spirit did operate in the New Testament as a person, but it is different in the *Tanakh* in that He did His work in the form of acts without using a personal description of Himself.

The Holy Spirit Is a Person

If the plurality of God is true and can stand on its own in the *Tanakh* without the well-documented New Testament to add to its weight, then perhaps we can search the Hebrew Scriptures to see if the tri-unity we see in the New Testament was first established in the Hebrew Scriptures as well. We will look now at evidence in the Hebrew Scriptures for the tri-unity of God in relation to the Holy Spirit, then later in relation to the Second Person, the Messiah.

Morey argues that whatever approach to finding biblical evidence is used to show the Son as the Second Person of the Godhead, the same approach must be taken in relation to discovering evidence of the Holy Spirit as the Third Person:

> The biblical evidence that convinced us that the Father and the Son are Persons, is the exact same kind of evidence that demonstrates

---

[602] VanGemeren, ed., *Dictionary of Old Testament and Exegesis,* 3:1073-1076.

CHAPTER 7: HOLY SPIRIT

that the Spirit is a Person. Thus, to deny the evidence when we apply it to the Spirit, but to accept it when we apply it to the Father or to the Son is sheer hypocrisy as well as being self-refuting. If the evidence is valid for One, then it is valid for all Three.[603]

Passages that affirm the Holy Spirit's personality will be examined first. Both David L. Cooper and Robert Morey express this point:

> Turning back to our original passage, Isaiah 63:8-10, we see God who becomes the Savior of Israel (vs. 8). In verse 9 the Angel of His presence saved her in that He carried out the actual plan of the Almighty. Then in verse 10 we note the Holy Spirit whom she grieved and against whom she rebelled. Thus in these three verses we see three divine personalities.[604]

> First, Isaiah says that קָדְשׁוֹ "His Holy Spirit" was וְעִצְּבוּ "grieved to the point of being provoked." The word וְעִצְּבוּ is a waw consecutive participle of עָצַב and means to feel profound hurt, pain, and grief. For example, the word עָצַב was used to describe the inward pain felt by David when he heard that his son Absalom was dead (2 Samuel 19:1-2). His weeping reveals how deeply he felt the pain. It was even used of God in Genesis 6:6, where we are told, "He was grieved in His heart." Secondly, only a Person can be grieved by מָרוּ "rebellion" against Him. Thus, the Holy Spirit is a Person and not an impersonal force.[605]

Walvoord agrees with Cooper and Morey that the Isaiah 63:10 expresses the personality of the Holy Spirit.[606] Here the Holy Spirit is not only recognized as a person but as a distinct person from the other members of the tri-unity.

In Micah 2:7 the author expresses the fact that the Holy Spirit is capable of being impatient. Being impatient is a quality of a person. A wind or force does not have the personal capacity to be annoyed or be impatient. Morey states that fact:

> The word translated "impatient" is הֲקָצַר which is a qal perfect of the word קָצֵר which means to be impatient. It is used in this sense in such places as Numbers 21:4; Judges 10:16; 16:16, etc. The question,

---

[603] Morey, *The Trinity: Evidence and Issues,* 188.
[604] David L. Cooper, *The God of Israel,* 80.
[605] Morey, *The Trinity: Evidence and Issues,* 189.
[606] John F. Walvoord, *The Holy Spirit* (Findlay, OH: Dunham Publishing, 1958), 7.

"Is the Spirit of the LORD impatient?" reveals that the Jews believed that the Holy Spirit was a Person capable of becoming annoyed with the sin of man.[607]

Further statements on the personality of the Holy Spirit are given by Payne in referring to Moses. Payne states that God said to Moses, *the Spirit,* not *My Spirit,* which would not indicate the Spirit of the Father, but the Spirit who is distinct from Himself:

> The personality of the Spirit was first revealed to Moses. Specifically, God informed Moses relative to the seventy elders who were to assist him in government: "I will take of the Spirit who is upon you and I will place [Him] upon them, so they may bear the burden of the people with thee" (Numbers 11:17). This statement indicates that the Spirit is distinct from *Yahweh,* that He is personal (giving judicial advice), and that He is divine (guiding Israel).[608]

Payne's statement shows the distinctness between two members of the tri-unity. It also shows that the Holy Spirit will guide, which is something that a person does, as He guides the 70 elders in administering judicial advice to the people of Israel. Payne also references Isaiah 48:16, *and the Lord God has sent Me and His Spirit*, and shows the Holy Spirit to be a personality that is distinct from the Father.[609] Kirkpatrick also affirms the personality of the Holy Spirit in referencing some of the same passages already cited:

> Passages like these which imply that the spirit of Jehovah personally acts, prepare the way for the New Testament revelation concerning Him, and can be used in the fullest Christian sense.[610]

A further confirmation on the personality of the Holy Spirit is seen in Creation with the act of intelligence in relation to creation of the world. To be involved in the creation of the universe and the creation of man shows a tremendous, complex mind far beyond human understanding. Ryrie refers to Job 26:13 and 33:4 where Job references the Spirit of God as the Creator.[611] In Psalm 104:30, the psalmist says, *You send forth Your Spirit, they are created; and You renew the face of the ground.* Lockyer states the following in relation to this verse:

---

[607] Morey, *The Trinity: Evidence and Issues,* 190.
[608] Payne, *The Theology of the Older Testament,* 173.
[609] Payne, *The Theology of the Older Testament,* 173.
[610] A. F. Kirkpatrick, *The Book of Psalms* (Cambridge: The University Press, 1914), 2:293.
[611] Charles Caldwell Ryrie, *The Holy Spirit* (Chicago, IL: Moody, 1965), 31.

CHAPTER 7: HOLY SPIRIT

It is evident from the immediate context that the "all" and the "they" refer to the living creatures of the whole world, and to beasts, birds, and fish in particular.[612]

Enns also expresses the personality of the Holy Spirit in showing His omnipotence and omnipresence in Job 33:4 and also alludes to Psalm 139:7-10.[613]

Not only does the "Spirit" guide and show intelligence, but also speaks, as we see in 2 Samuel 23:1-2 when David was on his deathbed. In this very fascinating statement, David says the Holy Spirit spoke through him. Speaking would be another act of personality, as seen in that verse:

> These are the last words of David: The utterance of David the son of Jesse, the utterance of the man set on high, the anointed of the God of Jacob, the favorite of Songs of Israel: The spirit[614] of the LORD has spoken through me, His message is on my tongue.

How much of the tri-unity of God did David understand? That may never be known. But this text and others clarify that David minimally understood the plurality of God. Morey makes a summary statement in relation to the Holy Spirit as a person speaking through David:

> The personhood of the Spirit is as certain as the inspiration of the Psalms of David. Notice that it is the Spirit's word which is the word of God. Only a Person can speak the word of God. Only a self-conscious living, person speaks.[615]

Once again in Nehemiah 9:30, the personality of the Holy Spirit is given in that He testified against rebellious Israel. Morey makes a firm statement that only a person has the capability of "testifying" or giving witness":

> The word translated "testified against" is וַתָּעַד which is a waw consecutive imperfect and means to bear witness, testify, or protest against someone. It is used of God (Psalm 50:7; 81:8) as well as man

---

[612] Herbert Lockyer, *All About the Holy Spirit* (Peabody: Hendrickson, 1995), 46.
[613] Enns, *The Moody Handbook of Theology*, 250.
[614] All Jewish bibles have a small "s" for spirit, but the KJV, NKJV, NASV, NIV, and the ESV all capitalize spirit. This Scripture reference, like most in this book, is from the Jewish Study Bible.
[615] Morey, *The Trinity: Evidence and Issues*, 190-191.

(Genesis 43:3; Deuteronomy 8:19). An impersonal force or power cannot bear witness, testify or protest anything.[616]

Ezekiel gives a very clear example of the personality of the Holy Spirit in Ezekiel 2:2; 8:3; 11:1. Here the Lord God tells Ezekiel to *get up,* and then Ezekiel says the *Spirit entered me.* In the other two passages, Ezekiel says the *Spirit lifted me up.* This is giving the activity of the Holy Spirit in His act of lifting up Ezekiel.[617] These previous verses cited serve as several examples to substantiate the personality of the Holy Spirit. Again, as Morey has stated, the same approach used to find evidence of the personality of the Second Person of the tri-unity should be applied to find evidence for the personhood of the Holy Spirit.

The Holy Spirit in Creation

Pache relates that the account of Creation is an allusion to the Trinity and indirectly to the Spirit. *Elohim* (discussed in chapter two as a plural noun) could be just as easily translated in Genesis 1:1 as "Gods," as follows: *In the beginning, the Gods created.* Again, in verse 26, God shows His plurality by referring to Himself with a plural personal pronoun.[618] The only other Person of God that is mentioned in the Creation passage is in Genesis 1:2 where Moses says that God, the Spirit, hovered, moved, or brooded over the face of the waters. Several Jewish and Christian authors attribute the "wind," as being the impersonal force from God. Towner makes a statement that *spirit* here should not be capitalized because the Priestly (P) writers knew nothing about the Trinity.[619]

Modern scholars using higher criticism have concluded that different authors using different documents composed the Pentateuch. This documentary hypothesis identified passages by supposed sources into the terms known today as Yahwistic (J); Elohistic (E), Deuteronomic (D), and Priestly (P), codes that were combined to form the Pentateuch. Gunkel in his book even divides his table of contents to reflect this view: The primeval History according to J, then primeval History in P, and Abraham Legends of J and E.[620] These are completely fictitious authors that liberal theologians have concocted to explain the Old Testament in secular terms and remove the supernatural aspect of the Inspiration of Scripture. They have lost sight of the fact

---

[616] Morey, *The Trinity: Evidence and Issues,* 191-192.
[617] Erickson, *Christian Theology,* 2nd Ed.,882.
[618] Rene Pache, *The Person and Work of the Holy Spirit* (Chicago, IL: Moody, 1954), 29.
[619] Towner, *Westminster Bible Companion: Genesis,* 17.
[620] Hermann Gunkel, *Mercer Library of Biblical Studies: Genesis* (Macon, GA: Mercer University Press, 1997), contents.

that God is the author of the Bible, and He wrote through the agency of man. His Word was written exactly as He wanted it written, when He wrote it, and by whom He said wrote it. The net result is that by 1890, this new secular approach had rejected the Mosaic authorship of the Pentateuch, except for conservative biblical scholars who hold to verbal plenary inspiration of the Scriptures.[621] It was not the Priestly (P) authors that wrote Genesis 1:2, but God who wrote it through Moses, and God knows His own nature. It is the conclusion of this author that Moses also was aware of God's nature because God was revealing Himself to Moses directly. So Towner's comment on not capitalizing *spirit* in Genesis 1:2 to void a reference to the Holy Spirit in Creation is not consistent with the Word of God. Far from editing backwards from a Trinitarian Christian perspective, we would be guilty of overlooking a unique aspect of the original Word of God without basis.

In returning to Genesis 1:2, Hildebrandt refers to Rabbi Zlotowitz who states "and the divine presence hovered upon the surface of the water."[622] Zlotowitz argues that the "Spirit of God" was an impersonal force, not the "Holy Spirit," that was the active one in verse 2. Both Hildebrandt[623] and Allen Ross[624] recognize in verse 2 the personality of the Holy Spirit in Creation. They refer to Deuteronomy 32:11 in relation to the Spirit who moved upon the waters. Hildebrandt disagreed with the Jewish Rabbi Zlotowitz who wanted to suppress the thought of the personality of God in Genesis 1:2. Wood makes the following statement in affirming the personality of the Holy Spirit:

> There are several Scripture passages that speak of the Holy Spirit's having had a part in the creative work. The most significant is Genesis 1:2, "And the Spirit of God moved upon the face of the water." The important word here is moved (*merahapeth*). The Hebrew form is a piel participle, connoting continued action. The thought in view is well illustrated in Deuteronomy 32:11, where the only other piel form of the word in the Old Testament is found. In this passage God's care of Israel in the wilderness is likened to an eagle fluttering over her young in providing for them. The idea of the word in Genesis 1:2, then, is that the Holy Spirit "fluttered over," "took care of," "moved upon" the chaotic state of the world in the interest of bringing order and design. Since the indication comes immediately before the description of the six-day creative activity,

---

[621] Alexander and Baker, *Dictionary of the Old Testament Pentateuch*, 61-62.
[622] Rabbi M. Zlotowitz, *Bereishis: Genesis* (Brooklyn, NY: Mesorah Press, 1986), 1:38.
[623] Hildebrandt, *An Old Testament Theology of the Spirit of God*, 36.
[624] Allen P. Ross, *Creation & Blessing: Genesis* (Grand Rapids: Baker, 1988), 107.

the implication is that the work of the six days was performed by the Spirit.[625]

Walvoord states that all the host of heaven was made by the Holy Spirit (Psalm 33:6). He expresses the creative act as a beautiful picture painted of the heavens being designed and embellished by the Holy Spirit (Job 26:13). These heavens that the Holy Spirit has made *declare the glory of God* (Psalm 19:1). The heavens that the Holy Spirit created have a distinctive characteristic of being designed to bring glory to the Father and Son. It is understood from the New Testament in John 16:13-14 that the Holy Spirit does not glorify Himself but brings glory to the Son. Walvoord sums up his statement on the Holy Spirit and His active part in Creation by saying:

> The work of the Holy Spirit ever bears this characteristic, as it reflects the glory of God, the Holy Spirit not being in the foreground. In the work of creation itself, then, the Holy Spirit is revealed to have a distinct character of operation. He brings order to creation; He is the Giver of life; and shapes creation to achieve it significant purpose of bringing all glory to God.[626]

Walvoord states that even the term *Elohim* implies a work not done by one Person but all the members of the triune God.[627] So when Genesis 1:1 speaks of God creating, it involves all the Godhead, as the Son is also involved in Creation according to Isaiah 48:13 and Zechariah 12:1. Solomon, in Ecclesiastes 12:1, also implies that all the members of the triune God were involved in creation and are to be remembered. Walvoord then proceeds to reference Isaiah 40:12-14 to show that the Spirit is revealed as the Creator by implication:

> The Holy Spirit is described as the untaught, uncounselled, and omnipotent God, who without need of instruction or assistance measured the waters, the heavens, the dust of the earth, and the mountains. His intimate connection with the plan and management of the universe is apparent.[628]

Since *Elohim* created the universe and the earth, R. A. Torrey continues the argument that *Elohim* is plural, which includes the Father, Son, and Holy Spirit in

---

[625] Leon J. Wood, *The Holy Spirit in the Old Testament*, 30.
[626] Walvoord, *The Holy Spirit*, 42.
[627] Walvoord, *The Holy Spirit*, 39.
[628] Walvoord, *The Holy Spirit*, 37-38.

CHAPTER 7: HOLY SPIRIT

Creation. He states the following in relation to *Elohim*, implying the Holy Spirit, as well as the Father and Son, were active in Creation as *Elohim*:

> Why did the Hebrews, with their unquestionable and intense monotheism, use a plural name for God? This was the question that puzzled the Hebrew grammarians and lexicographers of the past, and the best explanation that they could arrive at was the plural of God here used was "the pluralis majestatis," that is, the plural of majesty. But this explanation is entirely inadequate. To say nothing of the fact that the pluralis majestatis in the Old Testament is a figure of very doubtful occurrence – I have not been able to find any place in the Old Testament where it is clear that the pluralis majestatis is used – but in addition to that, even if it were true that the pluralis majestatis does occur in the Old Testament, there is another explanation for the use of a plural name for God that is far nearer at hand and far more adequate and satisfactory, and that is, that the Hebrew inspired writers used a plural name for God, in spite of their intense monotheism, because there is a plurality of person in the one Godhead.[629]

Even though Torrey does not speak specifically of the Holy Spirit, he is dealing with the whole of the triune God in the word *Elohim*, which includes the Holy Spirit. So whether dealing with the passages in Genesis 1:2, 26; Deuteronomy 32:11; Job 26:13; or Psalm 19:1 or with the name of God (*Elohim*), the use of this plural name for God implies that the Holy Spirit was involved in Creation.

Finally, the great evangelist of the twentieth century, Billy Graham, states that the Holy Spirit was involved in Creation by tying together Job 33:4 with Genesis 2:7:

> When God "formed man of dust from the ground" (Genesis 2:7), the Holy Spirit was involved. We learn this indirectly in Job 33:4, "The Spirit of God has made me, and the breath of the Almighty gives me life." A play on words here shows how intimately God's Spirit and our breath are related: both "Spirit" and "breath" are from the same Hebrew word.[630]

---

[629] R. A. Torrey, *The Holy Spirit* (New York: Revell, 1927), 21-22.
[630] Billy Graham, *The Holy Spirit* (Waco, TX: Word, 1978), 25.

There are numerous references in the *Tanakh* that specifically state, and others that strongly imply, that the Holy Spirit who was involved in creation was a person.

Holy Spirit Is Distinct from the Father and Son

In previous chapters it was shown that the Messenger (Angel) of the *Yahweh* was distinct from *Yahweh* and yet *Elohim*. The *Shechinah* was distinct from *Yahweh*, and yet His presence was the presence of *Elohim* or *Yahweh*. Also, it was seen that even *Yahweh* was distinct from *Yahweh*! All of these were representations of the Son being distinct from the Father.

Now the next logical step is to distinguish the Holy Spirit from both the Father and the Son. David, the Psalmist, in Psalm 143:10 gave the distinctiveness of the Holy Spirit:

Teach me to do Your will; for You are my God: Your spirit is good; lead me into the land of uprightness.

Here David is asking the Spirit to lead him in righteousness as the Spirit indwells and guides him.[631]

In Haggai 2:1-9, the one speaking is *Yahweh*. Yet in verse 5, *Yahweh* speaks as the covenant maker with Israel, whom He brought out of Egypt. He speaks to the fact that His Spirit abode among them. According to Cooper, the Holy Spirit came and dwelt in Israel when the Lord God, through the Angel of His presence, delivered her, making the Holy Spirit distinct from the one who made the covenant with them.[632]

In Nehemiah 9:20 the Holy Spirit is given to the people by God to instruct them:

You gave your good Spirit to instruct them and did not withhold your manna from their mouth and gave them water for their thirst. (ESV)

This verse shows two aspects of His Person: First, He is distinct from the LORD (Yahweh, the Father); and, secondly, He teaches, which only a person can do.

---

[631] Payne, *The Theology of the Older Testament*, 174.
[632] David L. Cooper, *The God of Israel*, 80.

CHAPTER 7: HOLY SPIRIT

Using Isaiah 48:16, Cooper shows the distinctiveness between all three members of the tri-unity:

Come near to Me, hear this: I have not spoken in secret from the beginning; from the time that it was, I was there. And now the Lord God and His Spirit have sent Me. (NKJV)

Cooper makes the following statement:

Along with the Messiah, God sends His spirit. The latter here is as much a person as the Creator, whom God dispatches to the earth.[633]

We see additional references to the Holy Spirit as a person in Isaiah 61 and 63. In Isaiah 61:1, the passage that *Yeshua* read in the Nazareth synagogue (Luke 4:16-30), also points out that the *Servant* has been anointed by *Yahweh* for a distinct ministry *to preach the good tidings* and that the *Spirit of the LORD* is upon Him, so we see three Persons referenced in this key passage that Yeshua shared.

In Isaiah 63:7-10, 14, the distinction of the Holy Spirit from the other members of the tri-unity is clear.

⁷ I will recount the kind acts of the LORD, the praises of the LORD, for all that the LORD has wrought for us, the vast bounty to the House of Israel that He bestowed upon them according to His mercy and His great kindness. ⁸ He thought: Surely they are My people, children who will not play false. So He was their Deliverer. ⁹ In all their troubles He was troubled, and the angel of His Presence delivered them. In His love and pity He Himself redeemed them, raised them, and exalted them all the days of old. ¹⁰ But they rebelled, and grieved His holy spirit; then He became their enemy, and Himself made war against them.

¹⁴ Like a beast descending to the plain? Twas the spirit of the LORD gave them rest; thus did You shepherd Your people to win for Yourself a glorious name.

In verse 7 the LORD (**Yahweh**) is referenced, and the Messenger (Angel) of His Presence (the Son as a visible manifestation of God) is referenced in verse 9. These two personalities are distinct from the Holy Spirit in verse 10. Cooper makes the following observation:

---

[633] David L. Cooper, *The God of Israel*, 117.

> We must also remember Jehovah made His Holy Spirit to dwell in the midst of Israel and that later she rebelled against Him and grieved Him. Thus the Holy Spirit is recognized as God and as being separate and distinct from the Lord Jehovah.[634]

The distinction is continued in verse 14 where it says that *the Spirit of the LORD gave them rest*. So Isaiah 63 presents the distinction of the personalities of the tri-unity. In concluding this section, Feinberg states that even though the *Tanakh* does not explain how the Godhead is identical and yet distinct, it does show the tri-unity of God:

> In light of this evidence, it is hard to think that the Spirit of God or Holy Spirit is less than divine. Moreover, several passages cited distinguish him from Y*ahweh*, so the Holy Spirit is somehow both identical and distinct from the Lord. The respects in which he is identical and different are not explained in the OT, but a fairly straightforward reading of the OT about the Spirit of God suggests that there is plurality in the Godhead. Moreover, attributes and actions that could only be true of God are attributed to the Holy Spirit."[635]

Holy Spirit's Coming Upon and Indwelling

There is a difference of opinion and often confusion over the ministry of the Holy Spirit in relation to how He ministered to human beings then and today. What will be observed is that the Holy Spirit functioned differently with Old Testament saints than with New Testament saints.

Several things need to be noted about the ministry of the Holy Spirit under the dispensation of Law. Pache brings out two distinctions: First, "the Spirit is not given to all" and second, "the Spirit was temporarily given, and could be withdrawn."[636] Ryrie states it a little differently when he gives three divisions that are related to the nature of the Holy Spirit's work. First, "the Spirit was in certain ones," which is illustrated with the Spirit of God in Joseph and Daniel. Second, "the Spirit is said to have come upon many" as illustrated in the book of Judges (chapters 3, 6, 11, 13-15) and upon Saul (1 Samuel 10). Third, "the Spirit is said to have filled some" as

---

[634] David L. Cooper, *The God of Israel*, 84-85.
[635] John S. Feinberg, *No One Like Him*, 454-455.
[636] Pache, *The Person and Work of the Holy Spirit*, 30.

CHAPTER 7: HOLY SPIRIT

recorded with Bezaleel (Exodus 31:3; 35:31).[637] Ryrie summarizes his three previous statements:

> What do these examples indicate? Simply that, although the Spirit did indwell men of Old Testament times, it was a selective ministry, both in regard to whom He indwelt and for how long.[638]

What should be understood is that the Spirit's activity of coming upon, or in, or filling, had nothing to do with the person or his/her spiritual salvation. Walvoord also sees the Holy Spirit in this light when he says:

> It will be noted, first, that the coming of the spirit to indwell individuals has no apparent relation to spiritual qualities.[639]

It is important to understand that the Holy Spirit's ministry was selective as to whom He came upon, in, or filled to accomplish the specific tasks or purposes that He desired. Walvoord clarifies this by saying:

> Only a few were indwelt by the Holy Spirit, and these were known for their distinctive gift, were sought out as leaders and prophets, and were usually marked men."[640]

David, in his confession of his sin in Psalm 51:11, pleads with the Lord not to remove His Holy Spirit from him. David remembered vividly what happened to Saul. Because of his sin and lack of repentance, Saul had the Holy Spirit removed from him (1 Samuel 16:14). So the fact was that the Holy Spirit could come and leave, totally unlike the ministry of the Holy Spirit in the New Testament (John 14:17). The Holy Spirit came upon people for specific tasks. Wood states once that task was completed, He would leave:

> The Spirit came upon the persons involved for the activity concerned and then left them when that activity had been completed.[641]

The empowering presence of the Holy Spirit upon a person for a specific task was the norm during the Old Testament period.[642] Different aspects of the Holy

---

[637] Ryrie, *The Holy Spirit*, 41-42.
[638] Ryrie, *The Holy Spirit*, 42.
[639] Walvoord, *The Holy Spirit*, 72.
[640] Walvoord, *The Holy Spirit*, 72.
[641] Leon J. Wood, *The Holy Spirit in the Old Testament*, 43
[642] VanGemeren, ed., *Dictionary of Old Testament Theological and Exegesis*, 3:1076.

Spirit's ministry of empowering will come out clearly as the different individuals in the *Tanakh* are studied.

It appears that the Holy Spirit had a broader ministry than is generally recognized. Walter Kaiser expresses that the Holy Spirit also regenerated people in the Old Testament as referenced in Jesus' conversation with Nicodemus in John 3:3-10.[643] The Holy Spirit had a ministry among Old Testament saints, but little attention has been given to that aspect of the Holy Spirit's Old Testament ministry.

Holy Spirit's Ministry to Individuals in the *Tanakh*

The Holy Spirit had a ministry among Old Testament saints, but little attention has been given to that aspect of the Holy Spirit's Old Testament ministry. In the forthcoming examples of the Holy Spirit's ministry to Old Testament believers, it will be observed that the Holy Spirit came upon, filled, indwelt, and left because of sin or the completion of a task. (Those aspects will be in bold font.)

BEZALEEL

Feinberg points out that in Exodus 31:2-3 God **filled** Bezaleel to do the work of an artisan as he prepared the Tabernacle:

> *In wisdom, in understand, and in knowledge and in all craftsmanship, to make artistic designs for work in gold, in silver and in bronze, and in the cutting of stones for setting, and in the carving of wood that he may work in all kinds of craftsmanship.*

So as an artisan, in the construction of the Tabernacle, Bezaleel was enabled, by the Holy Spirit, to do and complete the task laid out before him. Moses concurs with what God said in Exodus 35:31.[644]

UNNAMED TAILORS

In Exodus 28:3, God tells Moses that the tailor had been **endowed with the Spirit of wisdom** to make all the High Priestly garments.[645]

---

[643] Walter C. Kaiser, The Christian and the "Old" Testament (Pasadena, CA: William Carey Library, 1998), 223-224.
[644] John S. Feinberg, *No One Like Him*, 454.
[645] Walvoord, *The Holy Spirit*, 71.

> *And you shall make holy garments for Aaron your brother, for glory and for beauty. And you shall speak to all the skillful persons* **whom I have endowed with the Spirit of wisdom,** *that they make Aaron's garments to consecrate him, that he may minister as priest to Me. And these are the garments which they shall make: a breast piece and an ephod and a robe and a tunic of checkered work, a turban and a sash, and they shall make holy garments for Aaron your brother and his sons, that he may minister as priest to Me.*

SEVENTY ELDERS

In Numbers 11:17, 25 the LORD told Moses that He would take some of the Spirit that he had and place it **upon the seventy elders** so they could bear the burden of the people with him.

> *Then I will come down and speak with you there, and I will take of the Spirit who is* **upon you***, and will put Him* **upon them***; and they shall bear the burden of the people with you, so that you shall not bear it all alone.*

> *Then the LORD came down in the cloud and spoke to him; and He took of the Spirit who was* **upon him** *and placed Him* **upon the seventy elders***. And it came about that when the Spirit rested upon them, they prophesied.*

So Moses gathered the elders together, in obedience to God, for the partial transference of the Spirit to the elders. Hildebrandt gives added information to this movement of the Spirit as some of the Spirit is transferred from Moses to the 70 elders:

> Moses gather[ed] the seventy elders in obedience to *Yahweh's* direction so that *Yahweh* could "take" from the *ruach* on him and bestow some of the *ruach* on each of the elders. The verb *asal* indicates the "withholding" of a portion of the *ruach* that is on Moses for his leadership duties and is then distributed among the elders for their new responsibilities. The term emphasizes the great endowment of Spirit on Moses and is conceived of materially and quantitatively.[646]

---

[646] Hildebrandt, *An Old Testament Theology of the Spirit of God,* 157.

The immediate consequence of the *ruach* resting on the seventy elders was their spontaneous expression of *prophesying*. In verse 29, two of the elders continued to prophesy; and Joshua objected. Moses responded by saying he wished all of the Lord's people were prophets and that the LORD would put His Spirit **upon them**. What is immediately apparent was that the Spirit was resting on only certain people, in this case the elders. We also see that the Spirit here is distinct from *Yahweh*, and that this Spirit is personal in giving divine judicial advice in His guidance of Israel.[647]

BALAAM

There is one non-Israelite example of the Holy Spirit coming upon a false prophet who knew the God of Israel (Numbers 22:8-35). Balaam was from Mesopotamia (Deuteronomy 23:4); and, according to the *Tanakh*, his reputation was that whomever he blessed would be blessed, and whomever he cursed would be cursed (Numbers 22:6). Balak, King of Moab, called for Balaam to curse Israel. In Numbers 23:5, the Scriptures say that the LORD put the words in Balaam's mouth; he could only speak what God put in his mouth. Then in Numbers 24:2, the Scriptures distinctly say, *and the Spirit of God* **came upon him**. Balaam was unable to curse Israel because the Spirit of God came **upon him** and he had to bless Israel.[648]

> *And Balaam lifted up his eyes and saw Israel camping tribe by tribe;*
> *and the Spirit of God* **came upon him**.

This is a difficult passage in that Balaam was not a genuine prophet but rather a diviner. While he knew God, he did not follow God. This passage shows God's covenantal protection of Israel in taking over Balaam's mouth.[649]

JOSHUA

> *So the LORD said to Moses, take Joshua the son of Nun, a man* **in whom is the Spirit**, *and lay your hand on him.* (Numbers 27:18)

Joshua was prepared by the Spirit of God to be the successor of Moses and to lead Israel into the Promised Land. He was a man of God, **filled with the Spirit of wisdom** (Deuteronomy 34:9), to do a very difficult job to lead Israel and conquer the Land.

In entering the period of the Judges, the Holy Spirit came upon the Judges for the purpose of delivering Israel from its oppressors after they repented of following

---

[647] Payne, *The Theology of the Older Testament*, 173.
[648] Leon J. Wood, *The Holy Spirit in the Old Testament*, 44.
[649] Lockyer, *All About the Holy Spirit*, 55.

other gods. Four judges are specifically mentioned as having the *Spirit of the LORD come upon* them: Othniel, Gideon, Jephthah, and Samson. Several authors, such as Wood,[650] Hildebrandt,[651] Lockyer,[652] Walvoord,[653] Erickson,[654] Butler,[655] and Enns,[656] state that the Spirit, as a person, came upon the judges as they delivered Israel. Morey in referring to Othniel, states that the Spirit came upon him and instructed him or enabled him. Only a person can instruct or enable judges, not a force or power.[657]

OTHNIEL

> *...Othniel the son of Kenaz, Caleb's younger brother. And the Spirit of the LORD* **came upon him***, and he judged Israel.*
>
> (Judges 3:9b-10)

Block, in His discussion on the first judge, Othniel, refers to the Spirit of God, calling Him a member of the Trinity. However, at the same time, Block seems to want to make *the Spirit of the LORD* a power or force rather than a distinct person. In contrast, the above authors distinctly imply the Spirit of God is a person coming upon Othniel and enabling him to have victory over the enemy. Block's statement on the personality of the Holy Spirit is confusing because of his statement that the Holy Spirit is an extension of the LORD's personality:

> Similarly, the Spirit of God is the agency/agent through which God's will is exercised, whether it be in creation, his dispensing of life, his guidance and providential care, the revelation of his will, his renewal of unregenerate hearts, or his sealing of his covenant people as his own. The Spirit of God is not a self-existent agent operating independently but "an extension of the LORD's personality," the third member of the Trinity, by which God exercises influence over the world.[658]

---

[650] Leon J. Wood, *The Holy Spirit*, 25, 53-55. Also see: Leon J. Wood, *Distressing Days of the Judges* (Grand Rapids, MI: Zondervan, 1975), 161-171, 201-233, 278-340.
[651] Hildebrandt, *The Holy Spirit in the Old Testament*, 114-117.
[652] Lockyer, *All About the Holy Spirit*, 55.
[653] Walvoord, *The Holy Spirit*, 71, 74.
[654] Erickson, *Christian Theology*, 2nd Ed, 884.
[655] Butler, *Butler's Bible Works*, 3:179, 210, 230, 237.
[656] Enns, *The Moody Handbook of Theology*, 260-261.
[657] Morey, *The Trinity: Evidence and Issues*, 192.
[658] Daniel I. Block, *The New American Commentary: Judges, Ruth*. (vol. 6. Nashville: Broadman & Holman, 1999), 6:154-155.

Block's statement is unclear. Does he see the *Spirit of God* here as a distinct person from the Father, or is he making the *Spirit of God* simply an "extension" of, rather than distinct from, God? He seems to be sitting on the fence.

GIDEON

> *So the* **Spirit of the LORD came upon** *Gideon; and he blew the trumpet, and the Abiezrites were called together to follow him.*
> (Judges 6:34 KJV)

What is significant about Gideon is that he was very hesitant to become the *valiant warrior*, as the Messenger (Angel) of *Yahweh* referred to him in Judges 6:12. He questioned God about the *wondrous deeds* He performed in the past (v. 13). His excuse, in verse 14, showed his reluctance and low position in his father's house. Then in verse 17, he asks for a sign because of his timidity in pulling down the altar of Baal by night because of the fear of his father's household and the town's people. Then, in verse 36, Gideon made the request for the fleece test. His faith was not strong. Nestled between all this is the statement in verse 34: *The spirit of the LORD enveloped* or came upon him. The Holy Spirit's personal presence came upon Gideon as He gave him divine enablement to blow the shofar and begin to muster the men for battle.[659]

Block makes an interesting statement as to the response of the people to Gideon:

> This raises an extremely important question: Why are Gideon's clansmen, tribesmen, and countrymen so ready to respond to him? Are they impressed with his leadership ability or his courage? Do they recognize him as the "valiant warrior," whom the messenger of *Yahweh* had addressed in v. 12? Not if one may judge from the expressed perception of his standing within his own family and tribe (v. 15) when God calls him to military leadership or from the trepidation with which he destroyed the Baal cult site in the preceding account (v. 31). From the succeeding narrative of the dew and the fleece (vv. 36-40) it seems that nothing has changed internally or personally. Gideon remains hesitant. Juxtaposed with a text that portrays Gideon doing all he can to avoid a leadership role, the answer must lie in the opening clause of v. 34: the Spirit of *Yahweh* "clothed" Gideon. This idiom expresses in more dramatic

---

[659] John F. Walvoord and Ray B. Zuck, *The Bible Knowledge Commentary: Old Testament* (Wheaton, IL: Victor Books, 1985), 393.

form the notion expressed earlier in 3:10: "The Spirit of the LORD came upon Othniel," that is[,] the Spirit took possession of the man.[660]

What is obvious is that the Spirit of the LORD that came upon him caused him to become the *valiant warrior*, and that the people flocked to join him to fight the Midianites.

JEPHTHAH

> *Then the* **Spirit of the LORD came upon** *Jephthah, and he passed over Gilead, and Manasseh, and passed over Mizpah of Gilead, and from Mizpah of Gilead he passed over unto the children of Ammon.*
> (Judges 11:29 KJV)

This statement of Scripture is the same as that of Othniel and Gideon. The Spirit of the LORD came upon them, as in this case, upon Jephthah. There seems to be three general ways this passage is viewed by authors: First, some authors, such as Grudem,[661] Wolf,[662] Keil, and Delitzsch,[663] acknowledge that the Spirit of the LORD did come upon Jephthah, but they did not interact with the passage in relation to the Holy Spirit. Second, others, such as Garstang[664] and Schneider,[665] do not even refer to the Spirit of the LORD in their discussion of Jephthah. Lastly, some authors, such as McCann,[666] state that Jephthah "looks worse than bad" while Soggin[667] states that this section of Scripture on Jephthah was a later interpretation so as to make Jephthah a major Judge rather than a minor Judge. McCann and Soggin both have a tendency to discredit the person and judgeship of Jephthah.

This passage on Jephthah where it references the *Spirit of the LORD* is neglected by many authors. This author believes the passage is too challenging, so it

---

[660] Block, *The New American Commentary: Judges, Ruth,* 6:271-272.
[661] Grudem, *Systematic Theology*, 636.
[662] Herbert Wolf. *The Expositor's Bible Commentary* (12 vols. Grand Rapids: Zondervan, 1992), 3:455.
[663] Keil and Delitzsch, *Commentary on the Old Testament*, 2:384.
[664] John Garstang, *The Foundations of Bible History: Joshua Judges* (Grand Rapids: Kregel, 1978), 329-333.
[665] Tammi J. Schneider, *Berit Olam: Studies in Hebrew Narrative and Poetry, Judges* (Collegeville, MN: The Liturgical Press, 2000), 169-183.
[666] J. Clinton McCann, *Interpretation: A Bible Commentary for Teaching and Preaching: Judges* (Louisville, KY: John Knox Press, 2002), 85.
[667] J. Alberto Soggin, *The Old Testament Library: Judges*, (trans. John Bowden; Philadelphia: Westminster, 1981), 206-207.

is passed over due to *the Spirit of the LORD* coming upon him and the problem with Jephthah's daughter. Yet, God found the events of this Judge's life worthy of mention in Hebrews 11:32, even with this problematic passage. The simple question that must be asked is: If the Holy Spirit came upon the others that have been previously mentioned in this chapter, wouldn't it be equally true in relationship to Jephthah's judgeship?

SAMSON

We see a number of references to *the Spirit of the LORD* in relation to Sampson in the book of Judges.

> *And the* **Spirit of the LORD began to stir** *him in Mahaneh-dan, between Zorah and Eshtaol.* (Judges 13:25)

> *And the* **Spirit of the LORD came upon him** *mightily, so that he tore him as one tears a kid though he had nothing in his hand; but he did not tell his father and mother what he had done.* (Judges 14:6)

> *Then the* **Spirit of the LORD came upon him** *mightily, and he went down to Ashkelon and killed thirty of them and took their spoil, and gave the changes of clothes to those who told the riddle. And his anger burned, and he went up to his father's house.* (Judges 14:19)

> *When he came to Lehi, the Philistines shouted as they met him.* **And the Spirit of the LORD came upon him** *mightily so that the ropes that were on his arms were as flax that is burned with fire, and his bonds dropped from his hands. And he found a fresh jawbone of a donkey, so he reached out and took it and killed a thousand men with it.* (Judges 15:14-15)

The ministry of the Holy Spirit in the life of Samson is unique to the Judges. Four times the Spirit of the LORD came upon Samson as God used him in judging the Philistines. Only with Gideon (6:11-22) and Samson (13:3-23) is the Messenger (Angel) of *Yahweh* involved in their lives. Only with the promise and birth of Samson is the Messenger (Angel) of *Yahweh* involved with his birth. Each of the four judges mentioned in this section had a special empowerment to carry out God's assigned tasks. Because Samson was designated as a Nazirite (13:14), it seems that the Holy Spirit came upon him until Delilah cut his hair (16:18-20). The Holy Spirit came upon him on several occasions, with special empowerment, as illustrated by in Judges 13:25; 14:6, 19; 15:14-15.

Samson was also unique among Israel's Judges in that God instructed him to fight the Philistines alone rather than to raise an army. On four occasions, he received a special enablement for a major display of strength.[668] *Yahweh*'s active participation with Israel is seen with the involvement of the Messenger (Angel) of *Yahweh* as well as the Holy Spirit coming upon these individuals when the nation repented and called for deliverance.[669]

It should also be noted that respected scholars such as Woods,[670] Walvoord, and Zuck[671] refer to *the Spirit of the LORD* as *the Holy Spirit*. Most authors do not make that specific designation in relationship to the Spirit passages in Judges. This designation of the Holy Spirit is important because the Jewish response is that the Spirit is God's Spirit, not a distinct member of the Godhead. The lack of designation is expressed frequently by Schneider when she says, of the Spirit of the LORD, that He was "moved by the spirit of the deity."[672] The usage of the term *Elohim* here specifies and clarifies a distinction by denoting God as a plurality. Hence, when the Hebrew Scriptures refer to the Spirit of *Yahweh*, or the Spirit of God, or by the statement that the Spirit of the LORD came upon an individual, the *Tanakh* is referring to the Holy Spirit, the Third Person of the Godhead of *Elohim*.

One final note on Samson and the ministry of the Holy Spirit in his life: Even though Samson was anointed as a Judge, there were periods of godless disobedience in his life. Both the personal and official blessedness of the Spirit were removed. This is not an issue of keeping or losing personal salvation, then or now, but of being anointed for high office or specific skillful tasks.

SAUL

There are four basic passages that speak of the Spirit of God in relationship to Saul. Three references are found in 1 Samuel 10 and 11 and one in chapter 16, which refers to both Saul and David. The first reference is a prophecy by Samuel that the Spirit of the LORD would come upon Saul and make him into a different man:

> *And the* **Spirit of the LORD will come upon thee**, *and you shall prophesy with them, and shall be turn into another man.*
> (1 Samuel 10:6 KJV)

---

[668] Leon J. Wood, *The Holy Spirit in the Old Testament*, 55.
[669] Hildebrandt, *An Old Testament Theology of the Spirit of God*, 117.
[670] Leon J. Wood, *Distressing Days of the Judges*, 311-312.
[671] Walvoord and Zuck, *The Bible Knowledge Commentary: Old Testament*, 404.
[672] Schneider, *Berit Olam: Judges*, 202.

The second reference is the recorded fulfillment of Samuel's words to Saul. Samuel gives Saul three signs that will confirm God's choice of him as king. This is most significant because when *the Spirit of God* came upon Saul, it caused him to prophesy with a band of prophets:

> *When they came to the hill there, behold, a group of prophets met him; and the* **Spirit of God came upon him** *mightily, so that he prophesied among them.* (1 Samuel 10:10 KJV)

Hildebrandt makes this comment in connection to Saul prophetic experience and *Yahweh*'s confirmation of him as the first king:

> The act of prophesying by Saul and the band of prophets is to be distinguished from that of prophetic inspiration, which conveys a message to the recipient. The ecstatic element indicates an encounter with the *ruach yhwh* that brings about external manifestations in additions to verbal utterances. In this instance, the fulfillment of the three signs would confirm that *Yahweh* is with Saul.[673]

The Spirit of God came upon Saul, as with the Judges, to equip him to fulfill the task of being king:

> *And the* **Spirit of God came upon Saul** *when he heard those tidings, and his anger was kindled greatly.* (1 Samuel 11:6 KJV)

Walvoord and Zuck affirm that the Spirit of God came upon Saul to equip him because he was inexperienced and unlettered and unable to assume kingly responsibilities in much the same way that the judges did before him.[674] Barber concurs and continues the same idea when he says:

> It seems most likely that God gave to Saul that which he lacked by training and heredity. He provided him with the inner disposition to fulfill the tasks of a king. He equipped him, as He had done the judges, so that Saul would be able to deliver his people from those who sought to oppress them. When the transitory enthusiasm of his meeting with the prophets passed, it left Saul with a certain inner sense that could not be satisfied without further communion with the Lord.[675]

---

[673] Hildebrandt, *An Old Testament Theology of the Spirit of God,* 120.
[674] Walvoord and Zuck, *The Bible Knowledge Commentary: Old Testament,* 441.
[675] Cyril J. Barber, *The Books of Samuel.* (vol. 1. Neptune, NJ: Loizeaux, 1994), 116.

CHAPTER 7: HOLY SPIRIT

So the coming of the Spirit of God upon Saul was not only to let him know that God was with him, but was also to equip him for his task as king.

One other point that Bergen brings out is the contrast between the use of the terms *Spirit of God* and the *Spirit of the LORD*. He observes that elsewhere in the *Tanakh*, when the Holy Spirit came upon an individual, it states that the Spirit of the LORD came upon them. However, here, and only one other place, does it say that the *Spirit of God* came upon him. Even though both terms refer to the same Person of God, the Spirit of God is used only with one other person, Balaam. The reason for God's choice of words is not clear, but as Balaam was unfaithful to God, Saul was also unfaithful.[676] Bergen's observation is interesting but not valid. For the *Spirit of God* also came upon others such as Bezaleel in Exodus 31:2-3; Azariah, a prophet who gave a warning to Asa in 2 Chronicles 15:1; and Zechariah, the priest in 2 Chronicles 24:20. Bergen's statement is inconclusive because among these references, two people acted in disobedience, two people acted in obedience, and another, an artisan, prepared the Tabernacle.

When the Spirit of God came upon Saul, it was permanent (ongoing) because of his office; but it turned out to be temporary. Having the Spirit of God come upon the other Judges was temporary because their ministries were limited in scope, with the possible exception of Samson. In 1 Samuel 16, the passage indicates that had Saul not sinned by his incomplete obedience but instead had remained faithful, the Spirit would have remained with Saul throughout his life as king.[677]

> Divine spirit follows immediately upon the anointing and remains "from that day forward." Moreover, as we are about to discover, *Yahweh*'s spirit has departed from Saul (16:14).[678]

DAVID AND SAUL

> *13 Then Samuel took the horn of oil and anointed him in the midst of his brothers; and the* **Spirit of the LORD came mightily upon** *David from that day forward. And Samuel arose and went to Ramah.*
> *14 Now the* **Spirit of the LORD departed from Saul,** *and an evil spirit from the LORD terrorized him.*   (1 Samuel 16:13-14)

What is seen here is that the Holy Spirit came upon Saul and was with him up to 1 Samuel 16:14. Then the Lord sent an evil spirit to terrorize him because God

---

[676] Bergen, *The New American Commentary: 1 and 2 Samuel*, 7:136.
[677] Leon J. Wood, *The Holy Spirit in the Old Testament*, 62.
[678] P. Kyle McCarter, Jr. *The Anchor Bible: 1 Samuel* (vol. 8. Garden City, NY: Doubleday, 1980), 8:276.

had now rejected Saul and had Samuel anoint David to be king. These two events occurred in close sequence to each other. Once the Holy Spirit came upon David, the Holy Spirit left Saul. When the Holy Spirit left Saul, it did not mean that he was not a believer on the God of Israel, but rather that the enabling power of God left him and was given to David.[679]

DAVID

> The **Spirit of the LORD spoke by me** *and His word was on my tongue. The God of Israel said, The Rock of Israel spoke to me.*
> (2 Samuel 23:2-3a)

> *Do not cast me away from Your presence, and* **do not take Your Holy Spirit from me.** (Psalm 51:11)

In 1 Samuel 16, it was observed that the Spirit of the LORD came upon David and was with him throughout his lifetime. That is seen by two things: first, the Holy Spirit spoke by David; and second, the Holy Spirit's words were on his tongue. Bergen speaks of David as being in the passive role as the Holy Spirit spoke through him as he makes the following observation:

> Thus David has now been portrayed throughout the books of Samuel as king, priest, and prophet....Since David, the first member of Israel's royal messianic line, functioned in these three roles, it seems appropriate that Jesus the Messiah should not only be depicted by the New Testament writers as inheriting these roles but superseding David's accomplishments in them. He did not choose this role but accepted it when the Spirit of the Lord spoke through him. David's role was essentially passive in this event. When he spoke, it was the Lord's "word" not his own that was on his "tongue."[680]

Youngblood makes the observation that as God, He spoke through the mouth of Balaam (24:2, 4), and the Spirit of the LORD spoke through David. Youngblood makes the following connection with *Yeshua*:

> That David spoke "by the Spirit" on another occasion is affirmed by Jesus Himself (Matthew 22:43), and David's use of the phrase "spoke through" represents a clear claim to divine inspiration. David

---

[679] Ronald Youngblood, *The Expositor's Bible Commentary*, 12 vols. (Grand Rapids: Zondervan), 3:688.
[680] Bergen, *The New American Commentary: 1, 2 Samuel*, 465-466.

was conscious of the fact that the "word" of the Lord was on his "tongue" and that the mighty "Rock of Israel" had spoken to him.[681]

Youngblood was referring to 2 Samuel 23:2-3 where David said:

> *² The spirit of the LORD has spoken through me, His message is on my tongue; ³ The God of Israel has spoken, the Rock of Israel said concerning me: He who rules men justly, he who rules in awe of God.*

It is clearly presented by David that the Holy Spirit, who is distinct from *Yahweh*, spoke to and through him.

Also, it can be observed that David pleaded with the Lord (Psalm 51:11) not to take his Holy Spirit from him. David wanted the presence of God with him to guide him and enable him as King of Israel. David also remembered very clearly what happened to Saul because of his sin. David wanted to walk righteously before his God as his Psalms so aptly speak.

MICAH

> *On the other hand I am* **filled** *with power – With the Spirit of the LORD.* (Micah 3:8)

In this verse Micah, a contemporary of Isaiah in the eighth century B.C.E., spoke of himself as being *filled with the Spirit of the LORD*. He traces the power of his prophetic ministry to the Holy Spirit.[682] Just as Bezaleel was filled with the Spirit, so was Micah. This filling of the Holy Spirit equipped Micah to deal with the corruption among the leaders of Israel (3:1-3; 7:1-4) and among the priest and prophets themselves (2:6, 11; 3:5-7).[683]

ISAIAH

The prophet Isaiah had a vision of the Lord, but nowhere does he say that the Spirit of the LORD was upon him as others did. Obviously the Spirit of the LORD was upon him, but it is not stated. What we do see in Isaiah is that the Spirit will be upon the Messiah and the future nation of Israel when all of Israel confesses the corporate sin of rejecting the Messiah. The next verse is an example of the Spirit being upon Israel because of the New Covenant:

---

[681] Youngblood, *The Expositor's Bible Commentary*, 3:1082.
[682] Walvoord, *the Holy Spirit*, 50.
[683] Hildebrandt, *An Old Testament Theology of the Spirit of God*, 190-191.

> *And as for Me, this is **My covenant** with them, says the LORD: "**My spirit which is upon you**, and My words which I have put in your mouth, shall not depart from your mouth, nor from the mouth of your offspring, nor from the mouth of your offspring's offspring," says the LORD "from now and forever."* (Isaiah 59:21)

This verse is connected to three themes in the book of Isaiah, as well as to the books of Jeremiah and Ezekiel, where the New Covenant of Jeremiah 31:31-34 is discussed along with the roles of the Messiah and the Holy Spirit. Walter Kaiser connects the *My covenant* in the above verse to the New Covenant of Jeremiah 31.[684]

Motyer also connects the Isaiah 59:21 passage with the ministry of the Servant of the LORD in the servant passages of Isaiah.[685] Enns connects the fulfillment of the New Covenant to the return of the Messiah and the forgiveness of Israel.[686] Wolf connects the covenant with the Servant of the Lord and relates it to the New Covenant.[687]

The fact is that Isaiah 59:21 pertains to Israel's future where the New Covenant is God's future blessing on Israel, even though they grieved His Holy Spirit (63:10). The Holy Spirit was grieved and turned away; but the New Covenant speaks of the pouring out of God's Spirit (44:3). But in Jeremiah 31:31-37, which was connected to Isaiah 59:21, is a promise by God, through His New Covenant, that *My spirit* will be upon them and *My words* will be put in their mouths and will not depart from them from generation to generation even *from now and forever*. So in Isaiah 59:21 God promises His spirit would come upon them, that His words will be in their mouths, and all will come to pass in the New Covenant and through the Messiah, the Servant of the LORD. Christians recognize that the New Covenant is the indwelling of the Holy Spirit in the lives of believers, both Jew and Gentile; however, this New Covenant will not be totally fulfilled until Israel embraces *Yeshua* as her own personal Messiah and trusts in Him.

EZEKIEL

In the following verses, references to the Spirit's actions are in bold, which is my emphasis:

> *And as He spoke to me **the Spirit entered me** and set me on my feet; and I heard Him speaking to me.* (Ezekiel 2:2 NASV)

---

[684] Kaiser, *Toward an Old Testament Theology*, 231.
[685] J. Alec Motyer, *The Prophecy of Isaiah* (Downers Grove, IL: InterVarsity, 1993), 492.
[686] Enns, *The Moody Handbook of Theology*, 68.
[687] Wolf, *Interpreting Isaiah*, 235.

And He stretched out the form of a hand and caught me by a lock of my head; and **the Spirit lifted me up** *between earth and heaven and brought me in the visions of God to Jerusalem, to the entrance of the north gate of the inner court, where the seat of the idol of jealousy, which provokes to jealousy, was located.* (Ezekiel 8:3 NASV)

Moreover, **the Spirit lifted me up** *and brought me to the east gate of the LORD's house which faced eastward. And behold, there were twenty-five men at the entrance of the gate, and among them I saw Jaazaniah son of Azzur and Pelatiah son of Benaiah, leaders of the people.* (Ezekiel 11:1 NASV)

And the **Spirit lifted me up** *and brought me in a* **vision by the Spirit of God** *to the exiles in Chaldea. So the vision that I had seen left me.* (Ezekiel 11:24 NASV)

The Hand of the LORD was upon me, and He brought me out **by the Spirit of the LORD** *and set me down in the middle of the valley; and it was full of bones.* (Ezekiel 37:1 NASV)

Most authors do not interact with the plurality of God that is present in these passages. In all these passages there is a plurality of persons involved with Ezekiel and his visions. It is disheartening to notice that scholars, such as Feinberg[688] and Cooper,[689] do not interact with the Spirit that is so prevalent in these passages. In fact, Taylor states that according to Ezekiel 2:2, the Spirit is "spiritual energy" and not a person.[690] Yet, each of these passages clearly indicate two members of the Godhead. In looking at the description in Ezekiel 1:26, God is appearing in a human form. In fact, Alexander refers to this section of Scripture as a "theophany,"[691] God appearing in human form. Studying these verses in parallel highlights the personalities in each verse, as seen in the table below:

In each instance and in each verse, in the immediate context, there are two personalities engaged with Ezekiel. A man appears in 1:26, 8:2, 10:2, 11:16-17, and 37:1. This author believes that these appearances of a man are theophanies of the Second Person of the Godhead. The other personality mentioned in 2:2, 8:2, 10:2,

---

[688] Charles L. Feinberg, *The Prophecy of Ezekiel: The Glory of the Lord* (Chicago: Moody, 1969).
[689] Lamar Eugene Cooper, Sr. *The New American Commentary: Ezekiel* (vol. 17) (Nashville: Broadman and Holman, 1994).
[690] John B. Taylor, *Ezekiel* (Downers Grove: InterVarsity, 1974), 61.
[691] Ralph H. Alexander, *The Expositor's Bible Commentary: Ezekiel* (vol. 6. Grand Rapids: Zondervan, 1986), 6:761.

11:24, and 37:1 is continually called the Spirit, which is the Third Person of the Godhead, the Holy Spirit. These two, the Man and the Spirit, are members of the God-

Multiple Persons of God in Ezekiel's Vision

Ezekiel	The Man / The Spirit
1:26a	*"a figure with the* **appearance of a man**" /
2:2	"**Spirit** *entered me and set me on my feet*"
8:2	*"a likeness as the* **appearance of a man**" /
8:3	"*the* **Spirit** *lifted me up between heaven and earth*"
10:2	*"And He spoke to the* **man** *clothed in linen"* (10:2) /
11:1	"*the* **Spirit** *lifted me up and brought me to the east gate*"
11:16-17	*"Thus says the* **Lord God**" (11:16-17) /
11:24	*"And the* **Spirit** *lifted me up and brought me in a vision by the* **Spirit of God**"
37:1a	*"The* **hand of the** LORD *was upon me,* /
37:1b	*"and He brought me out by the* **Spirit of the LORD** *and set me down"*

head who are working with Ezekiel. One is interacting with words, and the other in lifting Ezekiel up to take him to the locations of the visions that God wants him to see. Cooke makes the following remarks along the same lines:

> This was no messenger, no angel. As at the inaugural vision, so now, it is Jehovah Himself in human form, glowing with supernatural splendour, who appears to the prophet, and speaks to him, and announces the hour of visitation....The distinction between the hand of Jehovah and the spirit seems to be that the one gave the impression of a visible, the other of an invisible agency: the hand

appeared to grasp the prophet by the forelock, the spirit impelled his movement.[692]

In each of these passages there is a clear distinction between the theophany of God (appearance of a man) and the Spirit of God. These two Persons are addressed and treated as being distinct.

Inspiration of the Scriptures

The word "inspiration" comes from the Latin Vulgate Bible in which the verb "inspire" appears in 2 Timothy 3:16 and 2 Peter 1:21. However, the word *inspiration* in the Greek is actually used only once, in 2 Timothy, to translate the word *theopneustos*. *Theopneustos*, which means "God-breathed" emphasizes the exhalation of God. *God-breathed* would be more accurate since it emphasizes that Scripture is the product of the breath of God. The Scriptures are not something breathed *into* by God. Rather, the Scriptures have been breathed *out* by God.[693]

The Greek word that is used for the English word *Scripture* is *graphe*, which simply means "writing."[694] The written Word of God was given by God, and it was recorded in writing as He willed. The writings that He wanted preserved as Scripture have become what is called today The Bible.

Inspiration and how is it to be understood in the Hebrew Scriptures, as well as the New Testament, is important to understand. Walvoord lays out a clear statement as to the meaning of inspiration:

> That God so supernaturally directed the writers of Scripture that without excluding their human intelligence, their individuality, their literary style, their personal feelings, or any other human factor, His own complete and coherent message to man was recorded in perfect accuracy, the very words of Scripture bearing the authority of divine authorship. Nothing less than a plenary and verbal inspiration will satisfy the demands of the Scripture themselves and give to faith the confidence in the Word of God which is essential to faith and life.[695]

Geisler also gives the same kind of definition of inspiration as Walvoord:

---

[692] G. A. Cooke, *The International Critical Commentary: The Book of Ezekiel*, (Edinburgh: T. & T. Clark, 1936), 89-91.
[693] Enns, *The Moody Handbook of Theology*, 160.
[694] Enns, *The Moody Handbook of Theology*, 153.
[695] Walvoord, *The Holy Spirit*, 58.

> Inspiration is the supernatural operation of the Holy Spirit, who through the different personalities and literary styles of the chosen human authors invested the very words of the original books of Holy Scripture, alone and in their entirety, as the very Word of God without error in all that they teach or imply (including history and science), and the Bible is thereby the infallible rule and final authority for faith and practice of all believers.[696]

God worked with individual personalities and literary styles so that when the Word of God was given to human authors, there was an absence of any formal argument to prove the inspiration of their writings because none was deemed necessary. The character of the Scriptures themselves were sufficient evidence for both the authors and the readers.

The term *inspiration* makes other declarations as expressed by Geisler and Nix:

(1) The claim of inspiration has several other characteristics that need to be mentioned. First, inspiration is verbal, meaning that it "extends to the very words of Scripture" (Exodus 24:4; Isaiah 8:1; 30:8).

(2) Inspiration makes the Scripture unbreakable or infallible (Psalm 82; John 10:35).

(3) The Scriptures are irrevocable, meaning that they cannot be changed and will be fulfilled (Matthew 5:18; Luke 16:17; 24:44).

(4) Inspiration makes the Scriptures the final authority (Matthew 4:4, 7, 10). Nothing will supersede the written Word of God.

(5) Inspiration is plenary, meaning that it is full, complete, extending to every part[697] (2 Timothy 3:16).

There is one thing that needs to be made clear concerning the work of the Holy Spirit in inspiration. The Holy Spirit did not inspire men, but inspired his Word. Gray makes the distinction in the work on the Holy Spirit when he says:

---

[696] Geisler, *Systematic Theology*, 1:241.
[697] Norman L. Geisler and William E. Nix, *A General Introduction to the Bible* (Chicago: Moody, 1968), 48-51.

CHAPTER 7: HOLY SPIRIT

When we speak of the Holy Spirit coming upon the men in order to the composition of the books [sic], it should be further understood that the object is not the inspiration of the men but the books – not the writers but the writings. It terminates upon the record, in other words, and not upon the human instrument who made it.[698]

The more we think upon it the more we must be convinced that men unaided by the Spirit of God could neither have conceived, nor put together, nor preserved in its integrity that precious deposit known as the Sacred Oracles.[699]

There are two key verses in the New Testament that clearly point to the inspiration of the *Tanakh*. Paul states that *all Scripture is given by inspiration of God* in 2 Timothy (3:16) and attributes inspiration of the *Tanakh* to the ministry of the Holy Spirit. Peter affirms in 2 Peter 1:20-21 (to Jewish believers in Messiah who had been scattered in the Diaspora) that the writings of the *Tanakh* did not come from the will or intellect of man but *holy men of God spoke as they were moved by the Holy Spirit*.[700]

The writers of the *Tanakh*, when referring to the Hebrew Scriptures as the authoritative Word of God, gave their testimony and bore witness to the divine inspiration of God's Word: the Law (Exodus 20:1; 32:16; Leviticus 27:34; Numbers 36:13) and the Prophets (Joshua 24:26-27; 1 Samuel 3:18-19; Isaiah 1:1-2; Jeremiah 1:1-2; Ezekiel 1:3).[701]

A valid point needs to be injected here on a particular Jewish consideration of what is inspired. Jewish rabbis treat the Oral Law (*Talmud*) as equal to Scripture, although they would say that they don't. The *Talmud* has become their primary source of interpretation of Scripture. They ignore the Scriptures that refer to Moses writing down all that God gave him (Exodus 24:4; Deuteronomy 31:9, 24; Joshua 24:26).[702] As a result, this Oral Law and not the written Word of God has become the source of all rabbinic authority.

---

[698] James M. Gray, *The Fundamentals,* Ed. Torrey, R. A. and A. C. Dixon (Reprinted without alteration or abridgement from the original four volume edition issued by the Bible Institute of Los Angeles in 1917. Grand Rapids: Baker, 1980), 2:11.

[699] Gray, *The Fundamentals*, 2:18-19.

[700] Gray, *The Fundamentals*, 2:20.

[701] Barackman, *Practical Christian Theology,* 27.

[702] **Oral Law**: Judaism states that Moses received two Laws, one written and one oral. Now Judaism will not call the Oral Law the Word of God; nevertheless, the authority placed upon the Oral Law practically places the Oral Law on equal footing and greater than the Written Law of God given to Moses. Rabbis will not interpret the Written Law without studying the

The children of Israel did not vow to keep the Oral Law. They made a commitment to *Yahweh* to keep the Written Law of God. Exodus 24:3-7 rules out a fictitious Oral Law as being given to Moses, then to Joshua, then the Judges, and on to the Prophets. The Oral Law is fictitious because nowhere in the whole of the *Tanakh* is there even a glimmer, let alone a clear statement, of this uniquely Jewish position about the Oral Law (*Talmud*) being given by God or recognized as being divinely authoritative. Oral Law has become an "idol" of words by the rabbis because the Jewish people bow to its authority rather than the authority of the Written Word of God (which is what they vowed to keep), which *Elohim* over and over again confirmed in His Scriptures. The Oral Law has no confirmation by God in the *Tanakh*. Verbal Inspiration deals with the very words of God that He so carefully gave and preserved in His Word (see appendix three). The Oral Law is nothing more than the commentaries of the rabbis, their interpretations of the *Tanakh*.

The New Testament uses the phrase *it is written* over 90 times.[703] Jesus described the written word as that which *comes out of the mouth of God* (Matthew 4:4). So important were the exact words of God that Jeremiah was told:

> *This is what the LORD says: Stand in the courtyard of the Lord's house and speak to all the people of the towns of Judah who come to worship in the house of the LORD. Tell them everything I command you; do not omit a word.* (Jeremiah 26:2)

Other New Testament testimony of the *Tanakh* comes from *Yeshua* as a witness to divine inspiration:

(1) *Yeshua* recognized the whole of the *Tanakh* (John 5:39; Luke 24:44-46) and its three divisions (Mark 7:8-13; Matthew 13:13-14; John 10:34-35).

(2) *Yeshua* made reference to 14 books of the *Tanakh, as follows*: Genesis (Mark 10:6-8), Exodus (Luke 18:20), Numbers (John 3:14), Leviticus and Deuteronomy (Luke 10:26-28), 1 Samuel (Mark 2:25), 1 Kings (Matthew 12:42), Psalms (Mark 12:10), Isaiah (Luke 4:17-21), Daniel (Matthew 24:15), Hosea (Matthew 9:13), Jonah

---

Oral Law which cannot be substantiated anywhere in the entire *Tanakh*. The actual origin of the Oral Law occurred after the return from captivity. A need to read the Word of God in Hebrew arose, as indicated in Nehemiah 8:8, and to then translate it into Aramaic and apply it to daily life. The generation after Ezra began to expand the Written Law by adding manmade rules and regulations to each of the 613 Written Laws of Moses and giving it equal and greater authority than the Scriptures themselves.

[703] Geisler, *Systematic Theology*, 1:236.

(Matthew 12:40), Zechariah (Matthew 26:31), and Malachi (Matthew 11:10).

(3) *Yeshua* believed in the historicity of persons, such as Abel (Luke 11:51), Noah and the Flood (Matthew 24:37-39), Moses (John 3:14), David (Luke 20:41), Jonah (Matthew 12:40), God's creation of man and the divine institution of marriage (Matthew 19:4-7), and the prophet Daniel (Matthew 24:15).

(4) *Yeshua* submitted Himself to the authority of the Hebrew Scriptures (Matthew 5:17; 26:54; Luke 18:31).

(5) *Yeshua* had complete trust in the writings and teachings of the *Tanakh*. This is indicated by His appeal to them for God's will when He was tempted (Matthew 4:4, 7, 10), His referring to God's statement regarding marriage (Matthew 19:4-6), and His argument for the doctrine of the resurrection (Matthew 22:29-32).

(6) *Yeshua* declared that the Scriptures could not be broken (John 10:35). In context, the Lord said that the Scriptures (Psalm 82:6), which He identified as the Word of God, could not be annulled as though its declarations were untrue.[704]

The inspiration of the Holy Spirit is clearly seen in the New Testament. But how is it seen in the Hebrew Scriptures? In the Hebrew Scriptures there are two phrases that are literally used thousands of times. These key phrases are: *Thus says the Lord* and *The Word of the Lord came unto*, both of which distinctly refer to the inspiration of the Scriptures.[705] Waterhouse makes the following observation:

> Statements from the Law and the Prophets assert not only that the Old Testament is divine revelation, but, more specifically, that the words were at times given by God and at other times guided by God. This is verbal inspiration.[706]

Waterhouse goes on to quote references from the Hebrew Scriptures to show that God indeed spoke and guided the human authors of Scripture (Deuteronomy 18:18; 34:10; 2 Samuel 23:1-2; Isaiah 8:11, 20, 59:21; Jeremiah 1:9; 15:16; 30:2;

---

[704] Barackman, *Practical Christian Theology*, 27.
[705] Steven W. Waterhouse, *Not By Bread Alone: An Outlined Guide to Bible Doctrine* (Amarillo, TX: Westcliff Press, 2000), 4.
[706] Waterhouse, *Not By Bread Alone: An Outlined Guide to Bible Doctrine*, 4.

Ezekiel 3:1-4).[707] By closely observing 2 Samuel 23:2 and Isaiah 59:21, both David and Isaiah express the fact that the Holy Spirit spoke through them:

> *The Spirit of the LORD spoke by me, and His Word was in my tongue.* (KJV)

> *As for Me, this is My covenant with them, says the LORD; My spirit that is upon thee, and My words which I have put in your mouth.* (KJV)

Here the Holy Spirit is clearly seen as the one who is speaking through David and Isaiah in the *Tanakh*. Geisler continues by expressing phrases, such as *God said* (Genesis 1:3, 6), *the Word of the LORD came to me* (Jeremiah 34:1; Ezekiel 30:1), which are found hundreds of times in the Hebrew Scriptures. Geisler states:

> These reveal beyond question that the writer is claiming to give the very Word of God. In the book of Leviticus alone there are some 66 occurrences of phrases like "the LORD spoke unto Moses" (1:1; 4:1; 5:14; 6:1, 8, 19; 7:22).[708]

God used words and expected those words to be used exactly as He instructed. Using them otherwise would be a direct violation of verbal inspiration. This simply means that *words* were inspired, God's Word, not God's thoughts or dynamic equivalents, which is so popular today in our modern translations and paraphrases. It is God's Word, rather than inspired thoughts, that man is held accountable for (Exodus 24:3-7; Deuteronomy 18:18; 2 Samuel 23:2; Isaiah 59:21; 2 Chronicles 34:14; Zechariah 7:12). Geisler strongly affirms that Scriptures were not man's words or thoughts, but God's Word:

> So it wasn't simply God's message that men were free to state in their words; the very choice of words was from God....Sometimes we are reminded that even the tense of verbs are stressed by God.[709]

Inspiration usually has two other descriptive words to help clarify its meaning: "verbal" and "plenary." Inspiration, in being verbal, extends to every word as being inspired. Plenary further defines the term inspiration as "extending to every part of the words and all they teach or imply."[710] Barackman further conveys that *verbal* extends to each word of Scripture and "to the grammatical form of each

---

[707] Waterhouse, *Not By Bread Alone: An Outlined Guide to Bible Doctrine*, 4.
[708] Geisler, *Systematic Theology*, 1:234.
[709] Geisler, *Systematic Theology*, 1:236.
[710] Geisler, *Systematic Theology*, 1:236.

CHAPTER 7: HOLY SPIRIT

word," as well as speaking of plenary inspiration as not just the words but the equality of the words:

> Plenary Inspiration means that every part of the sixty-six canonical books of the Bible was a product of divine inspiration to an equal degree (2 Timothy 3:16).[711]

Plenary inspiration simply means that all Scripture is equally inspired of God. However, Judaism, as they deduce from Numbers 12:5-8, see three levels of inspiration: The Law (Torah) as the most inspired, then the Prophets – still inspired but to a lesser degree then the Torah – and, lastly, the Writings, also still inspired but to a lesser degree than the Law and the Prophets.

Methods of Revelation

When speaking of Divine Revelation in connection with the Bible, the English word *revelation* is derived from the Greek word *apokalupsis*, which means "disclosure" or "unveiling,"[712] signifying that God unveiled Himself to mankind through His written Word and through theophanies of Himself. Without revelation – if God did not disclose or unveil Himself to man – man would have no idea as to what God is like or how man could interact with Him. Thiessen gives a clear meaning of revelation in the following comment:

> That act of God whereby he discloses himself or communicates truth to the mind, whereby he makes manifest to his creatures that which could not be known in any other way. The revelation may occur in a single, instantaneous act, or it may extend over a long period of time; and this communication of himself and his truth may be perceived by the human mind in varying degrees of fullness.[713]

The Holy Spirit is also involved in revelation of God as is expressed in the following statement by Walvoord:

> The most prominent means of revelation is that of the spoken word. "Thus says Jehovah" is found in hundreds of instances in the Old Testament. A comparison of such passages as Isaiah 6:1-10 and Acts 8:25 will demonstrate that the Holy Spirit is the person of the

---

[711] Barackman, *Practical Christian Theology*, 25.
[712] Enns, *The Moody Handbook of Theology*, 155.
[713] Thiessen, *Lectures in Systematic Theology*, 7.

Trinity speaking in these instances. While the Old Testament used "Jehovah" and "Lord" as the speaker, the New Testament uses the title, Holy Spirit.[714]

In a broader use of the term revelation, God revealed Himself through Creation and history, through the Scriptures, and in the conscience of man. In general revelation, God revealed Himself in history and nature, while in "special" revelation, God revealed Himself in the Scriptures and in His Son.[715] His Spirit was involved with the other members of the Godhead in that revelation of God.

OT and NT comparisons of the Holy Spirit

Throughout the Hebrew Scriptures, there are times when the reader may not be able to determine that the One speaking is the Person of the Holy Spirit. Although this section is not an argument for the personality of the Holy Spirit from the *Tanakh*, this argument does show how the apostles in the first century C.E. understood the ministry of the Holy Spirit in the *Tanakh*.

Five verses quoted in the *Tanakh* by New Testament writers Matthew, Mark, Peter, Paul, and the author of Hebrews show their understanding that these verses contain references to the Holy Spirit. Matthew and John Mark were reporting the statements of *Yeshua*. Peter's reference was made just before the feast of Succoth (Pentecost). Paul was speaking to the Jewish leadership in Rome. The unknown author of Hebrews was writing to the suffering Jewish believers who lived in the Land. Each passage will be briefly discussed supporting the contention that these writers understood the Holy Spirit to be present and active in the Hebrew Scriptures.

Psalm 110:1 with Matthew 22:41-44

> [Ps 110:1] *The LORD says to my Lord, "Sit at My right hand while I make Your enemies Your footstool."*
>
> [Matt. 22:42] *While the Pharisees were gathered together, Jesus asked them, saying, what do you think of Christ [Messiah]? Whose son is He? They said unto Him, The Son of David.* [22:43] *He said to them, How then does David in the spirit call Him Lord, saying,* [22:44] *the*

---

[714] Walvoord, *The Holy Spirit*, 50-51.
[715] Tenney, *Zondervan Pictorial Encyclopedia of the Bible*, 5:86.

CHAPTER 7: HOLY SPIRIT

LORD said unto my Lord, [You come] sit on My right hand, till I make Your enemies Your footstool?

According to Ryrie, where this interchange occurs in the book of Matthew, *Yeshua* was asking the Pharisees a question concerning Psalm 110:1. *Yeshua*, at this point, was attributing to the Holy Spirit divine authorship of David's Psalm 110.[716] He then ties Psalm 110:1 to David's powerful statement of 2 Samuel 23:2-3 where David states that *the Spirit of the LORD spoke by Me*, connecting that further with David's Messianic Psalm 22. In Psalm 22, the Holy Spirit, who spoke through David, gives a very detailed description of what Yeshua would suffer on the cross. Walvoord points out the same incident from Mark 12:36 when David spoke by the Holy Spirit, thus attributing inspiration to the Holy Spirit.[717]

Psalm 41:9[10] with Acts 1:16

My ally in whom I trusted, even he who shares my bread, has been utterly false to me. (Psalm 41:9[10])

Yes, my own familiar friend, in whom I trusted, who ate of my bread, Has lifted up his heel against me. (Psalm 41:9 KJV)

Men and brothers, this scripture had to be fulfilled which the Holy Spirit by the mouth of David spoke before concerning Judas, which was [a] guide to them that took Jesus. (Acts 1:16)

Here again Peter gives testimony to the Holy Spirit as the authority of the word of David concerning Judas, who betrayed *Yeshua*.

Isaiah 6:9-10 with Acts 28:25-27

In the next passage, Paul ascribes to the Holy Spirit the words of Isaiah, a prophet 700 years before Messiah:

Isa 6:9 And He said, "Go, say to that people: Hear, indeed, but do not understand; 6:10 See, indeed, but do not grasp. Dull that people's mind, stop its ears, and seal it eyes – lest, seeing with its eyes and

---

[716] Ryrie, *The Holy Spirit*, 36.
[717] Walvoord, *The Holy Spirit*, 60.

THE TRI-UNITY OF GOD IS JEWISH

hearing with its ears, it also grasp with its mind, and repent and save itself."

^{Acts 28:25} *And when they did not agree among themselves, they departed, after that Paul had spoken one word, Well spoke the Holy Spirit by Isaiah the prophet to our fathers, Saying, ^{28:26} Go unto this people, and say, Hearing you shall hear, and shall not understand; and seeing you shall see, and not perceive: ^{28:27} For the heart of this people is waxed gross* [become calloused], *and their ears are dull of hearing, and their eyes have they closed; lest they should see with their eyes, and hear with their ears, and understand with their heart, and should be converted, and I should heal them.*

Psalm 95:9-11 with Hebrews 3:7-11

Here the unknown author of Hebrews related to his brethren concerning the hearts of the wilderness generation; and he attributed the words of the Psalmist to the Holy Spirit.

^{Ps. 95:9} *...When your fathers put Me to the test, tried Me, though they had seen My deeds. ^{95:10} Forty years I was provoked by that generation; I thought, "they are a senseless people; they would not know My ways." ^{95:11} Concerning them I swore in anger, "they shall never come to My resting-place!"*

^{Hebrews 3:7} *Wherefore as the Holy Spirit says, today if you will hear His voice, ^{3:8} harden not your hearts, as in the provocation, in the day of temptation in the wilderness: ^{3:9} When your fathers tempted Me, proved* [tested] *Me, and saw My works forty years. ^{3:10} Therefore I was grieved with that generation, and said, they do always err in their heart; and they have not known My ways. ^{3:11} So I swore in my wrath, they shall not enter into My rest.*

Jeremiah 31:33 with Hebrews 10:15-16

The unknown Jewish believer quotes the New Covenant reference in Jeremiah 31 in Hebrews and ascribes authorship by the Holy Spirit to the New Covenant being offered in that Hebrew Scripture passage.

CHAPTER 7: HOLY SPIRIT

Jer. 31:33 But such is the covenant I will make with the House of Israel after these days – Declares the LORD: I will put My teaching into their inmost being and inscribe it upon hearts. Then I will be their God, and they shall be My people.

Heb. 10:15 Whereof the Holy Spirit also is a witness to us: for after that He had said before, *10:16* This is the covenant that I will make with them after those days, says the LORD, I will put My laws into their hearts, and in their minds will I write them.

This reference to the Holy Spirit in the book of Hebrews confirms the Personhood of the Holy Spirit, as the author of Hebrews connects Him to Jeremiah 31 of the *Tanakh*. The New Covenant writers understood that the Holy Spirit was responsible for the inspiration of the Hebrew Scriptures.

New Covenant

The Holy Spirit has a role in the New Covenant of Jeremiah 31 as can be seen in several verses from the *Tanakh* which clarify the Holy Spirit's involvement. [Insert reference to your book or a quote from, *Israel's Only Hope,* here?] Pache, in citing these verses, makes four points in relationship to the Holy Spirit coming upon mankind:

(1) The Holy Spirit will be poured out upon all flesh according to Joel 2:28-29. We see the beginnings of that in Acts 2:16-17 when the Holy Spirit was poured out on the 120 in the upper room.[718] Even though the fulfillment of this prophecy on the coming of the Holy Spirit is still future, it is a reference from the *Tanakh*. This is also a reference to the pouring out of the Holy Spirit in Isaiah 44:3 and Ezekiel 39:29. All three of these verses relate to the same event when His Spirit is poured out upon Israel.

(2) The Holy Spirit that is given in the New Covenant according to Isaiah 59:21 will remain forever.

(3) In Ezekiel 36:26-27 [and] 37:14, it is very clear that the Holy Spirit will be placed within Israel. God through the Holy Spirit

---

[718] **Joel 2:28-29**: See Manuscript # 134 of Dr. Arnold Fruchtenbaum called "*How the New Testament Quotes the Old Testament.* See www.Ariel.org for Ariel Ministries in Tustin, CA

will give them a new heart[,] and the stony heart will be removed[;] and they will be placed in the Land. [That also ties together] with 1 Corinthians 3:16, where the indwelling Holy Spirit makes us a temple to the living God.

(4) It is clear that the Holy Spirit will rest upon the Messiah without measure as Isaiah 11:2; 42:1; [and] 61:1 indicate.[719]

Enns addresses another vital issue that *Yeshua*, in all likelihood, was referring to in John 3:10 in connection to Ezekiel 36. Enns continues by saying that the Holy Spirit, in Ezekiel 11:19 and 36:25-27 is promised by God to regenerate Israel during the Millennium.[720] These passages from the *Tanakh*, and *Yeshua's* discussion with Nicodemus, suggest that the Old Testament believers should have been aware of the work of regeneration by the Holy Spirit.

If the New Testament were to be considered in addition to the Hebrew Scriptures, it would be very simple to substantiate the personality of the Holy Spirit because Matthew, Mark, Luke, John, Paul, and Peter's writings are full of references to the Holy Spirit. When we look at the Hebrew Scriptures alone, we must remember that just as with the Second Person of the Godhead, that Scripture is progressive revelation. God did not choose to reveal everything about Himself at the start. That is equally true of the Third Person of the Godhead.

At the beginning of this chapter it was expressed that it is difficult to distinguish between the Holy Spirit and God because God, Himself, is pure Spirit. So how does one make a distinction between God the Father's Spirit and the Holy Spirit? In the New Testament, the personality of the Holy Spirit is clearly expressed by the authors. His Person is clearly defined and separated from the other members of the triune God. But in the *Tanakh* that pattern is not followed. Rarely is there an expression that relates directly to the Holy Spirit as a person. However, what is clearly seen in the *Tanakh* is the action or movement of the Holy Spirit, making it difficult to show His personhood. This means that the personhood of the Holy Spirit has been seen, but only to a limited degree, in the *Tanakh*. If we look closely, however, we do see some glimmers regarding the personhood of the Spirit. In the Hebrew Scriptures, the Spirit can be grieved (Genesis 6:3; Isaiah 63:10) and is distinct from God the Father and God the Son (Isaiah 48:16). The *Tanakh* implies the personhood of the Holy Spirit, but the New Testament fully lays out the personality of the Third Person of the Godhead.

---

[719] Pache, *The Person and Work of the Holy Spirit*, 34-35.
[720] Enns, *The Moody Handbook of Theology*, 260.

CHAPTER 8:
MESSIAH DIVINE?

In the *Tanakh* there are Scriptures written by Moses, David, Isaiah, Micah, Zechariah, and the unknown author(s) of Samuel and Chronicles that clearly present the Messiah, the Son of David as God! However, in Judaism there are several views concerning the Messiah. Two of the most prominent will be addressed. First, who is Messiah: God or man? Reform Judaism and Secular Jews do not believe that Messiah is a person but that a messianic age will evolve and universal peace will come. Below, we read the reflections of a messianic Jewish believer regarding Messiah as a personal savior versus an abstract messianic age.

> Messianism, which in the Bible is described as God's mighty interposition in human history, has become debased by contemporary Jewish spokesmen in something of a socio-economic program to be achieved by man alone by way of progressive, evolutionary fulfillment. The prophetic teachings concerning the day of judgment in which God will put an end to history as we know it are completely disregarded.[721]

> As can be clearly seen, there is no personal Messiah involved at all in Secular and Reform Judaism's ideology. Orthodox Judaism clearly believes that Messiah is a person, but they do not regard that person as God.[722] Ultra-orthodox Hasidim believe that, in the future, two Messiahs will come, due to the obvious portions of Scripture that point to two types of Messiahs. They identify the two as: (1) Messiah ben Joseph, who will come, suffer, and die (the suffering servant), and (2) and Messiah ben David, who will come and reign as king physically in Jerusalem.[723] A Jewish believer in *Yeshua*, the Messiah, relayed the following incident after being in an Orthodox Hasidic home in Brooklyn for Shabbat. The men sitting around the

---

[721] Kac. *The Spiritual Dilemma of the Jewish People*, 26-27.
[722] Jacobs, *A Jewish Theology*, 293.
[723] Joseph Klausner. *The Messianic Idea In Israel* (New York: Macmillan, 1955), 11, 519-531.

table were pounding their fists while singing songs with the words, "We want *Mashiach* now, we want *Mashiach* now." They were obviously acting out their fervent desire for the Messiah to come and fulfill the promise of God to Abraham. They obviously did not believe that the Messiah had already come in the person of Jesus (*Yeshua*) Christ (*ha Mashiach* or Messiah).

The term *Mashiach*, a Hebrew word meaning "anointed one," denotes two ideas of consecration and endowment of any object or person. The term appears 39 times in the Hebrew Scriptures and originally was used of the "anointed priest" (Leviticus 4:3, 4) and of kings when God referred to them as *My anointed* (1 Samuel 2:35), *Your anointed* (Psalm 84:9), and *His anointed* (1 Samuel 12:3, 5). By the time of the exile and post-exilic period, *Mashiach* had narrowed its meaning to the one who would fulfill the promises to Abraham and bring in the Kingdom and fulfill the covenant to David. So *Mashiach*, or Messiah, became the term for the long-awaited promised one who would bring in the Kingdom spoken of by the prophets.[724] In Daniel 9:26 the Scripture says that before the destruction of the city (Jerusalem) would occur, the *anointed* (מָשִׁיחַ) will be cut off. That verse uses the term *Messiah*, and history acknowledges that *Yeshua* was put to death 40 years prior to the destruction of the *city* and the *sanctuary*.

A clear understanding of the actual verses depends on the interpretation of two important Hebrew words: (1) עוֹלָם or *olam* and (2) עַד or *'ad*.[725] Both of these words are translated in the English text as *eternal, eternity, everlasting, forever, ever and ever, age,* or *ancient*.[726] In English such terms project beyond the end of time. However, in the Hebrew, there is no word that expresses the English concept of "eternal." Therefore, to understand the term in English, a reader needs to know what the word meant in the Hebrew language then.

Olam עוֹלָם

Olam (עוֹלָם), means "long duration, antiquity, futurity."[727] *Olam* is divided into two groups with numerous sections. It deals with time in the past, as well as indefinite futurity. However, the majority of references deal with man's life, a dynasty, or laws that were no longer in use as the Mosaic Law. The term *olam* deals

---

[724] James Smith. *The Promised Messiah*, 1-4.
[725] Botterweck, Ringgren, and Fabry. *Theological Dictionary of the Old Testament*, 10:456, 530
[726] Robert Young. *Young's Analytical Concordance to the Bible*, 310-312.
[727] Brown, Driver and Briggs, *A Hebrew and English Lexicon of the Old Testament*, 761-763.

CHAPTER 8: MESSIAH DIVINE

with families and relationships with nations or an age. What is obvious is that the term *olam* in the *Tanakh* is confined to time, except for God who is outside of time. When *olam* is used in connection with God, it indicates that eternity is to be understood when used of Him. Schoonhoven expresses it this way:

> The OT has no special term for "eternity" that can be contrasted with a term denoting "temporality." The Hebrew word most often used to express "eternity" is *olam*. It is the same word that expresses duration of time, and it designates eternity only in such statements as "from *olam*" and "until *olam*" (Psalm 90:2).[728]

The term *olam* is a very elastic term for time, stretching from a portion of time in man's life, to his whole life right through to a period of time that could be to the end of an age or time period. Schoonhoven's explanation follows:

> When viewed from the vantage point of the Bible, eternity is a term that includes temporal relations. Eternity is time stretching endlessly forward and backward, with the result that time itself must be regarded as a segment of eternity.[729]

Because God is outside of time, He is not governed by time. So *olam* refers to man's relationship to other men, nations, or to God for a period of time, whether that time is a man's lifetime or an age. The exception is when the reference is to God, as He is not bound by time. Below are some passages of how *olam* is used "generally to point to something that seems long ago, but rarely, if ever, refers to a limitless past."

Genesis 6:4	*Those were the mighty men who were of old* written from Moses' point in time.
Deuteronomy 32:7	to the time of one's elder
1 Samuel 27:8	*ancient times*
Isaiah 51:9	*days of old, the generations of long ago*
Isaiah 58:12	Rebuild the *ancient ruins*, a future prophecy, what they will do in relationship to their past.

---

[728] Bromiley. *The International Standard Bible Encyclopedia*, 2:162.
[729] Bromiley. *The International Standard Bible Encyclopedia*, 163.

Isaiah 63:9	carried them all the days of old
Jeremiah 6:16	*ancient paths* where the good way is and walk in it
Jeremiah 18:15	*ancient paths* they (Israel) have forgotten Me and do not walk in My paths
Jeremiah 28:8	prophets before me and you, from *ancient times*
Ezekiel 36:2	*ancient high places* (ASV)
Micah 7:14	*as in the days of old*
Malachi 3:4	*as in the days of old and as in former years*
Job 22:15	*ancient path* which wicked men trod
Proverbs 22:28	*ancient boundary* that your fathers have set
Ezra 4:15	[Aramaic] *have incited revolt within it in past days*
Ezra 4:19	[Aramaic] *that the city has risen up against the kings in past days*[730]

Olam is not only used of the past; the majority of the time it is used of some future period. It refers to a future time of limited duration or conditions that will exist continuously throughout a limited period of time, often a single lifetime. The following two examples express that position:

> *"as long as one lives"* (a slave for life) Exodus 21:16, (Deuteronomy 15:17; 1 Samuel 27:12)

> *"May my lord King David live forever"* 1 Kings 1:31 (Nehemiah 2:3; Daniel 2:4)[731]

Arnold Fruchtenbaum, speaking in relation to the Sabbath being kept *forever*, states that the word is used within time:

---

[730] Harris, Archer, and Waltke, *Theological Wordbook of the Old Testament*, 2:672-673.
[731] Botterweck, Ringgren, and Fabry. *Theological Dictionary of the Old Testament*, 10:535-536.

While the English terms tend to carry concepts of eternity, this is not the meaning of the Hebrew words themselves. Classical Hebrew had no word that actually meant "eternal." The Hebrew term for "forever" (*olam*) means "long duration," "antiquity," or "futurity." The Hebrew terms basically mean "until the end of a period of time." What that period of time is must be determined by the context of related passages. The period of time may have been to the end of a man's life, or an age, or dispensation, but not "forever" in the sense of eternity. This is very clear from examining the usage of the same terminology in other passages.[732]

Second, there are two Hebrew forms of *olam*. One is *le-olam*, which means "unto an age." The second form is *'ad-olam*, which means "until an age." However, neither of these forms carry the English meaning of "forever." Though it was translated that way in English, the Hebrew does not carry the concept of eternity as the English word "forever" does.

Third, the words *olam*, *le olam*, or *ad-olam*, sometimes mean only up to the end of a man's life. For example, it is used in Exodus 14:13 of someone's lifetime. It is used in Exodus 21:6, Leviticus 25:46, and Deuteronomy 15:17 of a slave's life. In 1 Samuel 1:22 and 2:35, it is used of Samuel's life. First Samuel 20:23 speaks of the lifetime of David and Jonathan. First Samuel 27:12 and 28:2 and 1 Chronicles 28:4 use the word of David's lifetime. While the English reads, *forever*, obviously from the context the Hebrew [equivalents do] not mean forever in the sense of eternity, but only forever up to the end of the person's life.

Fourth, *olam* sometimes means only "an age or dispensation." For example, Deuteronomy 23:3 uses the term *forever*, but it limits the term *forever* as only ten generations long. It obviously carries the concept of an age here. In 2 Chronicles 7:16 it is used only for the period of the First Temple. So, again, the word *forever* in Hebrew does not mean eternal, it means up to the end of a period of time which could either be a man's life or an age or a dispensation.

Fifth, the same word for *forever* is used of certain ceremonial facets of the Mosaic Law which everyone agrees has ended with the

---

[732] Arnold G. Fruchtenbaum, *The Sabbath: Manuscript # 176* (Tustin, CA: Ariel Ministries, 1991), 18.

coming of Christ. For example, the same word *forever* is used of the kindling of the Tabernacle lamp stands (Exodus 27:20; Leviticus 24:3): it is used of the ceremony of the showbread (Leviticus 24:8); it is used of the service of the brazen laver (Exodus 30:21); is used of the Levitical priesthood and Levitical garments (Exodus 28:43; 40:15; Leviticus 6:18; 10:9; Numbers 10:8; 18:23; 25:13; Deuteronomy 18:5; 1 Chronicles 15:2; 23:13); it is used of the sacrificial system, including the sacrifices and offerings (Exodus 29:28; Leviticus 7:34, 36; 10:15; Numbers 15:15; 18:8, 11, 19; 19:10); it is used of the Day of Atonement sacrifice (Leviticus 16:34); and, it is used of the red heifer offering (Numbers 19:10). It is used of all of these ceremonial facets that everybody agrees [have] been done away with in Christ.[733]

Within all these references to the term *olam*, the concept of "eternity" is conceptualized from the perspective of man – not God – who according to the prophets, dwells in heaven and is outside of time and unlimited by space as pointed out by Vos. God, with the character of immutability, is outside of time, separated from time and not governed by time. Vos states:

> That the prophets represent God as dwelling in heaven, unlimited by space, and yet they also say that He dwells in Zion and that Canaan is His land...the same relation applied as between Jehovah and time. In popular language, such as the prophets use, eternity can only be expressed in terms of time, although in reality it lies altogether above time."[734]

In his book, *On the Eternity of God*, Charnock does not use the Hebrew word *olam* to lay out the differences between time and eternity, for eternity is before and after time:

> Time hath a continual succession...We must conceive of eternity contrary to the notion of time; as the nature of time consists in the succession of parts, so the nature of eternity [is] an infinite immutable duration....So eternity is the duration of his essence; and when we say God is eternal, we exclude from him all possibility of beginning and ending, all flux and change. As the essences of God cannot be bounded by any place, so it is not to be limited by any

---

[733] Fruchtenbaum. *The Sabbath*, Manuscript #176, 18-19.
[734] Geerhardus Vos. *Biblical Theology, Old and New Testaments* (Grand Rapids: Eerdmans, 1948), 263.

time; as it is his immensity to be everywhere, so it is his eternity to be always...His duration is as endless as his essence is boundless: he always was and always will be, and will no more have an end than he had a beginning; and this is an excellency belonging to the Supreme Being....Time began with the foundation of the world; but God being before time, could have no beginning in time. Before the beginning of creation, and the beginning of time, there could be nothing but eternity...for as between the Creator and creatures there is no medium, so between time and eternity there is no medium.[735]

Charnock's whole chapter on the eternity of God is very worthwhile reading and meditating upon.

Several other authors, such as Botterweck,[736] VanGemeren,[737] and Harris[738] also lay out some excellent material on the word *olam*.

So what is the conclusion in relation to the word *olam*, and how it is to be understood in the *Tanakh*? Fruchtenbaum gives the clearest and simplest answer when he states that the context determines just how *olam* is to be understood.[739] The understanding of *olam* in reference to man or to God will be determined by its context. That context will determine whether *olam* is in the framework of time or whether *olam* is in relation to God and His nature, essence, and character as being outside of time, eternal. The following are two examples from Isaiah 60 where *olam* is used in reference to God and carries with it the English concept of eternity:

> *[19] No longer shall you need the sun for light by day, nor the shining of the moon for radiance [by night]; for the LORD shall be your light **everlasting**, your God shall be your glory.*
>
> *[20] Your sun shall set no more, your moon no more withdraw; for the LORD shall be a light to you **forever**, and your days of mourning shall be ended.*

---

[735] Steven Charnock. *Existence and Attributes of God* (Grand Rapids: Baker, 1996), 1:280-282. For some additional information see: L. Thomas Holdcroft, *The Doctrine of God* (Oakland, CA: Western Book Company, 1978), 21-23.
[736] Botterweck, Ringgren, and Fabry. *Theological Dictionary of the Old Testament*, 10:531-545.
[737] VanGemeren, ed.. *Dictionary of Old Testament Theology & Exegesis,* 3:345-350.
[738] Harris, Archer and Waltke. *Theological Wordbook of the Old Testament*, 2:672-673.
[739] Fruchtenbaum, *The Sabbath: Manuscript #176,* 18.

In this passage Isaiah states that there will be no more need for the sun and moon, for the *Shechinah* of God will be your light. Webb,[740] Wolf,[741] and Young[742] refer to Revelation 21:23 [22:5] where Apostle John states that after the destruction of the heavens and earth and once the new heavens and earth are in place, God's glory will be their light. Something beyond the physical earth and time are in view in connection with God's *Shechinah* light in this passage from Isaiah 60. Psalm 119:89 states, *The LORD exists forever; Your word stands firm in heaven*, meaning that the Word of God is settled in heaven, a place outside of the limits of earth and time. This verse declares that the Word of God is in the eternal heavens. According to Leupold, "the Word of God which comes from the eternal Lord of the heavens has its abiding, resting place and will, like [the heavens], endure forever."[743]

While *olam* is predominantly used in the context of time, it is also used outside of time in reference to God. So where *olam* is used of man and his relationship to others – whether other people or nations – it has a time context. Yet throughout the *Tanakh*, *olam*, when in context with God, has an eternal perspective beyond time.

'Ad - עד

The second word for eternity is *du* which means "perpetuity."[744] The word *perpetuity* reflects both time and eternity. This Hebrew word refers to "past time" and "future time." In past time, it is referenced only twice as the *ancient mountains* in Habakkuk 3:6 and in relation to the wicked in Job 20:4.[745] The other references refer to future time and deal with things earthbound or time-related, except with reference to God. The term *du* is used 48 times in the *Tanakh*: twenty-nine (29) times in the book of Psalms; eight times in Isaiah; twice in each of Micah, Job, and Proverbs; and once each in Ezekiel 15:18, Amos 1:11, Habakkuk 3:6, Daniel 12:3, and 1 Chronicles 28:9.[746] In these 48 references, *'ad* is used 19 times in conjunction with *olam*[747] as in Isaiah 45:17 (*olam*/everlasting; *'ad*/without end), Exodus 15:18 (*olam*/for ever; *'ad*/ever), and Daniel 12:3 (*olam*/forever; *'ad*/ever).

---

[740] Webb, *The Message of Isaiah*, 231.
[741] Wolf, *Interpreting Isaiah*, 238.
[742] Edward J. Young, *The Book of Isaiah*, 3:455.
[743] Leupold, *Exposition of the Psalms*, 842.
[744] Brown, Driver, and Briggs. *A Hebrew and English Lexicon of the Old Testament*, 723.
[745] Harris, Archer, and Waltke, *Theological Wordbook of the Old Testament*, 2:645.
[746] Jenni and Westermann, *Theological Lexicon of the Old Testament*, 2:837.
[747] Harris, Archer, and Waltke, *Theological Wordbook of the Old Testament*, 2:645.

CHAPTER 8: MESSIAH DIVINE

Brown, Driver, and Briggs, in reference to *du* or *'ad*, have two groupings of usages: (1) to past time as reflected in the above paragraph, and (2) to future time as reflected in *forever*, as during a lifetime, of a king, or of things, or of "the continuous existence of nations" as well as "divine existence."[748] In the future sense, *du* "always denotes the unforeseeable future," which does not necessarily imply eternity. However, when *du* is applied to God, it does imply eternity or everlasting.[749] Like *olam*, *'ad* must be understood and interpreted within the context in which it is given. It must be understood that time is only a segment of eternity, and God is outside of time.

Since no Hebrew word independently reflects eternity by itself, *olam* and *'ad* reflect time, which is only a part of eternity. God lives outside of time; He made time. Hence, He is not bound by time. But when *olam* and *'ad* are used of God, in relation to His being, it is understood to be a reference to eternity, beyond time. Therefore, interpreting *olam* and *'ad* requires the context and related passages to determine whether it is bound by time or whether it reflects eternity.

First Coming Messianic References

The English words *eternity*, *everlasting*, and *forever* play a critical role in understanding First Coming messianic references. However, before looking into these references, let us take a look at some *eternal* promises of God in the Hebrew Scriptures. In Genesis 12, 13, 15, 17, and 22, God makes a covenant called the Abrahamic Covenant, which is recognized as an *eternal* covenant.[750] Deuteronomy 30 is not only a promise of a Land Covenant[751] to be given to Abraham and to his descendents, (Genesis 15:4-5, 18), but it is also an *eternal* covenant.[752] Understanding the eternal nature of these promises is critical to gaining insight into the situation today in Israel. God is in the process of regathering Israel, as Deuteronomy 30 denotes, the fulfilling of His covenant to Abraham. Several years ago this author read a quote that is significant and well worth pondering:

---

[748] Brown, Driver, and Briggs, *A Hebrew and English Lexicon of the Old Testament*, 723.
[749] Harris, Archer, and Waltke, *Theological Wordbook of the Old Testament*, 2:645.
[750] Fruchtenbaum, *Israelology: The Missing Link in Systematic Theology*, 334
[751] **Land Covenant**: Traditionally the Land Covenant has been called the "Palestinian Covenant." To avoid confusion with the Palestinian Covenant as outlined in the Palestinian Liberation Organization (PLO) charter, which calls for the destruction of Israel; for the purposes of this study, the term *Land Covenant* is being used to identify the Covenant that God made with Israel in Deuteronomy 28-30.
[752] Fruchtenbaum, *Israelology: The Missing Link in Systematic Theology*, 572-581.

> The most central portion of all Scripture is the Abrahamic Covenant; everything else is commentary on it. (unknown)

Not only did God make an eternal covenant with Abraham and enlarge it to Israel in the Land Covenant, He also made an eternal covenant with David. These three covenants are eternal and, minimally, last through future time, or "long duration," until time and history close. The Hebrew Scripture reveals nothing beyond the Messianic Kingdom that is promised to Abraham and to David's eternal Son. Only in the New Testament, in the book of Revelation, is further revelation given, about an Eternal State. In dealing with the Davidic Covenant, there is an extremely strong indication that there is something here that has an eternal reference to the end of time into eternity. The coming verses will show that the promises of an eternal God, who is working to fulfill them through the eternal Son, who is the eternal Son of David.

In this section, there are several First Coming messianic references (2 Samuel 7:11-16; 1 Chronicles 17:11-14; Isaiah 9:6-7; Micah 5:2) that use the term *olam* or *'ad*. How are these verses to be understood when referring to the Messiah? These verses are very important because Judaism often recognizes them as messianic, even when the messianic person appears to be divine. Yet while rabbis recognize these verses as messianic, they will not embrace the idea that Messiah can be God. To them it is completely inconceivable that God would incarnate Himself as flesh and dwell among men.

Despite Judaism's disclaimers, the divinity of the Messiah is clearly indicated in two distinct categories of Hebrew Scriptures. The first involves passages in which *olam* is used. Second are passages that are recognized as messianic, where *Yahweh* is speaking of Himself, but we see clearly events that were experienced only by the Second Person of the tri-unity.

What has been established is that *olam* and *'ad* play a significant role in understanding the eternal aspect of the Abrahamic, Land, and Davidic Covenants, as well as the First Coming references of the Messiah that have direct bearing on those covenants and promises given by the prophets. But before these verses are discussed, one other observation is in order in relation to Genesis 3:15. This passage is commonly called the protevangelium, meaning that it is the prototype for the Christian gospel.[753] There is something that must be said about this verse that draws attention to the nature and essence of the Seed of the woman as it is related to the promise given by God to Satan concerning his undoing. First the verse:

---

[753] Mathews, *New American Commentary*, 247.

CHAPTER 8: MESSIAH DIVINE

> *And I will put enmity between you and the woman, and between your seed and her Seed; He shall bruise your head, and you shall bruise His heel.* (Genesis 3:15)

It is commonly recognized that Satan, originally called *Lucifer, son of the morning* (Isaiah 14:12), was most likely a very beautiful creature (Ezekiel 28:13). In Ezekiel 28:14[16], he is called *the anointed Cherub that covers*. Apparently, the Cherubim were the "guardians and proclaimers of God's glorious presence and holiness."[754] Cherubim seem to have the highest ranking among the angels and are also the closest to the presence of God.[755] Unger confirms Shower's statement:

> He is the highest and most exalted of heaven's beings, who became Satan when he led a celestial revolt that spread to myriads of the angelic beings."[756]

Satan, as a covering cherub, may have been one of the most powerful angels that God had created. So if the Seed of the woman were just a man, he could not have touched Satan. This verse strongly indicates that the Seed of the woman would have to be equal to or greater than Satan, himself, in order to defeat him. If that were the case, then the Seed of the woman would be the incarnation of God in flesh. It would have been impossible for this prophecy, given to Satan to be fulfilled without *the Seed of the woman* minimally being a supernatural person. This passage by itself does not necessarily establish that God, in human flesh, is the Seed of the woman; however it is the foundation for the messianic prophecy, and Eve understood it that way in Genesis 4:1. By the time the last prophet has come, and everything needed to identify this promised Deliverer has been revealed; this is the only possibility.

Messiah Divine!

A significant place to start an investigation of who the Messiah might be is an examination of the Davidic Covenant given in 1 Chronicles 17:10-14 and 2 Samuel 7:11-16. The significance of this covenant hinges on the direct relationship between the Davidic Covenant and the passages given by the prophets equating this physical son of David with the Messiah as God. Why are there two references to the Davidic Covenant? They are not totally the same. They are different, and yet they

---

[754] C. Fred Dickason, *Angels: Elect and Evil* (Chicago: Moody, 1975), 128.
[755] Renald Showers, *Those Invisible Spirits Called Angels*, (Bellmawr, NJ: Friends of Israel Gospel Ministry, 1997), 27-28.
[756] Merrill F. Unger, *Biblical Demonology* (Wheaton: Scripture Press, 1952), 15

have tremendous similarities. Observe the two passages with the personages, with the differences and similarities involved.

2 Samuel 7 and 1 Chronicles 17

2 Samuel 7:11-16	1 Chronicles 17:10-14
Olam House or Dynasty	*Olam* House or Dynasty
Olam Kingdom	*Olam* Kingdom
Olam Throne	*Olam* Throne
If he sins – chasten	No sin or chastening mentioned
Solomon in view	Someone beyond Solomon in view

Fruchtenbaum makes the following observation of these two passages of Scripture as to the differences and similarities:

> The parallel passage [to 2 Samuel 7:11-16] in 1 Chronicles 17:10b-14 is very similar, yet there are significant differences. In 2 Samuel the son is immediate; in 1 Chronicles he is distant. In 2 Samuel the son is a sinner; in 1 Chronicles there is no mention of sin. In 2 Samuel the reference is to Solomon; in 1 Chronicles the reference is to Messiah.
>
> The three promises of 2 Samuel are repeated here, but a fourth is also added: an eternal son. "I will settle him in my house forever." David's line will eventually culminate in the birth of an eternal Person whose eternity will guarantee David's dynasty, kingdom and throne forever.[757]

Olam is used three times both in the Chronicles and Samuel passages. These passages cannot be read without an understanding that God is making a perpetual covenant with David. This covenant will last through time and eternity because of the aspect brought out in the Chronicles passage concerning an eternal son, who is the Messiah.

---

[757] Fruchtenbaum. *Messianic Christology*, 79.

CHAPTER 8: MESSIAH DIVINE

What Ethan, the Ezrahite, who was in Solomon's court (1 Kings 4:30-31) wrote about David in Psalm 89, is significant. He wrote after the time of David and during Solomon's reign, giving important confirmation and understanding as to the interpretation of the Davidic Covenant. Look at some of the following verses from Psalm 89:

> *3-4 [4-5] I have made a covenant with My chosen one; I have sworn to My servant David; I will establish your offspring forever, I will confirm your throne for all generations. Selah.*

> *29 [30] I will establish his line forever, his throne, as long as the heavens last.*

> *34-37 [35-38] I will not violate My covenant, or change what I have uttered. I have sworn by My holiness, once and for all; I will not be false to David. His line shall continue forever, his throne, as the sun before Me, as the moon, established forever, and enduring witness in the sky. Selah*

> *51 [52] How Your enemies, O LORD, have flung abuse, abuse at Your anointed at every step.*

These statements of Scripture by the hand of Ethan the Ezrahite are clear and unmistakable. This Davidic Covenant is viewed by Ethan under the Inspiration of Scripture as being *forever*. The word *anointed* in verse 51 is the Hebrew word *Mashiach*, from which *Messiah* comes. The connection that Ethan makes between the eternal nature of the Davidic Covenant and the identity and role of *Mashiach* is significant.

One other dimension to be considered in understanding the nature of the timeframe of the Davidic Covenant is the Jeremiah 22:24-30 passage, which appeared to threaten the *forever* implications of the Davidic Covenant. This passage needs to be brought into view as to its direct relationship between Solomon and his kingly line which was cursed by God in Jeremiah 22:24-30. *Yeshua*, in the New Testament, could not get His right to rule from his stepfather, Joseph. *Yeshua* was of the Davidic line through *Miriam* (Mary); but there were many sons of David in the first century C.E. In the New Testament book of Luke, God, Himself, gives the right to rule to *Yeshua* at the time of His birth:

> *He shall be great, and shall be called the Son of the Highest: and the Lord God shall give unto Him the throne of His father David.* (Luke 1:32)

THE TRI-UNITY OF GOD IS JEWISH

This fulfilled what Nathan had told David: that his house, throne, and kingdom would be secure because one of his sons would be the eternal Son of God, whose incarnation would place Him physically in the house of David (1 Chronicles 17:11-14; Luke 3:23-31).

Another significant verse from the New Testament deals directly with the Davidic Covenant. *Yeshua*, near the end of His ministry, asked the Pharisees a question as to who the Messiah would be; however, they could not, and would not, answer. In Matthew 22:41-46, *Yeshua* was referring to Psalm 110:1:

> *^{41} While the Pharisees were gathered together, Yeshua asked them, saying, ^{42} What do you think of Messiah? Whose son is he? They said to Him, The Son of David. ^{43} He said to them, how then does David in spirit call Him Lord, saying, ^{44} The LORD said unto My Lord, You* [come] *sit on My right hand, till I make Your enemies Your footstool? ^{45} If David then called Him Lord, how is He His Son? ^{46} And no man was able to answer Him a word, neither durst* [dare] *any man from that day forth ask Him any more questions.*

The answer to the question, *If David then called Him Lord, how is He His Son*, was obviously, because David's Son would be God. Yeshua's question about Psalm 101:1 was a demonstration by Yeshua that their anticipated deliverer would be divine. However, the Pharisees would not answer His question.

Olam, in the 1 Chronicles account, points out clearly that a Son of the sons of David would reign on his throne for *olam*. Once again, the context definitely points to *olam* as the end of time. When Ethan, in Psalm 89, adds his understanding to the original passage; it becomes even clearer that the One who is settled by God, in His house and in His kingdom, shall be established and reign on the throne of David beyond the end of time into eternity, forevermore. Last, the curse of Jeremiah 22 totally disqualifies any descendent of Solomon from ever being King over Israel from the throne of David.

Isaiah 9:6-7

There are seven observations about this verse that point to this Child being uniquely different than anyone else born.

> *^{6} For unto us a child is born, unto us a son is given: and the government shall be upon His shoulder: and His name shall be called Wonderful, Counselor, the mighty God, the Everlasting*

CHAPTER 8: MESSIAH DIVINE

Father, The Prince of Peace. ⁷ Of the increase of His government and peace there shall be no end, upon the throne of David, and upon his kingdom, to order it, and to establish it with judgment and with justice from hence-forth even for ever. The zeal of the LORD of hosts will perform this. (KJV)

Verse 6-7 makes clear that God promised and named a child who would reign over Israel. Human parents name a child because they like the sound of the name. Some parents name a child because of the biblical meaning or because of the biblical character of the person that bore that name. Yet a human parent has absolutely no idea whether or not the child will live up to that name. Not so with God. When He names a child, He does so from His omniscience, knowing that the name He gives will exactly fit the character and purpose of that child. Therefore, the names given for Messiah, this child that will be born according to Isaiah 9, describe His character. Of the five descriptions given to Him, three of them are used only of God. Notice also that in verse 7, this person is directly tied to the throne of David. Who was this child? Jewish scholars teach that the "child" to be born was Hezekiah, a contemporary of Isaiah.[758] Cohen also argues that unlike his father Ahaz, who was a vassal to Assyria, Hezekiah was not a vassal. But Cohen's reasoning is not even logical. Hezekiah, King of Judah, led a vassal state under the Assyrians until he rebelled. Sennacherib, the King of Assyria (705-681), then descends upon Judah and totally destroys 46 major cities. The Oriental Institute Cylinder, a six-sided clay prism produced in the time of Sennacherib, records his third campaign, which was directed against Judah and Jerusalem:

As for himself (Hezekiah), like a bird in a cage is his royal city Jerusalem, I shut (him) up.[759]

Second Kings 18-20 makes it clear that Judah was a vassal state under Hezekiah's leadership. In fact, Hezekiah stripped the Temple of its gold and silver to try to get Assyria to stop attacking Judah. That does not sound like he could be the *child* as Cohen tries to state or the *Wonderful* or the *Mighty God*, let alone the *everlasting Father* referenced in Isaiah 9. Hezekiah, according to biblical history, did not have the character of any of these names.

Second, the word *wonderful* (Isaiah 9:6) in this passage is פֶּלֶא or *pele*, a variant of the Hebrew root word פָּלָא (*pala*).[760] Ranier Albertz, a contributing author

---

[758] A. Cohen, *The Soncino Chumash, Isaiah* (New York: The Soncino Press, 1983), 44.
[759] Joseph P. Free and Howard F. Vos, *Archaeology and the Bible History* (Grand Rapids: Zondervan, 1992), 180-181.
[760] Botterweck, Ringgren, and Fabry, *Theological Dictionary of the Old Testament*, 11:534.

to *Theological Lexicon of the Old Testament,* states that the verb occurs 78 times and means "to be wondrous" or "to fulfill" (a vow) "or to separate."[761] Albertz also states that:

> In the large, major category of its usage,...it indicates an event that a person, judging by the customary and the expected, finds extraordinary, impossible, even wonderful. *Pele* never hinges on the phenomenon as such but includes both the unexpected event as well as one's astonished reaction to it....The wonder, the astonishment, includes the recognition of the limits of one's own power to conceptualize and comprehend.[762]

This word *wonderful* is used in the context of something that is beyond human knowledge or ability as is stated by Conrad:

> The texts all deal with extraordinary phenomena, transcending the power of knowledge and imagination....In fact, the texts do not deal with circumstances presented simply as being extraordinary, but rather with certain goals impossible for humans to attain by their own devices or with actions and events directed toward them or affecting them that they are nevertheless unable to influence. In other words, they deal with acts and effects transcending human knowledge and imagination and hence above all transcending the powers of human agency....Primarily, the observation is made concerning a line that human beings cannot cross but that can be crossed from the other side. The word group thus also marks the contrast between the finitude of what is possible on one side of the line and infinite range of what is possible on the other side...but for the most part it applies to superhuman forces and powers, especially to God. The texts are concerned above all with the insurmountable contrast between what is possible for human beings and what is possible for God.[763]

What becomes rather obvious is that, even though *pele* is used of God rather than man, the context of verse 6 definitely links the word to God as well as a child that

---

[761] Rainier Albertz, a contributor to Jenni and Westermann, *Theological Lexicon of the Old Testament,* 2:982.

[762] Jenni and Westermann, *Theological Lexicon of the Old Testament,* 2:982.

[763] Botterweck, Ringgren, and Fabry, *Theological Dictionary of the Old Testament,* 11:534-535.

will bear all governmental responsibility and will sit on the throne of David. This verse states that a child will be born who will govern from the throne of David, and His name is Wonderful (*pele*), pointing to God, Himself. Clearly, this One will be God in flesh reigning on the throne of David.

Third, the name *Mighty God* (Isaiah 9:6) is even more perplexing concerning the Jewish dilemma of its dual reference to God and to a child. Jewish people do not believe the Messiah will be God, and yet here is a child that will be born in order to reign on the throne of David, and *His name shall be called…the mighty God."*

Yet Jeremiah 32:18 states, *The Great, the Mighty God, the LORD of host, is His name.* Even in the *Jewish Study Bible*, Jeremiah 32:18 does not remove its meaning: *O Great and mighty God whose name is the LORD of Hosts.* No Jewish person is going to question or doubt that the statement in Jeremiah is the LORD God Almighty, Himself. So how can the same truth be denied in Isaiah 9:6, that speaks of a child who would be born whose name is *El gibbor* (God almighty)? Isaiah 10:21 also refers to Israel returning to the *Mighty God.* God is consistent with His Word, even if man is not. It is tremendously inconsistent to say that the Jeremiah 32 and Isaiah 10 passages refer to God and the Isaiah 9:6 passage does not.

Fourth, the *Everlasting* as in *Everlasting Father* in Isaiah 9:6 is the Hebrew word עַד (*'ad*) which means "duration" or "perpetuity." This is a reference to God as the Father who is their guardian and protector. Fruchtenbaum notes that Isaiah 9:6 can be compared to Isaiah 63:16 which says: *You, O LORD, are our Father; our Redeemer from everlasting is Your name.*[764] Here the word *olam*, rather than *'ad*, is used, but both refer to eternity as unto the end of time and into eternity, when used in reference to God. Also Isaiah 63:16 states that *LORD, Father,* and *Redeemer* are from *everlasting* and so is His name, even as Isaiah 9:6 refers to the child to be born, that *His name will be called Everlasting Father*.

Fifth, the description used in verse 7 is *no end*, which in Hebrew is אֵין־קֵץ. Although Jenni claims that this word for *end* is "distributed throughout the entire Old Testament," he makes no reference to Isaiah 9:7.[765] Also, Talmon, on writing on the word קֵץ, does not reference Isaiah 9:7; but he does divide the meaning and usage of the word into four groups: (1) end as in lifetime, (2) end as a period of time, (3) end as a historical period and (4) eschatology.[766] Isaiah states of this child that will be born, that of His government there will be *no end* to its increase and peace. That seems to be self-explanatory. This usage seems to be unique because the other usages do reference a specific period of time; whereas, *no end* as used in this passage has

---

[764] Fruchtenbaum, *Messianic Christology*, 40.
[765] Jenni and Westermann, *Theological Lexicon of the Old Testament*, 3:1154.
[766] Botterweck, Ringgren, and Fabry, *Theological Dictionary of the Old Testament*, 13:82-83.

something in view beyond time. Hill and Matties show the usage of *end* as theological, as in divine judgment (Genesis 6:13); as in *end of time* and *end of human history* (Daniel 8:17, 19; 11:40; 12:4, 6); and even as in *end of wrongdoing* (Ezekiel 21:25, 29 [30, 34]). But because of the אין (no), the verse is stating that "a time of peace without end is expected."[767] So the אין gives it the opposite meaning, no ending, as is referenced by Brown, Driver, and Briggs.[768] Coppes very clearly shows that difference with the word אין (no) when he states: "Contrariwise, the Messiah's kingdom will know no end."[769] Clearly this word אין (no) is used not in a time frame but in the sense of eternity. Clearly the Messianic Kingdom referenced in verse 7 will have no end.

Jewish scholars recognize the enduring kingdom, but do not acknowledge that the Messiah will reign forever, but that God is reigning forever. The first paragraph is a comparison between Moses and Messiah ben David. Moses brought the people of the Exodus to the entrance of the Promised Land and Messiah ben David brings them to the Kingdom. The following quote coming from the *Messiah Texts* (Patai) (a scholarly Jewish work) will be viewed in four parts:

> With the death of **Moses, the earthly career of Israel's first Redeemer** comes to an end. In the Other World, of course, he continues to keep a watchful eye on his people, continues to intercede in their behalf. **Messiah ben David, too, nears the end of his ministry with his victory over the armies of Gog and Magog and over their satanic master Armilus, whom he kills with the breath of his mouth.** This latter detail, incidentally, is an eloquent indication of the kind of victory Jewish legend envisaged would be achieved by the Messiah. There was to be first of all, a holocaustal sequence of wars, myriads would be killed in actual combat, or by earthquakes and other great cataclysms, but the greatest of victories, that over Armilus himself, the evil incarnate, would be a spiritual one: his annihilation would be brought about by breath from the pure mouth of the Son of David, the elect of God, the Messiah.[770] (Emphasis mine)

---

[767] VanGemeren, ed. *Dictionary of Old Testament Theology & Exegesis,* article contributed by Andrew E. Hill and Gordon H. Matties, (Grand Rapids, MI: Zondervan, 1997) 3:955.
[768] Brown, Driver, and Briggs, *A Hebrew and English Lexicon of the Old Testament,* 892.
[769] Harris, Archer, and Waltke, *Theological Wordbook of the Old Testament,* 2:809.
[770] Raphael Patai, *The Messiah Texts* (Detroit: Wayne State University Press, 1979), xxxiii-xxxiv.

CHAPTER 8: MESSIAH DIVINE

What is so interesting in this section is that the Messiah ben David will bring them into the Kingdom, the enemy will be defeated, but then he will fade away into obscurity. The Rabbic Judaism premise is there must be two separate messiahs, of which neither is divine. They do not anticipate one Messiah who comes on two separate occasions.

> This greatest feat of the Messiah is, at one and the same time, also his last one. Just as Moses had brought the Children of Israel to the threshold of the Promised Land and then died, so the Messiah leads them to victory over Gog and Magog, culminating in the elimination of Armilus, **and then fades away, disappears from the scene. Nothing more is heard about him except some very vague and generalized statements to the effect that he would continue to rule over his people for an indeterminate period.** In all the great events which follow the victory over Armilus, the Messiah plays no role whatsoever.[771] (Emphasis mine)

To the Jewish rabbis the Messiah fades away into obscurity, while God the Father takes central stage in Jerusalem as the King and rules over the earth as the Son of David. That interpretation would make the Scriptures null and void! Messiah must rule according to Moses, Ethan, Isaiah, Micah, Jeremiah, Daniel, and Zechariah. This lapse is so heartbreaking because of Judaism blindness preventing them from seeing the multiple occasions where God showed Himself as a plurality (tri-unity). Because their premise is faulty, they mishandle or misinterpret the *Tanakh*.

> We know, or at least we are led to believe, that he is present at the Resurrection of the dead, at the Last Judgment, at the Messianic banquet, at the House of Study of the future in which the new, Messianic, Tora will be taught, but if he is, **no mention is made of his presence and he plays no role at all. In all those great occurrences and processes it is God, the Holy one, blessed be He, who Himself takes the central place on the stage**. It is God who resuscitates the dead, who judges the pious and the wicked, who sits with the saintly at the great feast, who pours wine into their cups, who entertains them by dancing before them, who teaches them the new Tora, and who received the homage of the entire rejuvenated, reformed and sanctified world. Where is the Messiah in all this? **We are told nothing of him**, and were it not that in the earlier phases of the Messianic myth we were assured that he would, after the ultimate

---

[771] Patai, *The Messiah Texts*, xxxiv.

> victory, reign in Jerusalem as the Prince of Peace, **we would not even suspect that he is present.**[772] (Emphasis mine)

Their conclusion is that just as Moses is a type of Messiah, both are redeemers, and neither has a part in the Promised Land or in the Kingdom.

> Thus, and in this primarily, the **Messiah proves to be essentially a Moses figure, and Moses to be the accurate prefiguration of the Messiah. Both are Redeemers**, but neither of them has a part in the great era to whose threshold they lead their people at the price of their lifeblood.[773] (Emphasis mine)

Both the beginning and ending of this statement from the *Messiah Text* compare Moses and Messiah as redeemers who do not enter the Promise. To them, Moses did not enter into the promised Land, and Messiah ben David will not enter the promised Kingdom. This parallel with Moses comes from the Torah in Deuteronomy 18:15-18 which speaks of a prophet like unto Moses. In the middle of the quote it refers to the Messiah that "fades away" as follows:

> And then fades away, disappears from the scene. Nothing more is heard about him except some very vague and generalized statements to the effect that he would continue to rule over his people for an indeterminate period.

Instead of the Messiah reigning, they see God the Father reigning in Jerusalem. Considering what has been seen in all of the previous chapters of this study on plural references of God to Himself, we can conclude that God is a tri-unity. With this understanding, we can recognize that *Yeshua*, who is the Messiah, is the one on record in the *Tanakh* as the ruler from Jerusalem during the Kingdom. It was also seen in those previous chapters that, without question, the plurality (tri-unity) of God is in the Hebrew Scriptures. The Scripture makes clear, simple statements about who the Messiah is. However, as with Judaism, if one's basic premise is wrong, then it would appear that the Messiah could not be God because God is one; the identity of the Messiah and His future reign is missed. The reason the Messiah does not permanently fade away is because He is God Almighty who will reign in Jerusalem as was promised to David. God the Father is not a descendent of David, but God the Son (as the Person being referenced here) is clearly understood from Psalm 110:1 and Matthew 22:41-46, which was even understood by the Pharisees in *Yeshua*'s day.

---

[772] Patai, *The Messiah Texts*, xxxiv-xxxv. Underlining is by this author.
[773] Patai, *The Messiah Texts*, xxxiv-xxxv. Bolding is by this author.

The words *no end* are very significant in Isaiah 9:7. These words are even more significant when the descriptions of the child to be born in verse 6 are placed alongside the fact that this child's Kingdom and peace will have *no end*. God's Kingdom will be ruled by God incarnate in the Person of Messiah. Although Isaiah 9:6-7 underscores that very powerful statement concerning the Person of Messiah who was to be born, Isaiah adds even more with the use of the term *no end* concerning His reign.

Sixth, the statement *upon the throne of David* (Isaiah 9:7) has a direct connection to the Davidic Covenant which was given 300 years earlier. This One, who will be human and yet is *Wonderful* (*pele*), the *mighty God*, and the *everlasting Father*, has a dual nature and is the fulfillment of the covenant promises to Abraham and to David. The promises to both will be fulfilled when this One, the God/man, actually reigns from the throne of David in Jerusalem, and His Kingdom will have *no end*.

Seventh is the statement concerning the Kingdom that says *hence forth even for ever* (Isaiah 9:7). The point is that a child would be born who would be God, Himself. He would personally fulfill His promise to Abraham, to Israel, and to David. As stated previously, His Kingdom will have *no end*. Isaiah reaffirms that the messianic person will personally reign on the throne from *hence forth even for ever* (עוֹלָם – olam).

Micah 5:2

> *But you, Bethlehem Ephratah, though you be little among the thousands of Judah, yet out of you shall He come forth unto Me that is to be ruler in Israel; whose goings forth have been from of old, from everlasting.* (KJV)

This verse is understood among Christians not only to give the birthplace of the Messiah but also His eternality. Jewish scholars likewise recognize this passage as being messianic. In fact, "all ancient Jewish interpreters regarded the ruler as the Messiah."[774] Barker goes on to comment that the Targums also favor the messianic interpretation of the prophecy. Goldman adds a divisive twist to the interpretation by stating that this passage refers to the House of David that originated in Bethlehem. Goldman quotes David Altschul who reflects his view:

---

[774] Kenneth L. Barker, *The New American Commentary: Micah* (21 vols. Nashville: Broadman, 1998), 97.

> Not that the Messiah will be born in Bethlehem, but that is [sic] his origin of old, through David, will be Bethlehem.[775]

The above statement is very convenient. The Jewish people today do not know what tribe they are from owing to the destruction of their ancestry records in 70 C.E. They know only that they are Jewish. Given this loss of documentation, how would a future Messiah prove Himself to be a descendent from the house of David? The fact is that if the Messiah would first appear today rather than before 70 C.E., He could not prove that He was from the line of David.

Some raise objections that the Messiah did not necessarily have to be born in Bethlehem. Hengstenberg gives a response to the Jewish authors who argue against this particular detail of messianic prophecy:

> The reference to the Messiah was, at all times, not the private opinion of a few scholars, but was publicly received, and acknowledged with perfect unanimity. As respects the time of Christ, this is obvious from Matthew 2:5. According to that passage, the whole Sanhedrin, when officially interrogated as to the birth place of the Messiah, supposed this explanation to be the only correct one. But if this proof required a corroboration, it might be derived from John 7:41-42. In that passage, several who erroneously supposed Christ to be a native of Galilee, objected to His being Messiah on the ground that Scripture says [the Messiah was to be born in Bethlehem.][776]

Hengstenberg makes it completely clear that the Messiah was to be born in Bethlehem, and that is exactly what the Jewish leadership understood when Herod inquired of the Messiah's place of birth (Matthew 2:4-8).

Two primary phrases need to be studied when investigating the divinity of the Messiah: (1) *whose goings forth have been from old* and (2) *from everlasting*. These are important because Jewish scholars state that Messiah is not eternal and is created by the Father.[777] So do these phrases reflect eternity or just an ancient origen? Barker points out that there are two possible readings of the text. One says, *whose origins are from of old, from ancient time,* which does not necessitate being eternal. He reflects their understanding in the following quote:

---

[775] S. Goldman, *The Soncino Books of the Bible: The Twelve Prophets* (New York: Soncino Press, 1994), 175.
[776] Hengstenberg, *Christology of the Old Testament,* 1: 491.
[777] Patai, *The Messiah Texts,* 16-17, 19.

> Those who prefer the main text that the expression *mime olam* refers to the ancient "origins" of the Messiah in the line of David....The stress is on the "origins" of the future Davidic ruler in the Davidic town of Bethlehem....The Davidic roots of the coming ruler are emphasized by the prophet Micah....Certainly the deity and eternality of the Messiah are still plainly taught in other passages.[778]

An NIV footnote provides an alternative rendering: *whose goings out are from of old, from days of eternity.* Many prefer the reading in the NIV footnote rather than the main text because of the use of the word *eternity*. Eternity, or *olam*, when used of God has eternity in view, but when used of man has only time in view. Jewish authors would like the main text interpretation because it falls in line with Goldman's argument that Messiah is only eternal in the mind of God:

> That "goings forth" reflect lineage, and "from ancient days" is taken to mean that the Messiah existed in the mind of God from time immemorial, as part of the Creator's plan at the inception of the universe."[779]

If Micah 5:2 were the only messianic reference, these arguments might carry more weight. However, God prepared His people for the Messiah through the words of Moses and the Prophets, plus all the plural references to God, making this view of a human, limited, non-divine Messiah difficult to accept. In the following statements, the reality of the eternality of the Messiah is more in line with the theme and content of the *Tanakh* and Micah.

It was noted at the beginning of this chapter that the word *olam* can carry two concepts, *time* and *eternity*. *Olam*, when used in conjunction with God, who is not confined or bound by time, who lives outside of space, refers to His eternality. The following author points to two perspectives, one by Jewish and liberal Christian scholars and the other by believers who take this passage (Micah 5:2), with all that the *Tanakh* has to say, to mean that the Messiah is eternal:

> "Goings forth;" "from of old;" "from everlasting." The Jewish rabbis in the Christian era refer these words either to the naming of the Messiah's name in eternity or to the idea of the Messiah existing in God's mind before the creation of the world. Rationalistic interpreters of the early nineteenth century generally adopted these interpretations. Modern Jewish and Protestant interpreters generally

---

[778] Barker, *The New American Commentary: Micah*, 97-98.
[779] Goldman, *The Soncino Books of the Bible: The Twelve Prophets*, 175.

refer "from of old," "from everlasting," to the time of the rise of the Davidic dynasty.[780]

Here Laetsch points not just to Micah 5:2 but to the many references to tracing one's heritage. He contends there is no special significance just in tracing one's lineage back to Abraham or Adam:

> Yet a lineage dating back to ancient times could not possibly have served as a special characteristic of the future Ruler. Every descendant of David and even of Abraham and Adam could trace his lineage back to creation. Nor can the words denote "the many preparations made by God from the earliest times in prophecy and history for the founding of the Messianic kingdom." For the words speak not of the founding of a kingdom, nor of the preparations for such a kingdom, nor of the prophecies of the going forth of the Ruler. The prophet here speaks of the goings forth and of the birth of a future Ruler.[781]

As Laetsch points out the Jewish view as well as the modern rationalistic interpretations of Protestants and Jewish interpreters, he gives a logical augment for viewing Messiah as eternal, before time, even without the use of the word *olam*. Feinberg, a Jewish believer, makes the following statement that the use of words in Micah 5:2 is the strongest possible expression for infinite duration and preexistence of the Messiah:

> These goings forth were in creation, in His appearances to the patriarchs and throughout the Old Testament history of redemption. The phrases of this text are the strongest possible statement of infinite duration in the Hebrew language (Psalm 90:2; Proverbs 8:22-23). The preexistence of the Messiah is being taught here, as well as His active participation in ancient times in the purposes of God.[782]

Henderson observes that Micah is speaking of one who is eternal and has been active in the affairs of man in the past:

---

[780] Laetsch, *The Minor Prophets*, 272.
[781] Laetsch, *The Minor Prophets*, 272.
[782] Charles L. Feinberg, *The Minor Prophets*, 173.

His goings forth, when He created the world, and appeared to Moses and the patriarchs, and revealed to them the Divine will.[783]

In discussing the concept that the Messiah is eternal, Hailey considers the verse with the same idea but with a different approach:

> From here would come the one through whom the "former dominion" would be restored. "Whose goings forth are from of old, from everlasting" indicates more than that He descends from an ancient lineage; it relates Him to God, the eternal One. His rule reaches back into eternity. The priests and scribes of Herod's day recognized that the Messiah would be born in Bethlehem.[784]

Barnes points out that the Messiah did not come forth from Bethlehem, but that His going forth was from eternity:

> *Whose goings forth* have been *from of old, from everlasting,* lit. *from the days of eternity. Going forth* is opposed to *going forth; a going forth out of* Bethlehem, to *a going forth from eternity; a going forth,* which then was still to come, (the Prophet says, shall go forth) to a *going forth* which had been long ago, not from the world but from the beginning, not in the days of time, but *from the days of eternity.*[785]

Lastly, Kaiser refers to the Hebrew word *olam* and the fact that, when used in conjunction with God, it refers to eternity:

> But this Ruler was not a recent creation, for even though He would be born in Bethlehem, He had existed from eternity. When the Hebrew word for "everlasting" *olam*, is used in connection with God, it can only mean "from eternity on" (Psalm 25:6; 90:2). That can be its only meaning here if the Ruler is none other than the Son of God, the Messiah.[786]

---

[783] Henderson, *Thornapple Commentaries: The Twelve Minor Prophets*, 249.
[784] Homer Hailey, *The Minor Prophets* (Grand Rapids: Baker, 1972), 209.
[785] Albert Barnes, *Barnes Notes: Minor Prophets* (2 vols. Grand Rapids: Baker, 1950), 2:70.
[786] Kaiser, *The Communicator's Commentary: Micah – Malachi*, 64.

Jeremiah 23:5-6

> *⁵ See, a time is coming, declares the LORD, when I will raise up a true Branch of David's line. He shall reign as King and shall prosper, and He shall do what is just and right in the land. In His days Judah shall be delivered and Israel shall dwell secure. And this is the name by which He shall be called: The LORD is our Vindicator. ⁶ Behold, the days come, says the LORD, that I will raise unto David a righteous Branch, and a King shall reign and prosper, and shall execute judgment and justice in the earth. In His days Judah shall be saved, and Israel shall dwell safely: and this is His name whereby* [by which] *He shall be called, THE LORD IS OUR RIGHTEOUSNESS.* (KJV)

In this passage it is necessary to understand both the historical and spiritual climate of Judah. We must understand that Jeremiah was speaking to the remaining Jewish tribes that had not been carried away by the Bablyonian captivity. He was warning Judah of impending, sure judgment, so the identification of a future Vindicator was a message of comfort in the midst of very bad news.

To briefly summarize, Judah had a series of wicked kings (Ahaz, Manasseh, and Amon) whose reigns totaled around 75 years full of wickedness and apostasy by the kings and the people. In fact, Manasseh reigned for 55 years and was the most wicked of all the Kings of Judah (2 Kings 21; 23:26-27; 24:3-4; 2 Chronicles 34:23-25; Jeremiah 15:4). The spiritual condition of Judah was very poor. The next king, Josiah, was a very righteous king and instituted a revival; but it was only a surface movement. After Josiah was killed in 609 B.C.E., each of his three sons (Jehoahaz, Eliakim/Jehoiakim, Mattaniah/Zedekiah), plus a grandson (Jehoiachin), would reign in turn on the throne. These three sons and grandson were all wicked, and Judah quickly lapsed back into sin and idolatry (Ezekiel 8-11). The common denominator is that these last four kings, who came to the throne in a short span of 22 years, did evil in the sight of the LORD, resulting in the kingdom of Judah becoming unstable and insecure. The spiritual state of Judah was in absolute rebellion against God as 2 Kings 23:30 – 25:30; 2 Chronicles 36, Ezekiel 8 – 11 and other passages bear out. As a result, God's judgment of Judah was harsh, culminating in Judah, Jerusalem, and the Temple being destroyed, and the people being taken into captivity by Babylon.

With this spiritual and historical background in view, there are two significant portions of Scripture in Jeremiah 22 and 23 which had a direct bearing on Judah, both then and for the distant future, one of judgment and the other of Promise.

CHAPTER 8: MESSIAH DIVINE

In Jeremiah 22:24-30 *Yahweh* curses Coniah or Jehoiachin (Josiah's grandson), the king, and his descendents, in a unbending statement that in the future not one of them would ever again reign on the throne of David.[787] When Coniah was deposed, his uncle Zedekiah was made king. In leading up to Jeremiah 23:5-6 *Yahweh* declares this: *Woe to the shepherds who are destroying and scattering the sheep of my pasture!* These evil kings, and the ones before them, had destroyed God's people, and God was about to deal with them and the people for their sins. God's promise in verses 5-6 is not a new promise but a clarification of the Davidic Covenant concerning a good Shepherd. *Yeshua* draws from Ezekiel 34 and Zechariah 11 as He refers to Himself as the Good Shepherd in John 10:11. This was not just an illustration; He was referencing back to the *Tanakh*.[788]

The first item in Jeremiah 23:5 to draw attention is the phrase, *when I will raise up a true branch of David's line* and that He will *reign as king and shall prosper, and he shall do what is just and right in the land.* Fruchtenbaum draws from the following comment that the Messiah will be a descendent of David:

> The kingship of Messiah is yet to come, but this verse clearly speaks of Messiah as a descendent of David and thus stresses His humanity.[789]

The one thing that rings clear, whether in Judaism or Christianity, the understanding of this verse is that it speaks of a human descendent of David that will be King and Shepherd over His people Israel. Keil and Delitzsch affirm that the one who is "raised up" is "my servant David":

> Neither of these sayings can be spoken of a series of kings. Besides, we have the passages Jeremiah 30:9; Ezekiel 34:23; 37:24, where the servant to be raised up to David by Jehovah is called "my servant David."[790]

In the beginning of 23:5, Jeremiah says, *See, a time is coming*. That phrase is a common expression for the messianic era as in Jeremiah 31:27-34.[791] Jeremiah

---

[787] **Davidic Kingly line**: David had several sons, the most famous being Solomon. But Solomon's line is the subject of Jeremiah. 22:24-30. Another lesser known son was Nathan who is not involved in the curse. Messiah could not come from Solomon's line, but Nathan's line was not involved in the curse of Coniah.
[788] Robert Davidson, *The Daily Study Bible Series: Jeremiah and Lamentations* (Philadelphia: Westminster, 1985), 25.
[789] Fruchtenbaum, *Messianic Christology*, 62.
[790] Keil and Delitzsch, *Commentary on the Old Testament*, 8:350.
[791] Laetsch, *Commentary on Jeremiah* (St. Louis: Concordia Publishing House, 1952), 189.

proceeds to use that phrase three times, emphasizing the messianic era (verses 27, 29, 31 – KJV *Behold, the days come*). The last usage in Jeremiah 31:31, is the promise of the New Covenant which started at Pentecost and will not be fulfilled until the end of the Tribulation when Israel says concerning Messiah *Yeshua, Blessed is He that cometh in the name of the Lord* (Psalm 118:26; Matthew 23:39). Clearly, these references verify that the Messiah is the son descended from David.[792]

The Messiah, whose human descent is through David's line, will reign in three descriptive ways, "righteously," "wisely," and "just." The Messiah who will reign "righteously," "wisely," and "just" is in stark contrast to the reign of Coniah and the curse placed upon his descendents in Jeremiah 22:24-30,[793] as well as the bad shepherds, the kings, priests, and other leaders in Jeremiah 23:1. Both Huey[794] and Davidson[795] point out an even sharper contrast between the meaning of Zedekiah's name, "the Lord our righteousness," and his reign, which was unlike the promised reign of the *righteous Branch*:

> This message was most likely delivered during the reign of King Zedekiah. His name means the Lord is righteous or the Lord is my righteousness. The name of the new ruler was intended as a repudiation of Zedekiah. He will be an exact opposite of rulers such as Zedekiah and Jehoiakim. He will be called "the Lord Our Righteousness." The name of this coming ruler implies that a time will come when all the people will acknowledge the Lord as the only source of righteousness.[796]

The word for *Branch* is the Hebrew word "*Zemach*," which is never used to denote a twig but to indicate a sprout growing directly out from the root of the original tree forming a new second tree.[797] This *Branch* will be righteous by nature, not an acquired righteousness. Feinberg clarifies that this reference to the Branch, which is called THE LORD OUR RIGHTEOUSNESS, is used symbolically of the Messiah. It is not being used horticulturally but is used as a technical term for the Messiah as Feinberg explains its usage:

> It is clear that the term "Branch" is symbolic of the Messiah because the adjective modifying it is a quality of persons and not plants. The

---

[792] Laetsch, *Commentary on Jeremiah*, 190.
[793] Walvoord and Zuck, *The Bible Knowledge Commentary: Old Testament*, 1158.
[794] F. B. Huey, *Bible Study Commentary: Jeremiah* (Grand Rapids: Zondervan, 1981), 77.
[795] Robert Davidson, *The Daily Study Bible Series: Jeremiah and Lamentations*, 25.
[796] F. B. Huey, *The New American Commentary: Jeremiah, Lamentations* (Nashville: Broadman, 1993), 212.
[797] Laetsch, *Commentary on Jeremiah*, 190.

shoot or sprout is a scion of the stock of David. "Branch" has a collective meaning when used horticulturally but not when used symbolically. "Branch,"...a Technical Term in the Prophets.[798]

In the post-exilic times, *the Branch* became a technical term for the expected ideal King as noted by the prophet Zechariah (3:8; 6:12).[799] Interestingly, Jeremiah was not the first to use the term *Branch*, for Isaiah had used it (Isaiah 4:2; 11:1-2) 100 years before Jeremiah.

All this groundwork from Jeremiah 23:5 as to the humanity and righteousness of the future son of David leads up to verses 6. Two items in verse 6 needs to be discussed: first, *his name,* and, second, *whereby he shall be called, THE LORD OUR RIGHTEOUSNESS*. When *Adonai Elohim* states the name of the son of David, it becomes clear that God is using this name because He knows the nature and essence of the future son of David, the Messiah:

> We must not overlook the unusual manner in which this name is introduced. The Lord does not merely say: ,His name is or shall be, nor: Call Him, nor: Call His name, nor: This shall He be called. He uses a phraseology unique in the entire Old Testament, occurring only here. "And this (is) His name which one shall call Him." That is not idle redundancy. Two facts of greatest importance are stressed. The first one: "This (is) His name." Name, as used here by the Lord, is not a mere label or tag, but designates the very nature, the essence and being of the Branch. And secondly, He expresses His will that mankind should know this *Zemach* and acknowledge Him and call Him by that name, given to Him by the Lord God of Hosts, which describes to us His inmost essence, as Jehovah Himself knows and understands it.[800]

The individual's name in Jeremiah 23:5, *THE LORD OUR RIGHTEOUSNESS* is *God*. This man who will be the Messiah, who will be the Righteous Branch and will be raised up unto David, is the LORD. This man's name, by the very mouth of *Adonai Elohim,* is *THE LORD OUR RIGHTEOUSNESS*. This Messiah is the God/man. Fruchtenbaum notes that even sources from rabbinic writings support that conclusion:

---

[798] Charles L. Feinberg, *Jeremiah* (Grand Rapids: Zondervan, 1982), 162.
[799] J. A. Thompson, *The New International Commentary on the Old Testament: The Book of Jeremiah* (Grand Rapids: Eerdmans, 1980), 489.
[800] Laetsch, *Commentary on Jeremiah,* 195.

> In the Midrash on Proverbs 19:21 (200 – 500 C.E.) it says: "Rabbi Hunah said Eight names are given to the Messiah which are: Yinnon, Shiloh, David, Menachem, Jehovah, Justi de Nostra, Tsemmach, Elias."[801]

Notice the fifth name (Jehovah) and seventh name (Tzemmach) from the quote just cited, coming from Jeremiah 23:6; and *Branch* based on Jeremiah 23:5. Observe three other references quoted from rabbinic sources:

> In the Midrash on Lamentation 1:16, it says, "What is the name of Messiah?" Rav Ava Ben Kahanna said, "Jehovah is his name and this is proved by, this is his name [quoting Jeremiah 23:6]."

Clearly, the name of the Messiah in this Midrash quotation sees the Messiah as Jehovah the LORD OUR RIGHTEOUSNESS.

> In the *Talmud* (Babba Bathra Tractate 75b) it says: Shmuel ben Nachman said in the name of Rabbi Yohanan, "the following three will be named with the name of the Holy One blessed by he – the upright, as it is said, [quotes Isaiah 43:7], the Messiah, as it is written and this is his name whereby he shall be called THE LORD OUR RIGHTEOUSNESS [quoting Jeremiah 23:6]."

In this tractate of the *Talmud*, one rabbi using the source authority of another rabbi clearly sees the Messiah as the LORD, for that is His name.

> In the Midrash on Psalm 21:1 it says: God calls King Messiah by his own name, but what is his name? The answer is "Jehovah is a man of war (Exodus 15:3)" and concerning Messiah we read "Jehovah our righteousness this is his name."[802]

When all of the factors are laid out from Jeremiah 23:5-6, along with the ancient Jewish commentary on the verse, the Messiah, the Promised One of Israel, is the physical son of David. God not only shows the humanity of the Messiah but that His name is to be called *THE LORD OUR RIGHTEOUSNESS*. This leaves no doubt that the Messiah is God incarnate, who came in the Person of *Yeshua* of Nazareth.

---

[801] Fruchtenbaum, *Messianic Christology*, 62.
[802] Fruchtenbaum, *Messianic Christology*, 62-63.

CHAPTER 8: MESSIAH DIVINE

Psalm 110:1-7

> *¹ The LORD said to My Lord, "sit Yourself at My right hand, while I make Your enemies Your footstool." ² The LORD will stretch forth from Zion Your mighty scepter; hold sway over Your enemies! ³ Your people come forward willingly on Your day of battle. In majestic holiness, from the womb, from the dawn, Yours was the dew of youth. ⁴ The LORD has sworn and will not relent, "You are a priest forever, a rightful king by My decree." ⁵ The Lord is at Your right hand. He crushes kings in the day of His anger. ⁶ He works judgment upon the nations, heaping up bodies, crushing heads far and wide. ⁷ He drinks from the stream on His way; therefore He holds His head high.*

This psalm is one of the most fascinating psalms in the *Tanakh* because of how *Yeshua* used it and how it relates to the equality of David's Lord with the LORD. There are four observations in this passage that need to be investigated.

1. First, David's son is his lord.

2. Second, this lord has enemies.

3. Third, this psalm ties together two positions that are forbidden in biblical Judaism. The kings of Israel (Judah) were not to be priests; yet in Psalm 110, the future reigning son of David is portrayed as a priest after the order of Melchizedek. This is unusual for a son of David of the Tribe of Judah to be both king and priest. When King Uzziah tried to officiate in a high priestly function thereby combining these two roles, God smote him with leprosy (2 Chronicles 26:16-21).

4. Fourth, this psalm is quoted in the New Testament more times than any other passage from the Hebrew Scriptures.

The Jewish response to this verse is very sharp and clear as Rabbi Singer explains that from the perspective of Rabbinic Judaism, it cannot refer to *Yeshua*:

> Psalm 110 represents one of the New Testament's most stunning, yet clever mistranslations of the Jewish Scriptures. Moreover, the confusion created by the Christianization of this verse was further perpetuated and promulgated by numerous Christian translators of

the Bible as well....The story of the church's tampering with Psalm 110 is so old that it begins in the Christian canon itself.[803]

Rabbi Singer, an anti-missionary for the Jewish people, makes some serious charges against the Christian interpretation of Psalm 110. However, in Michael Brown's book, it will be observed that Singer's problem is not with Christians but with the Jewish translators themselves. When translating the Greek Septuagint (LXX) from the Hebrew Scriptures, the sages' usage of the Greek word for lord, *kyrios,* lays at the heart of the controversy.[804] A part of this lengthy argument will be discussed later in this chapter.

Previously it was mentioned that four areas needed to be studied in reference to this verse: (1) David's son is his lord, (2) this lord has enemies, (3) this psalm ties together two positions, kingship and the priesthood, (4) this psalm is referenced in the New Testament more than any other passage from the *Tanakh.*

Regarding the first argument, David wrote Psalm 110:1 as being an oracle of *Yahweh!* David stated the following: *The LORD said to my Lord.* Philips is correct in seeing God as two distinct personalities, but his statement is too rash and abrupt. He gives no information as to how he arrived at his conclusion:

> Hebrew and Gentile scholars translate it the following way: "God said unto my God." This is very significant and revealing, for it presents two personalities: God number one and God number two. God number one spoke to God number two and said, "Sit thou at my right hand until I make thine enemies thy footstool."[805]

Phillips cannot mean Jewish Hebrew scholars because no Jewish scholar would make such rash and abrupt acknowledgement concerning God. Phillips does not explain how he arrived at his statement; he just makes it. Rabbi Singer has a valued point on the words for God; some versions give misleading translations by using two Lords, as representing two Gods.[806] Searching eight of nine popular versions confirms that only one of them replicates the emphasis of the original Hebrew. The King James Version uses *LORD* and *Lord* in that order. The problem of how *Lord* is used lies in the Greek Septuagint (LXX). In the Greek, "lord," "Lord," or "LORD" are all *kyrios,* which is translated lord or Lord in the New Testament. However, in the Hebrew text the first

---

[803] Tovia Singer, *http://www.OutReachJudaism.org/psalm110.html.*
[804] Michael L. Brown, *Answering Jewish Objections to Jesus: Messianic Prophecy Objections* (Grand Rapids: Baker, 2003), 133-145.
[805] O. E. Phillips, *Exploring the Messianic Psalms* (Philadelphia: Hebrew Christian Fellowship, 1967), 274.
[806] Tovia Singer, *http://www.OutReachJudaism.org/psalm110.html.*

CHAPTER 8: MESSIAH DIVINE

LORD is Israel's personal name for God (*Yahweh*); whereas, *adon* simply means "lord" or "master," not generally referring to God. Johnson states that *adon* is used 334 times (Genesis 18:12; 19:2; Ruth 2:13; 1 Samuel 1:15), and 300 times directly refers to a human lord and master. Only 30 times is the word used "of the divine Lord/Master, as in a divine title (Exodus 34:23; Deuteronomy 10:17)."[807] If only the first six words of Psalm 110:1 (*The LORD said unto my Lord*) are considered, it could very easily be seen as *Yahweh* speaking to the Messiah. However, those first six words would not necessitate the "lord" (*adon*) being God. In this instance, those six words are not isolated but are connected to *Sit at My right hand*, and that changes the whole prospective of the verse. That is a personal invitation by *Yahweh* for the Messiah to sit on the very throne of *Yahweh* at His right hand. Fruchtenbaum states that in the ancient Near East in Old Testament times, when a host king entertained a visiting king from another country, he would place him on his right side (1 Kings 2:19). This act of the host king was making a statement that the visiting king was his equal.[808] Keil and Delitzsch affirm that conclusion:

> The conclusion to be drawn from this psalm must have been felt by the Pharisees themselves, that the Messiah, because the Son of David and Lord at the same time, was of human and at the same time of superhuman nature; that it was therefore in accordance with Scripture if this Jesus, who represented Himself to be the predicted Christ, should as such profess to be the Son of God and of divine nature.[809]

A mere mortal will never sit on God's right hand. Angels don't even sit at God's right hand. So whoever the Messiah is, God Himself is making a statement that this physical seed of David is *Yahweh*'s equal. No human father, if he has any pride as a man, would ever call his physical son Lord! *Yahweh*'s invitation for an earthly monarch to sit on His right hand is momentous and even stupendous for the Hebrew mind. That is an understatement. The invitation between *Yahweh* and this future Lord of David's "shows an exceptional degree of intimacy between God and this 'new' monarch."[810] Phillips is correct in his statement that there are two Gods even though it does need to be tempered with explanation.

The second argument regards the enemies. *Yahweh* states, *while I make your enemies your footstool*. Phillips issues a very valued statement concerning who the

---

[807] VanGemeren, ed., *Dictionary of Old Testament Theology & Exegesis*, 1:257.
[808] Fruchtenbaum, *Messianic Christology*, 88.
[809] Keil and Delitzsch, *Commentary on the Old Testament: Psalms*, 5:185.
[810] Samuel Terrien, *Critical Eerdmans Commentary: The Psalms* (Grand Rapids: Eerdmans, 2003), 752.

enemies of God and who the son of David might be. When and where did God and His enemies ever have the acquaintance to meet each other to become enemies?

> God number two has some enemies...On further reflection, we realize that the enemies of God number two could not have been His enemies without knowing Him and having had some dealings with Him. The natural thought that comes to us is, who are these enemies? And when did they have an acquaintance with each other, and why did they become enemies?[811]

When will his enemies become the footstool of a king? When the enemies were defeated, the ancient practice of a victorious king was to symbolically place his foot on the neck of the defeated enemy who was lying on the ground. Smith refers to that very action as the practice of the ancient Near East:

> The allusion is to the custom of conquerors placing their feet upon the necks of the captured enemies as a symbolic token of total victory (Josh 10:24).[812]

Lay,[813] Pritchard,[814] and Howard[815] affirm Smith's statement by also referencing Joshua 10:24 as a biblical example of placing one's foot on the neck of the defeated enemy. *Yahweh* is saying that David's physical Lord, the Messiah, is invited to sit on His right hand because this son of David is His equal and He is going to make Messiah's enemies His footstool (He will give Messiah full victory, as shown in placing one's foot on the enemy's neck), and He will reign over all the earth. That verse is a powerful statement to show David's Lord is indeed the Lord, equal with the Father, and that He will reign from David's throne over all the earth.

Next is the argument about the forbidden area of intertwining the offices of the king and the priesthood. A king could be a prophet but not a high priest (Numbers 16:40; 18:7). A high priest could be a prophet but not a king. Merrill,[816] Smith,[817] and Geisler[818] express that these two offices were never to be combined in

---

[811] Phillips, *Exploring the Messianic Psalms*, 275.
[812] James Smith, *The Promised Messiah*, 187.
[813] Bromiley, *The International Standard Bible Encyclopedia*, 2:332.
[814] James B. Pritchard, *The Ancient Near East in Pictures* (Princeton, NJ: Princeton University Press, 1954), 285.
[815] David M. Howard, *The New American Commentary: Joshua*, 254.
[816] Eugene H. Merrill, *Kingdom of Priests* (Grand Rapids: Baker, 1987), 377.
[817] William Smith, *Old Testament History* (Joplin, MO: College Press, 1970), 639.
[818] Norman L. Geisler, *A Popular Survey of the Old Testament* (Grand Rapids: Baker, 1977), 155.

the same person, yet *Yeshua* will be King of Israel and also be a priest. The answer is not complex, for *Yeshua* was born of the house of David, the tribe of Judah, which would disqualify Him from serving in a priestly function under the Law. However, according to Psalm 110:4, this son of David, the Messiah, will serve as a priest-king even though God forbade that kind of dual role in the Mosaic Law. This son of David will not be a priest through the tribe of Levi, for David (and the author of the book of Hebrews) compares Him to a different High Priestly order *after the order of Melchizedek*, who was not Jewish but Canaanite. There is absolutely no way a mere human being of the house of David, of the tribe of Judah, could be a priest or Levite at the same time unless His priestly function came from a different order. The order of Melchizedek is a type of His High Priestly order. While this son of David is of the tribe of Judah, His origin is eternal; and Melchizedek is described as being *without father, without mother, without descent, having neither beginning of days, nor end of life* as Hebrews 7:1 clearly states. Messiah, after the *order of Melchizedek*, lays out the premise that the Mosaic Law has been discontinued because the Messiah is a priest and king, which simply means the Law cannot be in force during the dispensation of Grace, otherwise known as the Church age. Fruchtenbaum gives insight on this situation:

> The Law of Moses laid down that all priests had to be of the tribe of Levi and that kings had to be of the tribe of Judah. In order for this prophecy to be fulfilled, therefore, it is clear that it will be necessary for the Law of Moses and the Levitical Order to be removed.
>
> The New Testament (Hebrews 7:11-18) clearly teaches that with the death of Jesus, the Law of Moses was rendered inoperative by His fulfillment of it and was replaced with the Law of Christ. Under the new Law of Christ, the Order of Melchizedek is instituted in place of the Levitical Order; therefore, Messiah is indeed a priest and a king. Verse 4 states that Messiah's priesthood and kingship will be eternal.[819]

These four arguments clarify that Psalm 110 is a unique psalm that was used by *Yeshua* to silence the Pharisees and for the writers of Scripture to show that He is the Lord of all.

The forth argument for the identity of Lord is that Psalm 110:1-7 is the most-quoted passage in the Hebrew Scriptures found in the New Testament. Specifically, it is alluded to 14 times by the New Covenant writers. Wilson states that this verse, in each case, refers to *Yeshua*. *Yeshua* uses Psalm 110:1 with authority against the

---

[819] Fruchtenbaum, *Messianic Christology*, 89.

Pharisees, affirming that it was written by David under the inspiration of the Holy Spirit.[820] Echoing Wilson, Mays asserts that it is used more than any other reference from the *Tanakh* in reference to *Yeshua* (Matthew 22:44; Mark 14:62; 16:19; Luke 22:69; Acts 2:34-35; 7:55; Romans 8:34; Ephesians 1:20; Colossians 3:1; Hebrews 1:3, 13; 8:1; 10:12; 1 Peter 3:22).[821]

Daniel 9:24-27

> *²⁴ Seventy weeks are determined upon Your people and upon Your holy city to finish the transgression, and to make an end of sins, and to make reconciliation for iniquity, and to bring in everlasting righteousness, and to seal up the vision and prophesy, and to anoint the Most Holy. ²⁵ Know therefore and understand, that from the going forth of the commandment to restore and to build Jerusalem unto the Messiah the Prince shall be seven weeks, and threescore [60] and two weeks: the street shall be built again, and the wall, even in troublous times. ²⁶ And after threescore and two weeks shall Messiah be cut off, but not for Himself: and the people of the prince that shall come shall destroy the city and the sanctuary; and the end thereof shall be with a flood, and unto the end of the war desolations are determined. ²⁷ And he shall confirm the covenant with many for one week: and in the midst of the week he shall cause the sacrifice and the oblation to cease, and for the over-spreading of abominations he shall make it desolate, even until the consummation, and that determined shall be poured upon the desolate.* (KJV)

What is so powerful and convincing about this passage that rabbis do not want Jewish people to study it? In a personal conversation with this author, a Jewish believer stated that her rabbi said this passage was forbidden to study. She resented that, and as a result she read and studied it; and God had opened her eyes to see that if the Messiah is in this passage, then He had already come. The result of her investigation of this passage, and other passages, had brought her to a saving knowledge of her Messiah, *Yeshua*.

Other Christian scholars see this passage differently than is historically understood. Surprisingly, authors such as Charles,[822] Goldingay,[823] and Towner,[824]

---

[820] T. Ernest Wilson, *The Messianic Psalms* (Neptune, NJ: Loizeaux, 1978), 126.
[821] James L. Mays, *Interpretation: Psalms* (Louisville: John Knox Press, 1989), 350.
[822] R. H. Charles, *A Critical and Exegetical Commentary on the Book of Daniel* (Oxford: Clarendon Press, 1929), 246-247.

state that this passage was fulfilled during the time of the Maccabees (171 – 164 B.C.E.). One problem with this view is that they state that Onias III was the "anointed one" who is cut off.[825] He was the legitimate high priest at the time when Antiochus IV took over Israel from the Ptolemy's of Egypt, but Onias III had no spiritual impact on Judah at that time. By subtracting the 69 "weeks" or 483 years from 536 B.C.E. as the starting date, the cutting off of the Messiah would be approximately 73 B.C.E., and that is almost 100 years after the Maccabean Revolt. To those scholars, this passage is not to be understood as the promise of the coming of the Messiah to Israel, as in *Yeshua*, who was put to death or *cut off*. Nor do those same scholars see it as referring to the destruction of the city of Jerusalem and the Temple. This is liberal higher criticism in action. The biggest question defining the position that liberal higher critics take and the historical position is: When do the 70 weeks begin? Was the starting date 536 B.C.E. or approximately 444 B.C.E. with the decree of Artaxerxes? The purpose of this book is to substantiate the tri-unity of God, and in this particular passage, to examine the place of the Messiah in prophetic history, not to spend a multitude of pages showing why fundamental Christianity holds to 444 B.C.E. Sir Robert Anderson has written a whole book just dealing with this 444 B.C.E. dating of this prophecy and its fulfillment in *Yeshua*.[826] His writing does not need to be duplicated. So let us reflect on some additional sources.

There are two things that need to be observed concerning Daniel 9:24-27: First, Jewish scholars today generally do not view this text as referencing the first century and especially not referring to *Yeshua*. Second, from the standpoint of Christians, this prophecy of Messiah shows that the destruction of Jerusalem and the Temple would have a direct bearing on the deity of the Messiah.

Michael Brown quotes portions of Rashi, the respected Rabbi (1040-1105) of the eleventh century, from northern France[827] whose commentaries are included in the *Talmud*. To summarize Rashi's understanding and interpretation of Daniel 9:24-27, Brown makes the following comments from Rashi, that *anointed one* was the Judean King Agrippa, who was ruling at the time of the rebellion and destruction of Jerusalem and the Temple. Rashi interpreted the *prince* as Titus, the Roman General, who flooded the Land with Roman legions. What Rashi did was place the *anointed one* in the first century before the destruction – in the same century at *Yeshua*. Rashi ultimately does point to the Messiah and His reign, but His identification is

---

[823] John E. Goldingay, *Word Biblical Commentary: Daniel* (Dallas: Word Books, 1989), 30:266-268.
[824] W. Sibley Towner, *Interpretation: Daniel* (Atlanta: John Knox Press, 1984), 140-144.
[825] Towner, *Interpretation: Daniel*, 144.
[826] Sir Robert Anderson, *The Coming Prince* (Grand Rapids: Kregel, 1967), 1-304.
[827] Robinson, *Essential Judaism*, 300-301.

misplaced, being associated with the wrong people. In terms of God's purposes, the death of King Agrippa had absolutely no impact on His people Israel.[828] As far as the identification of the *prince* as being General Titus, that is impossible. Titus never made a 7-year (70th week) covenant with rebellious Israel, plus grammatically the *he* in verse 27 does not refer to Messiah but to a future *prince* that will come offering Israel a 7-year covenant, as Fruchtenbaum explains:

> The pronoun 'he" in verse 27 goes back to its nearest antecedent in verse 26, which is not the Messiah but "the prince who is to come." This "prince" has been a topic of Daniel's earlier prophecies in chapters 7 – 8. This political leader is better known to Christians as the Antichrist.[829]

So the *prince* is neither General Titus nor the Messiah, but the future Antichrist. That reality has startled more than one Jewish person. For example, when Rachmiel Frydland, a young Orthodox man, was confronted with the Messiah by a German missionary in pre-World War II Poland, using Daniel 9:24-27, he stated that as he looked through rabbinic commentaries, they were saying the same thing that Rashi stated centuries before.[830]

The reason why the rabbis have forbidden the reading and studying of Daniel 9:24-27 is because after the rejection of *Yeshua* as Messiah, rabbis over the centuries tried to figure out the time of the Messiah's coming and in the process had accepted many false messiahs, as is stated by Frydland:

> The Jewish people rarely study the Book of Daniel because many rabbinic Jews were misled attempting to interpret Daniel's cryptic "time." Some were led so far astray that they came to believe in false messiahs, and therefore Talmudic Jews frowned on students who studied Daniel with a view of finding out the time of the Messiah. However, religious Jews knew that this book revealed more about Messiah than any other book.[831]

Frydland's statement is absolutely true, for the Jewish people over the centuries, in trying to determine the time of the Messiah's coming, have followed 46 false messiahs.[832]

---

[828] Michael L. Brown, *Answering Jewish Objections*, 3:86-92
[829] Fruchtenbaum, *Messianic Christology*, 98.
[830] Rachmiel Frydland, *When Being Jewish Was A Crime* (Nashville: Nelson, 1978), 72-73.
[831] Frydland, *When Being Jewish Was a Crime*, 72.
[832] Smith, *The Promised Messiah*, 470-474.

CHAPTER 8: MESSIAH DIVINE

The impact of the 70 weeks of Daniel 9:24-27 will also be studied in determining whether they reference the Messiah as divine. These four verses will be observed in connection to the subject at hand. In verse 24, the 70 weeks that are determined need to be understood because of the confusion that has arisen over the centuries as to the meaning of the term *weeks:*

> Many English versions have translated the phrase to read seventy "weeks." But this translation is not totally accurate and has caused some confusion about the meaning of the passage. Most Jews know the Hebrew for "weeks" because of the observance of the Feast of Weeks, and that Hebrew word is *Shavuot*. However, the word that appears here in the Hebrew text is *shavuim*, which means "sevens." This word refers to a "seven" of anything with the context determining the content of the "seven." It is similar to the English word "dozen," which means twelve of anything based upon the context.[833]

The second item to be observed is the word "people." God's message is being relayed through Gabriel to Daniel to the Jewish people, not the Church. These three authors, Fruchtenbaum,[834] Lang,[835] and Feinberg,[836] among many others, identify six things in verse 24 that are determined upon *your people and your holy city*. Feinberg lists them as follows:

> During those seventy weeks of years, the great works to be accomplished were: first, "to finish the transgression"; second, "to make an end of sin"; third, "to make atonement for iniquity"; fourth, "to bring in everlasting righteousness"; fifth, "to seal up vision and prophecy"; and sixth, "to anoint the most holy place."[837]

These six areas are divided into two classes. The first three are concerned with the removal of sin, and the second three deal with bringing in righteousness. Walvoord points out that the first class all deal with sin named three ways: transgression, sin, and iniquity.[838] Each one of these phrases needs to be looked at individually.

---

[833] Fruchtenbaum, *Messianic Christology*, 94-95.
[834] Fruchtenbaum, *Messianic Christology*, 95-96.
[835] G. H. Lang, *The Histories and Prophecies of Daniel* (Grand Rapids: Kregel, 1940), 130-131.
[836] Charles L. Feinberg, *Daniel: The Kingdom of the Lord* (Winona Lake, IN: BMH Books, 1981), 127.
[837] Charles L. Feinberg, *Daniel: The Kingdom of the Lord*, 127.
[838] John F. Walvoord, *Daniel: The Key To Prophetic Revelation* (Chicago: Moody, 1971), 221.

Fruchtenbaum states that the words *to finish*, means "to restrain firmly," "to restrain completely," or "to bring to completion," while the word *transgression* is a very strong word for sin and means literally "to rebel." Also, in the Hebrew this word is with a definite article: *the transgression* or "the rebellion" indicates that some specific act of rebellion is finally going to be finished:

> The point is that some specific act of rebellion is finally going to be completely restrained and brought to an end. This act of rebellion or transgression is to come under complete control so that it will no longer flourish. Israel's apostasy is now to be firmly restrained in keeping with a similar prediction in Isaiah 59:20. Specifically, this is the rejection of the Messiah as dealt with in Isaiah 52:13 – 53:12.[839]

This understanding of the **first phrase**, *the transgression,* lends credence to Renald Showers' assertion that Israel has committed a particular transgression:

> With the word "the" in this context, it refers to the Jew's specific sin of rebellion against the rule of God. This rebellion was the root sin which prompted all of Israel's other sins. Gabriel was saying that Israel would not stop its rebellion against God's rule until these 490 years would run their course. In agreement with this, other scriptures indicate that Israel will not repent, turn to God and be saved until the second coming of Christ at the end of these 490 years (Zechariah 12:10 – 13:1; Romans 11:25-27).[840]

Showers clearly established the fact, with scriptural references, that Israel has been in a state of rebellion against God and against His Messiah, and will continue to do so until Messiah comes the second time. As was seen in the previous chapters in this study, *Yeshua* was very active as the God of Israel, and He was the ultimate theophany of God in flesh evidenced in such passages as Isaiah 9:6-7; 48:12-16; 50:1-7; and Micah 5:2. In other words, Walvoord adds to Showers' argument by stating that Israel's rebellion will only come to an end when *the transgression* is finished.

> The expression is derived from the *piel* verb form of the root *kala* meaning "to finish" in the sense of bringing to an end.[841]

---

[839] Fruchtenbaum, *Messianic Christology*, 95.
[840] Renald Showers, *The Most High God* (West Collingswood, NJ: The Friends of Israel Gospel Ministry, 1982), 118.
[841] Walvoord, *Daniel: The Key to Prophetic Revelation*, 221.

CHAPTER 8: MESSIAH DIVINE

The **second phrase** of six in Daniel 9:24 is *to make an end of sins*. This word is a more general word for transgressions that Israel has and is committing toward their God. The word "sin" also carries the idea of "missing the mark," as an arrow would miss its intended target. Miller expresses the word and concept as follows:

> "To put an end to sin" may either be translated *tamam*, "be complete, come to an end, finish," or *hatam*, "to seal, affix a seal, or seal up." Either translation would make sense and have basically the same meaning, for "sealing up" sin would be tantamount to putting an end to it. Yet "to put an end to" would fit the context better, a reading most scholars and translations accept.[842]

Accordingly, the transgression of Israel as they rebelled against *Yahweh* and His Messiah at His coming, along with all future individual acts of sins will be sealed up, end, or be finished. The way God intends to deal with the sins and transgression of Israel will be through atonement.

The **third phrase** of six in Daniel 9:24 is *to make atonement for iniquity*. The Hebrew word translated "to make an atonement" is *kaphar*. This word has the same root meaning as the word *kippur*, as in Yom Kippur, the Day of Atonement. In fact, this atonement is the means that God will use *to finish the transgression* and *to make an end of sins*. The word *iniquity* refers to the inward sin or what Christian theologians term the *sin nature*. However, that term *sin nature* would not be known in Judaism or be accepted by their leaders. The phrase that would be known to them is *yetzer hara* – "the evil inclination."[843] Fruchtenbaum expresses what the atonement is for and how the nation of Israel will be reconciled with their God:

> The third purpose of the Seventy Sevens is: to make reconciliation for iniquity. The Hebrew word for reconciliation is a word that means "to make an atonement." This is the means by which the first and second purposes will be accomplished. The means by which Israel's national sin of rejecting the Messiah will be removed and the means by which her daily sins will be removed is by an atonement.
>
> The third purpose is to make atonement specifically for iniquity. The word iniquity refers to the sin nature. The program of the Seventy Sevens is a cleansing of Israel that will include the removal of all

---

[842] Stephen Miller, *The New American Commentary: Daniel* (Nashville, Broadman, 2003), 260.
[843] Fruchtenbaum, *Messianic Christology*, 96.

three things; first, the national sin of rejecting His Messiahship; second, sinning daily; and third, dealing with the sin nature itself.[844]

Miller states in a brief summary of Daniel 9:24 that sin will be ended and transgression finished, for this would all be accomplished through *Yeshua*'s atonement for humanity's sin by the Messiah's substitutionary death upon the cross at Calvary. His blood was to be the atonement, or the covering for sin, reflected in this verse.[845]

These three purposes to *finish the transgression*, *make an end of sins*, and *make reconciliation for iniquity*, will deal with sin and the cleansing of Israel, which is today in a state of rebellion. Lang further states that this atonement for iniquity will be expiated by sacrifice.[846] These same three purposes mentioned at the beginning of this paragraph will bring about the three other remaining purposes. God will deal with the sin issue of Israel, as well as all of mankind, through the Messiah.

The **fourth phrase** of the six (first of the second group) purposes will be to *bring in everlasting righteousness*. Feinberg expresses that the atonement will be necessary to bring righteousness to Israel:

> He would first provide a basis on which men can become righteous, and then He will set up on earth an eternal kingdom of righteousness. Salvation and righteousness are, in fact, the chief characteristics of Messiah's coming rule on earth (Isaiah 45:17; 51:6-8; Jeremiah 33:14-16).[847]

Showers illustrates that in the past, Israel had revivals but fell again into sin. That righteousness was only temporary, but this future righteousness will be permanent:

> In the past, as the result of periodic revivals, Israel had experienced righteousness. However, that righteousness was temporary, for eventually the nation rebelled against God again. But when Israel repents and believes in Jesus Christ at His second coming, they will never rebel against God again (Jeremiah 31:31-34; Ezekiel 36:22-32). It will be given righteousness that will last forever.[848]

---

[844] Fruchtenbaum, *The Footsteps of the Messiah*, 192.
[845] Stephen Miller, *The New American Commentary: Daniel*, 260.
[846] Lang, *The Histories and Prophecies of Daniel*, 131.
[847] Charles L. Feinberg, *Daniel: The Kingdom of the Lord*, 127.
[848] Showers, *The Most High God*, 118-119.

CHAPTER 8: MESSIAH DIVINE

Israel's righteousness will be permanent, but when does this future righteousness come? The first three purposes (Daniel 9:24a) and the atonement for transgression, sin, and iniquity are tied to sacrifice; and that atoning sacrifice will bring in righteousness. That messianic person bringing in righteousness is the *righteous BRANCH* of Jeremiah 23:5-6 who is called *the LORD OUR RIGHTEOUSNESS*. In Daniel 9:24, one of the purposes of the Seventy Sevens is *to bring in everlasting righteousness*. Fruchtenbaum states that the word translated "everlasting" is the word *olam* and should be understood as being an "age" and not "eternity."

> This could be more literally translated "to bring in an age of righteousness," since the Hebrew *olam* is better translated as "age" rather than as "everlasting." This age of righteousness is to be the Messianic Kingdom spoken of in the Prophets (Isaiah 1:26; 11:2-5; 32:17; Jeremiah 23:5-6; 33:15-18). It is this very age that Daniel had been expecting to see established after the 70 years of captivity, but now he is told that that will only be after the 490 year period of the Seventy Sevens.[849]

The phrase *to bring in everlasting righteousness* is connected in the immediate context to the Messianic Kingdom and not in the context of eternity. The book of Revelation in the New Testament states that after this righteousness is brought in for the Messianic Kingdom, it will then go into the new order of the New Heavens, New Earth, and the New Jerusalem for eternity (Revelation 21-22), but the immediate context in Daniel only has the Kingdom in view.

The **fifth phrase** of six is *to seal up vision and prophecy* (Daniel 9:24). In Genesis 3, when sin came into the world, prophecy was introduced by God Himself in verse 15 as the method that He would use to reveal His plan of redemption from sin to mankind. Sin will be removed from Israel as referenced in the first half of Daniel 9:24. There will be no further need for prophecy and visions for sin will no longer be an issue.[850] Hence, *vision and prophecy* will be sealed up and removed in the future Messianic Kingdom. The actual Hebrew word *hatam* means to "seal, affix seal, seal up."[851] Showers' adds some additional insights as to future completion of the "seal[ing] up [of] the vision and prophecy":

> The thrust of this phrase seems to be as follows: revelation that comes through vision or prophecy no longer has to be of concern to

---
[849] Fruchtenbaum, *Messianic Christology*, 96.
[850] Lang, *The Histories and Prophecies of Daniel*, 132.
[851] Stephen Miller, *The New American Commentary: Daniel*, 261.

people once that revelation has been fulfilled. The vision of prophecy can be sealed up in the sense of being laid aside from the realm of active concern. The word translated "to seal up" is the same word which was translated "to make an end" in the phrase "to make an end of sins" earlier in this verse. It would appear that there is an intended relationship between the two phrases. That relationship is as follows: When Israel will make an end of its daily sins at the end of the 490 years, then all revelation that came through vision and prophecy concerning God's chastening of Israel can be sealed up. The people of Israel will no longer have to be concerned about that revelation, for all the foretold chastening will have been fulfilled. Since their sins which caused chastening will have ended, there will be no further need for chastening.[852]

When transgression, sin, and iniquity are removed (Leviticus 26:40-42; Jeremiah 3:11-18; Hosea 5:15) by the atoning work of Messiah (Isaiah 53), and the Jewish nation calls on Him (Psalm 80:1, 15-17; Daniel 7:13 with Matthew 26:64) and believes on Him, the Second Coming will occur (Psalm 118:26; Matthew 23:39). According to the New Covenant of Jeremiah 31 and Ezekiel 36, there will be no need for visions and prophecy because Israel will be saved and walking in His statutes.

The **last phrase** of the six is *to anoint the Most Holy* (place). This is the anointing of the Millennial Temple (Ezekiel 40-48). In other words, after all Israel's transgression, sin, and iniquity are removed by the anointing sacrifice of the Messiah, the Millennial Temple will be anointed.[853] The term "anointed" here is *Masah*, "to anoint" which means "to consecrate for religious service."[854]

Daniel 9:24 clearly shows that something supernatural will happen in regard to Israel and their sin in relationship to their God. That relationship between God and Israel is connected by two opposites: First, Israel's sin which keeps them in the state of rebellion. Second, in making reconciliation for iniquity, the sacrifice for sin will bring righteousness; visions and prophecy will come to an end and the Temple will be consecrated, all culminating in the Messiah, Himself, returning. The Messiah is interwoven throughout verse 24, as well as verses 25-27. In verse 26, only two words will be analyzed because of the impact they have on *Yeshua* in His First Coming: "Messiah" and being "cut off."

The term Messiah in the *Tanakh* denotes two ideas, one of consecration and endowment of either an individual, such as with Saul, David, and priests, or an object

---

[852] Showers, *The Most High God*, 119.
[853] Charles L. Feinberg, *Daniel: The Kingdom of the Lord*, 128.
[854] Stephen Miller, *The New American Commentary: Daniel*, 261.

such as the Tabernacle, the altar, or laver. Messiah comes from the Hebrew word *jvm* and is pronounced *Mashiach*, "anointed one," and occurs 39 times[855] in the Hebrew Scriptures.[856] Smith does not place the Daniel passage in with the listing of references (footnote 831), but Young's Concordance does,[857] as well as Oswalt, who states that the term *Messiah* developed in its understanding to focus in a person:

> This existence of the concept of "The Anointed One" in its own right, over and above the more narrowly prescribed historical functions of prophet, priest, and king, undoubtedly contributed to the rise of the concept of the eschatological Anointed One, the Messiah. Within the canon of the OT there are only two unambiguous references to this figure, both in Daniel 9:25, 26. Here Daniel predicts a time in the future when the Anointed One, who may well be the Most Holy who is anointed in 9:24, will appear and then be cut off with nothing.[858]

This term *Messiah* developed into the understanding of a messianic person in Jewish thinking from very early times, especially during the exile and post-exilic period. Oswalt expresses the fact that these two references in Daniel 9:25-26 are without a doubt a reference to the Messiah. The Jewish rabbis, from the post-exilic period into the time of *Yeshua*, had good reason to see Daniel 9 as a reference and a timetable for the coming of the messianic person. In the following statement, Rabbi Silver agrees that the messianic expectation was very high during the second quarter of the first century C.E.:

> Prior to the First Century (C.E.) the messianic interest was not excessive....The First Century, however, especially the generation before the destruction [of the Second Temple] witnessed a remarkable outburst of Messianic emotionalism. This is to be attributed, as we shall see, not to an intensification of Roman persecution, but to the prevalent belief induced by the popular chronology of that day that the age was on the threshold of the

---

[855] **Saul** - 1 Samuel 12:3, 5; 24:6, 10; 26:9, 11, 16, 23; 2 Samuel 1:14, 16, 21; **David** – 2 Samuel 19:21; 22:51; 23:1; Psalms 18:51; 20:6; 28:8; **Priest** – Leviticus 4:3, 5, 16; 6:22; **Reigning King** – Lamentations 4:20; Psalms 84:9; 89:38; **Patriarchs** – Psalm 105:15; 1 Chronicles 16:22; **Solomon** – 2 Chronicles 6:42; **Prospective King** – 1 Samuel 16:6; **Cyrus** – Isaiah 45:1; **Messiah** – 1 Samuel 2:10, 35; Psalms 2:2; 89:51; 132:10; Habakkuk 3:13 and Daniel 9:25-26.
[856] James Smith, *The Promised Messiah*, 1-3.
[857] Robert Young, *Young's Analytical Concordance to the Bible*, 39.
[858] VanGemeren, ed., *Dictionary of Old Testament & Exegesis*, 2:1126.

Millennium...When Jesus came into Galilee, "spreading the gospel of the Kingdom of God and saying the 'time is fulfilled' and the Kingdom of God is at hand," he was voicing the opinion universally held...the chronological fact [the timing of] which inflamed the Messianic hope rather than the Roman persecutions...Jesus appeared in the procuratorship of Pontius Pilate (26-36 C.E.)...It seems likely, therefore, that in the mind of the people the Millennium was to begin around the year 30 C.E. Be it remembered that it is not the Messiah who brings about the Millennium. It is the inevitable advent of the Millennium which carries along with it the Messiah and his appointed activities. The Messiah was expected around the second quarter of the First Century C.E. because the Millennium was at hand. Prior to that time he was not expected, because according to the chronology of the day the Millennium was still considerably removed.[859]

It is significant that a rabbi would acknowledge the time of the coming of the expected Messiah, even recognize *Yeshua*'s presence historically and yet miss *Yeshua* as the promised Messiah. These verses in Daniel 9:25-26 are very significant, powerful, and forceful in unambiguously pinpointing the time of the Messiah's coming. Even Moses, in a more general sense, spoke of the time of the Messiah in Genesis 49:10. The words *scepter will not depart from Judah until* He comes whose right it is,[860] clearly shows that Messiah's tribal identity must be present. Judah and all the other tribes lost their tribal identity when the Romans destroyed the Temple in 70 C.E. This simply means that in order for the Jewish people to identify the Messiah, and even identify their own tribal identity, the Messiah had to come before the destruction of the Temple because the genealogical records of the families and tribes were kept in the Temple which was destroyed in 70 C.E. Both Moses and Daniel predicted the time of the coming of the Messiah, but Daniel was more precise in regards to time and purpose of the Messiah's coming. This One, the Messiah, would deal with *the transgression, sin,* and *iniquity* of the people by His sacrifice or anointing work at Calvary.

The last words to be discussed in Daniel 9:26 are *cut off*. Examples of the term *cut off* are defined as follows: (1) as cutting off part of the body as the head or hands, or (2) the cutting off of the foreskin in the act of circumcision, or (3) the cutting down of trees, idols, to cut out or to eliminate, to kill or to cut (make) a

---

[859] Rabbi Abba Hillel Silver, *A History of Messianic Speculation in Israel*, (New York: Macmillan, 1927), 5-7

[860] Compare the words in Genesis 49:10 with Ezekiel 21:27. [Shiloh is not in the Genesis text.]

covenant.[861] The Messiah, in the context of Daniel 9, is viewed as being killed in the prophetic future. A violent death is seen by Walvoord,[862] Miller,[863] Lang,[864] Showers,[865] and Fruchtenbaum.[866] Walvoord states the verb rendered "to cut off" means to "destroy, to kill" and makes reference to Genesis 9:11, Deuteronomy 20:20, Jeremiah 11:19, Psalm 37:9. Miller relates the phrase *cut off* to the crucifixion of *Yeshua*. Lang relates the phrase *cut off* to the Passover sacrifice in the month of Nisan. Although Lang and Feinberg[867] suggest that Artaxerxes issued the decree in the month of Nisan, neither one has it documented. Showers connects the words *cut off* with the death penalty (Leviticus 7:20, 21, 25, 27) and with reference to a violent death (1 Samuel 17:51; Obadiah 9; Nahum 3:15). Being *cut off* is obviously a separation of body parts, foreskin, or the severing of a tree from its trunk; but it is also used in reference to death, a violent death. The context of Daniel 9:24-27 would lead very strongly to a death by execution, as the Romans did on their crosses.

This passage in Daniel 9 becomes quite powerful in that Israel's *transgression*, *sin*, and *iniquity*, are reconciled, and Israel will experience real righteousness for the first time through Jeremiah's New Covenant. The Millennial Temple is anointed, and there is an end to Israel's sins. Therefore, there is no further need for vision and prophecy, because all of the elements in Daniel 9:24-27 are focused in the Messiah, who was *cut off* in death as the substitutionary sacrifice for sin and was literally the "anointed one" who would and did come 483 years after the decree of Artaxerxes. A tremendous amount of power and time is compressed into these four verses of Daniel 9:24-27.

Isaiah Chapters 7 through 12

These six chapters of Isaiah are a unit called the "Book of Immanuel." Within the "Book of Immanuel," where Immanuel is referenced three times in Isaiah 7:14, 8:8, 10, there are three strategic portions of Scripture. Immanuel is the one born of a virgin in Isaiah 7:14. Isaiah states that this child which would be born would have some unique names for a human being and would reign from his father David's throne in Isaiah 9:6-7. Later Isaiah states that this one will be from the *stem*

---

[861] Harris, Archer, and Waltke, *Theological Wordbook of the Old Testament,* 1:456.
[862] Walvoord, *Daniel: The Key To Prophetic Revelation,* 229.
[863] Stephen Miller, *New American Commentary: Daniel,* 267.
[864] Lang, *The Histories and Prophecies of Daniel,* 134.
[865] Showers, *The Most High God,* 125.
[866] Fruchtenbaum, *Messianic Christology,* 97.
[867] Charles L. Feinberg, *Daniel: The Kingdom of the Lord,* 130.

of Jesse and that *the spirit of the LORD* will rest upon Him in Isaiah 11:1-2. The impact of the "Book of Immanuel" is significant, and that is where attention needs to be focused.

The person who will be born of a virgin in chapter 7 is called Immanuel, which means "God with us." The virgin will conceive and bear a son who will be "God with us!" For a further discussion on this section of Scripture, see Arnold Fruchtenbaum's work on Isaiah 7.[868]

Once again, Immanuel is referenced in Isaiah 8:8, 10 which leads up to another well-known passage in Isaiah 9:6-7. Here that virgin-born son, who is "God with us," is called names that only God is called (*wonderful* or "pele," *mighty God*, and the *everlasting Father*), as was already observed earlier in this chapter under the section on Isaiah 9:6-7. This Immanuel will be God/man and will reign on the throne of David, His father, forever because He is eternal.

In Isaiah 11:1-2, a further description is given of Immanuel or "God with us." Verse 1 identifies the humanity of Immanuel, and He is presented through the metaphor of Him coming from the stem of Jesse, a Branch growing out of his roots. This passage is echoed by two other passages, Jeremiah 23:5-6 where the Branch is called *the LORD OUR RIGHTEOUSNESS*, the Branch is "God with us." Also, in Isaiah 61:1, the Messiah is anointed by *the Spirit of the LORD God* and *the spirit of the Lord shall rest upon Him* in seven different manifestations as Isaiah 11:2 clearly states.

The Book of Immanuel has some tremendous portions of Scripture that speak of the one who is "God with us" as the God/man who was virgin-born, a son of David, who is also *Wonderful, mighty God,* and *everlasting Father*. What a significant section of Scripture Isaiah 7-12 is as it presents "God with us."

Isaiah 50:1a, 4-6

> *¹ Thus said the Lord:*
>
> *⁴ The Lord God has given me the tongue of the learned, that I should know how to speak a word in season to him that is weary: He wakens [Me] morning by morning, He wakens My ear to hear as a learned. ⁵ The Lord God has opened My ear, and I was not rebellious, neither did I turn back. ⁶ I gave My back to the smiters, and My cheeks to them that plucked off the hair: I hid not My face from shame and spitting.* (KJV)

---

[868] Fruchtenbaum, *Messianic Christology*, 32-37.

In relation to this verse and other verses in the *Tanakh*, a valid question can be asked: Who in history does this passage of Scripture describe? There can only be one answer: *Yeshua* of Nazareth. In verse 1, *Yahweh* is speaking; but then in verse 4, *Yahweh* states that the Lord (*Adonai*) God (*Elohim*) did something. Here are two personalities, *Yahweh* and the Lord God. Who is who? The answer comes in verse 6 where *Yahweh* gives a description of Himself:

> *I offered My back to the floggers and My cheeks to those who tore out My hair. I did not hide My face from insult and spittle.*

When did *Yahweh*, in history, give His back to the floggers or smiters? When did *Yahweh*, in history, allow His beard to be pulled from His face? When, in history, did *Yahweh* permit Himself to be shamed and spat upon? Before the answer is given, there are two points as to the personalities observed. First, there are two personalities represented here as God: *Yahweh* and the Lord God. Second, *Yahweh* allowed men to afflict Him with such beatings, shame, and spitting. The identity of *Yahweh* and what happened to Him is what happened to *Yeshua* who is the exact image of the Father, at Yeshua's trial before the Sanhedrin and before the Romans.

Isaiah is clearly presenting that a son will be born of a virgin and He will be "God with us." He will be born from the stem of Jesse of the house of David, and He will reign on David's throne forever. This one who is to reign on David's throne forever is named by God as *Wonderful, almighty God,* and the *everlasting Father*. He is introduced as the Servant of the Lord in chapters 42, 49, and 50 of Isaiah. This is the promised Messiah, the God/man repeatedly promised ever since Genesis 3:15.

Isaiah 52:13 – 53:12

Isaiah 53 introduces the suffering servant. The identity of the suffering servant brings controversy between Jewish and Christian adherences. Who is this Servant? Some Jewish scholars point to Isaiah, but predominantly to Israel as fulfilling the suffering Servant passage. This argument and the reasoning behind the rabbis changing their historic understanding were brought out by Victor Buksbazen, a Jewish believer in Messiah.[869] If a Jewish person is asked to read this passage and to identify the person, he or she invariably will say, upon reading Isaiah 53, that this passage comes from the Christian Bible (New Testament) and that this passage refers to Jesus. What a surprise it is for them when they realize that this passage comes from their own prophet Isaiah, and they themselves have identified *Yeshua* as the

---

[869] Victor Buksbazen, *The Prophet Isaiah* (Collingswood, NJ: Spearhead Press, 1971), 2:400-404.

THE TRI-UNITY OF GOD IS JEWISH

Suffering Servant. Isaiah 53 is not a passage of Scripture known by most Jewish people because it is forbidden by the rabbis to be read, and it is never read in the synagogue services. Rabbis in synagogue services end their reading at Isaiah 52:12 and pick up again at the beginning of Isaiah 54. That was not always the case, as Rabbi Moshe Alshekh of the sixteenth century states:

> [Our] Rabbis with one voice, accept and affirm the opinion that the prophet is speaking of king Messiah.[870]

There are many things that could be presented in this passage to show that this person is *Yeshua*. For a fuller treatment of this passage, there are numerous books that deal with each verse in depth as indicated in the footnote below.[871] One point that needs to be brought out in this passage is the identity of the speaker and the one of whom he is speaking. What will be addressed here are the personal pronouns in Isaiah 53 and to whom these pronouns refer within this passage.

The most common Jewish interpretation of Isaiah 53 is that it refers to Israel, for the nation of Israel is the servant of the Lord. This interpretation was given by Rashi, an eleventh-century rabbi. However, his contemporary, Maimonides, a rabbi from Egypt, took issue with Rashi. This interpretation did not become popular until the 1800s when Protestant missionaries began to use it with great success in sharing the Gospel of Messiah with the Jewish people in Europe.[872]

In Isaiah 53:2-7, a large number of pronouns are used. In these verses the pronoun *he* (used 12 times), *him* (used 7 times), and *his* (used 3 times) refer to the person who is the subject of this chapter. These 22 pronouns (*he, him* and *his*), within the space of six verses, all point to this person and describe him. Then in the same verses, numerous other pronouns *we* (8 times), *our* (6 times), and *us* (once) refer to someone else 15 different times. When totaling all of the pronouns used in these six verses, there are 37 personal pronouns.

A close examination of the text gives strong evidence that these pronouns, *we, our,* and *us* cannot be referring to God for God is not a sinner who has iniquities. These pronouns refer to Israel because they are sinners with iniquities. The *he, him,* and *his* clearly refer to the Servant of the Lord who is the Messiah because the

---

[870] Rachmiel Frydland, *What the Rabbis Know About the Messiah* (Cincinnati, OH: Messianic Publishing Co, 1991), 53.
[871] Arnold G. Fruchtenbaum, *Jesus Was a Jew* (Tustin, CA: Ariel Ministries Press, 1981); David Baron, *The Servant of Jehovah* (Jerusalem: Keren Ahvah Meshihit, 2000); Victor Buksbazen, *Isaiah's Messiah* (Bellmawr, NJ: Friends of Israel Gospel Ministry, 2002).
[872] Fruchtenbaum, *Messianic Christology*, 54. This whole section in Fruchtenbaum's book is very interesting and valuable (pp. 53-59.)

description cannot possibly be referring to Israel. If the suffering servant were Israel, then verse 8 would mean that Israel was *cut off*, executed, or dead. Also if Isaiah 53 is Israel, then who is the one referred to in the expression *for the transgression of my people was he stricken*? Israel just does not fit! But when the person of *Yeshua* is placed in the context of Isaiah 53, meaning the sins and iniquities of Israel were laid upon Him, that fits the context and the passage. In history, when Isaiah 53 is read, who does this passage fit? The answer is *Yeshua*.

Zechariah 11:12-14; 12:10; 13:7

These next three passages are all connected and should be approached as a unit because each one presents *Yahweh* as experiencing something that only a human being could experience. There are some key words in these passages, and they are tied together around one person, the Messiah: *Shepherd, pierced, My Shepherd* and *My Associate*. In Zechariah 11:12-14, 12:10, the question is who, in history, do these passages describe? There is not a lack of material as to the messianic references to *Yeshua* in these passages. Numerous scholars agree on the God/man aspect and see *Yeshua* as the central person fulfilling these passages: Baron,[873] Feinberg,[874] Fruchtenbaum,[875] Brown,[876] Unger,[877] Merrill,[878] Kaiser,[879] Hartman,[880] and Barrett.[881]

The Jewish interpretation is to distance themselves from anything that would even hint of *Yeshua* being the fulfillment of these passages because they do not believe in the tri-unity of God. These verses have had to be dealt with by the rabbis to suppress the obvious prophecies of *Yeshua* the Messiah as being *Yahweh*. These will be referenced just a little later as each passage is dealt with separately.

---

[873] Baron, *The Visions and Prophecies of Zechariah*, 379-380, 403-404, 437-440, 447-449, 474-477.
[874] Charles L. Feinberg, *God Remembers: A Study of the Book of Zechariah*, 208-209, 229-231, 244-246.
[875] Fruchtenbaum, *Messianic Christology*, 67-74.
[876] Michael L. Brown, *Answering Jewish Objections*, 3:37-38, 149-151.
[877] Unger, *Zechariah: Prophet of Messiah's Glory*, 199, 216-217, 230-232.
[878] Merrill, *An Exegetical Commentary: Haggai, Zechariah, Malachi*, 297-298, 320-321, 335-336.
[879] Kaiser, *The Communicators Commentary: Micah – Malachi*, 394-395, 405-406, 413.
[880] Fred Hartman, *Zechariah: Israel's Messenger of the Messiah's Triumph* (Bellmawr, NJ: Friends of Israel Gospel Ministry, 1994), 111-112, 129.
[881] Michael Barrett, *Beginning at Moses* (Greenville, SC: Ambassador-Emerald Int'l, 2001), 236-237.

> *¹² And I said to them, If you think good, give Me My price; and if not, forbear. So they weighed for My price thirty pieces of silver. ¹³ And the LORD said to Me, cast it to the potter: a goodly price that I was apprised at of them. And I took the thirty pieces of silver, and cast them to the potter in the house of the LORD.* (Zechariah 11:12-13)

Zechariah 11:4-14 speaks of the good *Shepherd* that ministers to the flock of Israel, but his leadership is not wanted by the *flock* or "people" of Israel. First, in 11:4, Zechariah speaking for God, refers to God as *Yahweh* my *Elohim* (LORD my God). The first person pronouns appear 19 times in these verses, three times in verse 6, five times in verse 7, once in verse 8, twice in verse 9, three times in verse 10, and once each in verses 12 and 14. The backdrop of this passage is that Zechariah is to act out the part of the shepherd for the LORD. *Yahweh* also took two staves called Beauty (v. 10) and Bands (v. 14) and cut them asunder, breaking His covenant with the nations and between Israel and Judah. Because of Israel's rejection of His leadership as the good *Shepherd*, *Yahweh*, the *Shepherd* asks them for His wages.

Before the wages issue is dealt with, it needs to be determined who the *Shepherd* is in Zechariah. On the surface, the *Shepherd* appears to be *Yahweh*, and He is. However, the picture that the *Shepherd* describes concerning His wages leads to an additional conclusion. David Baron adds some valuable insight as to the identity of the *Shepherd* who is also addressed as *Yahweh*. What is discovered is that *Yahweh* is *Yeshua*:

> But it practically comes to much the same thing, whether we regard the prophet as representing in his actions as shepherd, Jehovah, or more directly the Messiah, for the coming of the Messiah is often spoken of in the Old Testament as the coming of Jehovah. In Ezekiel 34 for instance, Jehovah Himself is represented, in His capacity as the true Shepherd of Israel, as seeking, saving, strengthening, healing, and satisfying His people; but as we read on in that chapter we become aware that it is not Jehovah directly who is going to do all this, but immediately through the Messiah. "And I will set them up one shepherd over them, and He shall feed them even My servant David; He shall feed them, and He shall be their shepherd" (Ezekiel 34:23) namely, the true David, the Messiah as the Jews themselves have always rightly interpreted this passage.[882]

We see the Shepherd is none other than *Yeshua*, the Good Shepherd (John 10:11). This will also be seen shortly as the rest of this passage is studied. The

---

[882] Baron, *The Visions and Prophecies of Zechariah*, 380.

good Shepherd asks for His wages. He did not give a demand, but asked for a voluntary response: "If you are satisfied, pay Me My wages; if not, don't." The good Shepherd was not looking for money but for spiritual qualities or spiritual fruit. Feinberg and Baron make similar observations concerning the wages that the good Shepherd desired:

> He was requesting of them fruitage from His ministry, such as piety, godly fear, devotion, and love and they gave Him instead that which was far worse than a direct refusal (Matthew 21:33-41).[883]

> The wages which He actually sought from them for all His Shepherd care, was, as the commentators rightly understand, the spiritual fruit of His labours – repentance, faith, true heart piety, humble obedience and grateful love. This is brought out clearly in the Lord's parable of the Vineyard, which is Israel, to whom He first sent His servants, and then His own son, "that He might receive the fruits of it."[884]

Instead of approving of Him, the Jewish leadership considered His entire ministry to them as worthless; and what they offered Him was an insult. Their response of 30 pieces of silver was a statement, not just an act of payment for services rendered. Their act of payment for how they viewed His ministry to them was that He was totally unworthy and worthless in their sight.[885] Giving the good *Shepherd* 30 pieces of silver, made the statement that He was worth no more than the price of a dead slave (Exodus 21:32).

What needs to be observed is that *Yahweh*, in Zechariah 11:4-14, was valued by the Jewish leadership as nothing more than a dead slave. Neither God the Father nor God the Holy Spirit took on humanity. Thus, neither could be betrayed or valued for 30 pieces of silver for Their services to them as a *Shepherd*. Only God the son, the Messiah, the son of David, the Branch, and the good Shepherd was valued for 30 pieces of silver. These verses show that *Yahweh*, in this passage, must have become a man in order to be betrayed in such a manner. This may not have been evident to the Jewish people before *Yeshua*'s coming, but after the death, burial, resurrection, and ascension of *Yeshua;* there is only one man in history, the God/man, that fits this description.

---

[883] Charles L. Feinberg, *God Remembers: A Study of the Book of Zechariah*, 209.
[884] Baron, *The Visions and Prophecies of Zechariah*, 403.
[885] Hartman, *Zechariah: Israel's Messenger of the Messiah's Triumph*, 111.

Zechariah 12:10

> *And I will pour upon the house of David, and upon the inhabitants of Jerusalem, the spirit of grace and of supplications: and they shall look upon Me whom they have pierced, and they shall mourn for Him, as one mourns for his only son, and shall be in bitterness for Him, as one that is in bitterness for his firstborn.* (KJV)

Zechariah 12:10 is another powerful statement because *Yahweh* states that something happened to Him that could only be experienced by human beings; He was pierced. So that the identity of the person speaking in verse 10 needs to be identified so that there is no confusion. By paying close attention to these first person pronouns, we can recognize the identity of the person in verse 10. The person speaking in verses 1 and 4 identifies Himself as *Yahweh* (LORD). Then He uses the first person pronouns in verse 2, *I will make Jerusalem*, verse 3, *In that day will I make*, verse 4, twice, *I will smite* and *I will open My eyes*, verse 6, *I will make the governors*, and verse 9, *I will seek to destroy*, in all these instances referring to the speaker *Yahweh*. Notice also that the speaker from verse 1 claims to be the Creator of the heavens and earth, just as the One who called Jacob, and identified Himself as the *first and the last* in Isaiah 48:13, 16. In Zechariah 12:10, *Yahweh* states that *I will pour upon the house of David*, and then continues with his powerful statement, *and they shall look upon Me whom they have pierced*. *Yahweh* is referring to a time when He was physically pierced, but that is impossible because Rabbinic Judaism believes that God is pure spirit and cannot, in any way, become a man. Yet, here *Yahweh* distinctly states that He was pierced, and the text does not call it to be read in a metaphorical sense. The literal sense of the verse is obvious. *Yeshua*, the Messiah, the God/man was pierced on Mt. Calvary, as the atonement (Daniel 9:24-25), the sin offering (Isaiah 53:10) for the sins of the world.

The Jewish response is to divert the natural meaning of Zechariah 12:10 away from any possibility of it implying that *Yeshua* could be the God/man promised by God from the very beginning when sin entered the world in Genesis 3 (v. 15). Brown references two Jewish interpretations of this text where they try to say that the "evil inclination" was pierced, or that the people of Israel will weep over Messiah ben Joseph being slain in the last Great War. These interpretations are not consistent with the text as Jewish scholars attempt to avoid having to admit that *Yeshua* is speaking in Zechariah 12:10:

> Zechariah 12:10 is discussed in the *Talmud* in b. Sukkah 55a. The verse – read with a singular, not plural, subject – is first interpreted to mean that it is the evil inclination (i.e., the sinful tendency in man)

that was slain, and the people wept when they saw how easily it could have been overcome. The second interpretation states that the people wept over Messiah son of Joseph who was slain fighting in the last great war (i.e., the last great future war) for his people, after which Messiah son of David asked God to raise him from the dead, and his request was granted. From this we learn two significant points: (1) The Hebrew was understood to be speaking of an individual person or thing, not of a plural subject (in other words, the one who was pierced through and slain, not those who were pierced through and slain); and (2) there was an ancient Jewish tradition interpreting the text in terms of a messianic figure who died and then was raised from the dead.[886]

Brown's point is that the text is speaking of an individual and not something collective, such as the "evil inclination." Brown's other point is that the text is speaking of the Messiah, but not just a mere man called Messiah ben Joseph. What the Jewish scholars do recognize in their interpretation is that the Messiah will be killed; they just misidentify who the Messiah is. The text is speaking of an individual and not something collective. Now in the same mental frame of reference, consider the translation given in the *Jewish Study Bible* for Zechariah 12:10 as they divert attention away from the Hebrew text, which clearly states, *and they look upon me whom they have pierced*. They rephrase it to say that Israel will lament to God for those who are slain:

> *But I will fill the House of David and the inhabitants of Jerusalem with a spirit of pity and compassion; and* **they shall lament to Me about those who are slain, wailing over them as over a favorite son** *and showing bitter grief as over a first-born.*

Kaiser also quotes this reference from the *Jewish Study Bible* as well as quoting from the 1896 Jewish translation:

> *And they* [i.e., the house of David and the inhabitants of Jerusalem] *shall look up to Me because of Him whom they* [i.e., the nations which came up against Jerusalem] *have pierced."*[887]

In the first quote, Jewish scholars have made two changes (bolded): First they removed the word *pierced* and inserted "slain." Second, they change the wording from *look upon me* to "lament to me." These changes effectively remove the intent of

---

[886] Michael L. Brown, *Answering Jewish Objections,* 148-149.
[887] Kaiser, *The Communicator's Commentary: Micah – Malachi,* 405-406.

what Zechariah was saying by removing the meaning in the verse that *Yahweh* was pierced, and that they would look upon Him. The second quote (immediate above) follows the Jewish interpretation that the nations pierced Messiah ben Joseph. If the passage is read naturally, without the preconception of the interpreter, then Messiah *Yeshua* is in view.

Next, the word *pierced* is a powerful word if kept within its context. This word *pierced* or דָּקַר (*daqaru*) is used 11 times in the Hebrew text (Numbers 25:8; Judges 9:54; 1 Samuel 31:4; 1 Chronicles 10:4; Isaiah 13:15; Jeremiah 37:10; 51:4; Lamentations 4:9; Zechariah 13:3) meaning to "pierce" or "thrust through."[888] Almost all references to being pierced in the *Jewish Study Bible* are all rendered as being "pierced through." So there is no doubt as to the meaning of this word in the text of this passage and its fulfillment in the crucifixion when *Yeshua* was pierced with the Roman spear (John 19:34), which is what Zechariah 12:10 references. Rabbinic Judaism believes that Messiah is not God, so the rabbis speak of two completely human Messiahs in the form of Messiah ben Joseph (the suffering Messiah) and Messiah ben David (the reigning Messiah) to try and avoid the obvious reference in Zechariah 12:10 that the Scriptures present the Messiah as the God/man. In contrast, if the text, as given in Zechariah 12:10, is taken for what it says, two messiahs are not needed because the same Messiah comes twice with two different purposes. The main issue for Jewish scholars is how to resolve the changing of the pronouns that God used of Himself, from *Me* to *Him* in this passage.[889] This shift in the pronouns goes from *Yahweh* as first person, *Me*, to the one who is mourned for in the third person, as *Him*. The lament for *Yahweh* who was pierced through, is viewed from *Yahweh*'s perspective as *Me*, whereas the *Him* is viewed from a future generation of Jewish people who will recognize *Yahweh* as *Him* the one they were responsible for piercing. The answer to the problem of the pronouns is a matter of viewpoint as both Barrett and Merrill express:

> The shift in pronouns from the first to the third person testifies to the distinctive association. That God would send His perfect representative, His Son, was the great message of hope.[890]

> From YHWH's viewpoint it is "Me" that is the focus; from the standpoint of the people it is "Him." Such a transition from one

---

[888] Unger, *Zechariah: Prophet of Messiah's Glory*, 216.
[889] Kaiser, *The Communicator's Commentary: Micah – Malachi*, 406.
[890] Barrett, *Beginning at Moses*, 237.

CHAPTER 8: MESSIAH DIVINE

person to another is not at all uncommon in Hebrew composition, especially in poetic and prophetic language.[891]

Yahweh, who is the obvious speaker in this passage, is the Messiah, the One who was physically pierced with a sword, the one for whom Israel will mourn bitterly. Kaiser mentions there is only one possible example of that kind of mourning in the biblical account, which was the death of King Josiah in 2 Kings 23:29 and 2 Chronicles 35:25.[892] Zechariah 12:10 states that Israel will weep for *Him* bitterly as one mourns for his only son, because to that future generation, *Yahweh* will be recognized as *Yeshua* who came as the Messiah twenty centuries ago. The word *only* is the Hebrew word *yachid* (discussed in chapter four of this book).

As can be clearly seen in Zechariah 12:10, *Yahweh* will pour on the house of David and Jerusalem the spirit of grace and supplication. He would be physically pierced, and Israel will someday mourn for Him greatly. This is one of the most gut-wrenching passages in Scripture, when the Jewish people realize that *Yeshua* was indeed the Messiah, God incarnate. They will weep and mourn, for they will then realize that all their fathers before them who worshipped *Yahweh* or *ha Shem*[893] with zeal were literally rejecting the One they said they worshipped. The last public words of *Yeshua* bring together the Persons Messiah and *Yahweh* in Matthew 23:37 as *Yeshua* speaks as *Yahweh*:

> *O Jerusalem, Jerusalem, you that kills the prophets, and stones them which are sent to you, how often would I have gathered your children together, even as a hen gathers her chickens under her wings, and you were unwilling!*

Notice as well in this verse that *Yeshua* is speaking as the God of Israel. The word *I* is *Yeshua* speaking, and He claims that He sent the prophets that they killed and stoned; and He, *Yeshua*, would have gathered them together to protect them but they were not willing.

---

[891] Merrill, *An Exegetical Commentary: Haggai, Zechariah, Malachi*, 320.
[892] Kaiser, *The Communicator's Commentary: Micah – Malachi*, 407.
[893] **HaShem**: Simply means "the Name." Because of Jewish sensitivity to the use of God's name, many Jewish people will avoid using the name of *Yahweh*, and insert *ha Shem* in its place.

Zechariah 13:7

> *Awake, O sword, against My shepherd, and against the man that is My Fellow [Associate], says the LORD of hosts: smite the Shepherd, and the sheep shall be scattered: and I will turn My hand upon [against] the little ones.*

Finally, Zechariah 13:7 is a very potent reference in connection to God the Father and God the Son being equals. There are numerous words such as *sword*, *man*, *My Shepherd* and *My Associate* in this verse. Each one needs to be dealt with individually, and then within the context, to see that *Yahweh* takes complete responsibility for the *sword* to be used against His Shepherd and His Associate, the Messiah.

First, the speaker is clearly *the LORD of hosts*, *Yahweh*. However, in this verse, the speaker is not the Messiah as in Zechariah 12:10 and 11:4-14. The *sword*, is told to awaken against *My Shepherd*. *Yahweh* is telling the sword to awaken against His Shepherd, the good Shepherd of chapter 11. The *sword* is a valid personification of the instrument of death and is instructed to move against the Shepherd, who is addressed as being *My Shepherd*.[894] The second term *My Shepherd* is the same shepherd of Zechariah 11:4-14, who is the personal Shepherd of *Yahweh*, *My Shepherd*. The term *Shepherd* also indicates that this is no ordinary shepherd but a particular Shepherd, *My Shepherd*.

The third and fourth words are *man*; that is, *My Associate* or My equal. The Hebrew word is עֲמִית or *amith*, which means "associate, fellow, relation,"[895] and is used in the *Tanakh* 11 times in Leviticus and this one time in Zechariah 13:7.[896] How does this word "*amith*" or "associate" relate to man and to *Yahweh* in this verse? First, the associate is a man, a human being that *Yahweh* designates as His associate. The word associate, as it is used in Leviticus, is a general term for "fellowman." Unger defines it as:

> The Hebrew word employed, *amith*, is used to denote persons associated together under common love for the enjoyment of common rights and privileges.[897]

---

[894] Kaiser, *The Communicator's Commentary: Micah – Malachi*, 413.
[895] Harris, Archer and Waltke, *Theological Wordbook of the Old Testament*, 2:675.
[896] Kohlenberger and Swanson, *Hebrew English Concordance to the Old Testament*, 1241-1242.
[897] Unger, *Zechariah: Prophet of Messiah's Glory*, 232.

CHAPTER 8: MESSIAH DIVINE

In Leviticus *amith* or *associate* is used as a neighbor who is one's equal. Here in Zechariah, God is calling His shepherd "His associate" or "His equal." Kaiser expresses that concept in this statement:

> This Shepherd is One who is side by side with, or the equal of, the Lord! The term "associate" (or companion) is used to refer to those who are close neighbors or close companions (Leviticus 6:2; 18:20; 19:15). The equality that such a relationship brings to mind is the equality with God claimed by Jesus in John 10:30 and 14:9. The Shepherd's close association with the Lord strengthens the case for identifying him as the Shepherd of 11:4-14 and the One who was pierced in 12:10.[898]

What has been established is that *Yahweh* has a man who is His Associate or equal. He then instructs a weapon of death (sword) to be against His Shepherd or Associate. It is no coincidence that chapter 11 speaks of a good Shepherd who is paid 30 pieces of silver for his leadership among His people, as an insult. This Shepherd is the one who was pierced in Zechariah 12:10, and the one upon whom the nation of Israel will look in the future. This Shepherd is a man, just as other messianic prophecies predicted; yet this man is also God, again as messianic prophecies predicted. Now this Shepherd, the man who is *Yahweh*'s equal, is having a sword instructed to be against Him.

The last phrase in Zechariah 13:7 states *smite the shepherd* or "kill the shepherd." Here *Yahweh* is instructing the sword to kill the Shepherd. It is not without significance that a sword is used, just as it was no coincidence that *Yeshua* was given 30 pieces of silver (an insult) as wages for His ministry as the good Shepherd in Zechariah 11:12-13. It is also significant that His death would come by being pierced and that a future generation will mourn for Him as Zechariah 12:10 clearly states. The word for *pierced* in Zechariah 12:10 is the same word used in Zechariah 13:3, where parents of a false prophet are to pierce their son or *thrust him through*. This verse shows how all of these passages are connected together in Zechariah chapters 11 and 12 with the same person in chapter 13. Also, it is important not to miss Zechariah 9:9, which *Yeshua* fulfilled on His entrance into Jerusalem a week before Passover. Taken together, these verses contain a wealth of information concerning God's working with Israel and the Messiah, His Shepherd.

The responsibility for killing Christ or the Messiah, needs to be examined. The Jewish people have taken the brunt of this for centuries by being called "Christ

---

[898] Kaiser, *The Communicator's Commentary: Micah – Malachi*, 413.

Killers." Let's set the record straight from a biblical perspective. The Jewish people were instruments in seeing Messiah killed, but so were the Romans! *Yeshua*, in Matthew 12, spells out very clearly that it was that generation, and not future generations, that was guilty of rejecting Him. All the hideous acts against the Jewish people have been inspired by Satan, who used ignorant "Christians" to keep the Jewish people from receiving the gospel. Barrett and Kaiser express the same idea in this quote:

> The sword is told, "Strike the Shepherd." This accords with what Isaiah taught: "Yet it pleased the LORD to bruise Him" (Isaiah 53:10). Thus Jesus was delivered up in accordance with the definite plan of God, although it is the men who did the deed who are culpable for what they did (Acts 2:23).[899]

> Although Zechariah 12:10 indicates that unbelievers were responsible for piercing the Messiah, 13:7 squelches any notion that Messiah's death was anything other than the eternal purposes of God. Zechariah advances Isaiah's announcement that it was God's pleasure or purpose to bruise the Servant (Isaiah 53:10) by revealing that Christ's execution was God's command.[900]

This subject of who was responsible for killing Messiah must be dealt with biblically. God the Father takes full responsibility for the death of Messiah; and, as Isaiah 53:10 clearly states, *if He was willing to be the guilt offering*. The sins of the world were placed on Jesus, on the cross, and the world stands guilty of His death, as being the free agent which committed the act. Jewish people have been persecuted by "Christians" for centuries for "killing Christ." Yet it is centrally significant that without His volunteer death, there could be no resurrection and no eternal life. The human race is completely helpless and lost in their sins, with absolutely no power to remedy the situation. Yes, the Jewish people and the Romans of the first century were the instruments that God used, yet God takes full responsibility. The Jewish people are no more "Christ's Killers" than any other person from among the nations, no better or worse than you or me since we have all sinned.

The impact of the tri-unity of God and the purpose of the Messiah's two comings are inseparable in understanding the redemptive purposes of God. First, the plurality of God is taught throughout the pages of the *Tanakh* and with passages showing that God would have to become man to redeem mankind from his sins. Second, the Scriptures show that the Messiah is God and will come twice, once to

---

[899] Kaiser, *The Communicator's Commentary: Micah – Malachi*, 413.
[900] Barrett, *Beginning at Moses*, 237.

CHAPTER 8: MESSIAH DIVINE

redeem the world from the curse of sin and again to redeem Israel and fulfill the promises made to Abraham in the future Millennial Kingdom. The Key factor is that God is a tri-unity who revealed Himself through the Messenger of *Yahweh*, and His Holy Spirit coming upon man is critical in comprehending the ministry of Messiah as given in the *Tanakh*. No one should even pretend to know or understand just how *Elohim* is plural and how He works within His Person. What is known is that the *Tanakh* as well as the New Covenant presents God operating in a triune form.

Finally, Josh McDowell estimated the chances of one "man" fulfilling all the major prophecies of the First Coming of Messiah was all but mathematically impossible. For Jesus Christ to fulfill eight of the major prophecies concerning His First Coming was 1 to the 17th power, or 1 to 100,000,000,000,000,000.[901] The eight prophecies are as follows:

(1) Born in Bethlehem – Micah 5:2;

(2) Preceded by a messenger – Isaiah 40:3;

(3) Entering Jerusalem on a donkey – Zechariah 9:9;

(4) Betrayed by a friend – Psalm 41:9 and hands and feet pierced – Psalm 22:16;

(5) Sold out for 30 pieces of silver – Zechariah 11:12;

(6) Money to be thrown into God's house – Zechariah 11:12 and price given for potter's field – Zechariah 11:13;

(7) Dumb before His accusers – Isaiah 53:7;

(8) Crucified with thieves.[902]

The probability that a single man could fulfill all 48 of the First Coming references is 10 to the 157th power.[903] That God used His Word to identify the man fulfilling these prophecies of Messiah's First Coming is beyond question an absolute miracle and gift from God.

This chapter has demonstrated that *Yeshua* is divine. He is the God/man that God promises, from the time of the Fall in Genesis 3:15 right up through the prophet Zechariah. The Scriptures are clear that *Yeshua* is both God and man, who will reign

---

[901] Josh McDowell, *Evidence That Demands a Verdict* (Nashville: Nelson, 1979), 1:167.
[902] McDowell, *Evidence That Demands a Verdict*, 1:141-166.
[903] McDowell, *Evidence That Demands a Verdict,* 1:167.

on the throne of David and fulfill the promises to Abraham, Isaac, and Jacob; to the Nation of Israel; and to David; all in the New Covenant of Jeremiah.[904]

---

[904] For more detail on the future fulfillment of the New Covenant given to Israel in Jeremiah 31:31-34, please refer to my book *Israel's Only Hope: The New Covenant*, (Keller, TX: Purple Raiment label of JHousePublishing, 2015).

CHAPTER 9:
SUMMARY

This author recognizes that above everything else: All Scripture is given by inspiration of God. The utmost point to be advanced is that the Scriptures, including the *Tanakh* and New Testament, are God's revelation of Himself. God had authors, such as Moses, use words to best describe His nature and character to human beings who could not have known Him at all unless He revealed Himself to them.

The purpose of this study is to analyze the prevalent Jewish teaching that the plurality of God is not inherent in the Hebrew Scriptures. Therefore, research was confined to the context of the *Tanakh*. As a Christian committed to the tri-unity of God, this writer's goal was to determine whether it is possible to substantiate a Trinitarian doctrine solely from the Hebrew Scriptures. After intense study and analysis, the conclusion is that the plurality (tri-unity) of God is unquestionably presented in the *Tanakh*. That conclusion is possible because, as Paul asserts, the *Tanakh* is the inspired Word of God (2 Timothy 3:16) used to reveal Himself to mankind through human authors.

In **chapter two**, we dealt with the image and likeness of God and understanding how God is a tri-unity by understanding that God also created us as a tri-unity.

As demonstrated in chapter three, God's names reflect His character and nature. Unlike human beings, who cannot look down through the life of their children when they are born, God's character is accurately reflected in His names. As parents, we choose names that sound good, or we name our child envisioning what we would like our child's character to be. Yet, whether the name and character of the child is compatible to his or her future life is totally unforeseen to earthly parents. However, God knows His nature, character, and who He is. Michael Barrett expresses the practice of naming children well and that God is capable of doing so with perfect knowledge of Himself:

> The point is that we use names without necessarily thinking about what the name means. That, however, was not the case for the writers of Scriptures. Names, particularly and especially the names of God, were never used haphazardly or casually in the Scripture.

Names conveyed something about the nature or character of the one so named. "Thou shalt call his name JESUS: for he shall save his people from their sins" (Matthew 1:21). That "Jesus" means "Jehovah saves" is certainly a significant statement given the purpose of the Savior's being born. What God called Himself was always an important means of His revealing Himself.[905]

When God used terms such as *Elohim, Eloah, Elah, El, Adonai,* and *Yahweh* to describe Himself, He did so with an intended meaning for the reader. God chose to violate Hebrew grammar by using the plural noun *Elohim* with a singular verb *create* in Genesis 1:1. This was so readers would recognize that God revealed Himself as one God (which the singular verb would affirm), but also that He showed Himself as a plurality (which the plural noun would affirm). God using *Elohim* 2,350 times to refer to Himself in the plural was not a mistake. God, who is one and a plurality, is not the author of confusion, so why are the very people He has revealed Himself to so unable to see the multitude of plural references to Himself He has made? This author believes that if God were one with no plurality at all, then He would have used *El, Elah,* or *Eloah* in the singular so that mankind would not be confused. However, if God is a tri-unity then the plural noun *Elohim* makes absolute logical sense.

The fact remains that God did use the plural noun *Elohim* with singular verbs. Coupled with that, God used on several occasions His personal name *YHVH* (*Yahweh* – LORD), which is a singular noun, not plural, in the *Tanakh* to refer to two *Yahwehs,* which again reveals plurality. God chose words to describe Himself in the plural, which is what confuses readers. As a human being and a singular being, readers are confused by God referring to Himself in both singular and plural ways and sometimes with the same combination of names as *Elohim* (plural) and *Yahweh* (singular). Added to that, God, Himself, and others refer to Him as Lord (*Adonai*), which again is a plural description of Him. Judaism has taken that plural form (*Adonai*) and they used it to replace the personal name for God, which is singular. God shows Himself to be a plural compound unity, while at the same time confirming the fact that He is *one*. All of these facts and references to *Elohim, Yahweh,* and *Adonai* show a significant number of times that God chose to represent Himself as a plural, while being *one* as discussed in this book. Here is a brief summary of the usages of God's names in the Hebrew Scriptures: (1) uses of *Elohim* as the true God – 2350 times; (2) two *Yahwehs* – 4 times; (3) uses of Lord when used with God – 449 times; (4) combination of *Elohim* and *Yahweh* – 930 times; (5) uses of two *Elohim*s – 1 time. Those usages of God, which He prompted the writers of Scripture to use of Himself, should not be overlooked or interpreted in ways that God

---

[905] Barrett, *Beginning At Moses*, 24.

SUMMARY

by inspiration did not intend. Those usages amount to a significant amount of plural references in the Hebrew Scriptures.

In **chapter four**, the theophanies of God – of the Messenger (Angel) of *Yahweh* and the *Shechinah* Glory of God – further build the case for the plurality of God. The Messenger (Angel) of *Yahweh* and the *Shechinah* of God are, without question, God yet are distinct from God. However, the fact and presence of these theophanies of God give great difficulty to Jewish scholars who attempt to explain away the significance of these passages throughout the *Tanakh*. These appearances of God before man are a precursor to the incarnation of God in the New Testament. These passages are generally held in common by Christians as the pre-incarnate Messiah, the Second Person of the Godhead. Barrett alone lists 25 references to the Messenger (Angel) of *Yahweh*.[906] This substantial number of references lays a strong foundation for the plurality (or tri-unity) of God.

In **chapter six**, the term *echad* in the *Shema* makes the point that God is *one* but also that oneness is made up as a compound or complex unity. The word *echad* is used 970 times throughout the *Tanakh*. Minimally, this word for *one* is in a plural context of others being involved. Some of these references relate specifically to a compound or complex unity. If Jewish scholars want to use *echad* to show oneness as to only *one*, their usage of *echad* does not accomplish that.

Chapter six deals with passages that have four types of plural descriptions of God and as a group are difficult to ignore. First, there are the plural personal pronouns in Genesis and Isaiah where God uses all His significant names of Himself, affirming plurality. Second, there are plural verbs with the plural noun *Elohim* that also point to the plurality of God. This is important because usually God uses the plural noun (*Elohim*) and a singular verb to show plurality and unity. However, in the four references cited; God has chosen to use the plural noun with plural verbs. While the plural noun with the singular verb departs from the pattern of Hebrew grammar, the plural noun and plural verb are in harmony with Hebrew grammar. Once again God affirms that He is one God with a plurality of Persons. Third, plural descriptions of Himself by the writers of Scripture affirm His plurality with the usage of plural modifiers of God. Fourth, there are three references in Isaiah that not only show plurality but also the tri-unity of God. Since God cannot make mistakes in the writing of His revelation of Himself to man, we can accept that these significant and numerous passages show not only His plurality but also the tri-unity of God in the *Tanakh*. One or two passages in the *Tanakh* would prove absolutely nothing; but when dealing with the number of references cited in this study, it becomes an overwhelming weight to affirm God's plurality.

---

[906] Barrett, *Beginning At Moses*, 160-162.

In **chapter seven**, the tri-unity of God becomes visible when the Person of the Holy Spirit is included in the plurality of God in the *Tanakh*. As was demonstrated, the Holy Spirit is not as visible in the *Tanakh* as in the New Testament. It is harder to see Him in the Hebrew Scriptures. It is harder because in the *Tanakh*, the Holy Spirit works as the active power of God. However, it was also seen from other passages that His personality is not removed from the pages of the *Tanakh*. He is never really given a name in either testaments, but his personality, character, and ministry are present in the *Tanakh*.

The Hebrew Scriptures do reveal His personality by being involved in Creation, being grieved, or being impatient, and that He can testify or give witness against rebellious Israel. All these aspects of His personality have been born out in chapter seven. Also His ministry has been seen to be different in the *Tanakh* than in the New Covenant. In the *Tanakh*, He came upon people to guide them, as with Saul and David, and to equip artisans to accomplish specific tasks in the making of the Tabernacle and High Priestly garments. He came upon others like the Judges to deliver the people. Isaiah alone is the prophet who couples together all three members of the tri-unity in the Godhead as three distinct persons (Isaiah 42:1, 48:16, 61:1, 63:7-14), all operating as God throughout the *Tanakh*.

So, once again the Hebrew Scriptures add more evidence to strengthen support for the triune nature of God. Even though it is the deeds of the Holy Spirit that are predominant, personality still comes through confirming Him as part of the unity of God, the triune God.

Chapter eight gives unquestioned evidence to the fact that Messiah is divine. This evidence substantiates that the Messiah is God and not just a man. The understanding of the English terms *forever, everlasting*, and *eternity* becomes helpful in understanding the usage of *olam* in connection with the Messiah. His divinity becomes so clear in passages such as 1 Chronicles 7; Isaiah 9; Micah 5:2; Jeremiah 23:5-6; Psalm 110:1; and Daniel 9:24-27. As these passages are added to the discussion, the evidence to the triune nature of God continues to build an insurmountable weight of evidence in substantiating the tri-unity of God in the *Tanakh*.

On the very first page of chapter one of this book, Rabbi Greenberg was quoted. In summary, he compared Judaism's and Christianity's belief in the oneness of God and that they are not compatible with each other. He spoke of the "overwhelming testimony" of the Bible that it speaks only of a monotheistic God. He insisted that whatever Christians call monotheism, it is not the monotheism of Judaism. However, after going through all the Hebrew Scriptures and analyzing a multitude of passages, I would challenge his point of view. It becomes clear to me that the *Tanakh* points without question to the plurality (tri-unity) of God. In summarizing his words from the context of the *Tanakh*, he believes the testimony of the Hebrew Bible flies in the face of Christianity's characterization of God as triune and supports Judaism's focus on God as an absolute *one*. Yet, as a result of my studies, I perceive that the whole tone of Scripture when read as God gave it clearly supports the plurality and tri-unity of God.

How can we explain the disconnects between Jewish and Christian doctrines on God's nature, and why do some Christian scholars overlook the plural references in the Hebrew Scripture? Does it make a difference if we pay attention or not?

Throughout this study, the question has been asked, have Christian scholars abandoned the Doctrine of the Triune God in the Hebrew Scriptures to rabbinic thought? It is only when man entangles himself with liberal humanistic thought that Christian scholars attempt to rewrite Scripture to suit their personal humanistic philosophy or pseudo-Christian bias. The reality is that Christian scholars have abandoned this doctrine not because of rabbinic teaching, but because of the secular humanism that has infiltrated the Church of the last 200 years or so. Wilson points out that the Church, up until modern times (the 1700s), saw the plurality and tri-unity of God in the Hebrew Scriptures.[907] Why did this viewpoint change? It is this author's opinion that secular humanistic thought could not accept the supernatural aspect of the Word of God. Modern humanistic thinkers had to find natural ways to get around the obvious intent of Scripture. Erickson speaks of this humanism as modernism:

> Basically, modernism retained the conception of the world but removed its supernatural or at least extra-natural basis. Thus, the vertical dualism was replaced by a horizontal dualism, in which the meaning or cause was found within or behind the natural world, rather than beyond or above it. The pattern of history is to be found within it rather than beyond it. Events are explained in terms of the social realities that cause them, rather than in terms of the purpose of a transcendent God.
>
> Modernism has been essentially humanistic. The human being is the center of reality, and in a sense everything exists for the sake of the human. In an earlier period, God had been thought of as the central and supreme object of value.[908]

---

[907] Marvin R. Wilson, *Our Father Abraham*, 54-55.
[908] Erickson, *Christian Theology* (2nd ed.), 161, 163.

A good example of humanism, or modern thinking, is expressed by Parkes. Even though he has some very valuable insights into the Jewish world of Paul's day, he does not see anything trinitarian in Paul or the *Tanakh:*

> His double experience of the atonement compelled him to think of Jesus Christ as more than human. But into what category was he then to place him? For as a Jew he recognized only one being to whom the category divine was fully applicable, and that was God himself. Paul was not a trinitarian; he had not the resources which were to be made available by several centuries of hammering on the anvil of both experience and philosophic thought. For him Jesus was never equal to God; whatever of divinity was to be ascribed to him was to be so ascribed because God had willed and planned it thus.[909]

> Undoubtedly the early Church was puzzled as to who Jesus was....The experience which they had undergone was an emotional and not an intellectual one....It is only as we understand this that we can appreciate the profound bewilderment which the Christian message caused in Jewish circles, and even among Jewish adherents of the new faith.[910]

As a scholar, Parkes has some very interesting information on the early first-century Jewish Church which was surrounded by Rabbinic Judaism's beliefs and concepts. It seems strange that anyone would say that Paul was not a trinitarian, but that is the context of Parkes' statement. He does not refer nor allude to Paul before his salvation but only after his conversion experience on the Damascus road.

This author's view is that Parkes' views are not consistent with the teachings of Scripture. This humanistic, modern thought sounds just like many rabbis who, not from a humanistic perspective but for religious reasons, reject the plurality of God. Modern humanistic thought has infected many Christian scholars in not accepting God's Word but instead finding humanistic reasons that leave out God and the supernatural. However, contrary to Parkes, the teaching of Paul and all the other New Testament writers clearly taught and understood the triune God from the *Tanakh* long before it was hammered out by experience and philosophic thought in the Nicean Council in 325 C.E. A careful observation of first-century Jewish believers in Messiah *Yeshua* clarifies one basic concept: these believers had no problem moving

---

[909] James Parkes, *The Foundations of Judaism and Christianity* (Chicago: Quadrangle Books, 1960), 219-220.
[910] Parkes, *The Foundations of Judaism and Christianity,* 215.

SUMMARY

from absolute monotheism to monotheism with three Persons making up that unity of God as a complex unity. Buswell expresses it clearly:

> In the section in which we called attention to the unity of God as taught in the New Testament, several passages were cited in which the divine unity is strongly affirmed, in direct conjunction with equally strong references to the deity of Jesus Christ. These passages are remarkable in that they contain no hint that the New Testament writers were at all conscious of any problem in the conjunction of these two ideas. That one God is complex in His being, and so subsists that there are personal distinctions within the Godhead, was no problem for the first-century Christians.[911]

It appears that many Christian scholars have abandoned the doctrine of the tri-unity of the Godhead in the Hebrew Scriptures not primarily by yielding to the unbelief of rabbinic scholars, but by yielding to the unbelief of humanistic "Christian" secularists who use the unbelief of "higher criticism" to reinterpret God.

This author sees three valuable benefits in having an understanding of the character and nature of God in the Hebrew Scriptures as shown in the plurality of the Godhead. With a clear, practical, and balanced understanding of the character and nature of God in the *Tanakh*, the Church today would be better equipped for living and witnessing for their Savior and Lord. First, having a practical understanding of the plurality of God in the *Tanakh* has been sadly neglected by the Church in America. The Church today primarily has a New Testament understanding of the character and nature of God. Second, this material on the plurality of God in the Hebrew Scriptures is not only valuable in witnessing to Jewish people, but also in witnessing to anyone who depreciates Christ, such as the cults. Third, tracing the triune nature of God through all of God's Word produces a better understanding of the Second Person of the Godhead as to His character of holiness, righteousness, and justice, demonstrated in the Hebrew Scriptures.

Understanding the plurality of God from the *Tanakh* is important because the Church teaches that God is immutable (Malachi 3:6); the consequence of ignoring the Hebrew roots of this has resulted in a lopsided view of Jesus when presenting relation to the true character and nature of God. The Church has depressed the holiness, righteousness, and justice of Jesus, who was very active in the Hebrew Scriptures as the Second Person of *Elohim*. At the same time, the Church has elevated the love of God totally out of proportion to the other characteristics of Jesus. *Yeshua* demonstrated His love by coming as the *Servant of the LORD* (Isaiah 42) and

---

[911] Buswell, *A Systematic Theology of the Christian Religion*, 120.

becoming the Lamb that God would provide (Genesis 22:8), the substitutionary sacrifice for the sins of the world. Thus, the Church today has an unbalanced view of the Person of Christ, which leads to a lack of fear, reverence, awe, and commitment to the Almighty God who is the active sustainer of the universe (Colossians 1:18).

When we lack understanding as to the plurality (and tri-unity) of God in the *Tanakh*, it negatively impacts evangelizing the Jewish people by discouraging them and keeping them from recognizing *Yeshua* as their Messiah (Hosea 5:15; Matthew 23:39). Ultimately they must believe the plurality (and tri-unity) of God and embrace that plural unity. Without believing in both the oneness and plurality of God, the reality that Jesus is God will continue to be a barrier. Despite the evidence in their own Scriptures, they will continue to reject Him as their Messiah and remain lost in their sins.

Zechariah 12:10 is one of the most gut-wrenching verses in Scriptures: *They shall mourn for Him, as one mourns for his only son.* When the Jewish nation as a whole realizes that *Yeshua* (Jesus) is the Messiah whom they rejected almost 2,000 years earlier and call for the One sitting on the Father's right hand (Psalm 80:17), then they will weep bitterly. Why? Because they and their fathers and their fathers' fathers will recognize they had been rejecting the very one in whom they said they trusted.

In closing, we see in Matthew 23:39 *Yeshua* making His last public statement to the Jewish nation, that they will not see Him again until they say the following words, *Blessed is He that cometh in the name of the Lord* (Psalm 118:22; Matthew 23:39). The rabbis say that when the Messiah comes they are to greet Him with these words. In fact only four days earlier in Matthew 21:9, they used these words as He entered Jerusalem riding on the donkey (Zechariah 9:9). But the statement was not accepted because the nation had already rejected Him by characterizing Him and all the works He had done by the power of the Holy Spirit as coming from the power of Beelzebub, the prince of the devils (Matthew 12:23-24). So the unpardonable sin, which was a national or corporate sin, had been committed and His Kingdom had been withdrawn for the time being, until He would be recognized for who He is, God incarnate, the Messiah of Israel, the Suffering Servant and the King of Kings. At that moment, His people will call for Him to come and He will respond; but until then, the Jewish nation will not see His face. The plurality of God is at the heart of Jewish evangelism, and being able to defend it from the Hebrew Scriptures is essential.

One final encouragement to Christians, God has given the responsibility to each believer to share the Gospel of Messiah to the world. The believing Church sends thousand of missionaries to every corner of the earth and to as many unreached people groups as possible. Many believers and more mission agencies have forgotten about God's chosen people, through whom every believer has received the legacy of Faith, and to whom we owe the careful preservation of God's Word.

The Church in past history has been the biggest obstacle for Jewish people to come to faith in Messiah Jesus, having been the largest anti-Semitic group in the world over the span of 1,800 years. Because of the Church's unbiblical treatment of Jewish people, they have become harder and more resistant to the Gospel of Messiah. Keep in mind, the Abrahamic Covenant: If we as Christians bless Israel, God will bless us. The reserve is also true: If we curse Israel, God will treat us in like manner.[912] It is the conviction of this author that worldwide missions would see more fruit for its labor if Missions agencies, and individual believers, would revisit the Jewish people and once again share the gospel with the Jew first.

Stan Telchin, a Jewish believer in Messiah, has said that the greatest act of anti-Semitism that the Church could commit is to withhold the Gospel of Messiah from the Jewish people.[913]

---

[912] For more insight on how God blessed and cursed individuals and nations following His covenant with Abraham and continues to do so today, see my book, *Poking God's Eye: A Theological and Historical View of Anti-Semitism Based on the Blessings and Cursings of Genesis 12:3*, (Keller, TX: Purple Raiment label of JHousePublishing, 2016).

[913] Stan Telchin, *Messianic Judaism IS NOT Christianity* (Grand Rapids: Chosen Books, 2004),

APPENDIX 1:
HOW TO BECOME ONE WITH G-D

To Be Reconciled To G-d

It is my prayer that upon reading this book your heart has been stirred as you recognized Jesus of Nazareth as the incarnation of G-d, He is *HaShem*. It has been demonstrated throughout this book that He is G-d Almighty, *Yahweh*, the Messenger (Angel) of *Yahweh*, the Son of David who sits at the right hand of G-d, the One for whom the Father will make His enemies His footstool (Psalm 110:1).

Below is a group of verses referred to as the Jerusalem Road to lead you into embracing the Messiah, the Son of David, *Yeshua*, as your Savior from sin. I know you do not consider yourself a great sinner. But consider in your *Tanakh* the G-d of your fathers Abraham, Isaac and Jacob, who is absolutely Holy, pure, and totally separated from sin. Open your Scripture and study His character and how He originally gave His covenant people, your fathers, sacrifices and priests to mediate between them and Himself. What was the need for the sacrifices and why did your fathers need a mediator to act on their behalf before G-d in His Temple? It is because they where sinners and needed a substitute to take *HaShem*'s wrath for their sins. That is what the sacrificial system was all about.

To sin against G-d is simply man's disobedience against His Law and against *HaShem* Himself. You may call it the "evil inclination," but whatever you call it, it is simply missing the mark of His holiness. In *HaShem*'s eyes little acts of sin are just as much sin as murder. Sinful things that you think or hide in your heart, even if you do not do them physically, are sins in *HaShem*'s eyes. If you in your mind, or your heart have lusted after a woman, you have committed adultery in your heart before *HaShem*. Ladies if you coveted something that is your neighbors, and want it to the point that you will obtain it at most any cost, G-d judges that as sin. Notice that in neither of these examples was the act literally committed, yet *HaShem* views your hearts from which wrong, evil, or sin comes from. Listen to the words of *Yeshua* from the New Testament:

> *But those things which proceed out of the mouth come forth from the heart; and they defile the man. For out of the heart proceed evil thoughts, murders, adulteries, fornication, thefts, false witness, blasphemies.* (Matthew 15:18-19)

Also the New Testament book that was written to Jewish believers in Messiah in the first century of the Common Era reflects the penetration of the Word of *HaShem*:

> *¹² For the word of God is quick, and powerful, and sharper than any two-edged sword, piercing even to the dividing asunder of the soul and spirit, and of the joints and marrow, and is a discerner of the thoughts and intents of the heart. ¹³ Neither is there any creature that is not manifest in His sight: but all things are naked and open unto the eyes of Him with whom we have to do.* (Hebrews 4:12-13)

That verse is simply stating that the Scriptures are like a double edged sword and can pierce into the spiritual part of man (soul and spirit), as well as the physical part of man (joints and marrow). It can even discern the very thoughts you think and the motivation behind them before you ever do them.

Nearly 2,000 years ago *HaShem* allowed Rome to destroy the Holy City and the Holy Temple, just as He allowed Babylon centuries before to destroy Jerusalem and Solomon's Temple. When G-d destroyed Jerusalem the first time, He gave Israel prophets, like Jeremiah, Ezekiel, and Daniel. He also gave them prophets after the return, like Haggai, Zechariah, and Malachi. G-d destroyed Jerusalem because of the sin of His covenant people, Israel. Notice that there has not been from Judaism's perspective a prophet to Israel since Malachi who lived 2,400 years ago. Now if the sacrificial system was *HaShem*'s picture of His Holy demands and man's complete inability to keep His laws, why did G-d remove the sacrificial system which was absolutely necessary, and why did He not replace it or even give a prophet with a word from *HaShem*? Or did He give a prophet (Deuteronomy 18:15-18), in the Person of His Son (Psalm 2:7-12; Proverbs 30:4), the Suffering Servant of Isaiah 53, the Servant of the LORD? In Rabbinic Judaism today, how do you get rid of your sins biblically? Rabbis have made substitutions, but not on *HaShem*'s authority, only on theirs. Since your eternal destiny is at stake, whose word is more important, the rabbis, or *HaShem* Himself through His Word? That is a question you must ask yourself. Who is my spiritual authority, rabbis or *HaShem*? *HaShem* loves you with an everlasting Love!

APPENDIX 1: HOW TO BECOME ONE WITH G-D

> *⁷ The LORD did not set his love upon you, nor choose you, because ye were more in number than any people; for ye were the fewest of all people: ⁸ But because the LORD loved you, and because he would keep the oath which he had sworn unto your fathers.* (Deuteronomy 7:7-8)

> *For thus says the LORD of hosts, "After glory He has sent me against the nations which plunder you, for he who touches YOU, touches the apple of His eye.* (Zechariah 2:8)

Search the Scriptures, ask the G-d of you fathers to show you what He has written in His Word that your prophets recorded for Him concerning His Son, your Messiah, the Son of David, the King of Israel, and your substitutionary sacrifice for your sin.

THE JERUSALEM ROAD

1. **"There is none without sin."**

   - **Psalm 14:3**
     They are all gone aside, they are all together become filthy: there is none that doeth good, not one.

   - **Psalm 51:5**
     Behold, I was shaped in iniquity; and in sin did my mother conceive me.

   - **Isaiah 53:6**
     All we like sheep have gone astray; we have turned every one to his own way; and the LORD hath laid on him the iniquity of us all.

   - **Jeremiah 17:9**
     The heart is deceitful above all things, and desperately wicked: who can know it?

   - **Isaiah 59:1-2**
     Behold, the LORD's hand is not shortened, that it cannot save; neither his ear heavy, that it cannot hear:

     But your iniquities have separated between you and your God, and your sins have hid his face from you, that he will not hear.

THE TRI-UNITY OF GOD IS JEWISH

- **Ecclesiastes 7:20**

   For there is not a just man upon earth, that does good, and sins not.

2. **Good deeds cannot purify.**

   - **Isaiah 64:6**

     But we are all as an unclean thing, and all our righteousness are as filthy rags; and we all do fade as a leaf; and our iniquities, like the wind, have taken us away.

   - **Habakkuk 2:4**

     Behold, his soul which is lifted up is not upright in him: but the just shall live by his faith.

   - **Jeremiah 18:20**

     Shall evil be recompensed for good? For they have digged [they dug] *a pit for my soul. Remember that I stood before thee to speak good for them, and to turn away they wrath from them.*

3. **God requires a blood sacrifice.**

   - **Leviticus 17:11**

     For the life of the flesh is in the blood: and I have given it to you upon the altar to make an atonement for your souls: for it is the blood that makes an atonement for the soul.

4. **Apply the blood of the Messiah.**

   - **Exodus 12:21-23**

     [21] *Then Moses called for all the elders of Israel, and said unto them, Draw out and take you a lamb according to your families and kill the Passover.* [22] *And ye shall take a bunch of hyssop, and dip it in the blood that is in the basin and strike the lintel and the two side posts with the blood that is in the basin; and none of you shall go out at the door of his house until morning.* [23] *For the LORD will pass through to smite the Egyptians; and when he sees the blood upon the lintel, and on the two side posts, the LORD will pass over the door, and will not suffer the destroyer to come in unto your houses to smite you.*

APPENDIX 1: HOW TO BECOME ONE WITH G-D

- **Leviticus 16:15-19**
  ^{15} *Then shall he kill the goat of the sin-offering, that is for the people, and bring his blood within the veil, and do with that blood as he did with the blood of the bullock, and sprinkle it upon the mercy seat, and before the mercy seat:* ^{16} *And he shall make an atonement for the holy place, because of the uncleanness of the children of Israel, and because of their transgressions in all their sins: and so shall he do for the tabernacle of the congregation, that remains among them in the midst of their uncleanness.* ^{17} *And there shall be no man in the tabernacle of the congregation when he goes in to make an atonement in the holy place, until he come out, and have make an atonement for himself, and for his household, and for all the congregation of Israel.* ^{18} *And he shall go out unto the altar that is before the LORD, and make an atonement for it; and shall take of the blood of the bullock, and of the blood of the goat, and put it upon the horns of the altar round about.* ^{19} *And he shall sprinkle of the blood upon it with his finger seven times, and cleanse it, and hallow it from the uncleanness of the children of Israel.*

- **Daniel 9:26**
  And after threescore and two weeks shall Messiah be cut off, but not for himself: and the people of the prince that shall come shall destroy the city and the sanctuary; and the end thereof shall be with a flood, and unto the end of the war desolations are determined.

- **Hebrews 9:12**
  Neither by the blood of goats and calves, but by his own blood he entered in once into the holy place, having obtained eternal redemption for us.

5. **Safety and refuge in God's Messiah**

- **Psalm 2:12**
  Kiss the Son, lest he be angry, and ye perish from the way, when his wrath is kindled but a little. Blessed are all they that put their trust in him.

- **Psalm 51:13**
  Then will I teach transgressors thy ways; and sinner shall be converted unto thee.

"WHO IS THIS MESSIAH?"

- **He was born of a virgin – Isaiah 7:14**

Therefore the Lord himself shall give you a sign; Behold, a virgin shall conceive, and bear a son, and shall call his name Immanuel.

- **Born in Bethlehem – Micah 5:2**

But thou, Bethlehem Ephratah, though thou be little among the thousands of Judah, yet out of thee shall he come forth unto me that is to be ruler in Israel; whose goings forth have been from of old, from everlasting.

- **Slain for our sins – Isaiah 53:5-6**

[5] But he was wounded for our transgressions, he was bruised for our iniquities: the chastisement of our peace was upon him; and with his stripes we are healed. [6] All we like sheep have gone astray; we have turned every one to his own way; and the LORD hath laid on him the iniquity of us all.

- **Resurrected – Psalm 16:10, Daniel 12:2**

For thou will not leave my soul in hell; neither wilt thou suffer thine Holy One to see corruption.

And many of them that sleep in the dust of the earth shall awake, some to everlasting life, and some to shame and everlasting contempt.

APPENDIX 1: HOW TO BECOME ONE WITH G-D

ISAIAH AVENUE

1. Sinners Before God – Isaiah 64:5-6

2. Separation From God – Isaiah 59:1-2

3. Salvation in God – Isaiah 53:6

4. Savior is God – Isaiah 9:5-6

5. Stayed Upon God – Isaiah 26:3

You will l keep him in perfect peace, whose mind is stayed on You: because he trusts in You.

ALL MEN ARE SINNERS

1 Kings 8:46

If they sin against You, (for there is no man that sins not), and You be angry with them, and deliver them to the enemy, so that they carry them away captives unto the land of the enemy, for or near;

Ecclesiastes 7:20

For there is not a just man upon earth, that does good, and sins not.

Psalm 14:1-3

[1] The fool hath said in his heart, there is no God. They are corrupt, they have done abominable works, there is none that does good. [2] The LORD looked down from heaven upon the children of men, to see if there were any that did understand, and seek God. [3] They are all gone aside, they are all together become filthy: there is none that does Good, no, not one.

Psalm 53:2-3

[2] God looked down from heaven upon the children of men, to see if there were any that did understand, that did seek God. [3] Every one of them is gone back: they are altogether become filthy; there is none that does good, no, not one.

THE TRI-UNITY OF GOD IS JEWISH

Psalm 130:3

If You, LORD, should mark iniquities, O Lord, who shall stand?

Isaiah 64:6

But we are all as an unclean thing, and all our righteousnesses are as filthy rags and we all do fade as a leaf; and our iniquities, like the wind, have taken us away.

Jeremiah 17:9

The heart is deceitful above all things, and desperately wicked: who can know it?

SIN SEPARATES US FROM G-D

Job 15:14-16

[1] What is man, that he should be clean? And he which is born of a woman, that he should be righteous? [2] Behold, he puts no trust in his saints; yes, the heavens are not clean in his sight. [3] How much more abominable and fifthy is man, [who] drinks iniquity like water?

Isaiah 59:2

But your iniquities have separated between you and your God, and your sins have hid his face from you, that he will not hear.

THE PENALTY OF SIN IS DEATH

Jeremiah 31:30

But every one shall die for his own iniquity.

Ezekiel 18:4, 20

[4] Behold, all souls are mine; as the soul of the father, so also the soul of the son is mine: the soul that sins, it shall die.

[20] The soul that sins, it shall die. The son shall not bear the iniquity of the father, neither shall the father bear the iniquity of the son: the

APPENDIX 1: HOW TO BECOME ONE WITH G-D

righteousness of the righteous shall be upon him, and the wickedness of the wicked shall be upon him.

Daniel 12:2

And many of them that sleep in the dust of the earth shall awake, some to everlasting life, and some to shame and everlasting contempt.

GOD PUNISHES FOR DISOBEDIENCE

Jeremiah 6:19-20

[19] "Hear, O earth: behold, I will bring evil upon this people, even the fruit of their thoughts, because they have not hearkened unto My words, nor to My law, but rejected it. [20] For what purpose does frankincense come to Me from Sheba, and the sweet cane from a distant land? Your burnt offerings are not acceptable, and your sacrifices are not pleasing to Me."

RESULTS OF DISOBEDIENCE

Jeremiah 5 (Please turn to and read this lengthy section)

Joshua 23:14-16

[14] And, behold, this day I am going the way of all the earth: and you know in all your hearts and in all your souls, that not one thing has failed of all the good things which the LORD your God spoke concerning you; all are come to pass unto you, and not one thing has failed thereof. [15] Therefore it shall come to pass, that as all good thing are come upon you, which the LORD your God promised you; so shall the LORD bring upon you all evil things, until he [will] have destroyed you from off this good land which the LORD your God has given you. [16] When you have transgressed the covenant of the LORD your God, which He commanded you, and have gone and served other gods, and bowed yourselves to them; then shall the anger of the LORD be kindled against you, and you shall perish quickly from off the good land which He has given unto you.

Deuteronomy 4:23-40

(Please turn to and read this lengthy section)

Deuteronomy 28

(Please turn to and read this lengthy section)

MEN MUST TURN FROM SIN

Ezekiel 33:10-11

[10] Therefore, O you son of man, speak unto the house of Israel; Thus you speak, saying, If our transgressions and our sins be upon us, and we pine [rotting] *away in them, how should we then live* [survive]? *[11] Say unto them, As I live, says the Lord God, I have no pleasure in the death of the wicked; but that the wicked turn from his way and live: turn ye, turn ye from your evil ways; for why will you* [do you want to] *die, O house of Israel?*

Hosea 14:1

Return, O Israel, unto the Lord your God; for you have stumbled in your iniquity.

INABILITY TO REDEEM OR CLEANSE OUR HEARTS

Psalm 49:7

None of them can by any means redeem his brother, nor give to God a ransom for him.

Proverbs 20:9

Who can say, I have made my heart clean, I am pure from my sin?

Jeremiah 2:22

For though you wash yourself with nitre [lye], *and take* [to wash yourself with] *much soap, yet your iniquity is marked before Me, says the Lord God.*

APPENDIX 1: HOW TO BECOME ONE WITH G-D

WE NEED A MEDIATOR and REDEEMER

Isaiah 59:16, 20

[16] And he saw that there was no man, and wondered that there was no intercessor: therefore his arm brought salvation unto them; and his righteousness, it sustained him.

[20] And the Redeemer shall come to Zion, and unto them that turn from transgression in Jacob, says the LORD.

BLOOD NEEDED FOR REMISSION OF SIN

Exodus 12:13

And the blood shall be to you for a token upon the houses where you are; and when I see the blood, I will pass over you, and the plague shall not be upon you to make an atonement for your souls; for it is the blood that makes an atonement for the soul.

Leviticus 17:11

For the life of the flesh is in the blood; and I have given it to you upon the altar to make an atonement for your souls; for it is the blood that makes an atonement for the soul.

A CIRCUMCISED HEART IS NEEDED

Deuteronomy 10:12-17

[12] And now, Israel, what does the LORD your God require of you, but to fear the LORD your God, to walk in all His ways, and to love Him, and to serve the LORD your God with all your heart and with all your soul, [13] To keep the commandments of the LORD, and His statutes, which I command you this day for your good? [14] Behold, the heaven and the heaven of heavens is the LORD's your God, the earth also, with all that therein is.

[15] Only the LORD had a delight in your fathers to love them, and He chose their seed after them, even you above all people, as it is this day.

¹⁶ Circumcise therefore the foreskin of your heart, and be no more stiffnecked. ¹⁷ For the LORD your God is God of gods, and Lord of lords, a great God, [the] *mighty, and a terrible* [awesome God], *who regards not persons, nor takes reward.*

Deuteronomy 30:6

And the Lord your God will circumcise your heart, and the heart of your seed, to love the Lord your God with all your heart, and with all your soul, that you may live.

Leviticus 26:40-42

⁴⁰ If they shall confess their iniquity and the iniquity of their fathers, with their trespass which they trespassed against me, and that also they have walked contrary unto me; ⁴¹ and that I also have walked contrary unto them and have brought them into the land of their enemies; if then their uncircumcised hearts be humbled, and they then accept of the punishment of their iniquity: ⁴² Then will I remember My covenant with Jacob, and also My covenant with Isaac, and also My covenant with Abraham will I remember; And I will remember the land.

Jeremiah 4:4

Circumcise yourselves to the Lord, and take away the foreskins of your heart, you men of Judah and inhabitants of Jerusalem: lest My fury come forth like fire, and burn that none can quench it, because of the evil of your doings.

Jeremiah 6:9, 10

⁹ Thus says the Lord of hosts, they shall thoroughly glean the remnant of Israel as a vine: turn back your hand as a grape gathered in the baskets. ¹⁰ To whom shall I speak, and give warning, that they may hear? Behold their ear is uncircumcised, and they cannot hearken: behold, the word of the Lord is unto them a reproach; they have no delight in it.

Jeremiah 9:25

Egypt, and Judah, and Edom, and the children of Ammon, and Moab, and all that are in the utmost corners, that dwell in the wilderness: for

APPENDIX 1: HOW TO BECOME ONE WITH G-D

all these nations are uncircumcised, and all the house of Israel are uncircumcised in the heart.

YOU MUST BE CONVERTED

Psalm 51:15

Then will I teach transgressors Your ways; and sinners shall be converted unto You.

Isaiah 6:10

Make the heart of this people fat, and make their ears heavy, and shut their eyes; lest they see with their eyes, and hear with their ears, and understand with their hearts, and convert, and be healed.

THERE WILL BE A RESURRECTION

Daniel 12:2

And many of them that sleep in the dust of the earth shall awaken some to everlasting life and some to shame and everlasting contempt.

Job 19:25-26

[25] *For I know that my Redeemer lives, and that He shall stand at the latter day upon the earth,* [26] *and after they have thus destroyed my skin yet from my flesh shall I see God.*

Psalm 49:16

But God will redeem my soul from the power of the grave: for He shall revive me.

Isaiah 25:8

He [Messiah] *will destroy death forever and the Lord God will wipe* [tears] *away from off all faces; and the rebuke of His people shall He take away from off all the earth, for the Lord has spoken it.*

THE TRI-UNITY OF GOD IS JEWISH

Isaiah 26:19

Thy dead men shall live, together with my dead body shall they rise.

Hosea 13:14

I will ransom them from the power of the grave; I will redeem them from death: O death, where are your plagues? O grave, where is your destruction?

PERSONAL INVITATION

Both the Hebrew Scripture and the New Testament present Jesus (*Yeshua*) as being equal with the Father (John 10:30). He became flesh and dwelt among us (John 1:14) and according to the Fathers plan, His Son, the Messiah, the Son of David was the final sacrifice for our sins which took place on the Feast of Passover. He was the perfect Unleavened Bread that came down from heaven (John 6:28-51). He then arose from the dead on the Feast of First Fruits (John 20:1), on the first day of the week becoming the first fruits of the resurrection (1 Corinthians 15:20-26). He ascending and was seated on the Father's right hand to make intercession for us and will return in the future to restore Israel and fulfill the promises to Abraham, Isaac and Jacob. Go to the Father and confess that you're a sinner, separated from Him, and acknowledging that Jesus is your savior from sin, your redeemer. Asking Him to come into your heart and life as your Messiah and Lord.

John 1:12

But as many as received Him (Yeshua), to them He gave the power to become the sons of God, even to them that believe on His name.

John 3:16-17, 36

[16] For God so loved the world, that He gave His only begotten Son, that whosoever believeth in Him should not perish, but have everlasting life. [17] For God sent not His Son into the world to condemn the world; but that the world through Him might be saved.

[36] He that believeth on the Son has everlasting life: and he that believeth not the Son shall not see life; but the wrath of God abides on him.

APPENDIX 1: HOW TO BECOME ONE WITH G-D

Acts 4:12

Neither is there salvation in any other: for there is none other name under heaven given among men, whereby we must be saved.

Romans 3:23

For all have sinned, and come short of the glory of God.

Romans 5:8

But God commends His love toward us, in that while we were yet sinners, Messiah died for us.

Romans 6:23

For the wages of sin is death; but the gift of God is eternal life through Yeshua Messiah our Lord.

Philippians 2:5-11

[5] Let this mind be in you, which was also in Messiah Yeshua: [6] Who, being in the form of God, thought it not robbery to be equal with God [because He is equal]: [7] But made Himself of no reputation, and took upon Him the form of a servant, and was made in the likeness of men: [8] And being found in fashion as a man, He humbled Himself, and became obedient unto death, even the death of the cross. [9] Wherefore God also has highly exalted Him, and given Him a name which is above every name: [10] That at the name of Yeshua every knee should bow, of things in heaven, and things in the earth, and things under the earth; [11] And that every tongue should confess that Yeshua Messiah is Lord, to the glory of God the Father.

Colossians 2:9-11

[9] For in Him dwells all the fullness of the Godhead bodily. [10] And you are complete in Him, who is the head of all principality and power: [11] In whom also you are circumcised with the circumcision made without hands, in putting off the body of sins of the flesh by the circumcision of Messiah:

THE TRI-UNITY OF GOD IS JEWISH

Hebrews 1:1-3

¹ *God, who at sundry times and in different Manners spoke in time past unto the fathers by the prophets,* ² *Has in these last days spoken unto us by His Son, whom He has appointed heir of all things, by whom also He made the worlds;* ³ *Who being the brightness of His glory, and the express image of His person, and upholding all things by the word of His power, when He had by Himself purged our sins, sat down on the right hand of the Majesty on high.*

Hebrews 10:10-18

¹⁰ *By the which will we are sanctified through the offering of the body of Yeshua Messiah once for all.* ¹¹ *And every priest stands daily ministering and offering oftentimes the same sacrifices, which can never take away sins:* ¹² *But this man, after He had offered one sacrifice for sin forever, sat down on the right hand of God;* ¹³ *From hence forth expecting till His enemies be made His footstool.* ¹⁴ *For by one offering He has perfected forever them that are sanctified.* ¹⁵ *Whereof the Holy Spirit also is a witness to us: for after that He had said before,* ¹⁶ *This is the covenant that I will make with them after those days, says the Lord, I will put My laws into their hearts, and in their minds will I write them;* ¹⁷ *And their sins and iniquities will I remember no more.* ¹⁸ *Now where remission of these is, there is no more* [any more need for an] *offering for sin.*

APPENDIX 2:
MOSES' USE OF ECHAD IN THE TORAH

This section will demonstrate the plurality of *echad* as Moses used it in the Torah. There are 382 references scattered throughout his writings. The Hebrew word *echad* is translated as *one*. There are three ways that scholars say *echad* is used: (1) *Echad* used as a unity, more than two things coming together in a unity of one, (2) *Echad* used in relationship to other things or persons but not as a compound unity, (3) *Echad* used to indicate the separateness or individuality of a person or thing. The third grouping is then divided into three parts: (a) first part denotes one standing by itself, (b) second part, called a "cardinal one" as Joshua enumerates the kings that he defeated in conquering the Land, (c) and an ordinal number expressed by the first of the week or month as in Exodus 40:17.

Jewish rabbis believe that the *echad*, in the *Shema* of Deuteronomy 6:4 (see chapter five), is an absolute one with absolutely no suggestion or hint of a plurality. In order to demonstrate the usage of *echad*, all the references of *echad* listed below show how this word is used and understood by Moses. It is my desire that Jewish people understand that the *echad* within the *Shema*, which is the cornerstone of their faith, that they see and understand that *echad* is consistently used in a plural context in all three divisions listed above.

As a Christian, this author was surprised to discover that the word for "one" in the *Shema* was not always a "one of unity." Forced by the evidence that has been observed, this author has revised his understanding of *echad*. The first division above, the unity of more than one thing, is less frequently used (34 times) of any of the other usages of the word *echad*. The second usage appears quite frequently (172 times). That usage is a context of plurality, not necessarily unity. It was also observed in the third section that even though a particular "one" is being referenced (176 times), it is also very often used in the context of plurality. It is never used as an absolute one like *yachid*, which is only *one* with absolutely no reference to plurality. Moses in his usage of *echad* used this word almost exclusively within a plural context. God is viewed in Judaism as "one" alone, and they would have people believe that *echad* is only "one," but that just does not fit the context of *echad* and how Moses used it.

Notice on the extended chart, in the first column are the scriptural references, in the second column are the quotations in which *echad* is found, and the third, fourth and fifth columns show the three areas of the third section mentioned above: (a) First *echad* denotes unity of one, (b) second denotes one is the context of plurality and (c) third, one as an individual one. In these quotations *echad* is italicized, and if the *echad* is translated with another word besides one, that is italicized as well.

After going through all 382 references, there is only one conclusion that a student of the Scriptures can come to: *echad* is not generally used as a unity of one, but in most instances it is used in the context of plurality. Clearly, Deuteronomy 6:4 evidences a plural context: *Hear, O Israel, the LORD our God, LORD is one*. The plural context is *elohenu* which is translated "our God(s)." *Elohim* is the plural form for God as was discussed in chapter two, and *elohenu* is translated "our God(s)." Moses was stating that *Yahweh* was their God(s), emphasizing God as a one of unity and as one within a plurality. Moses knew that at his disposal were the singular forms for God, like *El* or *Eloah* (*Elah* was not used until the time of the exile and post-exilic period), and yet he chose to use the plural form. According to rabbis, if *Yahweh* is "one," then Moses surely confused the issue when he used *echad* in Deuteronomy 6:4 to describe God. But if God chose to represent Himself as a plurality – as He did so frequently throughout the *Tanakh* – then the plural word *elohim* is correct, and the plural usage of *echad* is also correct.

In using the Hebrew Scripture published by assorted Jewish publishers, it should be noted that most often they treat *echad* the same way as translated in the King James Version or the New American Standard Version. Even passages that view *echad* within a plural context are also viewed in a plural context in their translations. So Judaism does understand that in Deuteronomy 6:4 *echad* is not an absolute one because Jewish scholars also translate *echad* as one in a plural context.

In investigating the usage of *echad* in different Jewish translations to see how they viewed *echad* in the Torah, the observation can clearly be seen that *echad* is used the same way as in the Christian bibles. **The chart that follows this section there are asterisks (*) preceding some of the verses that this author has checked in the following copies of the Hebrew Scriptures; *The Jewish Study Bible*,[914] *The Soncino Chumash*,[915] *The Harkavy Version*,[916] *The Pentateuch and Haftorahs*,[917] *Friedman's Commentary on the Torah*,[918] *The Holy Scriptures according to the***

---

[914] Berlin and Brettler, *The Jewish Study Bible*.
[915] Cohen, *The Soncino Chumash: The Five Books of Moses with Haphtaroth*.
[916] Harkavy, *The Twenty-Four Books of the Old Testament*.
[917] Hertz, *The Pentateuch and Haftorahs*.
[918] Richard Elliott Friedman, *Commentary on the Torah* (San Francisco: Harper Collins Publishers, 2001).

APPENDIX 2: MOSES' USE OF ECHAD IN THE TORAH

Masoretic Text,[919] **and the** *Isaac Leeser Version.*[920] **In going through the references of** *echad* **in all the Hebrew/English editions listed above,** *echad* **was used consistently the same way as in the KJV and the ASV.**

It is quite apparent that *echad* is primarily used in a plural context throughout the writings of Moses. That plural usage implies that *echad* is a unity of one, but even more so a plurality and is not used as an absolute one.

---

[919] The Jewish Publication Society, *The Holy Scriptures: According to the Masoretic Text* (Philadelphia: Jewish Publication Society, 1917).
[920] Isaac Leeser, *The Twenty-Four Books of the Holy Bible* (New York: Hebrew Publishing Co., 1913).

THE TRI-UNITY OF GOD IS JEWISH

Table: References of *Echad* in the Torah

1 = compound unity 2 = one as plural 3 = one among others	1	2	3
GENESIS			
Gen 1:5 — And the evening and the morning were the *echad-first* day.	■		
*Gen 1:9 — God said, Let the waters under the heaven to be gathered unto *echad* place,			■
*Gen 2:11 — The name of the *echad-first* is the Pishon;		■	
*Gen 2:21 — and he slept: and he took *echad* of his ribs, and closed up the		■	
*Gen 2:24 — and shall cleave unto his wife: and they shall be *echad* flesh.	■		
*Gen 3:22 — Behold, the man is become as *echad* of us, to know good and evil:	■		
*Gen 4:19 — the name of the *echad* (was) Adah, and the name of the other Zillah		■	
Gen 8:5 — on the *echad-first* (day) of the month,			■
Gen 8:13 — And it came to pass in the six hundredth and *echad-first* year,			■
Gen 8:13 — in the *echad-first* month,			■
*Gen 10:25 — And unto Eber were born two sons: the name of *echad* (was) Peleg		■	
*Gen 11:1 — And the whole earth was of *echad* language,	■		
*Gen 11:1 — and of *echad* speech.	■		
*Gen 11:6 — Behold, the people (is) *echad*,	■		
*Gen 11:6 — and they have all *echad* language;	■		

APPENDIX 2: MOSES' USE OF ECHAD IN THE TORAH

1 = compound unity 2 = one as plural 3 = one among others		1	2	3
*Gen 19:9	This *echad* came in to sojourn, and he will needs be a judge:			■
*Gen 21:15	and she cast the child under *echad* of the shrubs.			■
*Gen 22:2	a burnt-offering upon *echad* of the mountains which I will tell thee of.			■
Gen 26:10	*echad* of the people might lightly have lien with thy wife,			■
Gen 27:38	Hast thou but *echad* blessing, my father?			■
Gen 27:45	why should I be deprived also of you both in *echad* day?		■	
Gen 32:8	If Esau come to the *echad* company, and smite it,			■
Gen 33:13	and if men should overdrive them *echad* day, all the flock will die.		■	
Gen 34:16	and we will dwell with you, and we will become *echad* people.	■		
Gen 34:22	to be *echad* people, if every male among us be circumcised,	■		
Gen 37:20	and let us slay him, and cast him into *echad-some* pit,		■	
Gen 40:5	each man his dream in *echad* night,		■	
Gen 41:5	and behold, seven ears of corn came up upon *echad* stalk,	■		
Gen 41:11	And we dreamed a dream in *echad* night, I and he;		■	
Gen 41:22	and behold, seven ears came up in *echad* stalk, full and good:	■		
Gen 41:25	The dream of Pharaoh (is) *echad*: God hath shown Pharaoh	■		
Gen 41:26	and the seven good ears (are) seven years: the dream (is) *echad*.	■		

THE TRI-UNITY OF GOD IS JEWISH

1 = compound unity 2 = one as plural 3 = one among others		1	2	3
Gen 42:11	We (are) all *echad* man's sons: we (are) true (men),			✓
Gen 42:13	twelve brethren, the sons of *echad* man in the land of Canaan;			✓
Gen 42:13	the youngest is this day with our father, and *echad* is not.			✓
Gen 42:16	Send *echad* of you, and let him fetch your brother			✓
Gen 42:19	If ye (be) true (men), let *echad* of your brethren be bound in the house			✓
Gen 42:27	And as *echad* of them opened his sack to give his ass			✓
Gen 42:32	We (be) twelve brethren, sons of our father; *echad* (is) not,			✓
Gen 42:33	leave *echad* of your brethren (here) with me			✓
Gen 44:28	And the *echad* went out from me, and I said,			✓
Gen 48:22	Moreover I have given to you *echad* portion above your brethren,			✓
Gen 49:16	Dan shall judge his people, as *echad* of the tribes of Israel.			✓
EXODUS				
*Ex 1:15	Hebrew midwives, of which the name of the *echad* (was) Shiphrah			✓
*Ex 8:31	removed the swarms of (flies) from Pharaoh, . …Remained not *echad*			✓
Ex 9:6	but of the cattle of the children of Israel died not *echad*.			✓
Ex 9:7	And Pharaoh sent, and, behold, there was not *echad* of the cattle			✓
Ex 10:19	there remained not *echad* locust in all the coasts of Egypt.			✓

APPENDIX 2: MOSES' USE OF ECHAD IN THE TORAH

1 = compound unity 2 = one as plural 3 = one among others		1	2	3
Ex 11:1	Yet will I bring *echad* plague more upon Pharaoh,		■	
Ex 12:18	until the *echad* and twentieth day of the month at even,			■
Ex 12:46	In *echad* house shall it be eaten; thou shalt not carry forth		■	
Ex 12:49	*Echad* law shall be to him that is hometown,	■		
Ex 14:28	there remained not so much as *echad* of them.	■		
Ex 16:22	they gathered twice as much bread, two omers for *echad* (man)		■	
Ex 16:33	Take *echad-a* pot, and put a omer full of manna therein,		■	
*Ex 17:12	and Aaron and Hur stayed up his hands, the *echad* on the echad side		■	
*Ex 17:12	the echad on the *echad* side, and the other on the other side;		■	
Ex 18:3	of which the name of the *echad* (was) Gershom;		■	
Ex 18:4	And the name of the *other-echad* (was) Eliezer;		■	
Ex 23:29	I will not drive them out from before thee in *echad* year;			■
*Ex 24:3	and all the people answered with *echad* voice,	■		
Ex 25:12	and two rings shall be in the *echad* side of it,		■	
*Ex 25:19	And make *echad* cherub on the *echad* end,		■	
*Ex 25:19	and the *echad-other* cherub on the other end:		■	
Ex 25:32	three branches of the candlestick out of the *echad* side,		■	
Ex 25:33	with a knop and a flower in *echad* branch;		■	

THE TRI-UNITY OF GOD IS JEWISH

1 = compound unity 2 = one as plural 3 = one among others		1	2	3
Ex 25:33	and three bowls made like almonds in the *echad-other* branch,		■	
Ex 25:36	all it (shall be) *echad* beaten work (of) pure gold.	■		
*Ex 26:2	The length of *echad* curtain shall be eight and twenty cubits,		■	
*Ex 26:2	and the breadth of *echad* curtain four cubits:		■	
*Ex 26:2	and every *echad* of the curtains shall have echad measure		■	
Ex 26:2	and every echad of the curtains shall have *echad* measure	■		
Ex 26:4	And thou shalt make loops of blue upon the edge of the *echad* curtain		■	
Ex 26:5	Fifty loops shalt thou make in the *echad* curtain,		■	
Ex 26:8	The length of *echad* curtain (shall be) thirty cubits,		■	
Ex 26:8	and the breadth of *echad* curtain four cubits:		■	
Ex 26:8	and the eleven curtains (shall be all) of *echad* measure.	■		
*Ex 26:10	And thou shalt make fifty loops on the edge of the *echad* curtain		■	
*Ex 26:11	and couple the tent together, that it may be *echad*.	■		
Ex 26:16	and a cubit and a half (shall be) the breadth of *echad* board.		■	
Ex 26:17	Two tenons (shall there be) in *echad* board,		■	
Ex 26:19	two sockets under *echad* board for his two tenons,		■	
Ex 26:21	And their forty sockets of silver; two sockets under *echad* board,		■	

APPENDIX 2: MOSES' USE OF ECHAD IN THE TORAH

1 = compound unity 2 = one as plural 3 = one among others		1	2	3
Ex 26:24	they shall be coupled together above the head of it unto *echad* ring	■		
Ex 26:25	sixteen sockets; two sockets under *echad* board,		■	
Ex 26:26	five for the boards of the *echad* side of the tabernacle,		■	
Ex 27:9	the court of (fine) twined linen of a hundred cubits long for *echad* side:		■	
Ex 28:10	Six of their names on *echad* stone		■	
Ex 28:17	(even) four rows of stones: the *echad-first* shall be a sardius,		■	
Ex 29:1	Take *echad* young bullock, and two rams without blemish,			■
Ex 29:3	and thou shalt put them into *echad* basket,	■		
Ex 29:15	Thou shalt also take *echad* ram;		■	
Ex 29:23	And *echad* loaf of bread		■	
Ex 29:23	and *echad* cake of oiled bread,		■	
Ex 29:23	and *echad* wafer out of the basket of the unleavened bread		■	
Ex 29:39	The *echad* lamb thou shalt offer in the morning		■	
Ex 29:40	And with the *echad* lamb a tenth deal of flour mingled with		■	
Ex 30:10	*echad-once* in a year with the blood of the sin-offering of atonements:			■
Ex 30:10	*echad-once* in the year shall he make atonement upon it			■
Ex 36:9	The length of *echad* curtain was twenty and eight cubits		■	
Ex 36:9	and the breadth of *echad* curtain four cubits:		■	

THE TRI-UNITY OF GOD IS JEWISH

1 = compound unity 2 = one as plural 3 = one among others		1	2	3
*Ex 36:10	And he coupled the five curtains *echad* unto another;		X	
Ex 36:11	And he made loops of blue on the edge of *echad* curtain		X	
*Ex 36:12	Fifty loops made he in *echad* curtain,		X	
*Ex 36:12	the loops held *echad* curtain to another.		X	
*Ex 36:13	fifty taches of gold, and coupled the curtains *echad* unto another		X	
*Ex 36:13	so it became *echad* tabernacle.	X		
Ex 36:15	The length of *echad* curtain was thirty cubits,		X	
Ex 36:15	and four cubits (was) the breadth of *echad* curtain:		X	
Ex 36:15	the eleven curtains (were) of *echad* size.	X		
*Ex 36:18	to couple the tent together, that it might be *echad*	X	X	
Ex 36:21	and the breadth of a board *echad* cubit and a half		X	
Ex 36:22	*Echad* board had two tenons,		X	
Ex 36:22	equally distant *echad* from another:		X	
Ex 36:24	two sockets under *echad* board for his two tenons,		X	
Ex 36:24	and two sockets under *echad-another* board for his two tenons.		X	
Ex 36:26	And their forty sockets of silver; two sockets under *echad* board,		X	
Ex 36:26	and two sockets under *echad-another* board.		X	
Ex 36:29	and coupled together at the head thereof, to *echad* ring:		X	

APPENDIX 2: MOSES' USE OF ECHAD IN THE TORAH

1 = compound unity 2 = one as plural 3 = one among others		1	2	3
Ex 36:30	their sockets (were) 16 sockets of silver, under *echad-every* board			
Ex 36:31	five for the boards of the *echad* side of the tabernacle,			
Ex 37:3	even two rings upon the *echad* side of it,			
*Ex 37:8	*Echad* cherub on the end on this side,			
*Ex 37:8	and *echad-another* cherub on the (other) end on that side:			
Ex 37:18	three branches of the candlestick out of the *echad* side thereof,			
Ex 37:19	Three bowls made after the fashion of almonds in *echad* branch,			
Ex 37:19	and three bowls made like almonds in *echad-another* branch,			
Ex 37:22	all of it (was) *echad* beaten work (of) pure gold.	■		
Ex 39:10	And they set in it four rows of stones: the *echad* (first) row		■	
Ex 40:2	On the *echad-first* day of the first month thou shalt set up			■
Ex 40:17	on the *echad-first* day of the month, the tabernacle was reared up			■
LEVITICUS				
Lev 4:2	Speak unto the children of Israel, saying, If *echad-a* soul shall sin			
Lev 4:2	If echad-a soul shall sin through ignorance against *echad-any* of the			
Lev 4:2	commandments…and shall do against *echad-any* of them.			
Lev 4:13	and they have done (somewhat against) *echad-any* of the commandments			

317

THE TRI-UNITY OF GOD IS JEWISH

1 = compound unity 2 = one as plural 3 = one among others		1	2	3
Lev 4:22	When a ruler hath sinned, and done through ignorance (against) *echad-any*		■	
Lev 4:27	And if *echad* of the common people sin through ignorance,		■	
Lev 4:27	while he doeth (somewhat against) *echad-any* of the commandments of the		■	
Lev 5:4	then he shall be guilty in *echad* of these		■	
Lev 5:5	And it shall be, when he shall be guilty in *echad* of these (things),		■	
Lev 5:7	unto the LORD, *echad* for a sin-offering		■	
Lev 5:7	and the *echad-other* for a burnt-offering.		■	
Lev 5:13	In this way the priest will make atonement for him for *echad-any* of these		■	
*Lev 7:7	As their sin-offering (is), so is the trespass-offering: there is *echad* law	■		
Lev 7:14	And of it he shall offer *echad* out of the whole oblation		■	
Lev 8:26	he took *echad* unleavened cake			■
Lev 8:26	and *echad-a* cake of oiled bread,			■
Lev 8:26	and *echad* wafer, and put (them) on the fat			■
Lev 12:8	the *echad* burnt-offering,		■	
Lev 12:8	and the *echad-other* for a sin-offering;		■	
*Lev 13:2	then he shall be brought unto Aaron the priest, or unto *echad* of his sons		■	
*Lev 14:5	And the priest shall command that *echad* of the birds be killed		■	
Lev 14:10	and *echad* ewe lamb of the year without blemish,			■

APPENDIX 2: MOSES' USE OF ECHAD IN THE TORAH

1 = compound unity 2 = one as plural 3 = one among others	1	2	3
Lev 14:10 — mingled with oil, and *echad* log of oil.			■
Lev 14:21 — then he shall take *echad* lamb (for) a trespass-offering to be waved,			■
Lev 14:21 — to make an atonement for him, and *echad* tenth deal of fine flour		■	
Lev 14:22 — and the *echad* shall be a sin-offering		■	
Lev 14:22 — and the *echad-other* a burnt-offering.		■	
*Lev 14:30 — And he shall offer the *echad* of the turtledoves,		■	
Lev 14:31 — the *echad* (for) a sin-offering,		■	
Lev 14:31 — and the *echad-other* (for) a brunt-offering		■	
Lev 14:50 — And he shall kill the *echad* of the birds in an earthen vessel		■	
Lev 15:15 — the *echad* (for) a sin-offering,		■	
Lev 15:15 — and the *echad-other* (for) a burnt-offering;		■	
Lev 15:30 — And the priest shall offer the *echad* (for) a sin-offering,		■	
Lev 15:30 — and the *echad-other* (for) a burnt-offering;		■	
Lev 16:5 — two kids of the goats for a sin-offering, and *echad* ram for a burnt-offering			■
Lev 16:8 — And Aaron shall cast lots upon the two goats: *echad* lot for the LORD,		■	
Lev 16:8 — and the *echad-other* lot for the scapegoat.		■	
Lev 16:34 — make an atonement for the children of Israel for all their sins *echad* a year,			■
Lev 22:28 — ye shall not kill it and her young both in *echad* day.			■

THE TRI-UNITY OF GOD IS JEWISH

1 = compound unity 2 = one as plural 3 = one among others		1	2	3
Lev 23:18	seven lambs without blemish of the first year, the *echad* young bullock,			■
Lev 23:19	Then ye shall sacrifice *echad* kid of the goats for a sin-offering,			■
Lev 23:24	In the seventh month, in the *echad* (day) of the month,			■
Lev 24:5	two tenth deals shall be in *echad* cake.			■
*Lev 24:22	Ye shall have *echad* manner of law, as well for the stranger,			■
Lev 25:48	After that he is sold he may be redeemed again, *echad* of his brethren			■
Lev 26:26	ten women shall bake your bread in *echad* oven,			■
NUMBERS				
Num 1:1	on the *echad* (day) of the second month, in the second year			■
Num 1:18	And they assembled all the congregation together on the *echad* (day) of the			■
Num 1:41	of the tribe of Asher, (were) forty and *echad* thousand and five hundred			
*Num 1:44	(being) twelve men: each *echad* was for the house of his fathers.		■	
Num 2:16	in the camp of Reuben (were) an 100,000 and 50 and *echad* thousand and			
Num 2:28	and those that were numbered of them, (were) 40 and *echad* thousand			
Num 6:11	And the priest shall offer the *echad* for a sin-offering,		■	
Num 6:11	and the *echad-other* for a burnt-offering,		■	
Num 6:14	he shall offer his offering unto the LORD, *echad* he lamb of the first year			■

APPENDIX 2: MOSES' USE OF ECHAD IN THE TORAH

1 = compound unity 2 = one as plural 3 = one among others		1	2	3
Num 6:14	without blemish for a burnt-offering, and *echad* ewe lamb of the first year			■
Num 6:14	without blemish for a sin-offering, and *echad* ram without blemish			■
Num 6:19	and *echad* unleavened cake out of the basket			■
Num 6:19	and *echad* unleavened wafer,			■
Num 7:3	and twelve oxen; a wagon for two of the princes, and for each *echad* an ox:		■	
*Num 7:11	They shall offer their offering, *echad-each* prince on this day,		■	
Num 7:13	And his offering (was) *echad* silver charger,			■
Num 7:13	*echad* silver bowl of seventy shekels,			■
Num 7:14	*Echad* spoon of ten (shekels) of gold, full of incense:			■
Num 7:15	*Echad* young bullock			■
Num 7:15	*echad* ram,			■
Num 7:15	*echad* lamb of the first year, for a burnt-offering:			■
Num 7:16	*Echad* kid of the goats for a sin-offering:			■
Num 7:19	He offered (for) his offering *echad* silver charger,			■
Num 7:19	*echad* silver bowl of seventy shekels, after the shekel of the sanctuary;			■
Num 7:20	*Echad* spoon of gold of ten (shekels), full of incense:			■
Num 7:21	*Echad* young bullock,			■
Num 7:21	*echad* ram,			■

THE TRI-UNITY OF GOD IS JEWISH

1 = compound unity 2 = one as plural 3 = one among others	1	2	3
Num 7:21	*echad* lamb of the first year, for a burnt-offering:			
Num 7:22	*Echad* kid of the goats for a sin-offering:			
Num 7:25	His offering (was) *echad* silver charger, the weight whereof			
Num 7:25	*Echad* silver bowl of seventy shekels,			
Num 7:26	*Echad* golden spoon of ten (shekels), full of incense:			
Num 7:27	**Echad** young bullock			
Num 7:27	*echad* ram,			
Num 7:27	*echad* lamb of the first year, for a burnt-offering:			
Num 7:28	*Echad* kid of the goats for a sin-offering:			
Num 7:31	His offering (was) *echad* silver charger, the weight whereof			
Num 7:31	*echad* silver bowl of seventy shekels, after the shekel of the sanctuary;			
Num 7:32	*Echad* golden spoon of ten (shekels), full of incense:			
Num 7:33	*Echad* young bullock,			
Num 7:33	*echad* ram,			
Num 7:33	*echad* lamb of the first year, for a burnt-offering:			
Num 7:34	*Echad* kid of the goats for a sin-offering:			
Num 7:37	His offering (was) *echad* silver charger, the weight whereof			
Num 7:37	*echad* silver bowl of seventy shekels,			

APPENDIX 2: MOSES' USE OF ECHAD IN THE TORAH

1 = compound unity 2 = one as plural 3 = one among others		1	2	3
Num 7:38	*Echad* golden spoon of ten (shekels), full of incense:			
Num 7:39	*Echad* young bullock			
Num 7:39	*echad* ram,			
Num 7:39	*echad* lamb of the first year, for a burnt-offering:			
Num 7:40	*Echad* kid of the goats for a sin-offering:			
Num 7:43	His offering (was) *echad* silver charger, the weight whereof			
Num 7:43	*echad* silver bowl of seventy shekels, after the shekel of the sanctuary;			
Num 7:44	*Echad* golden spoon of ten (shekels), full of incense:			
Num 7:45	*Echad* young bullock			
Num 7:45	*echad* ram,			
Num 7:45	*echad* lamb of the first year, for a burnt-offering:			
Num 7:46	*Echad* kid of the goats for a sin-offering:			
Num 7:49	His offering (was) *echad* silver charger, the weight whereof			
Num 7:49	*echad* silver bowl of seventy shekels, after the shekel of the sanctuary;			
Num 7:50	*Echad* golden spoon of ten (shekels), full of incense:			
Num 7:51	*Echad* young bullock			
Num 7:51	*echad* ram,			
Num 7:51	*echad* lamb of the first year, for a burnt-offering:			

THE TRI-UNITY OF GOD IS JEWISH

1 = compound unity 2 = one as plural 3 = one among others	1	2	3
Num 7:52	*Echad* kid of the goats for a sin-offering:			
Num 7:55	His offering (was) *echad* silver charger, the weight whereof			
Num 7:55	*echad* silver bowl of seventy shekels, after the shekel of the sanctuary;			
Num 7:56	*Echad* golden spoon of ten (shekels), full of incense:			
Num 7:57	*Echad* young bullock			
Num 7:57	*echad* ram,			
Num 7:57	*echad* lamb of the first year, for a burnt-offering:			
Num 7:58	*Echad* kid of the goats for a sin-offering:			
Num 7:61	His offering (was) *echad* silver charger, the weight whereof			
Num 7:61	*echad* silver bowl of seventy shekels, after the shekel of the sanctuary;			
Num 7:62	*Echad* golden spoon of ten (shekels), full of incense:			
Num 7:63	*Echad* young bullock			
Num 7:63	*echad* ram,			
Num 7:63	*echad* lamb of the first year, for a burnt-offering:			
Num 7:64	*Echad* kid of the goats for a sin-offering:			
Num 7:67	His offering (was) *echad* silver charger, the weight whereof			
Num 7:67	*echad* silver bowl of seventy shekels, after the shekel of the sanctuary;			
Num 7:68	*Echad* golden spoon of ten (shekels), full of incense:			

APPENDIX 2: MOSES' USE OF ECHAD IN THE TORAH

1 = compound unity 2 = one as plural 3 = one among others		1	2	3
Num 7:69	*Echad* young bullock			
Num 7:69	*echad* ram,			
Num 7:69	*echad* lamb of the first year, for a burnt-offering:			
Num 7:70	*Echad* kid of the goats for a sin-offering:			
Num 7:73	His offering (was) *echad* silver charger, the weight whereof			
Num 7:73	*echad* silver bowl of seventy shekels, after the shekel of the sanctuary;			
Num 7:74	*Echad* golden spoon of ten (shekels), full of incense:			
Num 7:75	*Echad* young bullock			
Num 7:75	*echad* ram,			
Num 7:75	*echad* lamb of the first year, for a burnt-offering:			
Num 7:76	*Echad* kid of the goats for a sin-offering:			
Num 7:79	His offering (was) *echad* silver charger, the weight whereof			
Num 7:79	*echad* silver bowl of seventy shekels, after the shekel of the sanctuary;			
Num 7:80	*Echad* golden spoon of ten (shekels), full of incense:			
Num 7:81	*Echad* young bullock			
Num 7:81	*echad* ram,			
Num 7:81	*echad* lamb of the first year, for a burnt-offering:			
Num 7:82	*Echad* kid of the goats for a sin-offering:			

THE TRI-UNITY OF GOD IS JEWISH

1 = compound unity 2 = one as plural 3 = one among others		1	2	3
Num 7:85	His offering (was) *echad* silver charger, the weight whereof			■
Num 7:85	*echad* silver bowl of seventy shekels, after the shekel of the sanctuary;			■
Num 8:12	and thou shalt offer the *echad* (for) a sin-offering,		■	
Num 8:12	and the *echad-other* for a burnt-offering, unto the LORD		■	
Num 9:14	ye shall have *echad* ordinance, both for the stranger,	■		
Num 10:4	And if they blow (but) with *echad* (trumpet), then the princes,			■
Num 11:19	Ye shall not eat *echad* day, nor two days, nor five days, neither ten days,			■
*Num 11:26	and the name of the *echad* (was) Eldad, and the name of the other Medad:		■	
*Num 13:2	of every tribe of their fathers shall ye send *echad-a* man,		■	
*Num 13:2	every *echad* a ruler among them.		■	
*Num 13:23	and cut down from thence a branch with *echad* cluster of grapes,	■		
Num 14:15	Now (if) thou shalt kill (all) this people as *echad* man,	■		
Num 15:5	with a burnt-offering or sacrifice, for *echad* lamb.			■
Num 15:11	Thus shall it be done for *echad* bullock,			■
Num 15:11	or for *echad* ram,			■
Num 15:11	or for *echad-a* lamb,			■
Num 15:11	or *echad-a* kid.			■
Num 15:12	According to the number that ye shall prepare, so shall ye do to every *echad*		■	

APPENDIX 2: MOSES' USE OF ECHAD IN THE TORAH

1 = compound unity 2 = one as plural 3 = one among others		1	2	3
Num 15:15	*Echad* ordinance (shall be both) for you of the congregation,	■		
*Num 15:16	*Echad* law and echad manner shall be for you,		■	
*Num 15:16	*Echad* law and *echad* manner shall be for you,		■	
Num 15:24	that all the congregation shall offer *echad* bullock for a burnt-offering,		■	
Num 15:24	according to the manner, and *echad* kid of the goats for a sin-offering.		■	
Num 15:27	And if *echad-any* soul sin through ignorance,		■	
Num 15:29	You shall have *echad* law for him that sins through ignorance,		■	
Num 16:15	I have not taken *echad* ass from them, neither have I hurt echad of them.		■	
Num 16:15	I have not taken echad ass from them, neither have I hurt *echad* of them.		■	
Num 16:22	O God, the God of the spirits of all flesh, shall *echad* man sin,		■	
Num 17:3	for *echad* rod (shall be) for the head of the house of their fathers.		■	
*Num 17:6	and every *echad* of their princes gave him a rod apiece,		■	
*Num 17:6	each prince *echad*, according to their fathers' houses, (even) twelve rods:		■	
Num 28:4	the *echad* lamb shalt thou offer in the morning			■
Num 28:7	drink-offering thereof (shall be) the fourth (part) of an hin for the *echad* lamb			■
Num 28:11	two young bullocks, and *echad* ram, seven lambs of the first year without			■
Num 28:12	mingled with oil, the *echad* bullock;			■
Num 28:12	mingled with oil, for *echad* ram;			■

THE TRI-UNITY OF GOD IS JEWISH

1 = compound unity 2 = one as plural 3 = one among others		1	2	3
Num 28:13	flour mingled with oil (for) a meat-offering unto *echad* lamb;			■
Num 28:15	And *echad* kid of the goats for a sin-offering unto the LORD shall be offered,			■
Num 28:19	two bullocks, and *echad* ram, and seven lambs of the first year:			■
Num 28:21	A several tenth deal shalt thou offer for *echad-every* lamb,			■
Num 28:22	and *echad* goat (for) a sin-offering, to make an atonement for you.			■
Num 28:27	two young bullocks, *echad* ram, seven lambs of the first year;			■
Num 28:28	three tenth deals unto *echad* bullock, two tenth deals unto echad ram,			■
Num 28:28	three tenth deals unto echad bullock, two tenth deals unto *echad* ram,			■
Num 28:29	A several tenth deal unto *echad* lamb, throughout the seven lambs;			■
Num 28:30	(And) *echad* kid of the goats, to make an atonement for you.			■
Num 29:1	And in the seventh month, on the *echad-first* (day) of the month,			■
Num 29:2	*echad* young bullock, echad ram, (and) seven lambs of the first year			■
Num 29:2	*echad* young bullock, *echad* ram, (and) seven lambs of the first year			■
Num 29:4	And *echad* tenth deal for echad lamb, throughout the seven lambs;		■	
Num 29:4	And echad tenth deal for *echad* lamb, throughout the seven lambs;			■
Num 29:5	And *echad* kid of the goats (for) a sin-offering, to make an atonement for			■
Num 29:8	*echad* young bullock, echad ram, (and) seven lambs of the first year			■

APPENDIX 2: MOSES' USE OF ECHAD IN THE TORAH

1 = compound unity 2 = one as plural 3 = one among others		1	2	3
Num 29:8	echad young bullock, *echad* ram, (and) seven lambs of the first year			■
Num 29:9	three tenth deals unto *echad* bullock, two tenth deals unto echad ram,			■
Num 29:9	three tenth deals unto echad bullock, two tenth deals unto *echad* ram,			■
Num 29:10	three tenth deals unto echad bullock, two tenth deals unto *echad* ram,			■
Num 29:11	*Echad* kid of the goats for a sin-offering:			■
Num 29:14	three tenth deals unto *echad-every* bullock of the thirteen bullocks,		■	
Num 29:14	two tenth deals to *echad-each* ram of the two rams.		■	
Num 29:15	And a several tenth to *echad-each* lamb of the fourteen lambs:		■	
Num 29:16	And *echad* kid of the goats (for) a sin-offering,			■
Num 29:19	And *echad* kid of the goats (for) a sin-offering;			■
Num 29:22	And *echad* goat (for) a sin-offering, beside the continual burnt-offering,			■
Num 29:25	And *echad* kid of the goats (for) a sin-offering, beside the continual			■
Num 29:28	And *echad* goat (for) a sin-offering, beside the continual burnt-offering,			■
Num 29:31	And *echad* goat (for) a sin-offering, beside the continual burnt-offering,			■
Num 29:34	And *echad* goat (for) a sin-offering, beside the continual burnt-offering,			■
Num 29:36	*echad* bullock, echad ram, seven lambs of the first year without blemish:			■
Num 29:36	echad bullock, *echad* ram, seven lambs of the first year without blemish:			■

THE TRI-UNITY OF GOD IS JEWISH

1 = compound unity 2 = one as plural 3 = one among others		1	2	3
Num 29:38	And *echad* goat (for) a sin-offering, beside the continual burnt-offering,			■
Num 31:28	*echad* soul of five hundred, (both) of the persons, and of the beeves,		■	
Num 31:30	thou shalt take *echad* portion of fifty, of the persons, of the beeves,		■	
Num 31:47	Moses took *echad* portion of fifty, (both) of man and of beast,		■	
Num 33:38	in the *echad-first* (day) of the fifth month.			■
*Num 34:18	ye shall take *echad* prince of every tribe, to divide the land by inheritance.		■	
*Num 34:18	Any ye shall take echad prince of *echad-every* tribe, to divide the land by			■
Num 35:30	but *echad* witness shall not testify against any person (to cause him) to die.			■
Num 36:3	And if they be married to any of the sons of the *echad* tribes of the children		■	
Num 36:8	shall be wife unto *echad* of the family of the tribe of her father,			■
DEUTERONOMY				
Deut 1:3	in the fortieth year, in the eleventh month, on the *echad-first* (day) of the			■
*Deut 1:23	and I took twelve men of you *echad* of a tribe:			■
Deut 4:42	and that fleeing unto *echad* of these cities he might live:			■
Deut 6:4	Hear, O Israel: the LORD our God (is) *echad* LORD.	■		
*Deut 12:14	But in the place which the LORD shall choose in *echad* of thy tribes,		■	
*Deut 13:12	If thou shalt hear (say) in *echad* of thy cities,		■	
Deut 15:7	If there be among you a poor man of *echad* of thy brethren			■

APPENDIX 2: MOSES' USE OF ECHAD IN THE TORAH

1 = compound unity 2 = one as plural 3 = one among others		1	2	3
Deut 15:7	within *echad-any* of your gates in your land,		■	
Deut 16:5	You may not sacrifice the passover with *echad-any* of your gates,		■	
Deut 17:2	If there be found among you, within *echad-any* of thy gates		■	
Deut 17:6	(but) at the mouth of *echad* witness he shall not be put to death.			■
*Deut 18:6	And if a Levite come from *echad-any* of thy gates out of all Israel,		■	
Deut 19:11	and smite him mortally that he die, and flees into *echad* of these cities:			■
Deut 19:15	*Echad* witness shall not rise up again a man for any iniquity,			■
Deut 21:15	If a man have two wives, *echad* beloved,			■
Deut 21:15	and *echad-another* hated, and they have born him children,			■
Deut 23:16	(even) among you, in that place which he shall choose in *echad* of thy gates,		■	
Deut 24:5	(but) he shall be free at home *echad* year, and shall cheer up his wife			■
Deut 25:5	If brethren dwell together, and *echad* of them die, and have no child,			■
Deut 25:11	men strive together one with another, and the wife of the *echad* draws			■
Deut 28:7	they shall come out against thee *echad* way, and flee before you seven ways			■
Deut 28:25	you shalt go out *echad* way against them, and flee seven ways before			■
Deut 28:55	So that he will not give to *echad-any* of them of the flesh of his children		■	
Deut 32:30	How should *echad* chase a thousand, and two put ten thousand to flight,			■

1 = compound unity 2 = one as plural 3 = one among others	1	2	3
Totals for individual columns:	34	172	176
Grand total of *echad* references in the Five Books of Moses:			382

APPENDIX 3:
THE WORD:
VERBAL PLENARY INSPIRATION

The subject of Verbal Plenary Inspiration could easily fill a book; however, in this context only one aspect will be viewed in relation to the spoken or written Word of God. Chapter seven (pp. 220-227) defines Inspiration as well as the terms *verbal* and *plenary* so there is no need to address it again here. This is a challenge to both Christian and Jewish adherents to take another look at the doctrine of Inspiration.

The two purposes of this appendix are to draw attention to the Hebrew word(s) for the expression *the word of the Lord*, or similar expressions like *it is written*, that deal with the words of God that were given by God to the human authors and written in the Hebrew Scriptures. These two purposes are to draw the attention of Christians to how they interpret the word of God and to Jewish people concerning the Written Law versus the Oral Law.

The first purpose is to express the dire need in the twenty-first century for pastors and teachers to re-examine the doctrine of Inspiration as it is being presented in the Church today. The believing Church is quickly losing its biblical bearings as liberal scholars (higher criticism) have infected evangelical authors and translators who, as a result, are chipping away at this doctrine. They are aggressively flooding the "Christian" market place with books that reinterpret what God says into what they think God meant, or else they are giving the dynamitic equivalent to the words in the Bible (NIV, Living Bible, Good News, TNIV etc.) that God Himself inspired.

During a conversation with my writing coach[921] I discovered that the humanistic secular academic approach to all writings – including Scripture – is not the same today, in the postmodern world, as it was in previous years. She explained the new perspective: "the meaning lies – not in the text – but in the interpretation of the text." Fundamental Bible believers bristle at that statement because it undercuts their firmly held belief in verbal plenary inspiration of Scripture. The core of that postmodern perspective is a frontal attack on the very words that God used. Their implication is that all literature – including the Scriptures – is to be given over to the fallible mind of the humanistic secular person who wants to interpret all literature –

---

[921] In a private conversation with Dr. Elaine Huber

including the Scriptures – the same way. Many contemporary evangelical authors have adopted that view in relation to Scripture, even though they claim a belief in the Inspiration of Scripture.

Robert Wilkin expresses deep concern that some evangelicals are broadening their view of Inspiration:

> He [Wallace of Dallas Theological Seminary] suggested that the authors of the NT did not approach the reporting of history in the same way that current historians do. In order to interpret the NT correctly, we must be aware of this different approach. Practically speaking this brings into question the NT author's concern about historical accuracy in terms of the speaker, the location, the date, and the precise content of what was said.[922]

As Wilkin later points out that it is ludicrous to claim that the New Testament can contain historical inaccuracies and still be God-breathed, without error. God, who is the author, used words, precise words, to express His nature and His Person to mankind. It is troubling to see evangelical authors saying and implying that the Scriptures can't be trusted with the facts in history and science. History has demonstrated that it is finite man who cannot be trusted, when he moves away from what God said to reinterpret what God said.

In the process evangelicals move believers away from *Thus says the LORD* as the absolute final authority of Scripture. In their attempt to make the Scripture more readable to people, scholars have sacrificed one of the foundational doctrines of Scripture – Inspiration. Unfortunately, twenty-first-century evangelicals have taken it upon themselves to correct God's Word into what they think God meant. That is ludicrous – that an unreliable, fallible man, a creature made by infallible God, would take it upon himself to correct the Creator and Author of His own word.

The second purpose is to invite rabbis and Jewish people at large to reinvestigate the claims of *HaShem* that the words that He inspired, which He gave to Moses and the prophets were all written down. His word is supreme, not the writings of fallible men in their interpretations of the *Tanakh* in *Talmud* and other rabbinic commentaries. This next statement may be viewed as a harsh statement, but it is meant to be taken in love and to be thought through logically within the context of this book. Rabbinic Judaism has been the instrument to cause Jewish people to prostrate themselves before an idol, the god of the Oral Law, the one and only authoritative pillar of Rabbinic Judaism. Included in that call to investigate is the

---

[922] Robert N. Wilkin, "Toward a Narrow View of Ipsissima Vox," *JOTGES* 14, no. 26 (Spring 2001), 3-8.

APPENDIX 3: THE WORD, VERBAL PLENARY INSPIRATION

movement within Jewish believers of Messiah to lift up rabbinic practices and teaching in order to be more Jewish. The Hebrew Scriptures lifts up the Word of the LORD as being final to any opinion, theory or teaching of men. Nowhere in the Hebrew Scriptures did God even hint at another law, the Oral Law, running parallel to the Written Law. Where does God tell Jewish believers in Messiah to go back to rabbinic practices to be more Jewish? Jewish believers should be encouraged to read San Telchin's book, *Messianic Judaism IS NOT Christianity* or Baruch Maoz's book *Judaism is not Jewish*.[923] Judaism before the time of the destruction of Jerusalem and the Temple prefabricated the myth that *HaShem* gave two laws to Moses, the Written Law and Oral Law. Nowhere in the writings of Moses or the Prophets is there even a shred of evidence that *HaShem* did such a thing. The only possible reference to Oral Law in the Hebrew Scriptures is when the Written Law was read orally as Ezra did to the people (Nehemiah 8:1-8).

Let this be a challenge to any Jewish rabbis or Jewish persons to investigate for themselves the claims that *HaShem* makes concerning His own Word. Your eternal destiny hinges on what *HaShem* said versus what the rabbi said that *HaShem* said. The two are different and even contradictory. Stop accepting the words of the rabbis blindly. You are the most intelligent, blessed people of the world, which is a by-product of the Abrahamic Covenant. Investigate *HaShem*'s word with the minds that *HaShem* gave you, opening your minds and hearts to what *HaShem* said in His Word.

Moses, the prophets and other unknown writers of the *Tanakh* used several words to express the concept of words and writing:

אֹמֶר	emer (50)	words[924]
אִמְרָה	imra (36)	word, words, utterance[925]
דָּבַר	dabar – v (1140)	said, speak, spoken, spoke, speaking, tell[926]
דָּבָר	dabar – nm (1455)	word, words[927]
כָּתַב	katab – v (223)	written, write, wrote[928]
מִכְתָּב	miktab – nm (9)	writing[929]
פֶּה	peh – nm (498)	mouth[930]

---

[923] Baruch Maoz, *Judaism is not Jewish* (Ross-shire, Great Britain: Christian Focus, 2003).
[924] Botterweck, Ringgren and Fabry. *Theological Dictionary of the Old Testament*, 1:343.
[925] Harris, Archer, and Waltke, *Theological Wordbook of the Old Testament*, 1:55.
[926] VanGemeren, ed., *Dictionary of Old Testament Theology & Exegesis*, 1:912.
[927] VanGemeren, ed., *Dictionary of Old Testament Theology & Exegesis*, 1:913.
[928] Botterweck, Ringgren and Fabry. *Theological Dictionary of the Old Testament*, 7:373.
[929] Harris, Archer, and Waltke, *Theological Wordbook of the Old Testament*, 1:458.

THE TRI-UNITY OF GOD IS JEWISH

These Hebrew words which are generally translated as indicated in English word(s) refer to "words" that were spoken by *HaShem* directly or by *HaShem* through a human agent and "written down" by those human agents. These Hebrew words also refer to "words" spoken between mankind as well as directed from man to *HaShem*. "Writing" refers to several things: (1) "writing down" the very "words" that *HaShem* wanted in a book or scroll by the human agent, or whether *HaShem* to man, man to man, or man to *HaShem*, (2) *HaShem* personally has used "writing" as he wrote down the Ten Commandments with His finger, and (3) the word "mouth" refers to the "words" that come from the mouth, where they are formed and spoken. What is to be observed is that *HaShem* used "words" and "wrote down" the "words." *HaShem* did not give divine thoughts and leave it to the human agent to decide how to say or write His word. G-d the *Ruach HaKodesh* (Holy Spirit) so guided the authors of the "words" in such a way that *HaShem*'s "words" were spoken or "written down" without violating the personality and style of that particular human agent. If there is a conflict with some of the words that *HaShem* used, it is our lack of understanding, not *HaShem*'s inability to convey His word to us.

Below is a chart with references concerning the "word," "words" or all the words "written" by G-d or *HaShem*. In the first column is a Scriptural reference and in the second column is an actual quote. This is not a complete list, but a sampling from the Hebrew Scriptures. The list is intended to demonstrate that words used of God or man mean just that, God used words to express Himself to his people. Words make up phrases and sentences to express what God wants the reader to understand. Words that *HaShem* used points out strongly that His words were *written down*. In fact Moses is very clear that he wrote down *all* the words of *HaShem*. The Scriptures are the verbal plenary inspired word of God, and man should not be tampering with, or altering His word, to suit their personal bias or to meet "Christian" marketing needs.

---

[930] Harris, Archer, and Waltke, *Theological Wordbook of the Old Testament*, 2:718.

APPENDIX 3: THE WORD, VERBAL PLENARY INSPIRATION

"The Word:" Verbal Plenary Inspiration

Genesis				
Gen 15:1	After these things the **word** of the LORD came unto Abram in a vision,	dabar		
Gen 15:4	And, behold, the **word** of the LORD came unto him, saying	dabar		
Exodus				
Exod 17:14	And the LORD said unto Moses, **Write** this for a memorial in a book,		katab	
Exod 19:6	These are the **words** which thou shalt speak unto the children of	dabar		
Exod 19:7	and laid before their faces all these **words** which the LORD commanded him.	dabar		
Exod 19:8	All that the LORD hath spoken we will do. And Moses returned the **words** of the people	dabar		
Exod 20:1	And God spoke all these words, saying	dabar		
Exod 24:3	And Moses came and told the people **all the words** of the LORD…and said **all the words** which the LORD hath said will we do.	dabar		
Exod 24:4	And Moses **wrote all the words** of the LORD	dabar	katab	
Exod 24:8	behold the blood of the covenant, which the LORD hath made with you concerning **all the words**	dabar		
Exod 31:18	two tables of testimony, tables of stone, **written** with the finger of God	katab	katab	
Exod 32:16	tables were the work of God, and the **writing** was the **writing** of God,			miktab
Exod 33:4	And when the people heard these evil **tidings-words,**	dabar		

Exod 34:1	Hew thee two tables of stone like unto the first: and I will *write* upon these tables the *words* that were that were in the first tables	dabar	katab	
Exod 34:27	And the LORD said unto Moses, ***Write*** thou these ***words***: for after the tenor of these words I have made a covenant with thee and with Israel	dabar	katab	
Exod 34:28	And he *wrote* upon the tables the *words* of the covenant, the ten commandments	dabar	katab	
Exod 35:1	These are the *words* which the LORD hath commanded,	dabar		
Exod 39:30	And they made the plate of the holy crown of pure gold, and *wrote* upon it a ***writing***,		katab	miktab
Numbers				
Num 3:16	And Moses numbered them according to the *word* of the Lord,			peh
Num 3:51	according to the *word* of the LORD, as the LORD commanded			peh
Num 5:23	And the priest shall *write* these curses in a book,		katab	
Num 12:6	Hear now my *words*: If there be a prophet among you, I the LORD	dabar		
Num 15:31	Because he hath despised the *word* of the LORD, and hath broken his commandments	dabar		
Num 24:4	He hath said, which heard the *words* of God,			emer
Num 24:16	He hath said, which heard the *words* of God, and knew the knowledge of the most High,			emer
Num 33:2	And Moses *wrote* their goings out according to their journeys			peh

APPENDIX 3: THE WORD, VERBAL PLENARY INSPIRATION

Deuteronomy					
Deut 1:1	These be the **words** which Moses spoke unto all Israel on this side	dabar			
Deut 4:10	and I will make them hear my **words**, that they may learn to fear	dabar			
Deut 4:13	ten commandments and he **wrote** them upon two tables of stone			katab	
Deut 4:36	Out of heaven he made you to hear his voice,…and you heard his **words** out of the midst of the fire	dabar			
Deut 5:5	I stood between the LORD and you at that time, to shew you the **word** of the LORD	dabar			
Deut 5:22	These **words** the LORD spake unto all the assembly in the mount out of the midst of the fire, of the cloud, and of the thick darkness, with a great voice and he added no more, and he **wrote** them in two tables of stone and delivered them unto me.	dabar	katab		
Deut 8:3	but by every **word** that preceedeth out of the **mouth** of the LORD doth man live.				peh
Deut 9:23	then ye rebelled against the **commandment** of the LORD your God				peh
Deut 10:4	And he **wrote** on the tables, according to the first **writing,** the ten commandments,			katab	miktab
Deut 11:18	Therefore shall ye lay up these my **words** in your heart and in your soul, and bind them for a sign upon your hand,	dabar			
Deut 11:20	And thou shalt **write** them upon the door posts of thine house,			katab	
Deut 17:18	And it shall be, when he sitteth upon the throne of his kingdom, that he shall **write** him a copy of this law in a book			katab	
Deut 17:19	that he may learn to fear the LORD his God, to keep all the **words** of this law and these statutes, to do them.	dabar			
Deut 18:18	and I will put my **words** in his **mouth** and he shall speak unto them	dabar			peh

Deut 18:19	And it shall come to pass, that whosoever will not hearken unto my **words** which he shall speak in my name, I will require it of him.	dabar		
Deut 24:1	then let him **write** her a bill of divorcement,		katab	
Deut 24:3	if the latter husband hate her, and **write** her a bill of divorcement,		katab	
Deut 27:3	And thou shalt **write** upon them all the **words** of this law,	dabar	katab	
Deut 27:8	shalt **write** upon the stones all the **words** of this law very plainly.	dabar	katab	
Deut 27:26	Cursed be he that confirmeth not all the **words** of this law	dabar		
Deut 28:58	If thou wilt not observe to do **all the words** of this law that are **written** in this book	dabar	katab	
Deut 28:61	Also every sickness, and every plague, which is not **written** in the book of this law,		katab	
Deut 29:20	and all the curses that are **written** in this book shall lie upon him,		katab	
Deut 29:21	according to all the curses of the covenant that are **written** in this book of the law		katab	
Deut 29:27	to bring upon it all the curses that are **written** in this book		katab	
Deut 29:29	that we may do **all the words** of this law.	dabar		
Deut 30:10	to keep his commandments and his statutes which are **written** in this book of the law and his statutes which are written in this book		katab	
Deut 31:1	And Moses went and spake these **words** unto all Israel	dabar		
Deut 31:9	And Moses **wrote** this law, and delivered it unto the priests		katab	

APPENDIX 3: THE WORD, VERBAL PLENARY INSPIRATION

Deut 31:12	that they may hear, and that they may learn, and fear the LORD your God, and observe to do **all the words** of this law.	dabar		
Deut 31:19	Now therefore **write** ye this song for you and teach it		katab	
Deut 31:22	Moses therefore **wrote** this song the same day, and taught it the children of Israel.		katab	
Deut 31:24	when Moses had made an end of **writing** the **words** of this law in a book, until they were finished	dabar	katab	
Deut 31:28	that I may speak these **words** in their ears, and call heaven and earth to record against them.	dabar		
Deut 31:30	And Moses spake in the ears of all the congregation of Israel the **words** of this song	dabar		
Deut 32:1	Give ear, O ye heavens, and I will **speak**; and hear, O earth, the **words** of my **mouth**	dabar	Emer	peh
Deut 32:46	And he said unto them, Set your hearts unto all the **words** which I testify among you this day, which ye shall command your children to observe to do, all the **words** of this law.	dabar		
Joshua				
Josh 1:8	This **book of the law** shall not depart out of thy **mouth**,...that thou mayest observe to do according to all that is **written** therein		katab	peh
Josh 1:13	Remember the **word** which Moses the servant of the LORD	dabar		
Josh 1:18	Whosoever he be that doth rebel against thy **commandment**, and will not hearken unto thy **words** in all that thou commandest him,	dabar		peh
Josh 3:9	And Joshua said unto the children of Israel, Come hither, and hear the **words** of the LORD your God.	dabar		

THE TRI-UNITY OF GOD IS JEWISH

Josh 6:10	Ye shall not shout, nor make any noise with your voice, neither shall any **word** proceed	dabar		
Josh 8:31	As Moses the servant of the LORD commanded the children of Israel, as it is **written** in **the book of the law** of Moses,		katab	
Josh 8:32	And he **wrote** there upon the stone a copy of the law of Moses, which he **wrote** in the presence of the children of Israel.		katab	
Josh 8:34	And afterward he read all the **words** of the law, the blessings and cursings, according to all that is **written in the book of the law**	dabar	katab	
Josh 8:35	There was not a **word** of all that Moses commanded, which Joshua read not before all the congregation of Israel,	dabar		
Josh 10:13	Is not this **written** in the book of Jasher		katab	
Josh 18:4	and they shall rise, and go through the land, and **describe-write** it according to the		katab	
Josh 18:6	Ye shall therefore **describe-written** the land into seven parts saying go and walk through the land, and **describe-write** it and come again		katab	
Josh 18:9	And the men went and passed through the land, and **described-wrote** it by cities into seven parts in a book		katab	
Josh 23:6	Be ye therefore very courageous to keep and to do all that is **written in the book of the law** of Moses		katab	
Josh 24:26	And Joshua **wrote** these **words** in **the book of the law** of God,	dabar	katab	
Josh 24:27	for it hath heard all the **words** of the LORD which he spake unto us:			emer
Judges				
Judg 11:11	and Jephthah uttered al his **words** before the LORD in Mizpeh	dabar		

APPENDIX 3: THE WORD, VERBAL PLENARY INSPIRATION

1 Samuel				
1 Sam 3:1	And the **word** of the LORD was precious in those days;	dabar		
1 Sam 3:7	neither was the **word** of the LORD yet revealed unto him.	dabar		
1 Sam 10:25	Then Samuel told the people the manner of the kingdom, and **wrote** it in a book,			katab
1 Sam 15:10	Then came the **word** of the LORD unto Samuel, saying	dabar		
1 Sam 15:23	Because thou hast rejected the **word** of the LORD, he hath also rejected thee	dabar		
2 Samuel				
2 Sam 1:18	behold, it is **written** in the book of Jasher			katab
2 Sam 7:4	that the **word** of the LORD came unto Nathan,	dabar		
2 Sam 7:17	According to all these **words,** and according to all this vision,	dabar		
2 Sam 11:14	And it came to pass in the morning that David **wrote** a letter to Joab,			katab
2 Sam 11:15	And he **wrote** in the letter, saying, Set ye Uriah in the forefront of the hottest battle,			katab
2 Sam 12:9	Wherefore hast thou despised the **commandment-word** of the LORD	dabar		
2 Sam 22:31	As for God, his way is perfect; the **word** of the LORD is tried: he is a buckler to all them			imra
2 Sam 24:11	when David was up in the morning, the **word** of the LORD came unto the prophet Gad	dabar		
1 Kings				
1 Kgs 2:3	And keep the charge of the LORD thy God…as it is **written** in the law of Moses,		katab	
1 Kgs 6:11	And the **word** of the LORD came to Solomon, saying	dabar		

THE TRI-UNITY OF GOD IS JEWISH

1 Kgs 11:41	his wisdom, are they not **written** in the book of the acts of Solomon.			katab
1 Kgs 12:22	But the **word** of God came unto Shemaiah the man of God, saying,	dabar		
1 Kgs 13:1	there came a man of God out of Judah by the **word** of the LORD	dabar		
1 Kgs 13:2	And he cried against the altar in the **word** of the LORD	dabar		
1 Kgs 13:5	the sign which the man of God had given by the **word** of the LORD	dabar		
1 Kgs 13:9	For so was it charged me by the **word** of the LORD, saying	dabar		
1 Kgs 13:17	For it was said to me by the **word** of the LORD	dabar		
1 Kgs 13:20	as they sat at the table, that the **word** of the LORD came unto	dabar		
1 Kgs 13:26	the man of God, who was disobedient unto the **word** of the LORD:		peh	
1 Kgs 13:32	For the saying which he cried by the **word** of the LORD against the altar in Beth-el	dabar		
1 Kgs 14:19	behold, they are **written** in the book of the chronicles of the kings			katab
1 Kgs 14:29	are they not **written** in the book of the chronicles of the kings of			katab
1 Kgs 15:29	according unto the **saying-word** of the LORD	dabar		
1 Kgs 16:1	Then the **word** of the LORD came to Jehu the son of Hanani	dabar		
1 Kgs 16:34	according to the **word** of the LORD, which he spake by Joshua	dabar		
1 Kgs 17:2	And the **word** of the LORD came unto him (Elijah), saying	dabar		
1 Kgs 18:1	that the **word** of the LORD came to Elijah	dabar		
1 Kgs 22:19	and he said (Micaiah), Hear thou therefore the **word** of the LORD	dabar		

APPENDIX 3: THE WORD, VERBAL PLENARY INSPIRATION

2 Kings			
2 Kgs 15:12	This was the **word** of the LORD which he spake unto Jehu	dabar	
2 Kgs 22:11	when the king had heard the **words** of the book of the law,	dabar	
2 Kgs 22:13	concerning the **words** of this book that is found: …because our fathers have not hearkened unto the **words** of this book to do according unto all that which is **written** concerning us.	dabar	katab
2 Kgs 22:16	even all the **words** of the book which the king of Judah hath read:	dabar	
2 Kgs 22:18	As touching the **words** which thou hast heard:	dabar	
2 Kgs 23:2	and he read in their ears all the **words** of the book of the covenant which was found in the house of the LORD	dabar	
2 Kgs 23:16	and polluted it, according to the **word** of the LORD which the man of God proclaimed, who proclaimed these **words**.	dabar	
2 Kgs 24:2	according to the **word** of the LORD, which he spake by his servant the prophets	dabar	
1 Chronicles			
1 Chr 10:13	even against the **word** of the LORD, which he kept not,	dabar	
1 Chr 15:15	as Moses commanded according to the **word** of the LORD.	dabar	
1 Chr 16:15	Be ye mindful always of his covenant; the **word** which he commanded to a	dabar	
1 Chr 16:40	and to do according to all that is **written** in the law of the LORD, which he commanded		katab
1 Chr 17:3	that the **word** of God came to Nathan, saying	dabar	

2 Chronicles				
2 Chr 6:17	Now then, O LORD God of Israel, let thy *word* be verified, which thou hast spoken	dabar		
2 Chr 10:15	for the cause was of God, that the LORD might perform his *word*, which he spake by the hand of Ahigah	dabar		
2 Chr 11:2	But the *word* of the LORD came to Shemaiah the man of God,	dabar		
2 Chr 11:4	And they obeyed the *words* of the LORD, and returned from going	dabar		
2 Chr 12:7	And when the LORD saw that they humbled themselves, the *word* of the Lord	dabar		
2 Chr 21:12	And there came a *writing* to him from Elijah the prophet,			miktab
2 Chr 23:18	as it is *written* in the law of Moses, with rejoicing and with singing,		katab	
2 Chr 25:4	But he slew not their children, but did as it is *written* in the law in the book of Moses		katab	
2 Chr 29:15	according to the commandment of the king, by the *words* of the LORD, to cleanse	dabar		
2 Chr 30:12	one heart to do the commandment of the king .. the princes by the *word* of the LORD	dabar		
2 Chr 31:3	as it is *written* in the law of the LORD		katab	
2 Chr 33:18	and the *words* of the seers that spake to him in the name of the LORD God of Israel behold, they are *written* in the book of the kings	dabar	katab	
2 Chr 34:19	when the king had heard the *words* of the law, that he rent his	dabar		
2 Chr 34:21	concerning the *words* of the book that is found…Because our fathers have not kept the *word* of the LORD, to do after all that is *written* in this book.	dabar	katab	

APPENDIX 3: THE WORD, VERBAL PLENARY INSPIRATION

2 Chr 34:26	Thus saith the LORD God of Israel concerning the **words** which thou hast heard	dabar		
2 Chr 34:30	and he read in the ears all the **words** of the book of the covenant that was found in the	dabar		
2 Chr 34:31	to perform the **words** of the covenant which are **written** in this book.	dabar	katab	
2 Chr 35:4	according to the **writing** of David king of Israel, and according to the **writing** of Solomon		katab	miktab
2 Chr 35:12	to offer unto the LORD, as it is **written** in the book of Moses.		katab	
2 Chr 35:26	according to that which was **written** in the law of the LORD		katab	
2 Chr 36:16	But they mocked the messengers of God, and despised his **words,**	dabar		
2 Chr 36:21	To fulfill the **word** of the LORD by the **mouth** of Jeremiah,	dabar	peh	
2 Chr 36:22	that the **word** of the LORD spoken by the **mouth** of Jeremiah might be accomplished,...the spirit of Cyrus king of Persia, that he made a proclamation throughout all his kingdom, and put it also in **writing**,	dabar	Peh	miktab
Ezra				
Ezra 1:1	the first year of Cyrus king of Persia, that the **word** of the LORD by the **mouth** of Jeremiah might be fulfilled, and put it also in **writing**,	dabar	peh	miktab
Ezra 3:2	as it is **written** in the law of Moses the man of God		katab	
Ezra 3:4	They kept also the feast of Tabernacles, as it is **written**,		katab	
Ezra 9:4	Then were assembled unto me every one that trembled at the **words** of the God of Israel	dabar		

Nehemiah				
Neh 8:9	For all the people wept, when they heard the *words* of the law.	dabar		
Neh 8:12	because they had understood the *words* that were declared unto	dabar		
Neh 8:13	unto Ezra the scribe, even to understand the *words* of the law.	dabar		
Neh 8:14	And they found *written* in the law which the LORD had commanded		katab	
Neh 10:34	to burn the altar of the LORD our God, as it is *written* in the law		katab	
Neh 10:36	the firstborn of our sons, and of our cattle, as it is *written* in the law,		katab	
Psalms				
Psa 12:6	The *words* of the LORD are pure *words*: as silver tried in a furnace			imra
Psa 19:14	Let the *words* of my *mouth,* and the meditation of my heart,		emer	peh
Psa 33:4	For the *word* of the LORD is right and all his works are done in truth.	dabar		
Psa 33:6	By the *word* of the LORD were the heaven made;	dabar		
Psa 107:11	Because they rebelled against the *words* of God,			emer
Psa 119:9	by taking heed thereto according to thy *word.*	dabar		
Psa 119:13	With my lips have I declared all the judgments of thy *mouth.*			peh
Isaiah				
Isa 1:1	Hear the *word* of the LORD, ye rulers of Sodom;	dabar		
Isa 1:20	devoured with the sword: for the *mouth* of the LORD hath spoken it.			peh
Isa 2:3	and the *word* of the LORD from Jerusalem.	dabar		

APPENDIX 3: THE WORD, VERBAL PLENARY INSPIRATION

Isa 5:24	and despised the **word** of the Holy One of Israel.			imra
Isa 8:1	Take thee a great roll, and **write** in it with a man's pen		katab	
Isa 30:8	Now go, **write** it before them in a table, and note it in a book,		katab	
Isa 38:4	Then the **word** of the LORD came to Isaiah:	dabar		
Isa 38:9	The **writing** of Hezekiah king of Judah, when he had been sick,			miktab
Isa 41:26	there is none that declareth,...that heareth your **words**.			emer
Isa 58:14	for the **mouth** of the LORD hath spoken it.			peh
Isa 66:5	Hear the **word** of the LORD, ye that tremble at his **word**;	dabar		
Jeremiah				
Jer 1:2	To whom the **word** of the LORD came in the days of Josiah	dabar		
Jer 1:9	the LORD said unto me, Behold, I have put my **words** in thy **mouth**.	dabar		peh
Jer 2:1	Moreover the **word** of the LORD came to me, saying,	dabar		
Jer 6:10	behold, the **word** of the LORD is unto them a reproach;	dabar		
Jer 21:1	The **word** which came unto Jeremiah from the LORD,	dabar		
Jer 30:2	Thus speaketh the LORD God of Israel saying, **Write** thee all the **words** that I have spoken unto thee in a book	dabar	katab	
Jer 31:33	I will put my law in their inward parts, and **write** it in their hearts,		katab	
Jer 36:2	Take thee a roll of a book, and **write** therein all the **words** that I	dabar	katab	
Jer 36:4	Baruch **wrote** from the mouth of Jeremiah all the **words** of the LORD	dabar	katab	

Jer 36:6	Therefore go thou, and read in the roll, which thou hast **written** from my mouth, the **words** of the LORD in the ears of the people	dabar	katab
Jer 36:16	when they had heard all the **words,** they were afraid both one and other, and said…, We will surely tell the king of all these **words**.	dabar	
Jer 36:17	Tell us now, How didst thou **write** all these **words** at his mouth?	dabar	katab
Jer 36:18	He pronounced all these **words** unto me with his mouth and I **wrote** them with ink	dabar	katab
Jer 36:27	and the **words** which Baruch **wrote** at the mouth of Jeremiah,	dabar	katab
Jer 45:1	The **word** that Jeremiah the prophet spake unto Baruch the son of Neriah, when he had **written** these **words** in a book	dabar	katab
Lamentations			
Lam 2:17	he hath fulfilled his **word** that he had commanded in the days of old:			imra
Lam 3:38	Out of the **mouth** of the most High proceedeth not evil and good?			peh
Ezekiel			
Ezek 1:3	The **word** of the LORD came expressly unto Ezekiel the priest,	dabar	
Ezek 2:10	And he spread it before me; and it was **written** within and without; all my **words** that I shall speak unto thee receive in thine heart,	dabar	katab
Ezek 6:1	And the **word** of the LORD came unto me, saying	dabar	
Ezek 7:1	Moreover the **word** of the LORD came unto me, saying,	dabar	
Ezek 12:1	The **word** of the LORD also came unto me, saying	dabar	

APPENDIX 3: THE WORD, VERBAL PLENARY INSPIRATION

Ezek 37:4	and say unto them, O ye dry bones, hear the *word* of the LORD	dabar		
Ezek 38:1	And the *word* of the LORD came unto me, saying,	dabar		
Daniel				
Dan 9:2	whereof the *word* of the LORD came to Jeremiah the prophet,	dabar		
Dan 9:11	and the oath that is *written* in the law of Moses the servant of God		katab	
Dan 9:13	As it *written* in the law of Moses,		katab	
Hosea				
Hos 1:1	The *word* of the LORD that came unto Hosea, the son of Beeri,	dabar		
Hos 6:5	I have slain them by the *words* of my *mouth:*		emer	peh
Joel				
Joel 1:1	The *word* of the LORD that came to Joel the son of Pethuel.	dabar		
Amos				
Amos 3:1	Hear this *word* that the LORD hath spoken again you, O Children of	dabar		
Jonah				
Jonah 1:1	Now the *word* of the LORD came unto Jonah the son of Amittai,	dabar		
Micah				
Micah 1:1	The *word* of the LORD that came to Micah the Morasthite	dabar		
Micah 4:4	for the mouth of the LORD of hosts hath *spoken* it.			peh

Zephaniah		
Zeph 1:1	The word of the LORD which came unto Zephaniah the son	dabar
Haggai		
Hag 1:1	came the **word** of the LORD by Haggai the prophet unto	dabar
Zechariah		
Zech 1:1	second year of Darius, came the **word** of the LORD unto Zechariah,	dabar
Zech 8:18	And the **word** of the LORD of hosts came unto me, saying	dabar
Zech 12:1	The burden of the **word** of the LORD for Israel, saith the LORD,	dabar
Malachi		
Mal 1:1	The burden of the **word** of the LORD to Israel by Malachi	dabar

APPENDIX 4:
THE SERVANT OF THE LORD

Below are some passages of Scripture from two different versions. Yet they both say the same thing. The *Jewish Study Bible* is clear that the Servant of the LORD will suffer and die for the transgressions of His people. Once again check the pronouns; there is no possible way that this passage could be referring to the nation of Israel.

Isaiah 52:13 – 53:12

Jewish Study Bible

(13) Indeed, My servant shall prosper, Be exalted and raised to great heights. (14) Just as the many were appalled at him, so marred was his appearance, unlike that of man, His form, beyond human semblance, (15) Just so he shall startle many nations. Kings shall be silenced because of him, for they shall see what has not been told them, shall behold what they never have heard.

(1) Who can believe what we have heard? Upon whom has the arm of the LORD been revealed? (2) For he has grown, by His favor, like a tree crown, like a tree trunk out of arid ground. He had no form or beauty, that we should look at him: No charm, that we should find him pleasing. (3) He was despised, shunned by men, A man of suffering, familiar with disease. As one who hid his face from us, he was despised, we held him of no account. (4) Yet it was our sickness that he was bearing, Our suffering that he endured. We accounted him plagued, Smitten and afflicted by God; (5) But he was wounded because of our sins, crushed because of our iniquities. He bore the chastisement that made us whole, and by his bruises we were healed. (6) We all went astray like sheep, each going his own way; and the LORD visited upon him the guilt of all of us.

(7) He was maltreated, yet he was submissive, he did not open his mouth; Like a sheep being led to slaughter, like a ere, dumb before

THE TRI-UNITY OF GOD IS JEWISH

those who shear her, he did not open his mouth. (8) By oppressive judgment he was taken away, who could describe his abode? For he was cut off from the land of the living through the sin of my people, who deserved the punishment. (9) And his grave was set among the wicked, and with the rich, in his death, though he had done no injustice and had spoken no falsehood. (10) But the LORD chose to crush him by disease, that if he made himself an offering for guilt, he might see offspring and have long life, and that through him the LORD's purpose might prosper. (11) Out of his anguish he shall see it; he shall enjoy it to the full through his devotion. "My righteous servant makes the many righteous, it is their punishment that he bears; (12) Assuredly, I will give him the many as his portion, he shall receive the multitude as his spoil. For he exposed himself to death and was numbered among the sinners, whereas he bore the guilt of the many and made intercession for sinners.

Isaiah 52:13 – 53:12

King James Version

(13) Behold, my servant shall deal prudently, he shall be exalted and extolled, and be very high. (14) As many were astonished at thee; his visage was so marred more than any man, and his form more than the sons of men: (15) So shall he sprinkle many nations; the kings shall shut their mouths at him: for that which had not been told them shall they see; and that which they had not heard shall they consider.

(1) Who hath believed our report? And to whom is the arm of the LORD revealed? (2) For he shall grow up before him as a tender plant, and as a root out of a dry ground: he hath no form nor comeliness; and when we shall see him, there is no beauty that we should desire him. (3) He is despised and rejected of men; a man of sorrows, and acquainted with grief: and we hid as it were our faces from him; he was despised, and we esteemed him not. (4) Surely he hath borne our griefs and carried our sorrows: yet we did esteem him stricken, smitten of G-d and afflicted. (5) But he was wounded for our transgressions, he was bruised for our iniquities: the chastisement of our peace was upon him: and with his stripes we are healed. (6) All we like sheep have gone astray; we have turned every one to his own way; and the LORD hath laid on him the iniquity of us all.

APPENDIX 4: THE SERVANT OF THE *LORD*

(7) He was oppressed, and he was afflicted, yet he opened not his mouth: he is brought as a lamb to the slaughter, and as a sheep before her shearers is dumb, so he openeth not his mouth. (8) He was taken from prison and from judgment: and who shall declare his generation? For he was cut off out of the land of the living: for the transgression of my people was he stricken. (9) And he made his grave with the wicked, and with the rich in his death; because he had done no violence, neither was any deceit in his mouth. (10) Yet it pleased the LORD to bruise him; he hath put him to grief: when thou shalt make his soul an offering for sin, he shall see his seed, he shall prolong his days, and the pleasure of the LORD shall prosper in his hand. (11) He shall see of the travail of his soul, and shall be satisfied: by his knowledge shall my righteous servant justify many; for he shall bear their iniquities. (12) Therefore will I divide him a portion with the great, and he shall divide the spoil with the strong; because he hath poured out his soul unto death: and he was numbered with the transgressors; and he bare the sin of many, and made intercession for the transgressors.

APPENDIX 5:
THE DRIFT AWAY FROM THE BIBLE, A SUMMARY

from Arthur W. Kac's book,

The Spiritual Dilemma of the Jewish People

Published by

Baker Book House

In 1983

ISBN: 0-8010-5456-7

The following is a fair use summary of chapter seven of Dr. Kac's book, which is currently out of print. You may want to contact a used, on-line bookseller or do a inter-library loan from your public library to read this very significant chapter.

The Drift Away From the Bible
by Arthur W. Kac
from his book
The Spiritual Dilemma of the Jewish People

1. Works Versus Faith

In his first subdivision, "Works Versus Faith," Dr. Kac mentions two events that moved Judaism away from its Scriptural roots. One was the emergence of Christianity, which began in Jewish territory and credited itself with pointing to the fulfillment of the Jewish Scriptures. The second force was the destruction of the Temple in 70 C.E., which ended the sacrificial system that depended on it:

> The cessation of the sacrificial worship removed the priesthood as an influential force from Jewish life. Rabbinism was thus left free to pursue its course (p. 62).

> The cessation of the sacrificial worship in the first century disrupted the divinely instituted approach to God. The Jewish followers of Jesus saw in this event indirect proof that the atoning death of the Messiah had made the continuation of the Old Testament sacrificial cult unnecessary. (p. 62)

Dr. Kac was convinced that the formation of the Jewish cult of Rabbinic Judaism in reaction to the challenges of the Temple destruction and the emergence of Christianity as a sect of Judaism served an odd purpose. The effect was to create a hedge around the nationality of the Jews, preserving them through the centuries of history as a people, even when they no longer had the nation of Israel to identify them. Neither centuries in diaspora nor persecutions from all sides prevented them from continuing with a Jewish identity.

> And yet rabbinism fulfilled an important historical mission. With the loss of the Jewish national homeland a substitute had to be provided to safeguard Jewish nationality. Rabbinism produced this safeguard by creating a uniform religious way of life which served to cement unity between the Jewish communities dispersed all over the world. Humanly speaking, rabbinism saved Jewish nationally from extinction. (p. 63)

THE TRI-UNITY OF GOD IS JEWISH

Dr. Kac continues by pointing out that while this veering away from dependence on the literal Scriptures may have saved the identity of the Jewish people, it began a decided departure from the Scriptural basis of Judaism, which was then guided by the religion of the rabbis. The rabbis de-emphasized the messianic message of the Bible and emphasized good deeds and universal justice, which are both good religious principles. The changeover marked a transition from faith to deeds for the practice of Judaism. Accordingly, this led to "the exaltation of the Law by rabbinism as seen from representative passages from Talmudic writings" (p. 68).

In his subsection on "The Exaltation of the Torah," Dr. Kac explains next that the rabbis teach that the Torah is central to the practice of Judaism. While various teachings exist on what all is included in the Torah, the agreement rests on the importance of moral behavior based on Torah principles, which have been greatly debated and refined over the life of Israel by Jewish sages. They see the Torah as being created before the world and of having an eternal existence; and in this understanding, they fix it as the foundation of their teachings. In their view, the Torah itself acts as Israel's mediator between them and their God; and it is unchangeable. There is no need to look for another Moses or another Law. This contrasts to the teaching in the Gospel of John: "For the law was given by Moses, but grace and truth came by Jesus Christ" (1:17).

To Dr. Kac, it is clear that the Torah taught over all else the importance of relationship to God rather than moral justification. He looks at the teachings of Paul and also the Ten Commandments for clues. Let us look at a quote from Dr. Kac on Paul's teaching about the role of faith, and how that leads to a drift away from the biblical faith of Abraham and on to a form of humanism:

> In the third chapter of his letter to the Romans Paul discusses the matter of Abraham's justification by faith as recorded in the fifteenth chapter of Genesis. This statement in Genesis, that Abraham was considered righteous in the sight of God on the basis of his trust in God, is recorded before the Abrahamic Covenant was made and some time before the commandment of circumcision was given. To this the rabbinic answer was that the patriarchs observed the written and even the unwritten Law, notwithstanding the fact that the patriarchs lived centuries before the promulgation of the written law.
>
> Side by side with the emphasis of present-day Judaism on work versus faith there is a tendency to divorce ethical conduct from religion or faith in God. To be sure, this tendency is not confined to Judaism alone. (p.68)

APPENDIX 5 - "THE DRIFT AWAY FROM THE BIBLE"

Dr. Kac points out how this distancing from the power of the Word of God leads to a distancing from God, which is a familiar element of current post-modern philosophies:

> In a pamphlet seeking to explain the aims of the Jewish Reconstructionist movement, we are told that religion should not be viewed as a supernaturally revealed creed or code but rather as the affirmation of the worth-while-ness of life. This is the extreme logical development of the idealization and idolization of ethical conduct. If man's salvation is determined by his conduct rather than by his relation to God, then man can save himself and God can be dispensed with. This tendency to separate man's ethical conduct from faith in God, or the Law from God, may be seen in the following Talmudic passage: "Would that they [the Jewish people] would forsake Me but keep My Torah." (p. 68-69)

Dr. Kac tells a delightful story attributed to the ancient, traditional sage Rabbi Hillel the Elder:

> The story is told that a heathen asked him once to teach him the Law while standing on one foot; in other words, he wished Hillel to tell him what is the essence of the Jewish religion. The answer which Hillel gave is as follows: "Do not do to your fellow that which is hateful to you. This is the whole Law. The rest is its interpretation." (p.69)

Dr. Kac asks us to note that not a word was included about faith in God or man's relationship to God! The Greatest and First Commandment, to love God wholly and first, was noticeable only by its absence. He goes on to point out how this view departs from the Old Testament teachings:

> Of course, this exaltation of the Law by rabbinism is not quite in agreement with the teachings of the Old Testament. The Ten Commandments which represent the first body of laws given on Mount Sinai begin not with a commandment, but with a divine declaration. In this declaration God defines His ***relationship*** to Israel, based on what He has done for Israel, and not on what the Israelites have done for Him. "I am Jehovah thy God, who brought thee out of the land of Egypt, out of the house of bondage" (Exodus 20:2). (p.70) [Emphasis mine]

THE TRI-UNITY OF GOD IS JEWISH

Dr. Kac then points out the obvious, which is that Israel as a nation and the Jewish people as individuals, all broke the Law throughout all of biblical history. Not even Moses, Aaron, and Miriam were exempt from sin. Through Jeremiah, God promised to replace the Law, not with another Covenant of Law, but with a New Covenant of Grace (31:31-34). Paul agreed with this when he wrote Romans 3:20 reaffirming that we are not saved by works.

Dr. Kac provides various excerpts from the rabbis that show they were aware their teachings were not always in harmony with the Bible. This preference for their own logic and teachings led to a disengagement from biblical teachings from their own Scriptures. Here are two of several quotes he shared in his subsection, "Downgrading of the Bible":

> Our Rabbis taught, that to be engaged in the study of the Bible is neither good nor bad, but to be engaged in the study of the *Mishnah* is a good habit and it brings reward, while there is nothing better than the study of the Gemara (p. 71).

> It is a more serious matter to contradict the word of the Scribes [*Mishnah*] than the words of the Law of Moses (p. 71-72).

> He who interprets the Law [of Moses] not according to Halachah [i.e. in the manner of the rabbis], even though he possesses [the virtue of knowledge of] Torah and good deeds has no portion in the world to come. (p. 72).

Such teachings were probably aimed at Hebrew Christians, since at that time only Hebrew Christians, who were considered to be heretics because they followed the Old Testament Prophets and not the Jewish sages.

Dr. Kac states, "The Old Testament is frankly anthropomorphic," meaning that it describes God in human terms. He continues:

> There is a rabbinic saying to the effect that the Torah speaks the language of man, i.e., in His effort to communicate with man God adopts human ways. This is certainly correct; there could be no divine revelation unless God condescended to use human means by which to make Himself and His will known to man. But this is not all. Biblical anthropopathism reflects a truth which is basic in biblical theology, namely, that the same God who is everywhere, in, outside, and beyond His creation, is also the personal God of mankind. (p. 72-73)

APPENDIX 5 - "THE DRIFT AWAY FROM THE BIBLE"

Dr. Kac points out that as Jews adapted to Greek culture in the centuries before *Yeshua*'s Advent, they wanted to read their Bible, especially the first five books or the Pentateuch, in the language of the Greeks and to have it express the culture of the Greeks. In response, the Septuagint may have been the first definite attempt to weaken this Old Testament concept of a personal God. As a result, they removed anthropomorphic references to God as a person, as shown in the examples below (p. 73-74):

Exodus 24:11

> *And upon the nobles of the children of Israel He [God] laid not His hand* (Hebrew)

> *And of the elect of Israel not one uttered a dissenting voice* (Septuagint)

Exodus 25:22

> *And there I* [God] *will meet with thee* (Hebrew)

> *And thence I will be known to thee* (Septuagint)

Exodus 29:45

> *And I* [God] *will dwell in the midst of the children of Israel* (Hebrew)

> *And I will be invoked by the Children of Israel* (Septuagint)

Deuteronomy 33:27

> *The eternal God is a dwelling-place* (Hebrew)

> *The power of God will protect thee* (Septuagint)

Philo (c. 20 B.C.E. – c. 50 C.E.), an influential Greek Jewish philosopher of Alexandria, believed God was transcendent and not knowable, which reflected the thinking of the classical Greeks. He was an influence on the much later Jewish philosopher Maimonides (twelfth century), who also relied on a more allegorical rather than personal interpretation of Scriptures. Maimonides in particular was avoiding the personification of God that pointed to Jesus as a literal fulfillment of Scripture.

Dr. Kac points out that the Aramaic Translation of the Pentateuch known as the Targum Onkelos version was undertaken by Palestinian Jews and also echoed a less personal interpretation of God, but for a different reason than the Hellenistic Jews had sought a Greek translation. The reason the Targum drifted from the obvious Hebrew anthropomorphisms was "to counteract the doctrine of the Incarnation of the New Testament." He gives several examples, and lingers on the following one (p. 75):

Exodus 3:7

> *I* [Jehovah] *have surely seen the affliction of My people that are in Egypt . . .; for I know their sorrows* (Hebrew)
>
> *The bondage of My people which is in Egypt is verily disclosed before Me...; for their afflictions are disclosed before Me* (Targum)

On this Dr. Kac comments thus:

> The expression "I know" in the Hebrew version has the connotation of intimate knowledge, bordering on personal experience. We have here the beginning of one of the most precious teachings of the Bible, namely, that God identifies Himself with His people's joys and sorrows. This may be seen from the following passages: (1) "And His [God's] soul was grieved for the misery of Israel" (Judges 10:16), and (2) "In all their afflictions He [God] was afflicted, and the angel of His **presence saved them" (Isaiah 63:9).** (p. 75-76)

Dr. Kac also notes the importance of the biblical anthropomorphism in Isaiah 53, which presents the Suffering Servant that God used to identify Himself with His people in their "sins, sickness, and death." The personal reference to God in this passage has been a stumbling stone through the ages for the rabbis, resulting in the revisions that are currently taught today which focus more on a moral code rather than the personal God of Scripture.

In his section "The Depersonalization of the Messiah," Dr. Kac follows the tragic elevation of faith in man's accomplishments from the nineteenth century onward that encouraged many to believe in the goodness of mankind and the irrelevance of a God of redemption. This was aided by the long-standing absence of a physical State of Israel, so that many believed God had proven to be impotent in fulfilling His promise of restoration to the Land:

APPENDIX 5 - "THE DRIFT AWAY FROM THE BIBLE"

In the middle of the nineteenth century, newly formed Liberal Judaism in Germany took steps to introduce certain important changes in the ritual of the Synagogue. Among other things, it decided to delete from the Prayer Book all references to a national restoration of the Jews to Zion, as well as references to the coming of the Messiah. In place of "Redeemer" the word "Redemption" was substituted. For the first time in many centuries, Jews in the emancipated countries of Western Europe began to feel at home in the countries of their birth or residence. The petitions for a national restoration to Palestine lost all meaning to them. Since the hope of national restoration to Zion and the coming of the Messiah are closely related in the Jewish religion, the idea of a Messiah was discarded along with the hope of national restoration. However, subsequent events proved how wrong Liberal Judaism was in taking this stand.... (p. 76-77)

Joseph Albo (1380-1444), a Sephardic Jew, wrote *Ikarim* (*Principles*), a summary of the principles that make up Judaism, to show that Judaism was a true religion and that Christianity was false. He set out to show that belief in a personal Messiah was irrelevant to Jewish beliefs. Later, in the nineteenth century, this depersonalization of the Messiah resonated with Liberal Judaism.

In the words of Dr. Kac, so well stated that nothing can be added, the stage was set for a great tragedy that was about to unfold:

The great strides made in science, industry, education, and in the direction of attainment of democratic goals generated an atmosphere of optimism concerning human destiny." Man was believed to be essentially good. He was expected to receive from science all the power he needs; from education, all the knowledge he must have; from democracy, all the freedom he wants. The millennium was seen to be approaching, but it was a millennium which was indifferent to the actual spiritual state of man, a millennium without God. (p. 78)

At a rabbinical conference, ironically held in Germany at Frankfort-on-the-Main in 1845, the exuberant sense of mankind fulfilling the messianic role burst forth. It was tragic that German Jewry, the fountainhead of Liberal Judaism, should have seen in the prevailing state of affairs, with its materialistic mood, as the fulfillment of Israel's mission of the messianic hope of the prophets of the Old Testament. The effect which that era had on the German Jews may be seen from the following excerpts from addresses made at this rabbinical conference. One of the rabbis' comments, which in retrospect is eerie, was as follows:

> In our days... the ideals of justice and the brotherhood of men have been so strengthened through the laws and institutions of modern states, that they can never again be shattered; we are witnessing an ever nearer approach of the establishment of the Kingdom of God on earth through the strivings of mankind. (p 79)

In this way, the trend toward leaving out the prayers calling for the Messiah to come was advanced. However, one rabbi insisted that "this greatest and highest consummation of all, the ushering in of religious harmony, peace and brotherhood" (p. 79) might only be accomplished by one sent by God. His message was both biblical and foreshadowed the unthinkable events that would unfold regarding the Holocaust less than 100 years forward, the result of unregenerated human hearts in need of a Messiah.

In summary, the loss of the Temple and the associated sacrifice system created a dilemma of biblical proportions for the Jewish people. Dr. Kac sizes the situation up by writing:

> The two horns of this dilemma are the rejection of Jesus Christ and the cessation of the sacrificial worship of the Old Testament. In its persistent efforts to get away from Jesus, Judaism was forced to move further and further away from the Old Testament. In the process of this movement away from the Bible, many Jews lost faith in God's Word, faith in a Messiah, faith in a hereafter, and, finally, faith in God. This is the source of the spiritual conflict in the Jewish soul. (p. 82)

Again, there are many other extremely interesting facts included in the original text by Dr. Kac, and I highly recommend investing in the effort of obtaining a copy of his book, even though it is out of print, in order to gain deeper understanding of the drift that has affected Jewish thinking and also cast a shadow over traditional Christian thinking.

BIBLIOGRAPHY

Albertz, Ranier, a contributor to Jenni, Ernest and Claus Westermann. *Theological Lexicon of Old Testament*, Peabody, MA: Hendrickson, 1997.

Alexander, Ralph H. *The Expositor's Bible Commentary: Ezekiel*. 12 vols. Grand Rapids: Zondervan, 1986.

Alexander, T. Desmond and David W. Baker. *Dictionary of the Old Testament Pentateuch*. Downers Grove, Ill: InterVarsity, 2003.

Anderson, Sir Robert. *The Coming Prince*. Grand Rapids: Kregel, 1967.

Ankerberg, John and John Weldon. *Fast Facts on Islam*. Eugene, OR: Harvest House Publishers, 2001.

Atkinson, Basil R. C. *The Pocket Commentary of the Bible: Genesis*. Chicago: Moody, 1957.

Baker, Charles F. *A Dispensational Theology*. Grand Rapids: Grace Bible Publications, 1971.

Bancroft, Emery H. *Christian Theology*. Grand Rapids: Zondervan, 1964.

Barackman, Floyd H. *Practical Christian Theology: Examining the Great Doctrines of the Faith*. 4th ed. Grand Rapids: Kregel, 1998.

Barber, Cyril J. *The Books of Samuel*. 2 Vols. Neptune, NJ: Loizeaux, 1994.

Barker, Kenneth. *The New American Commentary: Micah*. 21 vols. Nashville: Broadman, 1998.

Barnes, Albert. *Barnes' Notes: Minor Prophets*. 2 vols. Grand Rapids: Baker, 1950.

Baron, David. *The Visions and Prophecies of Zechariah*. Jerusalem: Keren Ahvah Meshihit, 2000.

Barrett, Michael P. V. *Beginning At Moses*. 2nd ed. Greenville, SC: Ambassador-Emerald International, 2001.

Beale, Todd S. , William A. Banks, and Colin Smith *Old Testament Parsing Guide: Job-Malachi*.

Benach, Henry. *Go To Learn*. Chattanooga: International Board of Jewish Missions, 1997.

Bergen, Robert D. *The New American Commentary: 1 and 2 Samuel*. 21 Vols. Nashville: Broadman, 2002.

Berger, David. *The Rebbe, The Messiah and the Scandal of Orthodox Indifference*. Portland: The Littman Library of Jewish Civilization, 2001.

Berkhof, L. *Systematic Theology*. Grand Rapids: Eerdmans, 1941.

Berlin, Adele, and Marc Zvi Brettler. *The Jewish Study Bible*. New York: Oxford University, 2004.

Block, Daniel I. *The New American Commentary: Judges, Ruth*. Nashville: Broadman and Holman, 1999.

Botterweck, G. Johannes, Helmer Ringgren and Heinz-Josef Fabry. *Theological Dictionary of the Old Testament*. Grand Rapids: Eerdmans, 1977.

Briggs, Charles A. *Messianic Prophecy*. Peabody, MA: Hendrickson, 1988

Briscoe, Stuart. *The Communicator's Commentary: Genesis*. Waco, TX: Word Books, 1987.

Bromiley, Geoffrey W. *The International Standard Bible Encyclopedia*. 4 vols. Grand Rapids: Eerdmans, 1988

Brown, Francis, S. R. Driver, and Charles A. Briggs. *A Hebrew and English Lexicon of the Old Testament*, Oxford: Clarendon, n.d.

BIBLIOGRAPHY

Brown, Michael L. *Answering Jewish Objections to Jesus.* Vol. 2 of *Answering Jewish Objections.* Grand Rapids: Baker Books, 2000.

Brown, Michael L.. *Answering Jewish Objections to Jesus: Messianic Prophecy Objections* (Grand Rapids: Baker, 2003).

Brueggemann, Walter. *Theology of the Old Testament.* Minneapolis: Fortress Press, 1997.

Buksbazen, Victor. *Isaiah's Messiah.* Bellmawr, NJ: Friends of Israel Gospel Ministry, 2002.

Buksbazen. Victor. *The Prophet Isaiah.* 2 vols. Collingswood, NJ: Spearhead Press, 1971.

Buswell, James Oliver. *A Systematic Theology of the Christian Religion.* Grand Rapids: Zondervan, 1962.

Butler, J. Glentworth. *Butler's Bible Work.* 6 vols. New York: Funk & Wagnalls, 1889.

Buttrick, George Arthur. *The Interpreter's Bible.* Nashville: Abingdon, 1953.

Campus Crusade for Christ. *The Exodus Revealed, Search for the Red Sea Crossing.* Irvine CA: Discovery Media Productions, 2001, videotape.

Cassuto, U. *A Commentary on the Book of Genesis: Part One.* Jerusalem: Magnes Press, 1961.

Chafer, Lewis Sperry. *Systematic Theology.* 8 vols. Dallas: Dallas Seminary Press, 1964.

Charnock, Steven. *Existence and Attributes of God.* Grand Rapids: Baker, 1979.

Charles, R. H.. *A Critical and Exegetical Commentary on the Book of Daniel.* Oxford: Clarendon Press, 1929.

Cohen, A. *The Soncino Chumash, Isaiah.* New York: The Soncino Press, 1983.

Cohen, A. *The Soncino Chumash, The Five Books of Moses with Haphtaroth.* New York: The Soncino Press, 1993.

Cooke, G. A. *The International Critical Commentary: The Book of Ezekiel.* Edinburgh: T. & T. Clark, 1936.

Cooper, David L. *God's Gracious Provision for Man.* Los Angeles: Biblical Research Society, 1953.

Cooper, David L. *The God of Israel.* Los Angeles: Biblical Research Society, 1945.

Cooper, David L., *What Men Must Believe* (Los Angeles: Biblical Research Society, 1943), 105.

Cooper, Lamar Eugene. *The New American Commentary: Ezekiel.* vol. 17. Nashville: Broadman and Holman, 1994.

Craigie, P. C. *The New International Commentary on the Old Testament, The Book of Deuteronomy.* Grand Rapids: Eerdmans, 1976.

Crenshaw, James. *The Old Testament Library, Ecclesiastes.* Philadelphia: Westminster Press, 1987.

Criswell, W. A. *The Criswell Study Bible.* Nashville: Nelson, 1979.

Dahood, Mitchell. *The Anchor Bible: Psalms 101-150.* Garden City, NY: Doubleday, 1970.

Davidson, A. B. *The Theology of the Old Testament.* New York: Scribner's, 1928.

Davidson, Robert. *The Daily Study Bible Series: Jeremiah and Lamentations.* Philadelphia: Westminster, 1985.

Dickason, C. Fred. *Angels: Elect and Evil.* Chicago: Moody, 1975.

Dockery, David S. *Biblical Illustrator, Monotheism in the Scriptures.* Nashville, TN: Sunday School Board of the Southern Baptist Convention, 1991.

BIBLIOGRAPHY

Driver, S. R. *Westminster Commentaries, the Book of Genesis*. London: Methuen & Co. 1911.

Driver, S. R., A. Plummer, and C. A. Briggs, eds. *The International Critical Commentary: Genesis*. Edinburgh: T & T Clark. 1930.

Dyrness, William. *Themes in Old Testament Theology*. Downers Grove: InterVarsity, 1977.

Elwell, Walter A. *Evangelical Dictionary of Theology*. Grand Rapids: Baker Book House, 1984.

Enns, Paul. *The Moody Handbook of Theology*. Chicago: Moody Press, 1989.

Erickson, Millard J. *Christian Theology*. 2nd ed. Grand Rapids: Baker Books, 1998.

Erickson, Millard J. *Introducing Christian Doctrine*. Grand Rapids: Baker, 1992.

Evans, William. *The Great Doctrines of the Bible*. Chicago: Moody, 1974.

Feinberg, Charles L. , *Daniel: The Kingdom of the Lord* (Winona Lake, IN: BMH Books, 1981).

Feinberg, Charles L. *God Remembers, A Study of the Book of Zechariah*. New York: American Board of Missions to the Jews, 1965.

Feinberg, Charles L. "The Image of God," Bib Sac 129:515 (July 1972):237.

Feinberg, Charles L. *Jeremiah* (Grand Rapids: Zondervan, 1982).

Feinberg, Charles L. *The Minor Prophets* (Chicago: Moody, 1952), 328.

Feinberg, Charles L. *The Prophecy of Ezekiel: The Glory of the Lord*. Chicago: Moody, 1969.

Feinberg, John S. *No One Like Him*. Wheaton: Crossway Books, 2001.

Fischer, John, "*Yeshua*: The Deity Debate." *Mishkan* issue 39 (2003): 20-28.

Frame, John M. *The Doctrine of God*. Phillipsburg, NJ: P & R Publishers, 2002.

Free, Joseph P., Howard F. Vos. *Archaeology and the Bible History*. Grand Rapids: Zondervan, 1992.

Friedman, Richard Elliott. *Commentary on the Torah*. San Francisco: Harper Collins Publishers, 2001.

Fruchtenbaum, Arnold. *Genesis*. Tapes. Tustin, CA: Ariel Ministries, n.d.

Fruchtenbaum, Arnold. *Israelology, the Missing Link in Systematic Theology*. Tustin, CA: Ariel Ministries, 1993.

Fruchtenbaum, Arnold G. . *Jesus Was a Jew*. Tustin, CA: Ariel Ministries Press, 1981.

Fruchtenbaum, Arnold G., "Jewishness and the Trinity," n.p. [last accessed 11/4/2019]. Available online: www.Messiahnj.org/af-tri-unity.htm.

Fruchtenbaum, Arnold G. *Messianic Christology*. Tustin, CA: Ariel Ministries, 1998.

Fruchtenbaum, Arnold G. *The Footsteps of Messiah*. Tustin, CA: Ariel Ministries, 2003.

Fruchtenbaum, Arnold. *The Sabbath, Manuscript #176*. Tustin, CA: Ariel Ministries, 1991.

Fruchtenbaum, Arnold G., *The Trinity – Manuscript #50*. Tustin, CA: Ariel Ministries, 1983.

Frydland, Rachmiel. *What the Rabbis Know About the Messiah*. Cincinnati, OH: Messianic Publishing Co, 1991

Frydland, Rachmiel. *When Being Jewish Was a Crime*. Nashville: Nelson, 1978.

Fuchs, Daniel. *Israel's Holy Days*. Neptune, NJ: Loizeaux Brothers, 1985.

BIBLIOGRAPHY

Fuller, Reginald H. "The Vestigia Trinitatis in the Old Testament." Page 507 in The Quest for Context and Meaning, Edited by Craig A. Evans and Shemaryahu Talmon. Leiden, Netherlands: Brill, 1997.

Garstang, John. *Joshua – Judges: Foundations of Bible History*. Grand Rapids: Kregel, 1978.

Geisler, Norman L. , *A Popular Survey of the Old Testament*. Grand Rapids: Baker, 1977.

Geisler, Norman. *Systematic Theology*. 4 vols. Minneapolis: Bethany House, 2003.

Geisler, Norman L. and William E. Nix. *A General Introduction to the Bible*. Chicago, IL: Moody Press, 1968.

Goldberg, Louis. "The Deviation of Jewish Thought from an Old Testament Theology in the Intertestamental Period." Doctor of Theology. diss., Winona Lake, IN: Grace Theological Seminary,1963.

Goldberg, Louis. *Our Jewish Friends*. Neptune, NJ: Loizeaux Brothers, 1983.

Goldingay, John E. *Word Biblical Commentary: Daniel*. Dallas: Word Books, 1989.

Goldman, S. *The Soncino Books of the Bible: The Twelve Prophets* (New York: Soncino Press, 1994).

Gordis, Robert. *Koheleth, The Man and His World, A Study of Ecclesiastes*. New York: Schocken Books, 1968.

Graham, Billy. *The Holy Spirit*. Waco: Word, 1978.

Gray, James M. *The Fundamentals*. Ed. Torrey, R. A. and A. C. Dixon. Grand Rapids: Baker, 1980.

Grudem, Wayne. *Evangelical Feminism & Biblical Truth*. Sisters, OR: Multnomah Publishers, 2004.

Grudem, Wayne. *Systematic Theology*. Grand Rapids: Zondervan, 1994.

Gunkel, Hermann. *Mercer Library of Biblical Studies: Genesis*. Macon, GA: Mercer University Press, 1997.

Hailey, Homer. *The Minor Prophets*. Grand Rapids: Baker, 1972.

Hamilton, Victor P. *The New International Commentary on the Old Testament. Genesis Chapters 1-17*. Grand Rapids: Eerdmans, 1990.

Hamilton, Victor P. *The New International Commentary on the Old Testament*. Genesis Chapters 18-50. Grand Rapids: Eerdmans, 1990.

Harkavy, Alexander. *The Twenty-Four Books of the Old Testament*. 2 vols. New York: Hebrew Publishing Co, 1916.

Harris, R. Laird, Gleason L. Archer, Jr., and Bruce K. Waltke, eds., *Theological Wordbook of the Old Testament,* Chicago: Moody, 1981.

Hartman, Fred. *Zechariah: Israel's Messenger of the Messiah's Triumph.* Bellmawr, NJ: Friends of Israel Gospel Ministry, 1994.

Harvey, Richard. "Jesus the Messiah in Messianic Jewish Thought: Emerging Christologies." *Mishkan* (issue 39, 2003): 4-19.

Hasel, Gerhard F. "The Meaning of "Let Us" in Genesis 1:26." *Andrews University Seminary Studies* 13 Spring (1975) 58-66.

Heinze, E. Charles. *Trinity & Triunity*. Dale City, VA: Epaphras Press, 1995.

Henderson, Ebenezer. *Thornapple Commentaries: The Twelve Minor Prophets*. Grand Rapids: Baker, 1980.

Hendren, Noam. "The Divine Unity and the Deity of Messiah." *Mishkan* (issue 39, 2003): 36-47.

Hengstenberg, E. W. *Christology of the Old Testament*. 4 vols. Grand Rapids: Kregel, 1956.

Hertz, J. H. *Pentateuch and Haftorahs*. London: Soncino Press, 1952.

Heydt, Henry J. *Studies in Jewish Evangelism*. New York: American Board to the Jews, 1951.

BIBLIOGRAPHY

Hildebrandt, Wilf. *An Old Testament Theology of the Spirit of God*. Peabody, MA: Hendrickson, 1995.

Hill, Andrew E. and John H. Walton. *A Survey of the Old Testament*, Grand Rapids: Zondervan, 1991.

Hinson, David F. *Theology of the Old Testament*. London: Society for Promoting Christian Knowledge, 2001.

Hodge, Charles. *Systematic Theology*. 3 vols. Grand Rapids: Eerdmans, 1970.

Hoekema, Anthony A. *The Four Major Cults*. Grand Rapids: Eerdmans, 1963.

Holdcroft, L. Thomas. *The Doctrine of God*. Oakland, CA: Western Book Company, 1978.

House, Paul. *Old Testament Theology*. Downers Grove: InterVarsity, 1998.

Hubbard, David A. and Glenn W. Barker. *Word Biblical Commentary: Genesis 1-15*. 52 vols. Waco, Tex: Word Books, 1987.

Huey, F. B. *Bible Study Commentary: Jeremiah*. Grand Rapids: Zondervan, 1981.

Huey, F. B. *The New American Commentary: Jeremiah, Lamentations*. Nashville: Broadman, 1993.

Jacobs, Louis. *A Jewish Theology*. West Orange, NJ: Behrman House, Inc, 1973.

Jamieson, Robert, A. R. Fausset and David Brown. *A Commentary: Critical Experimental and Practical on the Old and New Testaments*. 6 vols. Grand Rapids: Eerdmans, 1945.

Janzen, J. Gerald. "On the Most Important Word in the *Shema* (Deuteronomy VI 4-5)." *Vetus Testamentum* 37, no. 3 (1987): 280-300.

Jenni, Ernest and Claus Westermann. *Theological Lexicon of Old Testament*, Peabody, MA: Hendrickson, 1997.

Jocz, Jacob. "The Invisibility of God and the Incarnation." *Canadian Journal of Theology* (1958): 179-186.

Johnson, John J. "A New Testament Understanding of the Jewish Rejection of Jesus: Four Theologians on the Salvation of Israel." *Journal of the Evangelical Theological Society* (2000): 229-246.

Johnson, Paul. *A History of the Jews*. New York: HarperCollins, 1987.

Johnston, Patrick and Jason Mandryk. eds. *Operation World*, Waynesboro, GA: Paternoster USA, 2001.

Josephus, Flavius. *Josephus, Complete Works* (trans. William Whiston. Grand Rapids: Kregel, 1978), 436.

Jukes, Andrew. *The Names of God.* Grand Rapids: Kregel, 1980.

Kac, Arthur W. *The Messiahship of Jesus*. Grand Rapids: Baker Book House, 1986.

Kac, Arthur W. *The Spiritual Dilemma of the Jewish People: Its Cause and Cure*. Grand Rapids: Baker, 1983.

Kaiser, Walter C., Jr. *The Communicator's Commentary: Micah – Malachi*. Vol. 21. Waco, TX: Word Books, 1992.

Kaiser, Walter C., Jr. *The Christian and the "Old" Testament*. Pasadena, CA: William Carey Library, 1998.

Kaiser, Walter C., Jr. *The Messiah in the Old Testament*. Grand Rapids: Zondervan, 1995.

Kaiser, Walter C., Jr. *Toward an Old Testament Theology*. Grand Rapids: Zondervan, 1991.

Kaplan, Aryeh. *The Real Messiah? A Jewish Response to Missionaries*. New York: National Conference of Synagogues, 1985.

Keil, C. F. and F. Delitzsch. *Commentary on the Old Testament*. Translated by James Martin. 10 vols. Grand Rapids: Eerdmans, 1973.

BIBLIOGRAPHY

Keiser, Thomas A., "The Divine Plural Contextual Presentation of Plurality in the Godhead." A paper presented March 24, 2006, to Evangelical Theological Society, Southwest Region.

Kelley, Page H.. *Biblical Hebrew: An Introductory Grammar.* Grand Rapids: Eerdmans, 1992.

Kirkpatrick, A. F. *The Book of Psalms.* Cambridge: The University Press, 1914.

Klausner, Joseph. *The Messianic Idea In Israel.* New York: Macmillan, 1955.

Knight, George A. F. *A Christian Theology of the Old Testament* (Carlisle, UK: Paternoster Publishing, 1998),

Kohlenberger, John R., III. *The Interlinear NIV Hebrew-English Old Testament.* Grand Rapids: Zondervan, 1987.

Kohlenberger, John R., III. and James A Swanson. *The Hebrew English Concordance to the Old Testament.* Grand Rapids: Zondervan, 1998.

Laetsch, Theodore. *Commentary on Jeremiah.* St. Louis: Concordia Publishing House, 1952.

Laetsch, Theodore. *The Minor Prophets.* St. Louis: Concordia, 1956.

Lang, G. H. *The Histories and Prophecies of Daniel.* Grand Rapids: Kregel, 1940.

Lange, John Peter. *Lange's Commentary on the Holy Scriptures.* Translated by Philip Schaff. 12 vols. Grand Rapids: Zondervan, 1960.

Leeser, Isaac. *The Twenty-Four Books of the Holy Bible.* New York: Hebrew Publishing Co., 1913.

Leupold, H. C. *Exposition of Genesis.* Grand Rapids: Baker Book House, 1942.

Leupold, H. C. *Exposition of Ecclesiastes.* Columbus, OH: Wartburg Press, 1952.

Leupold, H. C. *Exposition of the Psalms*. Grand Rapids: Baker Book House, 1959.

Livingston, G. Herbert. *The Pentateuch in Its Cultural Environment*. 2nd ed. Grand Rapids: Baker Book House, 1987.

Lockyer, Herbert. *All About the Holy Spirit*. Peabody: Hendrickson, 1995.

Lockyer, Herbert. *All the Divine Names and Titles in the Bible*. Grand Rapids: Zondervan, 1975.

Loewen, Jacob A. "The Names of God in the Old Testament." *The Bible Translator* 35, no. 2 (1984): 201-207.

Longman, Tremper, III. *The New International Commentary on the Old Testament: Ecclesiastes*. Grand Rapids: Eerdmans, 1998.

Macdonald, G. Jeffrey, *Press Republican* (Plattsburgh, NY; September 13, 2002), A7.

McCann, J. Clinton. *Interpretation, A Bible Commentary for Teaching and Preaching: Judges*. Louisville, KY: John Knox Press, 2002.

McCarter, P. Kyle, Jr. *The Anchor Bible: 1 Samuel*. vol. 8. Garden City, NY: Doubleday, 1980.

McConville, J. G. *Apollos Old Testament Commentary: Deuteronomy*. vol. 5. Downers Grove, IL, 2002.

McDowell, Josh. *Evidence That Demands a Verdict*. 2 vols. Nashville: Nelson, 1993.

Maoz, Baruch. *Judaism is not Jewish*. Ross-shire, Great Britain: Christian Focus, 2003.

Mathews, Kenneth. *The New American Commentary: Genesis 1:11:26*. 21 vols. Nashville: Broadman & Holman Publishers, 1996.

Mays, James L. *Interpretation: Psalms*. Louisville: John Knox Press, 1989.

BIBLIOGRAPHY

Merrill, Eugene H. *An Exegetical Commentary: Haggai, Zechariah, Malachi.* Chicago: Moody, 1994.

Merrill, Eugene H. *Kingdom of Priests.* Grand Rapids: Baker, 1987.

Merrill, Eugene H. "Rashi, Nicholas de Lyra, and Christian Exegesis." *Westminster Theological Journal 38*, (Fall 1975): 66-79.

Merrill, Eugene H. *The New American Commentary: Deuteronomy.* 21 vols. Nashville: Broadman & Holman Publishers, 1994.

Miller, H. S. *General Biblical Introduction.* Houghton, NY: Word Bearers, 1960.

Miller, Paul A. *Gramcord.* Vancouver, Wash: Gramcord Institute, 1999, www.gramcord.org.

Miller, Stephen *The New American Commentary: Daniel.* Nashville, Broadman, 2003.

Moeller, Henry R. *The Legacy of Zion.* Grand Rapids: Baker, 1977.

Moore, George Foot. *Intermediaries in Jewish Theology: Memra, Shekinah, Metatron.* Boston: Harvard University Printing Office, 1922.

Morey, Robert. *The Trinity: Evidence and Issues.* Grand Rapids: Word Publishers, 1996.

Morris, Henry M. *The Genesis Record.* Grand Rapids: Baker Book House, 1980.

Morris, Robert. *Anti-Missionary Arguments, The Trinity.* Irvine, CA: HaDavar Messianic Ministries,

Motyer, J. Alec. *The Prophecy of Isaiah.* Downers Grove, IL: InterVarsity, 1993.

Nachman, Moshe ben. *Ramban (Nachmanides), Commentary on the Torah – Genesis.* Translated by Chavel. New York: Shilo Publishing Inc.

Neusner, Jacob. *An Introduction to Judaism*. Louisville: Westminster/John Knox Press, 1991.

Neusner, Jacob and William Scott Green. *Dictionary of Judaism in the Biblical Period*. Peabody, MA: Hendrickson, 1999.

Niehaus, Jeffrey J. *God at Sinai*. Grand Rapids: Zondervan, 1995.

Nixon, Jim. "The Doctrine of the Trinity in the Old Testament." Th.M. thesis., Dallas Theological Seminary, 1974.

Oehler, Gustave Friedrich. *Theology of the Old Testament*. Grand Rapids: Zondervan, 1883.

Ogden, Graham and Lynell Zogbo. *A Handbook On Ecclesiastes*. New York: United Bible Societies, 1997.

Orr, James. *The International Standard Bible Encyclopedia*. 5 vols. Grand Rapids: Eerdmans, 1939.

Owens, John Joseph. *Analytical Key to the Old Testament*. Grand Rapids: Baker Book House, 1989.

Pache, Rene. *The Person and Work of the Holy Spirit*. Chicago: Moody, 1954.

Parkes, James. *The Foundations of Judaism and Christianity*. Chicago: Quadrangle Books, 1960.

Patai, Raphael. *The Messiah Texts*. Detroit: Wayne State University Press, 1979.

Payne, J. Barton. *The Theology of the Older Testament*. Grand Rapids: Zondervan, 1962.

Pfeiffer, Charles F. *Old Testament History*. Grand Rapids: Baker, 1973.

Phillips, John. *Exploring Genesis*. Chicago: Moody, 1980.

Phillips, O. E. *Exploring the Messianic Psalms* (Philadelphia: Hebrew Christian Fellowship, 1967).

BIBLIOGRAPHY

Picker, Chaim. *"Make Us A God!" A Jewish Response to Hebrew Christianity: A Survival Manual for Jews*. New York: iUniverse Press, 2005.

Preuss, Horst Dietrich. *Old Testament Theology*. 2 vols. Translated by Leo G. Perdue. Louisville: Westminster John Knox, 1995.

Pritchard, James B. *The Ancient Near East in Pictures*. Princeton, NJ: Princeton University Press, 1954.

Pryor, Dwight A. "One God and Lord," *Mishkan* (issue 39 2003), 56.

Rendsburg, Gary. "Dual Personal Pronouns and Dual Verbs in Hebrew." *Jewish Quarterly Review* 73, no. 1 (July 1982): 38-58.

Reyburn, William D. and Euan McG. Fry. *A Handbook on Genesis*. New York: United Bible Societies, 1997.

Reymond, Robert L. *Jesus: Divine Messiah*. Ross-shire, Scotland: Mentor Imprint, 2003.

Reznick, Leibel. *The Holy Temple Revisited*. Northvale, NJ: Jason Aronson, Inc, 1993.

Robinson, George. *Essential Judaism*. New York: Pocket Books, 2000.

Root, Gerald. "A Critical Investigation of Deuteronomy 6:4." B.D. thesis., Grace Theological Seminary, 1964.

Rosenthal, Stanley. *One God or Three?* Bellmawr, NJ: Friends of Israel Gospel Ministry, 1978.

Ross, Allen P. *Creation & Blessing: Genesis*. Grand Rapids: Baker, 1988.

Ross, Allen P. *Introducing Biblical Hebrew*. Grand Rapids: Baker Academics, 2001.

Ryle, Herbert E. *Cambridge Bible, the Book of Genesis*. London: Cambridge University Press, 1914.

Ryrie, Charles Caldwell. *The Holy Spirit*. Chicago: Moody, 1965.

Sacchi, Paolo. *The History of the Second Temple Period*. Sheffield, England: Sheffield Academic Press, 2000.

Sailhamer, John H. *The Expositor's Bible Commentary: Genesis*. 12 vols. Grand Rapids: Zondervan, 1990.

Sailhamer, John H. *The Pentateuch as Narrative: A Biblical-Theological Commentary*. Grand Rapids: Zondervan, 1992.

Sandler, Abe. "God's Chosen People," *The Alliance Life Magazine,* Christian & Missionary Alliance (Vol. 153, issue 2, March/April 2018).

Sarna, Nahum M.. *The JPS Torah Commentary, Genesis*. Philadelphia: The Jewish Publication Society, 1989.

Saucy, Robert L. *The Church in God's Program.* Chicago: Moody, 1972.

Schiffman, Michael. *Return of the Remnant*. Baltimore: Lederer, 1992.

Schneider, Tammi J. *Berit Olam: Judges*. Collegeville, MN: Liturgical Press, 2000.

Schultz, Samuel J. *The Old Testament Speaks*. New York: Harper & Row, 1970.

Schurer, Emil, *A History of the Jewish People in the Time of Jesus Christ.* Peabody, Mass: Hendrickson, Division two, 1890, 2:160-162.

Schurer, Emil. *A History of the Jewish People in the Time of Jesus Christ*. 5 vols. Trans by John Macpherson. Peabody, MA: Hendrickson, 2003.

Scott, J. Julius. *Jewish Backgrounds of the New Testament*. Grand Rapids: Baker Books, 1995.

Shorrosh, Anis A. *Islam Revealed: A Christian Arab's View of Islam*. Nashville: Nelson, 1988.

Showers, Renald. *The Most High God*. West Collingswood, NJ: The Friends of Israel Gospel Ministry, 1982.

BIBLIOGRAPHY

Showers, Renald E. *There Really is a Difference!* Bellmawr, NJ: Friends of Israel Gospel Ministry, 1990.

Showers, Renald. *Those Invisible Spirits Called Angels.* Bellmawr, NJ: Friends of Israel Gospel Ministry, 1997.

Silver, Rabbi Abba Hillel. *A History of Messianic Speculation in Israel.* New York: Macmillan, 1927.

Singer, Isidore. *The Jewish Encyclopedia.* New York: Funk and Wagnalls Co, 1906.

Singer, Tovia . Tovia. *http://www.OutReachJudaism.org/psalm110.html.*

Skinner, John. *The International Critical Commentary: A Critical and Exegetical Commentary on Genesis.* Edinburgh: T & T Clark, 1969.

Sloan, W. W. *Between the Testaments.* Paterson, NJ: Littlefield, Adams & Co, 1964.

Slotki, I. W. *The Soncino Books of the Bible, Isaiah,* New York: The Soncino Press, 1983.

Smith, Henry. *The Religion of Israel.* New York: Charles Scribner's Sons, 1914.

Smith, James. *The Promised Messiah.* Nashville: Thomas Nelson, 1993.

Smith, Payne. *The Handy Commentary, Genesis.* Ed. Charles John Ellicott. London: Cassell & Company, n.d.

Smith, Ralph L. *Old Testament Theology, Its History, Method, and Message.* Nashville: Broadman & Holman, 1993.

Smith, William. *Old Testament History.* Joplin, MO: College Press, 1970.

Soggin, J. Alberto. *The Old Testament Library: Judges.* Translated by John Bowden. Philadelphia: Westminster, 1981.

Speiser, E. A. *The Anchor Bible: Genesis.* Garden City, NY: Doubleday & Company, 1964.

Steinberg, Milton. *Basic Judaism.* New York: Harvest/HBJ Book, 1947.

Stone, Nathan. *Names of God.* Chicago: Moody, 1944.

Strong, Augustus H. *Systematic Theology*, Westwood, NJ: Revell, 1907.

Talbot, Gordon. *A Study of the Book of Genesis.* Harrisburg, PA: Christian Publications, 1981.

Tanenbaum, Marc H. and Marvin R. Wilson, A. James Rudin. *Evangelicals and Jews in Conversation on Scripture, Theology, and History.* Grand Rapids: Baker Book House, 1978.

Taylor, John B. *Ezekiel.* Downers Grove: InterVarsity, 1974

Telchin, Stan. *Messianic Judaism IS NOT Christianity*, Grand Rapids: Chosen Books, 2004

Telchin, Stanley. *Abandon.* Grand Rapids: Baker Book House, 1997.

Tenney, Merrill C. *The Zondervan Pictorial Encyclopedia of the Bible.* 5 vols. Grand Rapids: Zondervan Publishing House, 1975.

Terrien, Samuel. *Critical Eerdmans Commentary: The Psalms.* Grand Rapids: Eerdmans, 2003.

Thiessen, Henry C. *Lectures in Systematic Theology.* Grand Rapids: Eerdmans, 1979.

Thomas, Thomas A. "The Trinity in the Old Testament." Th. M. diss., Dallas Theological Seminary, 1952.

Thompson, J. A.. *The New International Commentary on the Old Testament: The Book of Jeremiah.* Grand Rapids: Eerdmans, 1980.

Torrey, R. A. *The Holy Spirit.* New York: Revell. 1927.

Towner, W. Sibley. *Interpretation: Daniel.* Atlanta: John Knox Press, 1984.

Towner, W. Sibley. *Westminster Bible Companion: Genesis.* Louisville, KY: Westminster John Knox Press, 2001.

BIBLIOGRAPHY

Tregelles, Samuel Prideaux, *Gesenius' Hebrew and Chaldee Lexicon to the Old Testament Scriptures*. Grand Rapids: Eerdmans, 1957.

Turner, Laurence A. *Genesis*. Sheffield, England: Sheffield Academic Press, 2000.

Unger, Merrill F. *Biblical Demonology*. Wheaton: Scripture Press, 1952.

Unger, Merrill F. *Unger's Bible Dictionary*. Chicago: Moody Press; 3rd edition, 1966.

Unger, Merrill F. *Zechariah: Prophet of Messiah's Glory*. Grand Rapids: Zondervan, 1963.

VanGemeren, Willem A. *Dictionary of Old Testament Theology & Exegesis*. Grand Rapids: Zondervan, 1997.

Vine, W. E. *Isaiah*. Grand Rapids: Zondervan, 1946.

Vos, Geerhardus. *Biblical Theology, Old and New Testament*. Grand Rapids: Eerdmans, 1948.

Vriezen, Th. C. *An Outline of Old Testament Theology*. Newton, Mass: Charles T. Branford Company, 1970.

Walvoord, John F. *Daniel: The Key to Prophetic Revelation*. Chicago: Moody, 1971.

Walvoord, John F. *Jesus Christ Our Lord*. Chicago: Moody Press, 1969.

Walvoord, John F. *The Holy Spirit*. Findlay, OH: Dunham Publishing, 1958.

Walvoord, John F. and Roy B. Zuck. *The Bible Knowledge Commentary: Old Testament*. Wheaton: Victor Books, 1985.

Warfield, Benjamin Breckinridge. *Biblical and Theological Studies*. Philadelphia: Presbyterian and Reformed Publishing, 1968.

Waterhouse, Steven W. *Not By Bread Alone: An Outlined Guide to Bible Doctrine*. Amarillo, TX: Westcliff Press, 2000.

Webb, Barry G. *The Message of Isaiah*. Downers Grove, IL: Inter-Varsity, 1996.

Weinfeld, Moshe. *The Anchor Bible: Deuteronomy 1-11*. New York: Doubleday, 1991.

Weiss-Rosmarin, Trude. *Judaism and Christianity, the Differences*. Middle Village: Jonathan David Publishers, Inc, 1997.

Wenham, Gordon. *Word Biblical Commentary: Genesis 16-50.* Waco, Tex: Word, 1987.

Westermann, Claus. *Genesis 1-11: A Continental Commentary*. Translated by John J. Scullion. Minneapolis: Fortress Press, 1994.

Whiston, William. *Josephus' Complete Works*. Grand Rapids: Kregel, 1978.

Wigram, George V. *The Englishman's Hebrew Concordance of the Old Testament*. Peabody, MA: Hendrickson Publishers, 1996.

Wilkin, Robert N. "Toward a Narrow View of Ipsissima Vox." *JOTGES* 14, no 26 (Spring 2001): 3-8.

Wilson, Marvin R. *Our Father Abraham*. Grand Rapids: Eerdmans, 1989.

Wilson, T. Ernest. *The Messianic Psalms*. Neptune, NJ: Loizeaux, 1978.

Wolf, Herbert M. *Interpreting Isaiah*. Grand Rapids: Baker, 1985.

Wolf, Herbert M. *The Expositor's Bible Commentary: Judges*. 12 vol. Grand Rapids: Zondervan, 1992.

Wood, B. G. "Prophecy of Balaam Found In Jordan." *Bible and Spade* 6 (Autumn 1977): 121-124.

Wood, Leon J. *Distressing Days of the Judges*. Grand Rapids: Zondervan, 1975.

Wood, Leon J. *The Holy Spirit in the Old Testament*. Eugene, OR: Wipf and Stock, 1998.

BIBLIOGRAPHY

Young, Edward J. *The Book of Isaiah*. 3 vols. Grand Rapids: Eerdmans, 1972.

Young, Robert. *Analytical Concordance to the Bible* (22nd Edition). Grand Rapids: Eerdmans, n.d.

Youngblood, Ronald. *New Illustrated Bible Dictionary*. Nashville: Thomas Nelson, 1995.

Youngblood, Ronald. *The Book of Genesis*. 2nd ed. Eugene, OR: Wipf and Stock, 1999.

Youngblood, Ronald. *The Expositor's Bible Commentary*. 12 vols. Grand Rapids: Zondervan, 1992.

Youngblood, Ronald. *The Genesis Debate*. Nashville: Nelsons, 1986.

Zimmerli, Walter. *Ezekiel 1*. Philadelphia: Fortress, 1979.

Zlotowitz, Meir. *The Family Chumash Bereishis: Genesis*. Brooklyn: Mesorah Press, 1986.

AUTHOR INDEX

Albertz, Rainier 233, 234
Alden, Robert L. 81
Alexander, Ralph H. 205, 367
Alexander, T. Desmond 13, 30, 36, 51, 53, 56, 58, 62, 82, 91, 103, 104, 185, 367
Anderson, Sir Robert 255, 367
Ankerberg, John 39, 367
Archer, Gleason L., Jr. ... 12, 23, 24, 26, 50, 51, 52, 55, 57, 61, 70, 80, 81, 97, 116, 119, 121, 122, 130, 179, 222, 225, 226, 227, 236, 265, 276, 335, 336, 374
Atkinson, Basil R. C. 29, 367
Baker, Charles F. 77, 78, 367
Baker, David W. 13, 30, 36, 51, 53, 56, 58, 62, 82, 91, 103, 104, 185, 367
Bancroft, Emery H. 72, 367
Banks, William A. 160, 368
Barackman, Floyd H. 29, 45, 56, 72, 77, 81, 171, 172, 209, 211, 212, 213, 367
Barber, Cyril J. 200, 367
Barker, Glenn W. 141, 375
Barker, Kenneth L. ... 239, 240, 241, 367
Barnes, Albert 243, 367
Baron, David ... 165, 167, 268, 269, 270, 271, 368
Barrett, Michael P. V. 269, 274, 278, 281, 282, 283, 368
Beale, Todd S. 160, 368
Benach, Henry 132, 368
Bergen, Robert D. 201, 202, 368

Berger, David 7, 368
Berkhof, L. 11, 29, 72, 171, 173, 368
Berlin, Adele 59, 98, 163, 169, 308, 368
Block, Daniel I. 195, 196, 197, 368
Botterweck, G. Johannes..... 25, 53, 81, 82, 104, 116, 118, 122, 220, 222, 225, 233, 234, 235, 335, 368
Brettler, Marc Zvi 59, 98, 163, 169, 308, 368
Briggs, C. A. 371
Briggs, Charles A. 43, 130, 131, 166, 220, 226, 227, 236, 368
Briscoe, Stuart 65, 151, 368
Bromiley, Geoffrey W. 89, 101, 221, 252, 368
Brown, David ... 135, 162, 163, 375
Brown, Francis .. 43, 130, 131, 220, 226, 227, 236, 368
Brown, Michael L. ... 129, 132, 166, 250, 255, 256, 269, 272, 273, 369
Brueggemann, Walter 12, 369
Buksbazen, Victor ... 165, 267, 268, 369
Buswell, James Oliver 72, 99, 287, 369
Butler, J. Glentworth .. 53, 195, 369
Buttrick, George Arthur ... 126, 369
Campus Crusade for Christ 103, 369
Cassuto, U. 138, 139, 369
Chafer, Lewis Sperry 8, 83, 91,

92, 100, 127, 128, 132, 369
Charles, R. H. 254, 369
Charnock, Steven 224, 225, 369
Cohen, A. ... 74, 233, 308, 369, 370
Cooke, G. A. 151, 207, 370
Cooper, David L. 16, 17, 63, 69, 73, 74, 75, 76, 79, 86, 129, 130, 132, 161, 162, 181, 188, 189, 190, 370
Cooper, Lamar Eugene 205, 370
Craigie, P. C. 123, 370
Crenshaw, James 163, 370
Criswell, W. A. 132, 370
Dahood, Mitchell 164, 370
Davidson, A. B. 150, 370
Davidson, Robert 245, 246, 370
Delitzsch, F. 54, 147, 159, 164, 167, 197, 245, 251, 377
Dickason, C. Fred 229, 370
Dockery, David S. 5, 6, 371
Driver, S. R. 43, 130, 131, 147, 149, 150, 157, 158, 220, 226, 227, 236, 368, 371
Dyrness, William 79, 179, 371
Ellicott, Charles John 153
Elwell, Walter A. 83, 89, 104, 177, 371
Enns, Paul 1, 83, 89, 109, 117, 123, 183, 195, 204, 207, 213, 218, 371
Erickson, Millard J. 17, 72, 113, 176, 177, 178, 184, 195, 285, 371
Evans, William 371
Fabry, Heinz-Josef .. 25, 53, 81, 82, 104, 116, 118, 122, 220, 222, 225, 233, 234, 235, 335, 368
Fausset, A. R. 135, 162, 163, 375
Feinberg, Charles L. 26, 98, 167, 205, 242, 246, 247, 257, 260, 262, 265, 269, 271, 371

Feinberg, John S. 176, 190, 192, 372
Fischer, John 4, 10, 372
Flavius, Josephus 376
Frame, John M. 42, 44, 372
Free, Joseph P. 233, 372
Friedman, Richard Elliott. 308, 372
Fruchtenbaum, Arnold G. .. ix, 1, 8, 9, 26, 59, 61, 64, 70, 71, 81, 85, 86, 101, 128, 132, 147, 148, 156, 160, 162, 166, 217, 222, 223, 224, 225, 227, 230, 235, 245, 247, 248, 251, 253, 256, 257, 258, 259, 260, 261, 265, 266, 268, 269, 372
Frydland, Rachmiel.. 256, 268, 372
Fuchs, Daniel 8, 373
Fuller, Reginald H. 124, 125, 373
Garstang, John.................. 197, 373
Geisler, Norman L. ... 49, 133, 134, 207, 208, 210, 212, 252, 373
Goldberg, Louis 5, 40, 41, 128, 132, 134, 176, 373
Goldengay, John E. 255, 373
Goldman, S. 373
Gordis, Robert 163, 373
Graham, Billy 187, 373
Gray, James M. 208, 209, 373
Green, William Scott 19, 81, 82, 145, 380
Grudem, Wayne 37, 38, 65, 71, 72, 86, 197, 374
Gunkel, Hermann 149, 184, 374
Hailey, Homer 243, 374
Hamilton, Victor P. .. 137, 148, 149, 151, 152, 153, 158, 159, 374
Harkavy, Alexander 59, 79, 161, 308, 374
Harris, R. Laird . 12, 23, 24, 26, 50, 51, 52, 55, 57, 58, 61, 70, 80, 81, 97, 116, 119, 121, 122, 130,

SCRIPTURE INDEX

179, 222, 225, 226, 227, 236, 265, 276, 335, 336, 374
Hartman, Fred 269, 374
Harvey, Richard 3, 374
Hasel, Gerhard F. 145, 146, 374
Heinze, E. Charles......... 30, 31, 374
Henderson, Ebenezer 167, 242, 243, 374
Hendren, Noam 56, 131, 374
Hengstenberg, E. W. . 99, 167, 240, 374
Hertz, J. H. 151, 152, 157, 308, 375
Heydt, Henry J. 128, 132, 375
Hildebrandt, Wilf 176, 178, 185, 193, 195, 199, 200, 203, 375
Hill, Andrew E. 2, 236, 375
Hinson, David F. ... 11, 12, 124, 375
Hodge, Charles............. 11, 72, 375
Hoekema, Anthony A. . 24, 34, 375
Holdcroft, L. Thomas....... 225, 375
House, Paul 11, 125, 375
Hubbard, David A. 141, 375
Huey, F. B. 246, 375
Jacobs, Louis..... 9, 60, 61, 79, 112, 219, 375
Jamieson, Robert..... 135, 162, 163, 375
Jamieson, Robert A. 135
Janzen, J. Gerald 119, 375
Jenni, Ernest.... 28, 53, 57, 81, 118, 123, 160, 226, 234, 235, 367, 376
Jocz, Jacob 1, 2, 376
Johnson, John J. 8, 376
Johnson, Paul 115, 376
Johnston, Patrick 21, 376
Jukes, Andrew.................... 12, 376
Kac, Arthur W. 3, 103, 139, 219, 357, 359, 360, 361, 362, 363, 364, 365, 366, 376

Kaiser, Walter C. 192
Kaiser, Walter C., Jr. . 86, 165, 167, 172, 173, 204, 243, 269, 273, 274, 275, 276, 277, 278, 376
Kaplan, Aryeh 46, 377
Keil, C. F. ... 54, 159, 164, 167, 197, 245, 251, 377
Keiser, Thomas A. . . 32, 35, 37, 377
Kelley, Page H. 70, 71, 377
Kirkpatrick, A. F. 182, 377
Klausner, Joseph 219, 377
Knight, George A. F. 65, 69, 377
Kohlenberger, John R., III .. 43, 51, 130, 136, 159, 161, 162, 276, 377
Laetsch, Theodore... 167, 242, 245, 246, 247, 377
Lang, G. H. 257, 260, 261, 265, 377
Lange, John Peter..... 160, 162, 377
Leeser, Isaac..................... 309, 377
Leupold, H. C. 54, 139, 162, 226, 378
Livingston, G. Herbert 150, 378
Lockyer, Herbert 12, 54, 183, 194, 195, 378
Loewen, Jacob A.............. 137, 378
Longman, Tremper, III ... 162, 163, 378
Macdonald, G. Jeffrey.......... 8, 378
Mandryk, Jason................. 21, 376
Maoz, Baruch................... 335, 378
Mathews, Kenneth A. . . 36, 60, 137, 138, 139, 140, 228, 379
Matties, Gordon H. 236
Mays, James L. 379
McCann, J. Clinton 197, 378
McCarter, P. Kyle 201, 378
McConville, J. G. 117, 118, 378
McDowell, Josh 279, 378

Merrill, Eugene H. .. 123, 133, 141, 148, 167, 168, 252, 269, 274, 275, 379
Miller, H. S. 15, 379
Miller, Paul A.... 43, 137, 159, 162, 379
Miller, Stephen........ 259, 260, 261, 262, 265, 379
Moeller, Henry R. 107, 379
Moore, George Foot........... 41, 379
Morey, Robert ... 14, 15, 89, 90, 91, 93, 95, 129, 130, 180, 181, 182, 183, 184, 195, 379
Morris, Henry .. 138, 139, 141, 144, 379
Morris, Robert......................... 379
Motyer, J. Alec................. 204, 379
Nachman, Moshe ben....... 153, 154, 380
Neusner, Jacob .. 5, 19, 81, 82, 145, 380
Niehaus, Jeffrey J......... 79, 80, 102, 104, 105, 106, 380
Nix, William E. 208, 373
Nixon, Jim........................ 128, 380
Oehler, Gustave Friedrich .. 50, 380
Ogden, Graham S..... 162, 163, 380
Orr, James 102, 380
Owens, John Joseph........ 136, 137, 160, 164, 380
Pache, Rene..... 184, 190, 217, 218, 380
Parkes, James 286, 380
Patai, Raphael . 236, 237, 238, 240, 380
Payne, J. Barton 12, 13, 51, 57, 62, 79, 99, 100, 118, 119, 182, 188, 194, 380
Pfeiffer, Charles F. 107, 380
Phillips, John.......... 25, 26, 27, 380
Phillips, O. E. ... 250, 251, 252, 381

Picker, Chaim..................... 46, 381
Plummer, A. 371
Preuss, Horst Dietrich .. 51, 62, 381
Pritchard, James B. 252, 381
Pryor, Dwight A... 10, 11, 115, 381
Rendsburg, Gary 76, 381
Reyburn, William D......... 152, 157, 158, 381
Reymond, Robert L............ 92, 381
Reznick, Leibel 8, 381
Ringgren, Helmer.... 25, 53, 81, 82, 104, 116, 118, 122, 220, 222, 225, 233, 234, 235, 335, 368
Robinson, George 4, 131, 255, 381
Root, Gerald..... 112, 126, 127, 381
Rosenthal, Stanley..... 64, 128, 132, 381
Ross, Allen P............. 75, 185, 381
Rudin, A. James 384
Ryle, Herbert E. 148, 149, 151, 152, 382
Ryrie, Charles Caldwell .. 182, 190, 191, 215, 382
Sacchi, Paolo................... 107, 382
Sailhamer, John H... 33, 34, 35, 36, 75, 382
Sandler, Abe...................... 21, 382
Sarna, Nahum M. 57, 382
Saucy, Robert L. 6, 382
Schiffman, Michael. 10, 58, 73, 74, 382
Schneider. Tammi J. 197, 199, 382
Schultz, Samuel J............... 51, 382
Schurer, Emil 5, 107, 382
Scott, J. Julius 4, 382
Scott, Jack B....... 56, 58, 69, 70, 80
Shorrosh, Anis A............... 77, 382
Showers, Renald E. ... 63, 229, 258, 260, 261, 262, 265, 383
Silver, Rabbi Abba Hillel. 264, 383

Singer, Isidore .. 101, 106, 107, 383
Singer, Tovia 249, 250, 383
Skinner, John 29, 383
Sloan, W. W. 107, 383
Slotki, I. W. 147, 166, 169, 170, 172, 383
Smith, Colin 160, 368
Smith, Henry 65, 383
Smith, James 6, 51, 167, 168, 220, 252, 256, 263, 383
Smith, Payne 153, 383
Smith, Ralph L. 118, 383
Smith, William 252, 383
Soggin, J. Alberto 197, 383
Speiser, E. A. ... 142, 143, 158, 384
Steinberg, Milton 114, 384
Stone, Nathan 12, 65, 82, 384
Strong, Augustus H. 72, 171, 384
Talbot, Gordon 31, 32, 384
Tanenbaum, Marc H. 4, 384
Taylor, John B. 205, 384
Telchin, Stan 115, 289, 335, 384
Tenney, Merrill C. 89, 90, 100, 214, 384
Terrien, Samuel 251, 384
Thiessen, Henry C. 80, 213, 384
Thomas, A. Keiser 33
Thomas, Thomas A. 127, 384
Thompson, J. A. 384
Torrey, R. A. 186, 187, 384
Towner, W. Sibley 66, 137, 138, 184, 185, 254, 255, 384, 385
Tregelles, Samuel Prideaux 54, 385
Turner, Laurence A. 152, 385
Unger, Merrill F. 102, 167, 229, 269, 274, 276, 385
VanGemeren, Willem A. 12, 23, 24, 25, 27, 28, 55, 56, 101, 117, 120, 121, 123, 178, 180, 191, 225, 236, 251, 263, 335, 385

Vine, W. E. 96, 164, 170, 171, 173, 385
Vos, Geerhardus 224, 385
Vos, Howard F. 233, 372
Vriezen, Th. C. 385
Waltke, Bruce K. 12, 23, 24, 26, 50, 51, 52, 55, 57, 58, 61, 70, 80, 81, 97, 116, 119, 121, 122, 130, 179, 222, 225, 226, 227, 236, 265, 276, 335, 336, 374
Walton, John H. 2, 375
Walvoord, John F. 108, 181, 186, 191, 192, 195, 196, 199, 200, 203, 207, 213, 214, 215, 246, 257, 258, 265, 385
Warfield, Benjamin Breckinridge .. 6, 73, 385
Waterhouse, Steven W. 211, 212, 386
Webb, Barry G. 170, 226, 386
Weinfeld, Moshe 160, 386
Weiss-Rosmarin, Trude 84, 85, 112, 113, 114, 386
Weldon, John 39, 367
Wenham, Gordon 157, 386
Westermann, Claus 28, 53, 57, 81, 118, 123, 149, 151, 152, 158, 160, 226, 234, 235, 367, 376, 386
Whiston, William 107, 376, 386
Wigram, George V. 54, 386
Wilkin, Robert N. 334, 386
Wilson, Marvin R. 4, 125, 285, 384, 386
Wilson, T. Ernest 253, 254, 386
Wolf, Herbert M. 116, 121, 122, 166, 170, 197, 204, 226, 386
Wood, B. G. 13, 386
Wood, Leon J. .. 175, 178, 185, 186, 191, 194, 195, 199, 201, 386, 387

Young, Edward J..... 165, 166, 169, 171, 173, 226, 387
Young, Robert..... 57, 58, 220, 263, 387
Youngblood, Ronald... 61, 62, 139, 140, 141, 154, 155, 156, 202, 203, 387

Zimmerli, Walter.............. 133, 387
Zlotowitz, Meir 185, 387
Zogbo, Lynell........... 162, 163, 380
Zuck, Roy B.... 196, 199, 200, 246, 385

SCRIPTURE INDEX

Also see tables in Appendices 2 and 3 for additional references specific to *echad* in the Torah and *The Word*, respectively.

Genesis
1 ...... 21, 27, 32, 37, 49, 61, 66, 67, 73, 75, 102, 135, 138, 139, 153, 154, 155, 165, 169, 171
1, 2 30
1:1 .... 30, 31, 61, 77, 137, 172, 184, 186, 282
1:1 – 2:3 .... 57, 135
1:1, 27 58
1:1-3 62
1:2 .... 180, 184, 185
1:2, 26 .... 80, 187
1:3 212
1:3, 6, 9, 11, 14, 20, 24 27
1:3, 6, 9, 14, 20 137
1:5 .... 117, 125, 127, 131
1:26 ...... 20, 23, 25, 27, 28, 29, 32, 34, 35, 47, 66, 69, 77, 135, 136, 137, 138, 140, 141, 142, 145, 146, 148, 149, 150, 151, 152, 153, 163, 172
1:26, 27 34
1:26-27 .... 27, 28, 33, 34
1:27 .... 30, 32, 33, 34, 35
1:28 36
1:29 58
2:3 135
2:3-4 58
2:4 82
2:4-5 57
2:7 .... 24, 30, 187
2:8-9, 15 58
2:16 .... 30, 58
2:17 30
2:24 .... 34, 64, 117, 119, 125, 126, 127, 131
2:27 30
3 .... 77, 102, 261
3:1, 3 58
3:5 .... 77, 78
3:8 .... 40, 58, 91, 102, 179
3:15 .... 228, 229, 267, 272, 279
3:21 39
3:22 ...... 66, 69, 77, 135, 136, 140, 141, 142, 145, 146, 148, 149, 151, 172
4:1 .... 34, 229
4:25 58
5 28
5:1 .... 33, 58
5:1-02a 33
5:1-3 .... 25, 28, 33, 34
5:2 35
5:24 58
6 102
6:3 .... 176, 218
6:6 181
6:13 .... 102, 236
6:17 179
6:19 35
6:22 58
7:3, 9, 16 35
7:9-16 58
8:15 58

8:21	40	20:1, 17	158
9	28	20:3	90
9:6	23, 28, 33, 45	20:13	20, 72, 76, 156, 157, 158, 160, 165
9:8, 12, 17	58	21:2	58
9:11	265	21:4, 12	58
9:16	58	21:15	120
9:27	58, 101, 102	21:17	58
11:1	119, 144	21:33	83, 84
11:3	143	22	92, 94
11:3-4	143	22:1	94
11:4	143	22:1-2	94
11:6	126	22:1-19	94
11:7	66, 69, 135, 136, 142, 144, 145, 146, 151, 152, 172	22:2, 12, 16	128
12	95	22:8	58, 288
12, 13, 15, 17, 22	227	22:11	95
12:1-3	7	22:11-12	94
14:18	52	22:12	95
14:18-20, 22	52	22:14	83
15	91, 95, 103, 169	22:15-16	94, 95
15:1	90	22:16	95
15:2, 8	81	26:35	179
15:4-5, 18	227	28:4	58
15:9-18	102	28:12	158
15:12-18	103	30:17, 22	58
16:3	51	30:18, 20	58
16:7, 13	98	31:1, 11	58
16:7-14	12	31:7, 9, 16	58
16:13-14	52	31:10	90
17:1	52	31:11-13	98
17:3, 23	58	31:16, 24	58
17:9	58	31:29	57
17:9, 16	58	32:24-30	85, 98, 99
18	5, 58, 84, 85, 91, 98, 108	33:13	121
18:9	84	34:22	120
18:12	251	35:7	20, 72, 76, 147, 156, 158, 165
18-19	84	35:7, 2	158
19:1	84	35:11	52
19:2	251	35:15	58
19:13-23	84	37:5	90
19:24	12, 18, 84, 85, 97, 167		

43:3 184
45:5, 7 58
45:8-9 81
45:27 179
46:2 58
49:10 ....7, 264
50:20 58

Exodus
1:20 58
2:24 58
3 ....91, 103, 108
3:2 103
3:4-5 99
3:7 364
3:13-15 82
3:14 ....82, 171
3:15 82
6:3 82
6:9 179
8:19 107
10:13 179
12:13 301
12:21-23 294
13:21-22 103
14:9 99
14:13 223
14:19 103
15:3 248
15:11 53
15:18 226
15:26 8
17:12 120
17:15 83
18:11 13
18:23 58
19:16-20 104
20:1 209
20:2 ....84, 361
20:2-3 ....17, 61
20:3 61
20:3-4 23

20:4 25
21:5-6 78
21:6 ....78, 223
21:16 222
21:32 ....167, 168, 271
22:8, 9, 28 78
23:17 81
23:20-23 ....91, 96, 106, 173
23:23 ....19, 104
23:29 121
24:3 ....119, 126
24:3-7 ....210, 212
24:4 ....208, 209
24:9-11 ....23, 89
24:11 363
24:16 104
25:9 25
25:19 120
25:22 363
25:36 120
27:20 224
28:3 192
28:43 224
29:28 224
29:45 363
30:21 224
31:2-3 ....192, 201
31:3 191
31:13 83
31:18 107
32:15-16 107
32:16 209
32:34 ....96, 97, 104
33:2-3 ....95, 96, 97
33:3 104
33:14-16 97
33:17-23 30
34:1 107
34:23 ....57, 251
35:6-7 55
35:30-31 134

35:31	191, 192
40:15	224
40:17	121, 307
40:34	101
40:34-35	104
40:36-38	103

Leviticus

1:1	212
4:1	212
4:3, 4	220
4:5	263
5:14	212
6:1, 8, 19	212
6:2	277
6:18	224
6:22	263
7:20, 21, 25, 27	265
7:22	212
7:34, 36	224
9:23 – 10:2	91
9:23-24	105
10:1-2	104
10:9	224
10:15	224
12:8	120
16:15-19	295
16:34	224
17:11	294, 301
18:20	277
19:2	83, 84
19:15	277
20:26	84
21:8	84
23:18	121
24:3	224
24:8	224
25:46	223
26:40-42	262, 302
27:34	209

Numbers

6:11	121
7:11-82	121
7:13-82	121
10:8	224
11:1-2	91, 105
11:12	44
11:12a	43
11:17	182, 193
11:23	40
11:31	179
12:2	91
12:2-5	105
12:5-8	7, 63, 213
12:6	90
12:6-8	58
12:13	52
13:23	119, 125, 127
14:10	105
14:11	105
14:15	120
14:23	105
14:27, 35	105
15:15	224
16:1-40	105
16:40	252
16:42, 49	105
18:7	252
18:8, 11, 19	224
18:23	224
19:10	224
20:16	99
21:4	181
22:6	194
22:7-13	13
22:8-35	194
23:5	194
23:19	52
23:22	52
24:2	194
24:2, 4	202

25:8	274
25:13	224
27:175	42
27:18	194
29:1-38	121
33:52	23
33:56	25
36:13	209

Deuteronomy

4:12	104
4:23-40	300
4:24	84
4:26	154
4:31	52
5:7	118
5:8	25
5:9	83, 84, 122
5:10	116, 122
5:22	104
5:23	160
6:4	1, 4, 9, 11, 15, 16, 19, 61, 77, 84, 100, 111, 116, 117, 119, 120, 121, 122, 123, 125, 126, 127, 128, 129, 131, 132, 133, 134, 144, 169, 307, 308
6:4-5	119
6:4-9	111
6:5	119, 122
7:7-8	293
7:9	52
8:3	40
8:19	184
9:10	107
10:12-17	301
10:17	81, 161, 251
10:17-18	58
11:12	40
13:2	61
15:17	222, 223
17:6	121
18:5	224
18:15-18	238, 292
18:15-19	7
18:16	104
18:18	211, 212
20:20	265
21:15	121
23:3	223
23:4	194
28	300
28 – 30	227
28:1-14	8
28:15	8
28:15-68	2
28:16-68	8
30	227
30:6	14, 302
30:19	154
31:9, 24	209
31:28	154
32	42
32:11	185, 187
32:12	116
32:15-17	55
32:18	43, 52
33:27	363
34:9	134, 194
34:10	58, 211

Joshua

3:10	160
3:11, 13	81
4:2	121
5	91
5:13-15	85, 91
5:14-15	98, 99
5:15	19
7:7	81
10:24	252
10:42	120
12:9-24	121
22:22	52, 74, 75
23:14-16	299

24:14-15	80
24:19	15, 161, 162, 165
24:26	209
24:26-27	209

Judges

2	80
2:1	12, 92, 95, 96, 97, 99, 102, 169
2:11	81
3, 6, 11, 13-15	190
3:9b-10	195
6:8	95
6:11-24	99
6:12	196
6:13	196
6:14	196
6:17	196
6:24	83, 196
6:34	196
6:36	196
7:13	90
8:3	179
9:23	180
9:45	274
9:53	121
10:16	181, 364
11:29	197
11:34	130
13:2-24	99
13:25	198
14:6	198
14:6, 19	198
14:19	198
15:14-15	198
15:19	179
16:16	181
16:29	120
19:26-27	81
20:1	119, 127
20:5	25

Ruth

1:22	76
2:13	251

1 Samuel 210

1:2	121
1:3	83
1:15	251
1:22	223
2:2	42
2:10, 35	263
2:35	220, 223
3:18	209
6:5	23
6:5, 11	23
10	190
10, 11, 16	199
10:6	199
10:10	200
11:6	134, 200
11:07b	120
12:3, 5	220, 263
16	201, 202
16:6	263
16:13	134
16:13-14	201
16:14	134, 191, 201
16:14-16	180
17:26	162, 165
17:36	160
17:51	265
18:10	180
19:9	180
20:23	223
24:6, 10	263
26:8	121
26:9, 11, 23	263
29:8	81
30:12	179
31:4	274

2 Samuel 230

1:14, 16, 21	263

SCRIPTURE INDEX

7:10-14 20
7:11-16 .... 228, 229, 230
7:23 .... 20, 63, 64, 72, 156, 159, 160, 165
12:1 120
12:3 121
19:1-2 181
19:21 263
21:5 25
22:2-3, 32, 47 42
22:47 160
22:51 263
23:1 263
23:1-2 .... 183, 211
23:2 212
23:2-3 .... 203, 215
23:2-03a 202
24:14 152
24:16 92

1 Kings 210
1:31 222
2:16 121
2:19 251
3:25 121
4:30-31 231
8:10-11 106
8:46 297
9:3 106
11:13 121
15:13 87
18:9-18 91
18:20-40 91
18:45 179
19:12 91
21:5 179
22 149
22:13b 120
22:19 .... 138, 147, 148

2 Kings
3:17 179
6:5 121
8:26 121
11:18 23
16:10 25
17:10 87
19:4, 16 160
19:3 99
21 244
23:26-27 244
23:29 275
23:30 – 25:30 244
24:3-4 244

1 Chronicles 230, 232
3:21f 101
7 284
10:4 274
15:2 224
16:22 263
17:10-14 .... 7, 230
17:10b-14 230
17:11-14 .... 20, 228, 232
17:19-14 229
19:1 121
23:13 224
28:4 223
28:9 226
28:12 180

2 Chronicles
3:17 121
4:3 25
5:13 120
6:42 263
7:1 106
15:1 201
17:16 223
18:7 121
19:3 87
23:17 23
24:20 201
26:16-21 249
30:12 120
33:19 87

Reference	Page
34:14	212
34:14-28	2
34:23-25	244
35:25	275
36	244

Ezra

Reference	Page
3:1	119
4:15	222
4:19	222
6:21-22	54

Nehemiah

Reference	Page
1:6	68
2:3	222
8:1	120
8:8	210
8:9	348
8:12	348
8:13	348
8:14	348
9:20	188
9:30	183
10:34	348
10:36	348
8:1-8	335

Job

Reference	Page
1	138
1:6	148
1:38	149
2	138
12:10	179
15:14-16	298
17:1	179
19:17	179
19:25-26	303
20:4	226
21:4	179
22:15	222
26:13	182, 186, 187
33:4	180, 182, 183, 187
41:16	178

Psalms

Reference	Page
2:2	263
2:7	133, 138
2:7-12	292
2:12	295
8:3	107
8:5-8 [6-9]	28
12:6	42
14:1-3	297
14:3	293
16:10	296
18:47	160
18:51	263
19:1	186, 187
19:7[8]	11
20:6	263
21:1	248
22	7, 215
22:1	52
22:16	279
22:20	130
25:6	243
28:8	263
29:1	53
33:6	186
37:9	265
41:9[10]	215, 279
42:3	160
45:6-7[7-8]	18, 71
45:7	138
48:7[8]	179
48:10[9]	25
49:7	300
49:16	303
50:7	183
50:21	25
51:5	293
51:11[13]	180, 191, 202, 203
51:13	295
51:15	303
53:2-3	297

SCRIPTURE INDEX

58:4 25
58:11 .... 20, 72, 156, 158
58:11[12] 72, 159
68:6 130
68:18 [19] 57
68:31 58
68:35 52
69:23 59
77:20 42
80:1, 15-17 262
80:17 288
81:8 183
82 208
82:6 .... 49, 211
89 .... 231, 232
89:3-4[4-5] 231
89:6[7] 53
89:7[6] 25
89:9 .... 220, 263
89:29[30] 231
89:34-37[35-38] 231
89:38 263
89:51[52] 231, 263
90:2 .... 52, 221, 242, 243
95:9-11 216
96:5 75
97:7 79
101:1 232
102:7[6] 25
104:29 180
104:30 182
105:15 263
110 .... 215, 249, 250, 253
110:1 ...... 138, 214, 215, 238, 250,
                   251, 253, 284, 291
110:1-7 .... 249, 253
110:4 253
110:41 232
111:7 40
118:22 288
118:26 .... 246, 262

119:89 226
130:3 298
132:10 263
136:26 52
138:1 78
139:7 176
139:7-10 183
143:10 188
144:4 25
146:5 52
149:2 .... 15, 164

Proverbs
1:14 120
8:22-23 242
14:29 179
17:3 42
19:11 179
19:21 248
20:9 300
30:4 292
31:10-31 38

Ecclesiastes
7:20 .... 294, 297
12:1 .... 15, 20, 162, 165, 186

Isaiah 210
1:1-2 209
1:9 25
1:15 41
1:26 261
4:2 247
5 42
6 .... 91, 106
6:1 90
6:1-3 106
6:1-6 148
6:1-10 213
6:3 .... 83, 145
6:4 145
6:5 .... 41, 145
6:6 69

6:8	..66, 135, 136, 138, 145, 146, 147, 149, 152, 172
6:9-10	215
6:10	303
7	266
7 – 12	168, 265
7:2	179
7:12	266
7:13-14	65
7:14	265, 296
8:1	208
8:8, 10	265, 266
8:11, 20	211
9	233, 284
9:5-6	7, 297
9:6	233, 235, 239
9:6-7	..20, 52, 228, 232, 239, 258, 265, 266
9:7	235, 239, 266
10	235
10:7	25
10:21	235
11:1	266
11:1-2	247, 266
11:2	173, 218, 266
11:2-5	261
13:4	25
13:15	274
13:17	81
14:12	229
14:24	25
19:3	179
25:4	178, 179
25:8	81, 303
26:3	297
26:19	304
29:24	180
30:8	208
32:17	261
36:18-20	17
37:4, 17	160
38:5	41
38:16	179
40:3	279
40:12-14	186
40:13	154
40:18	25
40:18, 25	25
41:4	84
42	168, 267, 287
42:1	173, 218, 284
42:5	179
42:8	96
42:14	44
42:17	165
43:7	248
44	81
44:3	204, 217
44:6	1, 84, 87, 167
45:1	263
45:5, 14, 18, 21	84
45:15	52
45:17	226, 260
45:18	58
46:5	25
48:9	173
48:10, 14	174
48:11	96
48:12	84
48:12-13	169
48:12-16	168, 169, 258
48:13	186
48:13, 16	272
48:16	77, 108, 138, 169, 170, 171, 172, 173, 182, 189, 218, 284
48:16c	170
49	168, 267
49:1-6	165
50	168, 267
50:1	166
50:1-6	165

SCRIPTURE INDEX

50:1-7 258
50:01a, 4-6 266
50:4 166
50:4-9 165
50:5-6 166
50:6 166
51:6-8 260
52:12 268
52:13 – 53:12 .... 267, 353, 354
52:13-15 354
53 .... 9, 132, 168, 262, 267, 268, 269, 292, 364
53:2 67
53:2-7 268
53:3 67
53:4 67
53:5 67
53:5-6 296
53:6 .... 293, 297
53:7 279
53:10 .... 7, 272, 278
53:13-15 353
54 .... 168, 268
54:1-6 354
54:1-7 353
54:4-5 165
54:5 .... 15, 42, 58, 164
54:5 – 53:12 165
54:7-12 .... 354, 355
54:13 – 53:12 258
59:1-2 .... 293, 297
59:2 298
59:16, 20 301
59:20 258
59:21 .... 204, 211, 212, 217
60 .... 225, 226
60 – 66 168
60:13 41
61 189
61:1 . 168, 172, 173, 189, 218, 266
61:1-02a 172

63 .... 189, 190
63:7 173
63:7-10 173
63:7-10, 14 189
63:7-14 .... 168, 173, 284
63:9 .... 97, 364
63:9, 10 172
63:10 .... 181, 204, 218
63:10-11 180
63:16 235
64:5-6 297
64:6 .... 294, 298
64:8 42
68:8-10 181

Jeremiah
1:1-2 209
1:9 211
2:5 – 3:10 2
2:5, 11 84
2:22 300
3:11-18 262
4:4 302
5 299
6:9, 10 302
6:19-20 299
9:25 302
9:25-26 14
10:10 160
11:8 2
11:19 265
15:4 244
15:16 211
17:9 .... 293, 298
18 - 19 42
18:17 179
18:20 294
22 .... 232, 244
22:24-30 .... 231, 245, 246
23 244
23:1 246
23:5 .... 245, 247, 248

23:5-6 ......21, 244, 245, 248, 261, 266, 284
23:6 ....83, 247, 248
23:36 160
26:2 210
30:1-10 2
30:2 211
30:9 245
31 ....204, 216, 217, 262
31:27, 29, 31 246
31:27-34 245
31:30 298
31:31 246
31:31-34 ....204, 260, 280
31:31-37 204
31:33 216
32 235
32:18 235
32:39 120
33:14-16 260
33:15-18 261
34:1 212
37:10 274
49:36 179
51:1 274

Lamentations
2:13 25
2:17 350
3:38 350
4:9 274
4:20 263

Ezekiel
1 ....91, 106
1:1 90
1:3 209
1:5, 10, 13, 16, 22, 26, 28 25
1:26 205
1:26a 206
2:2 ....184, 204, 205, 206
3:1-4 212
3:2 25
3:14 179
5:10-12 179
7:20 23
8 – 11 ....106, 244
8:1 106
8:2 ....205, 206
8:3 ....184, 205, 206
9:3 106
10:1, 21, 22 25
10:2 ....205, 206
10:18 106
11:1 ....184, 205, 206
11:5-6 180
11:16-17 ....205, 206
11:19 218
11:23 106
11:24 ....205, 206
12:14 179
15:18 226
16:17 23
17:10 179
17:21 179
18:4, 20 298
18:25 81
20:32 180
21:21 133
21:25, 29 [30, 34] 236
21:27 264
21[16] 133
23:14 23
23:15 25
26 218
28:13 229
28:14[16] 229
30:1 212
31:2, 8 25
31:18 25
33:10-11 300
34 ....245, 270
34:23 ....245, 270
36 262

SCRIPTURE INDEX

36:22-32 260
36:25-27 218
36:26-27 217
37:1 .... 205, 206
37:01a 206
37:01b 206
37:5-14 179
37:9 179
37:14 217
37:17, 19, 22 119
37:24 245
38:10 180
39:29 217
40 – 48 262

Daniel 210, 211, 261
2:4 222
2:13 90
2:31, 32, 34, 35 23
3:1-3, 5, 7, 10, 12, 14, 15, ...
 18, 19 23
3:25 25
4:14 149
5:5 107
7:2 179
7:5 25
7:10 149
7:13 262
8:17, 19 236
9 .... 263, 265
9:24 .... 257, 259, 260, 261,
 262, 263
9:24-25 272
9:24-27 ...... 7, 254, 255, 256, 257,
 265, 284
9:24a 261
9:25, 26 263
9:25-26 .... 263, 264
9:26 .... 3, 220, 264, 295
10:16 25
11 178
11:36 .... 52, 53

11:40 236
12:2 .... 296, 299, 303
12:3 226
12:4, 6 236

Hosea 210
1 97
1:1-7 86
1:1-10 160
1:2, 7 70
1:4-7 167
1:7 86
4:1-6 2
4:2, 3, 6 86
5:15 .... 106, 262, 288
9:1-9 2
12:3-5 85
13:7-8 42
13:14 304
13:15 179
14:1 300

Joel
1:1 351
2:17 177
2:28-29 217

Amos
1:11 226
5:26 23
7:7-8 81
7:10-17 2
8:11-12 59
9:1 81

Obadiah
9 265

Jonah 52, 210
1:1 351
4:2 52
4:8 179

Micah
2:6, 11 203
2:7 181
3:1-3 203

3:5-7	203
3:8	203
5:2	7, 21, 228, 239, 241, 242, 258, 279, 284, 296
5:14	87
7:1-4	203
7:14	222

Nahum
3:15	265

Habakkuk
1:11	178
2:4	8, 294
3:6	226
3:13	263

Zephaniah
1:1	352

Haggai
2:1-9	188
2:5	188

Zechariah 211
1:12	133
1:12-14	99
2:6[10]	179
2:6-11	171
2:8	86, 293
2:8-9	18, 86, 108, 167
2:9	86
3:1	98
3:1-10	92, 97, 98
3:2	98
3:4	98
3:5	98
3:6	98
3:6-8	99
3:7	98
3:8	247
6:12	247
7:12	212
9:9	277, 279, 288
11	167, 245
11, 12	277
11:1-17	3
11:4	270
11:4, 6-10, 12-14	168
11:4-13	168
11:4-14	167, 270, 271, 276, 277
11:6	270
11:7	270
11:8	270
11:9	270
11:10	270
11:12	168, 270, 279
11:12-13	167, 270, 277
11:12-14	269
11:13	279
11:14	270
12:1	186
12:10	3, 130, 269, 272, 273, 274, 275, 276, 277, 278, 288
12:10 – 13:1	258
12:13	168
13	277
13:3	274, 277
13:7	269, 276, 277

Malachi 211
1:26	29
2:10	120
2:15-16	179
3:2	42
3:6	287

Matthew 214
1:21	282
2:4-8	240
2:5	240
3:16	173
3:17	91
4:4	210
4:4, 7, 10	208, 211
5:17	211
5:18	208
9:13	210
11:9	288

SCRIPTURE INDEX

11:10	93, 211
12	278
12:22-42	155
12:23-24	288
12:31-45	105
12:40	211
12:42	210
13:13-14	210
15:18-19	292
17:1-8	109
19:4-6	211
19:4-7	211
20:1-16	42
21:33-41	271
22:29-32	211
22:41-44	214
22:41-46	232, 238
22:43	202
22:44	254
23:37	168, 275
23:37-39	106
23:39	246, 262, 288
24:1-2	3
24:15	210, 211
24:37-39	211
26:31	211
26:54	211
26:63-66	16
26:64	262
27:26, 30-31	166

Mark

2:25	210
7:8-13	210
10:6-8	210
12:10	210
12:36	215
13:1-2	3
14:62	254
16:19	254

Luke

1:31	231
3:23-31	232
4:16-22	172
4:16-30	189
4:17-21	210
5:21	16
10:26-28	210
11:51	211
16:17	208
18:20	210
18:31	211
20:41	211
21:5-6	3
21:20-24	3
22:69	254
24:25-27	16
24:25-27, 44-48	109
24:44	208
24:44-46	210

John

1:1-3	60
1:12	304
1:14	102, 304
1:18	108
3:3-10	192
3:10	218
3:14	210, 211
3:16-17, 36	304
4:24	30
5:36-38	108
5:39	15, 210
5:46	15
6:28-51	304
7:41-42	240
8:6	107
8:54-59	9
10:11	245, 270
10:30	70, 108, 277, 304
10:30-31	9
10:32-33	5
10:33	16
10:34-35	210

10:35	208, 211
14:9	277
14:9-11	109
14:17	191
16:13-14	186
19:34	274
20:1	304

Acts
1:16	215
2	165
2:16-17	217
2:16-21	177
2:23	278
2:34-35	254
3:11-19	14
4:12	305
8:25	213
8:26-37	14
28:25	216
28:25-27	215

Romans
1	154
1:18-32	80
1:21-23	80
3:20	362
3:23	305
5:8	305
6:23	305
8:34	254
11:10	59
11:25-27	258
16:25-26	6

1 Corinthians
2:7	6
3:16	218
8:4	61
8:6	1
15:20-26	304

2 Corinthians
5:17	36

Ephesians
1:20	254
3:4-10	6
5:18 – 6:4	36

Philippians
2:5-11	305

Colossians
1:15	28, 33
1:15-17	60
1:18	288
1:26-27	6
2:9-11	305
2:11	14
3:1	254
3:1 – 4:6	36

2 Timothy
1:9	139
3:16	50, 207, 208, 209, 213, 281

Hebrews ... 214, 217
1:1-3	109, 306
1:2	60
1:3, 13	254
3:7-11	216
4:12-13	292
7:1	253
7:11-18	253
8 - 10	8
8:1	254
9:12	295
10:10-18	306
10:12	254
10:15-16	216, 217
11:32	198

James
3:9	45

1 Peter
1:1-25	115
1:20	139
2:21-24	115
3:22	254
4:11	115

SCRIPTURE INDEX

2 Peter
- 1:16, 18 115
- 1:20-21 .... 50, 209
- 1:21 .... 50, 207
- 2:12 45

John
- 1:1 155

Jude
- v25 115

Revelation
- 17:8 139
- 21 – 22 261
- 21:23[22:5] 226

www.ingramcontent.com/pod-product-compliance
Lightning Source LLC
Chambersburg PA
CBHW082104230426
43671CB00015B/2599